W9-DIS-461

Spelling Workout

Phillip K. Trocki

MODERN CURRICULUM PRESS

COVER DESIGN: Pronk & Associates

ILLUSTRATIONS: Eric Larsen. 32-33, 48, 49: Jim Steck. 49: *cupcake*: Chris Knowles. 49: *peas*: Eric Larsen. 64: Jim Steck. 80: Jim Steck. 96: Jim Steck. 97: *opera singer*: Jim Steck. 112: Jim Steck. 113: *lunar lander*: Jim Steck. 165: Jim Steck.

PHOTOGRAPHS: All photos © Pearson Learning unless otherwise noted.

Cover: background dandelion Andy Roberts/Stone. t.l., m.l. Artbase Inc. m.r. Stephen Dalton/Animals Animals. b.l., b.r. Artbase Inc. Page 5, 8: © Tom McHugh/Photo Researchers, Inc. 9: Myrleen Ferguson/PhotoEdit. 12: Ronnie Kaufman/Corbis Stock Market. 13: © François Gohier/Photo Researchers, Inc. 16: PhotoDisc, Inc. 17: Aaron Haupt/Stock Boston. 20: Steve Gorton/Dorling Kindersley. 21: Bob Daemmrich/Stock Boston. 24: SuperStock, Inc. 29: Ryan McVay/PhotoDisc, Inc. 32: © Aaron Haupt/Photo Researchers, Inc. 33: Zig Leszczynski/Animals Animals. 36: Don Farrall/PhotoDisc, Inc. 37: SuperStock, Inc. 40: CMCD/PhotoDisc, Inc. 41: Courtesy of muralist John Pugh, Illusion Art. 44: Art Resource, NY. 53: Bill Ross/Corbis. 56: Ted Streshinsky/Corbis. 57: Charles Peale Polk "General Washington at Princeton". Oil on Canvas. 35 15/16" X 27 13/16". National Gallery of Art, Washington, DC. 61: AP/Wide World. 64: Vince Laforet/Allsport Photography, Inc. 65: Olaf Veltman/Creative Management Partners. 68: Annie Griffiths Belt/Corbis. 69: Cary Wolinski/Stock Boston. 72: D. Young-Wolff/PhotoEdit. 77: Richard T. Nowitz/Corbis. 80: Rob Rossi/Outside Images/PictureQuest. 81: Jerry Howard/Stock Boston/PictureQuest. 85: Paul A. Souders/Corbis. 88: Robert Dowling/Corbis. 89: Academy of Natural Sciences of Philadelphia/Corbis. 92: Bill Aron/PhotoEdit/PictureQuest. 93: Patrick Ward/Stock Boston/PictureQuest. 96: Leng/Leng/Corbis. 105: Andy Crawford/Dorling Kindersley. 108: Dave King/Dorling Kindersley. 109: Jeffrey L. Rotman/Corbis. 112: Joel W. Rogers/Corbis. 116: Tim Ridley/Dorling Kindersley. 117: Charles Gupton/Stock Boston/PictureQuest. 120: Tony Freeman/PhotoEdit. 122: Geostock/PhotoDisc, Inc. 125: t. Corbis, b. Bettmann/Corbis. 128: Bettmann/Corbis. 129, 132: David Young-Wolff/PhotoEdit. 133: Library of Congress. 136: Statue of Liberty National Monument/United States Department of Interior. 137: Tim Flach/Stone. 140: Staffan Widstrand/Corbis. 141: Art Resource, N.Y. 144: SuperStock, Inc. 145: American Woodwork XVII, Spinning Wheel for flaxwool, The Metropolitan Museum of Art.

Acknowledgments

ZB Font Method Copyright © 1996 Zaner-Bloser.

Some content in this product is based upon *Webster's New World Dictionary for Young Adults*. © 2001 Hungry Minds, Inc. All rights reserved. Webster's New World is a trademark or registered trademark of Hungry Minds, Inc.

NOTE: Every effort has been made to locate the copyright owner of material reprinted in this book. Omissions brought to our attention will be corrected in subsequent editions.

Modern Curriculum Press
An imprint of Pearson Learning
299 Jefferson Road, P.O. Box 480
Parsippany, NJ 07054-0480

www.pearsonlearning.com
1-800-321-3106

ISBN 0-7652-2492-5

14 15 16 V092 14 13

Table of Contents

4

Spelling Workout—Our Philosophy

Integration of Spelling with Reading and Writing

In each core lesson for *Spelling Workout*, students read spelling words in context in a variety of fiction and nonfiction selections. The reading selections provide opportunities for reading across the curriculum, focusing on the subject areas of science, social studies, health, language arts, music, and art.

After students read the selection and practice writing their spelling words, they use list words to help them write about a related topic in a variety of forms such as descriptive paragraphs, stories, news articles, poems, letters, advertisements, and posters. A proofreading exercise is also provided for each lesson to help students apply the writing process to their own writing and reinforce the use of spelling words in context.

The study of spelling should not be limited to a specific time in the school day. Use opportunities throughout the day to reinforce and maintain spelling skills by integrating spelling with other curriculum areas. Point out spelling words in books, texts, and the student's own writing. Encourage students to write, as they practice spelling through writing. Provide opportunities for writing with a purpose.

Phonics-Based Instructional Design

Spelling Workout takes a solid phonic and structural analysis approach to encoding. The close tie between spelling and phonics allows each to reinforce the other. *Spelling Workout* correlates closely to *MCP Phonics*, although both programs are complete within themselves and can be used independently.

Research-Based Teaching Strategies

Spelling Workout utilizes a test-study-test method of teaching spelling. The student first takes a pretest of words that have not yet been introduced. Under the direction of the teacher, the student then self-corrects the test, rewriting correctly any word that has been missed. This approach not only provides an opportunity to determine how many words a student can already spell but also allows students to analyze spelling mistakes. In the process students also discover patterns that make it easier to spell list words. Students study the words as they work through practice exercises, and then reassess their spelling by taking a final test.

High-Utility List Words

The words used in *Spelling Workout* have been chosen for their frequency in students' written and oral vocabularies, their relationships to subject areas, and for structural as well as phonetic generalizations. Each list word has been cross-referenced with one or more of the following:

Carroll, Davies, and Richman. *The American Heritage Word Frequency Book*

Dale and O'Rourke. *The Living Word Vocabulary*

Dolch. *220 Basic Sight Words*

Fry, Polk, and Fountoukidis. *Spelling Demons—197 Words Frequently Misspelled by Elementary Students*

Green and Loomer. *The New Iowa Spelling Scale*

Hanna. *Phoneme Grapheme Correspondences as Cues to Spelling Improvement*

Harris and Jacobson. *Basic Elementary Reading Vocabularies*

Hillerich. *A Written Vocabulary of Elementary Children*

Kucera and Francis. *Computational Analysis of Present-Day American English*

Rinsland. *A Basic Vocabulary of Elementary Children*

Sakiey and Fry. *3000 Instant Words*

Thomas. *3000 Words Most Frequently Written*

Thomas. *200 Words Most Frequently Misspelled*

A Format That Results in Success

Spelling Workout treats spelling as a developmental process. Students progress in stages, much as they learn to speak and read. In *Spelling Workout*, they move gradually from simple sound/letter relationships to strategies involving more complex word-structure patterns.

Sample Core Lesson

- **Spelling Words in Action** presents an engaging and informative reading selection in each lesson that illustrates the spelling words in context.

- The activity in the box at the end of the reading selection helps students focus on the spelling patterns of the list words presented in the lesson.

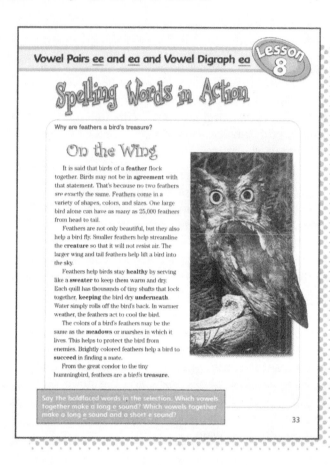

Vowel Pairs **ee** and **ea** and Vowel Digraph **ea**   Lesson 8

Spelling Words in Action

Why are feathers a bird's treasure?

On the Wing

It is said that birds of a **feather** flock together. Birds may not be in **agreement** with that statement. That's because no two feathers are exactly the same. Feathers come in a variety of shapes, colors, and sizes. One large bird alone can have as many as 25,000 feathers from head to tail.

Feathers are not only beautiful, but they also help a bird fly. Smaller feathers help streamline the **creature** so that it will not resist air. The larger wing and tail feathers help lift a bird into the sky.

Feathers help birds stay **healthy** by serving like a **sweater** to keep them warm and dry. Each quill has thousands of tiny shafts that lock together, **keeping** the bird dry **underneath**. Water simply rolls off the bird's back. In warmer weather, the feathers act to cool the bird.

The colors of a bird's feathers may be the same as the **meadows** or marshes in which it lives. This helps to protect the bird from enemies. Brightly colored feathers help a bird to **succeed** in finding a mate.

From the great condor to the tiny hummingbird, feathers are a bird's **treasure**.

Say the boldfaced words in the selection. Which vowels together make a long e sound? Which vowels together make a long e sound and a short e sound?

33

- The **Tip** explains the spelling patterns, providing a focus for the lesson.

- The **List Words** box contains the spelling words for each lesson.

- **Spelling Practice** exercises give students an opportunity to practice writing new words while reinforcing the spelling patterns.

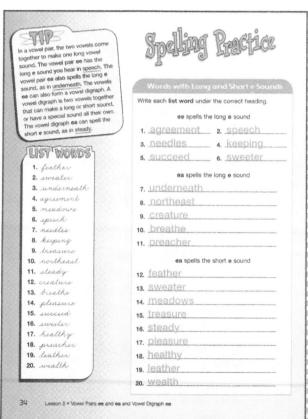

TIP

In a vowel pair, the two vowels come together to make one long vowel sound. The vowel pair **ee** has the long e sound you hear in speech. The vowel pair **ea** also spells the long e sound, as in underneath. The vowels **ea** can also form a vowel digraph. A vowel digraph is two vowels together that can make a long or short sound, or have a special sound all their own. The vowel digraph **ea** can spell the short e sound, as in steady.

LIST WORDS
1. feather
2. sweater
3. underneath
4. agreement
5. meadows
6. speech
7. needles
8. keeping
9. treasure
10. northeast
11. steady
12. creature
13. breathe
14. pleasure
15. succeed
16. sweeter
17. healthy
18. preacher
19. leather
20. wealth

Spelling Practice

Words with Long and Short e Sounds

Write each **list word** under the correct heading.

ee spells the long e sound
1. agreement   2. speech
3. needles   4. keeping
5. succeed   6. sweeter

ea spells the long e sound
7. underneath
8. northeast
9. creature
10. breathe
11. preacher

ea spells the short e sound
12. feather
13. sweater
14. meadows
15. treasure
16. steady
17. pleasure
18. healthy
19. leather
20. wealth

34   Lesson 8 • Vowel Pairs **ee** and **ea** and Vowel Digraph **ea**

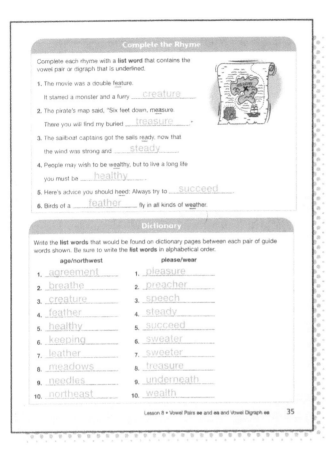

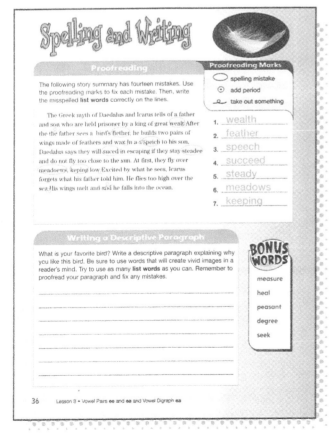

- Word meaning activities provide opportunities to practice list words while helping students develop their vocabularies.

- Activities such as crossword puzzles, riddles, and games help motivate students by making learning fun.

- **Spelling and Writing** reinforces the connection between spelling and everyday writing, and encourages students to apply the list words in different contexts.

- **Proofreading** practice builds proofreading proficiency and encourages students to check their own writing.

- **Writing** activities provide opportunities for students to use their spelling words in a variety of writing forms and genres. Write-on lines are provided. Students may also wish to use separate sheets of paper.

- **Bonus Words** offer more challenging words with similar spelling patterns. Activities in the *Teacher's Edition* give students the opportunity to practice the words with a partner.

Sample Review Lesson

- The **Review** lesson allows students to practice what they've learned.

- The spelling patterns used in the previous five lessons are reviewed at the beginning of the lesson.

- **Check Your Spelling Notebook** suggests that students look at their spelling notebooks to review any words that give them trouble. A partner activity provides practice for those words in a variety of learning modalities—kinesthetic, visual, and auditory.

- A variety of activities provides practice and review of selected list words from the previous lessons.

- **Show What You Know** is a cumulative review of the words in the five previous lessons using a standardized-test format.

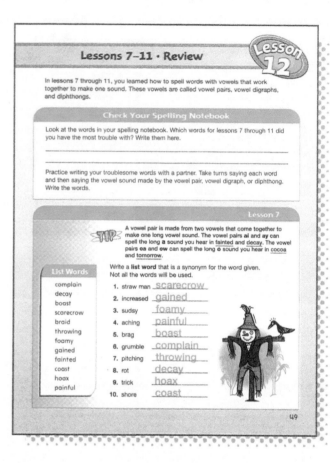

Lessons 7–11 · Review

Lesson 12

In lessons 7 through 11, you learned how to spell words with vowels that work together to make one sound. These vowels are called vowel pairs, vowel digraphs, and diphthongs.

Check Your Spelling Notebook

Look at the words in your spelling notebook. Which words for lessons 7 through 11 did you have the most trouble with? Write them here.

_____

Practice writing your troublesome words with a partner. Take turns saying each word and then saying the vowel sound made by the vowel pair, vowel digraph, or diphthong. Write the words.

Lesson 7

TIP A vowel pair is made from two vowels that come together to make one long vowel sound. The vowel pairs **ai** and **ay** can spell the long **a** sound you hear in <u>fainted</u> and <u>decay</u>. The vowel pairs **oa** and **ow** can spell the long **o** sound you hear in <u>cocoa</u> and <u>tomorrow</u>.

Write a **list word** that is a synonym for the word given. Not all the words will be used.

List Words

complain
decay
boast
scarecrow
braid
throwing
foamy
gained
fainted
coast
hoax
painful

1. straw man scarecrow
2. increased gained
3. sudsy foamy
4. aching painful
5. brag boast
6. grumble complain
7. pitching throwing
8. rot decay
9. trick hoax
10. shore coast

49

Show What You Know

Lessons 7–11 Review

One word is misspelled in each set of **list words**. Fill in the circle next to the **list word** that is spelled incorrectly.

1. ○ complain ○ meadows ○ lawyer ○ neither ● tosted
2. ○ joint ○ braid ○ speech ● straberries ○ northeast
3. ○ deceit ● croded ○ drains ○ keeping ○ caution
4. ○ saucers ○ thief ○ joined ○ coast ● conceve
5. ○ treasure ○ drawer ● achive ○ voyage ○ soiled
6. ○ decay ● stedy ○ vault ○ deceived ○ enjoyable
7. ○ roasting ○ creature ● naghty ○ received ○ counted
8. ○ powder ○ brief ● gnaing ○ breathe ○ throwing
9. ● tomorow ○ boast ○ pleasure ○ sweeter ○ awkward
10. ○ hawk ○ believe ○ review ○ oyster ● bondary
11. ○ poise ● infeeld ○ exhaust ○ succeed ○ borrow
12. ○ swallows ○ grief ○ poach ● squak ○ loyalty
13. ● freit ○ vein ○ faucet ○ author ○ healthy
14. ○ preacher ● lether ○ pause ○ shield ○ moisture
15. ○ poisonous ○ mountainous ○ pieces ○ eighty ● forny
16. ○ scarecrow ○ wealth ○ feather ● daghter ○ withdraw
17. ○ hauled ○ niece ● corageous ○ cocoa ○ fainted
18. ○ gained ○ sweater ○ awfully ○ unlawful ● yeld
19. ○ choir ○ toiled ○ either ○ needles ● underneth
20. ○ hoax ○ painful ○ agreement ● avoyd ○ broiled

Spelling Workout in the Classroom

Classroom Management

Spelling Workout is designed as a flexible instructional program. The following plans are two ways the program can be taught.

The 5-day Plan
Day 1 – Spelling Words in Action and Warm-Up Test
Days 2 and 3 – Spelling Practice
Day 4 – Spelling and Writing
Day 5 – Final Test

The 3-day Plan
Day 1 – Spelling Words in Action and Warm-Up Test/Spelling Practice
Day 2 – Spelling Practice/Spelling and Writing
Day 3 – Final Test

Testing

Testing is accomplished in several ways. A **Warm-Up Test** is administered after reading the **Spelling Words in Action** selection and a **Final Test** is given at the end of each lesson. Dictation sentences for each **Warm-Up Test** and **Final Test** are provided.

Research suggests that students benefit from correcting their own **Warm-Up Tests**. After the test has been administered, have students self-correct their tests by checking the words against the list words. You may also want to guide students by reading each letter of the word, asking students to point to each letter and circle any incorrect letters. Then, have students rewrite each word correctly.

Tests for review lessons are provided in the *Teacher's Edition* as reproducibles following each lesson. These tests provide not only an evaluation tool for teachers, but also added practice in taking standardized tests for students.

Individualizing Instruction

Bonus Words are included in every core lesson as a challenge for better spellers and to provide extension and enrichment for all students.

Review lessons reinforce correct spelling of difficult words from previous lessons.

Spelling Notebook allows each student to analyze spelling errors and practice writing troublesome words independently. Notebook pages appear as reproducibles in the *Teacher's Edition* and as pages at the back of the student book.

A reproducible individual **Student Record Chart** provided in the *Teacher's Edition* allows students to record their test scores.

Ideas for meeting the needs of ESL students are provided.

Dictionary

In the back of each student book is a comprehensive dictionary with definitions of all list words and bonus words. Students will have this resource at their fingertips for any assignment.

The Teacher's Edition
—Everything You Need!

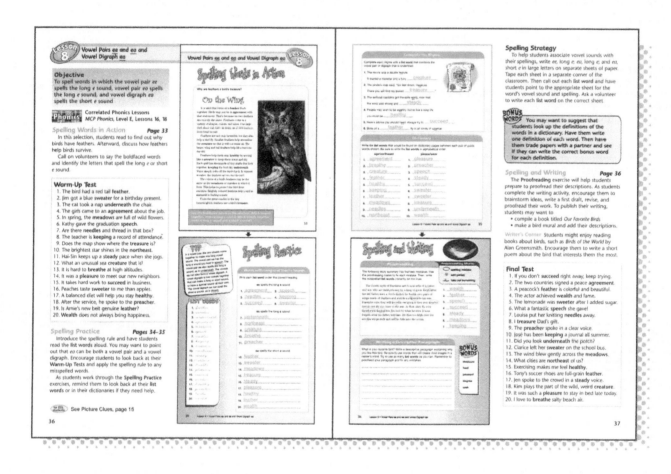

- The **Objective** clearly states the goals of each core lesson.

- Spelling lessons are correlated to *MCP Phonics*.

- Ideas for introducing and setting a purpose for reading are given for each reading selection.

- A **Warm-Up Test**, or pretest, is administered before the start of each lesson. Dictation sentences are provided.

- Concise teaching notes give guidance for working through the lesson.

- Ideas for meeting the needs of ESL students are highlighted.

- **Spelling Strategy** activities provide additional support for reinforcing and analyzing spelling patterns.

- Activities for using the **Bonus Words** listed in the student books are provided.

- **Spelling and Writing** includes suggestions for helping students use proofreading marks to correct their work. Suggestions for using the writing process to complete the writing activity are also offered.

- **Writer's Corner** extends the content of each reading selection by suggesting ways in which students can explore real-world writing.

- A **Final Test** is administered at the end of the lesson. Dictation sentences are provided.

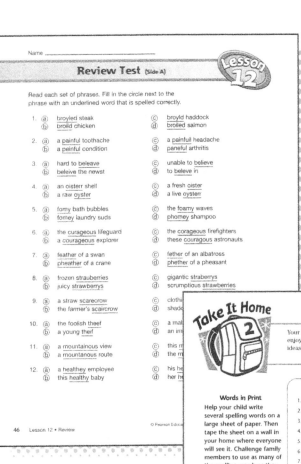

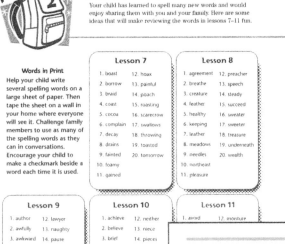

- **Review** lessons review spelling objectives, give guidance for further practice of list words, and provide dictation sentences for a **Final Test**. Reproducible two-page standardized tests to help prepare students for test-taking are supplied for assessment purposes after each **Review** lesson.

- Reproducible **Take It Home Masters** also follow each **Review** lesson and strengthen the school–home connection by providing ideas for parents and students for additional practice at home. Plus, they provide the complete set of spelling words for that group of lessons.

- Suggested games and group activities make spelling more fun.

Worksheet: Review Test (Side A) — Lesson 12

Name _____

Read each set of phrases. Fill in the circle next to the phrase with an underlined word that is spelled correctly.

1. (a) broyled steak (b) broil chicken (c) broyld haddock (d) broiled salmon
2. (a) a painful toothache (b) a peinful condition (c) a painfuil headache (d) paneful arthritis
3. (a) hard to beleave (b) believe the newst (c) unable to believe (d) to believe in
4. (a) an oisterr shell (b) a raw oyster (c) a fresh oister (d) a live oyster
5. (a) fomy bath bubbles (b) fomey laundry suds (c) the foamy waves (d) phomey shampoo
6. (a) the curageous lifeguard (b) a courageous explorer (c) the corageous firefighters (d) these couragous astronauts
7. (a) feather of a swan (b) pheather of a crane (c) fether of an albatross (d) phether of a pheasant
8. (a) frozen strauberries (b) juicy strawberrys (c) gigantic straberrys (d) scrumptious strawberries
9. (a) a straw scarecrow (b) the farmer's scaircrow (c) clothi... (d) shado...
10. (a) the foolish theef (b) a young therf (c) a mal... (d) an im...
11. (a) a mountainous view (b) a mountanous route (c) this m... (d) the m...
12. (a) a healthey employee (b) this healthy baby (c) his he... (d) her h...

46 Lesson 12 • Review   © Pearson Edu...

Worksheet: Take It Home 2

Your child has learned to spell many new words and would enjoy sharing them with you and your family. Here are some ideas that will make reviewing the words in lessons 7–11 fun.

Words in Print
Help your child write several spelling words on a large sheet of paper. Then tape the sheet on a wall in your home where everyone will see it. Challenge family members to use as many of the spelling words as they can in conversations. Encourage your child to make a checkmark beside a word each time it is used.

Lesson 7
1. boast 12. hoax
2. borrow 13. painful
3. braid 14. poach
4. coast 15. roasting
5. cocoa 16. scarecrow
6. complain 17. swallows
7. decay 18. throwing
8. drains 19. toasted
9. fainted 20. tomorrow
10. foamy
11. gained

Lesson 8
1. agreement 12. preacher
2. breathe 13. speech
3. creature 14. steady
4. leather 15. succeed
5. healthy 16. sweater
6. keeping 17. sweeter
7. leather 18. treasure
8. meadows 19. underneath
9. needles 20. wealth
10. northeast
11. pleasure

Lesson 9
1. author 12. lawyer
2. awfully 13. naughty
3. awkward 14. pause
4. caution 15. saucers
5. daughter 16. squawk
6. drawer 17. strawberries
7. exhaust 18. unlawful
8. faucet 19. vault
9. gnawing 20. withdraw
10. hauled
11. hawk

Lesson 10
1. achieve 12. neither
2. believe 13. niece
3. brief 14. pieces
4. conceive 15. received
5. deceit 16. review
6. deceived 17. shield
7. eighty 18. thief
8. either 19. vein
9. freight 20. yield
10. grief
11. infield

Lesson 11
1. avoid 12. moisture

48 Take It Home Master • Lessons 7–11   © Pearson Edu...

Spelling Enrichment

Bulletin Board Suggestion
Shoot for the Stars in Spelling Prepare a large rocket ship out of tagboard. Display it on the lower corner of a bulletin board so that it looks as if it is blasting off into space. Then cut large stars out of brightly colored construction paper. Encourage students to write spelling hints on the stars and add them to the bulletin board. The hint might be a spelling rule such as "i before e except after c . . . ." or it might suggest a funny pronunciation for one of the list words that will help students with an unusual spelling.

Group Practice
Fill-In Write spelling words on the board. Omit some of the letters and replace them with dashes. Have the first student in Row One come to the board to fill in one of the missing letters in any of the words. Then, have the first student in Row Two continue the procedure. Continue having students in each row take turns coming up to the board to fill in letters until all the words are completed. Any student who is able to correctly fill in a word earns a point for his or her row. The row with the most points at the end of the game wins.

Erase Write list words on the board. Then, ask the class to put their heads down while you call on a student to come to the board and erase one of the words. This student then calls on a class member to identify the erased word. The identified word is then restored and the student who correctly identified the erasure can be the person who erases next.

Crossword Relay First draw a large grid on the board. Then, divide the class into several teams. Teams compete against each other to form separate crossword puzzles on the board. Individuals on each team take turns racing against members of the other teams to join list words until all possibilities have been exhausted. A list word may appear on each crossword puzzle only once. The winning team is the team whose crossword puzzle contains the greatest number of correctly spelled list words or the team who finishes first.

Scramble Prepare letter cards sufficient to spell all the list words. Distribute letter cards to all students. Some students may be given more than one letter card. The teacher then calls out a list word. Students holding the letters contained in the word race to the front of the class to form the word by standing in the appropriate sequence with their letter cards.

Proofreading Relay Write two columns of misspelled list words on the board. Although the errors can differ, be sure that each list has the same number of errors. Divide the class into two teams and assign each team to a different column. Teams then compete against each other to correct their assigned lists by team members taking turns erasing and replacing an appropriate letter. Each member may correct only one letter per turn. The team that corrects its entire word list first wins.

Detective Call on a student to be a detective. The detective must choose a spelling word from the list and think of a structural clue, definition, or synonym that will help classmates identify it. The detective then states the clue using the format, "I spy a word that. . . ." Students are called on to guess and spell the mystery word. Whoever answers correctly gets to take a turn being the detective.

Spelling Tic-Tac-Toe Draw a tic-tac-toe square on the board. Divide the class into X and O teams. Take turns dictating spelling words to members of each team. If the word is spelled correctly, allow the team member to place an X or O on the square. The first team to place three X's or O's in a row wins.

Words of Fortune Have students put their heads down while you write a spelling word on the board in large letters. Then, cover each letter with a sheet of sturdy paper. The paper can be fastened to the board with magnets. Call on a student to guess any letter of the alphabet the student thinks may be hidden. If that particular letter is hidden, then reveal the letter in every place where it appears in the word by removing the paper.

The student continues to guess letters until an incorrect guess is made or the word is revealed. In the event that an incorrect guess is made, a different student continues the game. Continue the game until every list word has been hidden and then revealed.

Dictionary Activities
Around the World Designate the first person in the first row to be the traveler. The traveler must stand next to the student seated behind him or her. Then, dictate any letter of the alphabet at random. Instruct the two students to quickly name the letter of the alphabet that precedes the given letter. The student who is first to respond with the correct answer becomes the traveler while the other student sits at that desk. The traveler

162

Meeting the Needs of Your ESL Students

Spelling Strategies for Your ESL Students

You may want to try some of these suggestions to help you promote successful language learning for ESL students.

- Prompt use of spelling words by showing pictures or objects that relate to the topic of each selection. Invite students to discuss the picture or object.

- Demonstrate actions or act out words. Encourage students to do the same.

- Read each selection aloud before asking students to read it independently.

- Define words in context and allow students to offer their own meanings of words.

- Make the meanings of words concrete by naming objects or pictures, role-playing, or pantomiming.

Spelling is the relationship between sounds and letters. Learning to spell words in English is an interesting challenge for English First Language speakers as well as English as a Second Language speakers. You may want to adapt some of the following activities to accommodate the needs of your students—both native and non-English speakers.

Rhymes and Songs

Use rhymes, songs, poems, or chants to introduce new letter sounds and spelling words. Repeat the rhyme or song several times during the day or week, having students listen to you first, then repeat back to you line by line. To enhance learning for visual learners in your classroom and provide opportunities for pointing out letter combinations and their sounds, you may want to write the rhyme, song, poem, or chant on the board. As you examine the words, students can easily see similarities and differences among them. Encourage volunteers to select and recite a rhyme or sing a song for the class. Students may enjoy some of the selections in *Miss Mary Mack and Other Children's Street Rhymes* by Joanna Cole and Stephanie Calmenson or *And the Green Grass Grew All Around* by Alvin Schwartz.

Student Dictation

To take advantage of individual students' known vocabulary, suggest that students build their own sentences incorporating the list words. For example:

Mary ran.

Mary ran away.

Mary ran away quickly.

Sentence building can expand students' knowledge of how to spell words and of how to notice language patterns, learn descriptive words, and so on.

Words in Context

Using words in context sentences will aid students' mastery of new vocabulary.

- Say several sentences using the list words in context and have students repeat after you. Encourage more proficient students to make up sentences using list words that you suggest.

- Write cloze sentences on the board and have students help you complete them with the list words.

Point out the spelling patterns in the words, using colored chalk to underline or circle the elements.

Oral Drills

Use oral drills to help students make associations among sounds and the letters that represent them. You might use oral drills at listening stations to reinforce the language, allowing ESL students to listen to the drills at their own pace.

Spelling Aloud Say each list word and have students repeat the word. Next, write it on the board as you name each letter, then say the word again as you track the letters and sound by sweeping your hand under the word. Call attention to spelling changes for words to which endings or suffixes were added. For words with more than one syllable, emphasize each syllable as you write, encouraging students to clap out the syllables. Ask volunteers to repeat the procedure.

Variant Spellings For a group of words that contain the same vowel sound, but variant spellings, write an example on the board, say the word, and then present other words in that word family (*cake: rake, bake, lake*). Point out the sound and the letter(s) that stand for the sound. Then, add words to the list that have the same vowel sound (*play, say, day*). Say pairs of words (*cake, play*) as you point to them, and identify the vowel sound and the different letters that represent the sound (long *a: a_e, ay*). Ask volunteers to select a different pair of words and repeat the procedure.

Vary this activity by drawing a chart on the board that shows the variant spellings for a sound. Invite students to add words under the correct spelling pattern. Provide a list of words for students to choose from to help those ESL students with limited vocabularies.

Categorizing To help students discriminate among consonant sounds and spellings, have them help you categorize words with single consonant sounds and consonant blends or digraphs. For example, ask students to close their eyes so that they may focus solely on the sounds in the words, and then pronounce *smart, smile, spend,* and *special.* Next, pronounce the words as you write them on the board. After spelling each word, create two columns—one for *sm,* one for *sp.* Have volunteers pronounce each word, decide which column it fits under, and then write the word in the correct column. Encourage students to add to the columns any other words they know that have those consonant blends.

To focus on initial, medial, or final consonant sounds, point out the position of the consonant blends or digraphs in the list words. Have students find and list the words under columns labeled *Beginning, Middle,* and *End.*

Tape Recording Encourage students to work with a partner or their group to practice their spelling words. If a tape recorder is available, students can practice at their own pace by taking turns recording the words, playing back the tape, and writing each word they hear. Students can then help each other check their spelling against their *Spelling Workout* books. Observe as needed to be sure students are spelling the words correctly.

Comparing/Contrasting To help students focus on word parts, write list words with prefixes or suffixes on the board and have volunteers circle, underline, or draw a line between the prefix or suffix and its base word. Review the meaning of each base word, then invite students to work with their group to write two sentences: one using just the base word; the other using the base word with its prefix or suffix. For example: *My favorite mystery was due at the library Monday afternoon. By Tuesday afternoon the book was overdue!* Or, *You can depend on Jen to arrive for softball practice on time. She is dependable.* Have students contrast the two sentences, encouraging them to tell how the prefix or suffix changed the meaning of the base word.

Questions/Answers Write list words on the board and ask pairs of students to brainstorm questions or answers about the words, such as "Which word names more than one? How do you know?" (*foxes,* an *es* was added at the end) or, "Which word tells that something belongs to the children? How do you know?" (*children's* is spelled with an *'s*)

Games

You may want to invite students to participate in these activities.

Picture Clues Students can work with a partner to draw pictures or cut pictures out of magazines that represent the list words, then trade papers and label each other's pictures. Encourage students to check each other's spelling against their *Spelling Workout* books.

Or, you can present magazine cutouts or items that picture the list words. As you display each picture or item, say the word clearly and then write it on the board as you spell it aloud. Non-English speakers may wish to know the translation of the word in their native language so that they can mentally connect the new word with a familiar one. Students may also find similarities in the spellings of the words.

Letter Cards Have students create letter cards for vowels, vowel digraphs, consonants, consonant blends and digraphs, and so on. Then, say a list word and have students show the card that has the letters representing the sound for the vowels or consonants in that word as they repeat and spell the word after you. You may wish to have students use their cards independently as they work with their group.

Charades/Pantomime Students can use gestures and actions to act out the list words. To receive credit for a correctly guessed word, players must spell the word correctly. Such activities can be played in pairs so that beginning English speakers will not feel pressured. If necessary, translate the words into students' native languages so that they understand the meanings of the words before attempting to act them out.

Change or No Change Have students make flash cards for base words and endings. One student holds up a base word; another holds up an ending. The class says "Change" or "No Change" to describe what happens when the base word and ending are combined. Encourage students to spell the word with its ending added.

Scope and Sequence for MCP Spelling Workout

Skills	Level A	Level B	Level C	Level D	Level E	Level F	Level G	Level H
Consonants	1–12	1–2	1	1	1	1, 7, 9	RC	3
Short Vowels	14–18	3–5	3	2	RC	RC	RC	RC
Long Vowels	20–23	7–11, 15	4–5, 7–8	3	RC	RC	RC	RC
Consonant Blends/Clusters	26–28	13–14	9–10, 17	5, 7	RC	RC	RC	RC
y as a Vowel	30	16	11, 13	RC	RC	RC	27	RC
Consonant Digraphs—th, ch, sh, wh, ck	32–33	19–21	14–16	9	RC	RC	RC	RC
Vowel Digraphs		33	7–8	19–21, 23	8–10	11, 14–17	25	RC
Vowel Pairs	29		26	20, 22	7–8, 10	14	25	
r-Controlled Vowels		22, 25	19–20	8	RC	RC	RC	4
Diphthongs	24	32	31	22–23	11	17	RC	RC
Silent Consonants			28	11	4	8–9	RC	RC
Hard and Soft c and g		21	2	4	2	2	RC	
Plurals			21–22	25–27, 29	33–34	33	RC	RC
Prefixes		34	32–33	31–32	13–17	20–23, 25	7–8, 33	7–11, 19–20
Suffixes/Endings	34–35	26–28	21–23, 25, 33	13–17	25–29, 31–32	26–29, 31–32	5, 9, 13–14, 16, 26	5, 25–27
Contractions		23	34	28	20	RC	RC	RC
Possessives				28–29	20	RC	RC	RC
Compound Words				33	19	RC	34	RC
Synonyms/Antonyms				34	RC	RC	RC	RC
Homonyms		35	35	35	RC	34	RC	RC
Spellings of /f/: f, ff, ph, gh				10	3	3	RC	RC
Syllables					21–23	RC	RC	1
Commonly Misspelled Words					35	34	17, 35	17, 29, 35
Abbreviations						35	RC	RC
Latin Roots							11, 15, 31	13–16

Skills	Level A	Level B	Level C	Level D	Level E	Level F	Level G	Level H
Words with French or Spanish Derivations							10, 29	RC 28
Words of Latin/ French/Greek Origin								21–23, 28
List Words Related to Specific Curriculum Areas							31–34, 28, 32	
Vocabulary Development	•	•	•	•	•	•	•	•
Dictionary	•	•	•	•	•	•	•	•
Writing	•	•	•	•	•	•	•	•
Proofreading	•	•	•	•	•	•	•	•
Reading Selections	•	•	•	•	•	•	•	•
Bonus Words	•	•	•	•	•	•	•	•
Review Tests in Standardized Format	•	•	•	•	•	•	•	•
Spelling Through Writing								
Poetry	•	•	•	•	•	•	•	•
Narrative Writings	•	•	•	•	•	•	•	•
Descriptive Writings	•	•	•	•	•	•	•	•
Expository Writings	•	•	•	•	•	•	•	•
Persuasive Writings			•	•	•	•	•	•
Notes/Letters	•	•	•		•	•	•	•
Riddles/Jokes	•	•	•					
Recipes/Menus	•	•	•			•	•	
News Stories		•	•	•	•	•	•	•
Conversations/Dialogues	•	•		•	•	•		•
Stories	•	•	•	•	•	•	•	•
Interviews/Surveys		•			•	•	•	•
Logs/Journals	•	•	•	•	•	•	•	
Ads/Brochures		•	•	•	•	•	•	•
Reports					•	•	•	•
Literary Devices							•	•
Scripts		•					•	•
Speeches					•	•		•
Directions/Instructions	•	•		•				•

Numbers in chart indicate lesson numbers

RC = reinforced in other contexts

• = found throughout

Objective
To spell words with the sound of *k*, *kw*, and *n*

Correlated Phonics Lesson
MCP Phonics, Level E, Lesson 1

Spelling Words in Action   Page 5

In this selection, students read to find out what can happen during a violent earthquake. Ask students to share what they already know about earthquakes and whether they have ever experienced one.

Encourage students to look back at the boldfaced words. Ask volunteers to say each word and identify any sound that is not spelled the way it is pronounced.

Warm-Up Test

1. When the movie started, everyone was **quiet**.
2. After running the race, Tim had some **aches**.
3. Did you **shake** those apples off the tree?
4. Frank **knocked** on the door.
5. The author's picture was on the book **jacket**.
6. A **quarter** is one-fourth of a dollar.
7. Pablo **quickly** added up the numbers.
8. **Knowing** first aid is helpful when camping.
9. Marie had a **quarrel** with her best friend.
10. The audience listened to the **speaker**.
11. "Do you have any more **questions**?" asked Sam.
12. I was **kneeling** on the rug, picking up the toys.
13. What a powerful **earthquake** that was!
14. We called a **mechanic** to repair the car.
15. The **orchestra** tuned up before the concert.
16. This piece of wood has a **knothole**.
17. Did you **inquire** about the cost of the tickets?
18. Follow each step of the directions in **sequence**.
19. Some schools **require** you to take gym daily.
20. The main **character** in the story is a detective.

Spelling Practice   Pages 6–7

Introduce the spelling rule and have students read the **list words** aloud. Encourage students to look back at their **Warm-Up Tests** and apply the spelling rule to any misspelled words.

As students work through the **Spelling Practice** exercises, remind them to look back at their **list words** or in their dictionaries if they need help.

 for ESL students   See Tape Recording, page 15

Spelling Words in Action

What would you do if you felt an earthquake?

Earthquake

One moment it's **quiet**. The next, buildings **shake** and wobble. Dishes are **knocked** off shelves. Take cover **quickly**! It's an **earthquake**!

Though about a million quakes happen every year, most people have never felt one. This is because most tremors are small. Major earthquakes, big enough to knock buildings off their foundations, happen far less frequently. They can be very damaging, however, so schools in earthquake zones **require** students to know what to do in case of a quake. A **speaker** may talk to students about earthquake safety. Students might also practice taking shelter during earthquake drills.

Lots of people have **questions** about what to do if they feel a quake. **Knowing** a **sequence** of steps to follow can help people be safe during an earthquake. **Kneeling** under a strong piece of furniture or standing in a doorway gives some protection from falling objects. People should stay away from windows to avoid being hit by broken glass. People who are outside should go to an open space.

Families can work together to develop plans for earthquake safety at home. The best advice is to stay calm and to be prepared.

Say each boldfaced word in the selection. Which sounds are not spelled the way they are pronounced?

5

TIP
Sometimes a sound is not spelled the way you would expect. In the word earthquake, the sound for **kw** is spelled with the letters **qu**. The **n** sound in **knocked** is spelled with **kn**. The **k** sound can be spelled several ways: with **k**, as in shake; with **ch**, as in mechanic; and with **ck**, as in quickly.

Spelling Practice

Words with the Sound of k, kw, and n

Write each **list word** under the correct heading. You will use some words more than once.

LIST WORDS
1. quiet
2. aches
3. shake
4. knocked
5. jacket
6. quarter
7. quickly
8. knowing
9. quarrel
10. speaker
11. questions
12. kneeling
13. earthquake
14. mechanic
15. orchestra
16. knothole
17. inquire
18. sequence
19. require
20. character

kn spells the sound of n
1. knocked   2. knowing
3. kneeling   4. knothole

k spells the sound of k
5. shake   6. speaker
7. earthquake

ch spells the sound of k
8. aches   9. mechanic
10. orchestra   11. character

ck spells the sound of k
12. knocked   13. jacket
14. quickly

qu spells the sound of kw
15. quiet   16. quarter
17. quickly   18. quarrel
19. questions   20. earthquake
21. inquire   22. sequence
23. require

Puzzle

Read each clue. Write **list words** to complete the puzzle.

ACROSS
1. what we ask
4. twenty-five cents
8. short coat with sleeves
9. a group of musicians
10. silent
11. pains

DOWN
2. the person who is talking
3. tapped with your knuckles
4. in the fast way
5. a person who uses tools to work with machines
6. violent movement of the Earth's surface
7. order of things

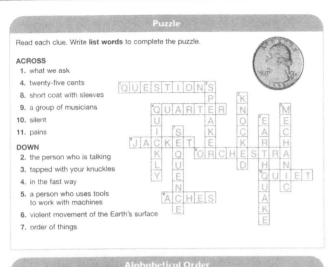

Alphabetical Order

Write each group of **list words** in alphabetical order.

earthquake	1. aches	orchestra	9. orchestra
kneeling	2. character	sequence	10. require
character	3. earthquake	require	11. sequence
aches	4. kneeling	shake	12. shake
knowing	5. inquire	quarter	13. quarrel
jacket	6. jacket	quickly	14. quarter
knothole	7. knothole	quarrel	15. questions
inquire	8. knowing	questions	16. quickly

Lesson 1 • Words with the Sound of k, kw, and n   7

Spelling and Writing

Proofreading

The following article has ten mistakes. Use the proofreading marks to fix the mistakes. Then write the misspelled **list words** correctly on the lines.

Scientists have been trying for years to accurately predict earthquakes. Knowing as quikely as possible when an earthquake will occur could save thousands of lives. In California in 1989, special sensors in a science lab picked up a rise in earth noise twelve days before a quake hit San Francisco. The noise, which increased greatly three hours before the earthquake hit, continued until power to the sensors was noacked out. Scientists still have quastons about these sensors. They think the sensors rekwire more testing to find out whether they can really help predict earthquakes.

Proofreading Marks
◯ spelling mistake
⌃ add something

1. knowing
2. quickly
3. earthquake
4. knocked
5. questions
6. require

Writing a Descriptive Paragraph

Special effects are used to create earthquakes and other disasters in the movies. What earthquake scenes can you imagine? Pretend that you are on a movie set watching a scene being filmed. Write a paragraph to describe what you see and hear. Try to use as many **list words** as you can. Remember to proofread your paragraph and fix any mistakes.

_____
_____
_____
_____
_____
_____

BONUS WORDS
qualify
hammock
kindness
knob
leprechaun

8   Lesson 1 • Words with the Sound of k, kw, and n

Spelling Strategy

Write *k, kw,* and *n* on the board as separate column headings. Then, write each **list word** in the correct column, leaving a blank for the letter or letters that spell the sound it contains. Call on volunteers to complete the words on the board.

BONUS WORDS   You may want to suggest that students write a sentence for each bonus word, leaving a blank for the word. Then have them trade papers with a partner and try to write the missing words.

Spelling and Writing   *Page 8*

The **Proofreading** exercise will help students prepare to proofread their writing. Before they begin, remind students that the proofreading mark ^ is used to add something, such as a space, a comma, a question mark, or an exclamation mark. As students complete the writing activity, encourage them to brainstorm ideas, write a first draft, revise, and proofread their work. To publish their writing, students may want to
- illustrate their descriptions
- read their descriptions aloud as radio broadcasts.

Writer's Corner The class can obtain important information about earthquakes by visiting the U.S. Geological Survey's Earthquake Hazards Program Web site at http://quake.wr.usgs.gov/. Encourage students to take notes as they click around the site.

Final Test
1. The librarian is a major **character** in the story.
2. He figured out the **sequence** of events.
3. There is a **knothole** in that piece of lumber.
4. I'd like to be a **mechanic** for the airlines.
5. The girls were **kneeling** down, playing marbles.
6. The **speaker** had a lot to say about pet care.
7. **Knowing** how to swim is important.
8. Does the daily paper cost only a **quarter**?
9. I **knocked** on the door, but no one answered.
10. I broke my leg a month ago, and it still **aches**.
11. When the crowd grew **quiet**, the concert began.
12. **Shake** the carton before you pour the juice.
13. I left my **jacket** in Pedro's truck.
14. Run **quickly** to catch him!
15. Why did you **quarrel** with your uncle?
16. Al skipped three of the **questions** on the test.
17. A small **earthquake** shook the town last night.
18. Derek plays the violin in the school **orchestra**.
19. I am here to **inquire** about a part-time job.
20. Will you **require** a deposit on that item?

19

Objective
To spell words with the hard and soft c and g sounds

 Correlated Phonics Lessons
MCP Phonics, Level E, Lessons 2–3

Spelling Words in Action   *Page 9*

In "Your Dog, Your Student," students read about dog training. Ask students why it would be important for a dog to learn to come when it is called.

Encourage students to look back at the boldfaced words. Ask volunteers to say each word and identify the sounds made by c and g.

Warm-Up Test
1. Connie went to a **concert** in the park.
2. Are you **certain** you spelled this word right?
3. Bill decided to join the **circus**.
4. Aunt Lisa and Uncle Frank are a great **couple**.
5. Give Joan a lot of **credit** for learning to ski.
6. How should we **celebrate** Mom's birthday?
7. About six hundred people live in that **village**.
8. Becky will **graduate** from high school in June.
9. We were **grateful** to receive Debbie's package.
10. Ms. Goff cut the **coupon** out of the newspaper.
11. The oil **shortage** made prices rise.
12. Waving to a friend is a nice **gesture**.
13. Rob is a **generous** boy who shares with others.
14. Next Saturday we must clean the **garage**.
15. My older brother just got his driver's **license**.
16. Do you want **sausage** and olives on your pizza?
17. This tool is an amazing **gadget**!
18. Try to go to the dentist on a **regular** basis.
19. The roads are **dangerous** when they are wet.
20. Sparkling silver **icicles** hung from the old barn.

Spelling Practice   *Pages 10–11*

Introduce the spelling rules and have students read the **list words** aloud. Encourage students to look back at their **Warm-Up Tests** and apply the spelling rules to any misspelled words.

As students work through the **Spelling Practice** exercises, remind them to look back at their **list words** or in their dictionaries if they need help. You may also want to call students' attention to words that contain both hard and soft c and g: *concert, circus, garage, gadget, icicles.*

 See Rhymes and Songs, page 14
for ESL students

20

Spelling Words in Action

How is training a dog at home like learning at school?

Your Dog, Your Student

You're a student all day at school. At home, your dog can be the student, and you can be the teacher!

Because dogs are pack animals, they love being told what to do. Just like people, dogs like **generous** praise when they do something right. Always make **certain** during training that you show your dog that you love it and that you are **grateful** for its efforts.

It is most important to teach your dog to come to you when called. This could save your dog from a **dangerous** situation someday. Call its name and use a hand **gesture** that signals the dog to come to you. Practice this a **couple** of times a day every day. Go easy, though! Training should be fun for the dog.

You can teach your dog to sit in a similar manner. With the dog on a leash, hold a treat just in front of its nose. Say "sit" and back the treat over its head, gently pushing its back end to the ground at the same time. When it sits, say "good dog" and give it the treat. Your dog deserves **credit** for working hard to learn a new skill.

Once your dog is a happy and well-behaved member of your family, both of you can **graduate** from dog training. **Celebrate** with something more than a **regular** treat. Training a dog can be a very rewarding experience for both you and your dog.

Look back at the boldfaced words. Say each word. What do you notice about the sounds that the letters c and g make?

4

Spelling Practice

TIP

The letter c can spell the hard sound heard at the beginning of cow. It can also spell the soft sound heard at the beginning of cent. The letter g can spell the hard sound in garden or the soft sound in danger.

When a c or g is followed by the vowel e, i or y, it usually spells its soft sound. When c or g is followed by a, o, or u, it usually spells its hard sound.

LIST WORDS
1. concert
2. certain
3. circus
4. couple
5. credit
6. celebrate
7. village
8. graduate
9. grateful
10. coupon
11. shortage
12. gesture
13. generous
14. garage
15. license
16. sausage
17. gadget
18. regular
19. dangerous
20. icicles

Words with Hard and Soft c and g

Write each **list word** under the correct heading. You will use some words more than once.

c as in cent	c as in cow
1. concert	15. concert
2. certain	16. circus
3. circus	17. couple
4. celebrate	18. credit
5. license	19. coupon
6. icicles	20. icicles

g as in danger	g as in garden
7. village	21. graduate
8. shortage	22. grateful
9. gesture	23. garage
10. generous	24. gadget
11. garage	25. regular
12. sausage	
13. gadget	
14. dangerous	

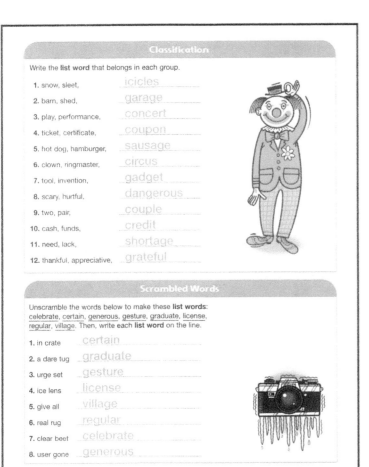

Classification

Write the **list word** that belongs in each group.

1. snow, sleet, _icicles_
2. barn, shed, _garage_
3. play, performance, _concert_
4. ticket, certificate, _coupon_
5. hot dog, hamburger, _sausage_
6. clown, ringmaster, _circus_
7. tool, invention, _gadget_
8. scary, hurtful, _dangerous_
9. two, pair, _couple_
10. cash, funds, _credit_
11. need, lack, _shortage_
12. thankful, appreciative, _grateful_

Scrambled Words

Unscramble the words below to make these **list words**: celebrate, certain, generous, gesture, graduate, license, regular, village. Then, write each **list word** on the line.

1. in crate _certain_
2. a dare tug _graduate_
3. urge set _gesture_
4. ice lens _license_
5. give all _village_
6. real rug _regular_
7. clear beet _celebrate_
8. user gone _generous_

Lesson 2 • Hard and Soft c and g   11

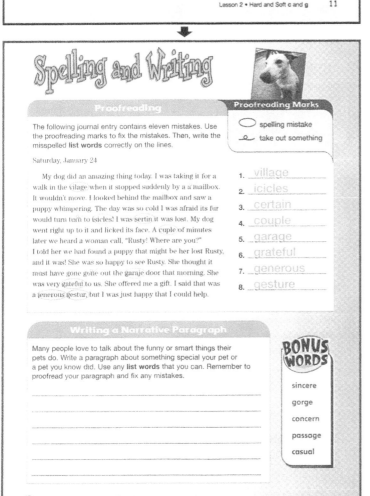

Spelling and Writing

Proofreading

The following journal entry contains eleven mistakes. Use the proofreading marks to fix the mistakes. Then, write the misspelled **list words** correctly on the lines.

Saturday, January 24

My dog did an amazing thing today. I was taking it for a walk in the vilage when it stopped suddenly by a mailbox. It wouldn't move. I looked behind the mailbox and saw a puppy whimpering. The day was so cold I was afraid its fur would turn turn to icicles! I was sertin it was lost. My dog went right up to it and licked its face. A cuple of minutes later we heard a woman call, "Rusty! Where are you?" I told her we had found a puppy that might be her lost Rusty, and it was! She was so happy to see Rusty. She thought it must have gone gone out the garaje door that morning. She was very gateful to us. She offered me a gift. I said that was a jenerous gestur, but I was just happy that I could help.

Proofreading Marks

⬭ spelling mistake
⤶ take out something

1. _village_
2. _icicles_
3. _certain_
4. _couple_
5. _garage_
6. _grateful_
7. _generous_
8. _gesture_

Writing a Narrative Paragraph

Many people love to talk about the funny or smart things their pets do. Write a paragraph about something special your pet or a pet you know did. Use any **list words** that you can. Remember to proofread your paragraph and fix any mistakes.

_____
_____
_____
_____
_____
_____
_____

BONUS WORDS

sincere
gorge
concern
passage
casual

12   Lesson 2 • Hard and Soft c and g

Spelling Strategy

Invite students to look at each **list word** and
- point to and name the vowel *e*, *i*, or *y*, if one of these letters follows the *c* or *g*
- say each word with the soft *c* or *g* sound; then complete these sentences, substituting the appropriate letters and word: "The vowel *e* follows the *c* in *certain*. *Certain* has the soft sound for *c*."

Guide students as they evaluate words that have both the soft and hard sounds, such as *concert* and *gadget*.

BONUS WORDS You may want to suggest that students try to use all five bonus words in a single sentence. Then have students pair up and compare sentences.

Spelling and Writing   *Page 12*

The **Proofreading** exercise will help students prepare to proofread their paragraphs. As students complete the writing activity, encourage them to brainstorm ideas, write a first draft, revise, and proofread their work. To publish their writing, students may want to send their stories to a magazine that publishes children's work.

Writer's Corner Students might enjoy visiting a local humane society and requesting information about caring for pets. Students can summarize what they learned by making a pet-care brochure.

Final Test
1. When does Jan **graduate** from college?
2. Liz has a **couple** of good ideas for the project.
3. Some **sausage** is made from ground pork.
4. The **icicles** look like giant glass needles.
5. Applause is a **gesture** that shows appreciation.
6. Kenneth wanted to move to a peaceful **village**.
7. The drought created a water **shortage**.
8. Larry and Nicolette sell popcorn at a **circus**.
9. Don't forget to renew the dog **license**.
10. What a **dangerous** situation you were in!
11. Where's that **gadget** for sharpening knives?
12. Danielle played the drums at the **concert**.
13. I deserve **credit** for my high marks in math.
14. I was **grateful** to receive the lovely necklace.
15. Thank you for your **generous** offer to help.
16. I'm **certain** I returned that library book!
17. How do you **celebrate** Independence Day?
18. My **coupon** is for a free ride on the Blue Racer.
19. What is your **regular** schedule?
20. Did you put your bike away in the **garage**?

Words with the Sound of f

Objective
To spell words in which *f*, *ff*, *gh*, and *ph* spell the *f* sound

 Phonics Correlated Phonics Lesson
MCP Phonics, Level E, Lesson 4

Spelling Words in Action   *Page 13*
Students learn some facts about dolphins in this selection. Ask students to share what they know about dolphins.

Encourage students to look back at the boldfaced words. Ask volunteers to say each word and identify the letter or letters that make the *f* sound.

Warm-Up Test
1. My sister was **frightened** by the loud noise.
2. When I have a bad headache, I really **suffer**.
3. Will you read the first **paragraph** of the article?
4. Andy made an **effort** to improve in math.
5. Tonya collects the **autographs** of famous people.
6. The **telephone** in my mother's office is cordless.
7. The **dolphins** learned to jump through hoops.
8. Did you leave yourself **enough** time to finish?
9. Comedians measure their success by **laughter**.
10. A **symphony** is a musical work in four parts.
11. Walking is a good form of **physical** exercise.
12. **Photography** is an art form.
13. I am learning about the **atmosphere** in science.
14. The crowd cheered the **flawless** performance.
15. Do you like to study **geography**?
16. Our **triumph** was the result of practice.
17. Do you know how **typhoid** is spread?
18. A compound word may contain a **hyphen**.
19. That was the worst **typhoon** yet!
20. A firefighter has a **tough** job.

Spelling Practice   *Pages 14–15*
Introduce the spelling rule and have students read the **list words** aloud. You may also want to discuss the meanings of words that may be unfamiliar (*typhoid*, *typhoon*). Encourage students to look back at their **Warm-Up Tests** and apply the spelling rule to any misspelled words.

As students work through the **Spelling Practice** exercises, remind them to look back at their **list words** or in their dictionaries if they need help.

for ESL students See Variant Spellings, page 14

22

Spelling Words in Action

What would you find most fun to do if you were a dolphin?

Dolphin Play

Dolphins love to play. They leap out of the water and dance in the waves made by boats.

When dolphins jump out of the water, it's called breaching. Many smaller dolphins will perform one fast breach after another. Some dolphins make small jumps that look like belly flops. Others use more **physical effort** when they jump. Bottle-nosed dolphins can jump 16 feet out of the water. These dolphins can perform **flawless** acrobatics in the air.

Dolphins are friendly animals that live in groups. They whistle, squeak, and click to each other under the water. They're making a dolphin **symphony**. What do these sounds mean? No one knows **enough** about dolphins to be sure. Perhaps the sounds are **laughter**, **frightened** cries, or friendly talk.

Dolphins enjoy being with people who feed them or play games with them. Dolphins can **suffer** because of humans, however. Even though there are laws against hunting dolphins, many are caught in nets meant to catch tuna. People fear that water shows with dolphin stunts may be **tough** on the dolphins. That is why there are laws that protect dolphins from abuse.

Look back at the boldfaced words. Say each word. What do you notice about the way the sound of f is spelled?

13

 **Spelling Practice**

TIP
The f sound can be spelled four ways:
- f as in frightened
- ff as in suffer
- ph as in paragraph
- gh as in enough

LIST WORDS
1. frightened
2. suffer
3. paragraph
4. effort
5. autographs
6. telephone
7. dolphins
8. enough
9. laughter
10. symphony
11. physical
12. photography
13. atmosphere
14. flawless
15. geography
16. triumph
17. typhoid
18. hyphen
19. typhoon
20. tough

Words with the Sound of f

Write each **list word** under the correct heading.

f spells the sound of f
1. frightened
2. flawless

ff spells the sound of f
3. suffer
4. effort

gh spells the sound of f
5. enough
6. laughter
7. tough

ph spells the sound of f
8. atmosphere 9. autographs
10. telephone 11. dolphins
12. symphony 13. physical
14. photography 15. paragraph
16. geography 17. triumph
18. typhoid 19. hyphen
20. typhoon

Synonyms

Synonyms are words that have the same or nearly the same meanings. Write the **list word** that is a synonym for each word given.

1. perfect _flawless_
2. strong _tough_
3. work _effort_
4. signatures _autographs_
5. plenty _enough_
6. victory _triumph_
7. scared _frightened_
8. storm _typhoon_
9. dash _hyphen_
10. disease _typhoid_

Move the Words

Each underlined **list word** in the sentences below must be moved to a different sentence to make sense. Write the correct **list word** in the blank at the end of the sentence.

1. No one likes to see an animal laughter. _suffer_
2. Learning photography helps you find places on maps. _geography_
3. For homework, write a telephone about dolphins. _paragraph_
4. There is concern about polluting the symphony. _atmosphere_
5. It's fun to talk to friends on the dolphins. _telephone_
6. A physical class teaches you how to use a camera. _photography_
7. Atmosphere usually swim and play in groups. _Dolphins_
8. The baby's geography made everyone smile. _laughter_
9. It takes a lot of suffer training to be a professional athlete. _physical_
10. The orchestra played a paragraph by Beethoven. _symphony_

Lesson 3 • Words with the Sound of f   15

Proofreading

The following poster has eleven mistakes. Use the proofreading marks to fix the mistakes. Then write the misspelled **list words** correctly on the lines.

Proofreading Marks
- ⟜ spelling mistake
- ⅃ add apostrophe

Come one, come all!
Dont wait!
Afternoon shows at Tyfoon Bay!

See the dofins perform with flauless grace.
Watch the sailors triumh over the pirates
in an exciting, noisy, and touf sea battle.
Join in with everyones laufter and cheers.
Hear the symfony play.
If you love fotography, be sure to bring your camera.
Telefone 555-3244 for more details.

1. _Typhoon_
2. _dolphins_
3. _flawless_
4. _triumph_
5. _tough_
6. _laughter_
7. _symphony_
8. _photography_
9. _Telephone_

Writing a Letter

Pretend that you are a sea-animal photographer. Write a letter telling a friend about one of the pictures you've taken. What animal does the picture show? Was it difficult to get the shot? Use any **list words** that you can. Remember to proofread your letter and fix any mistakes.

BONUS WORDS

waffle
festival
cough
telegraph
phonograph

16   Lesson 3 • Words with the Sound of f

Spelling Strategy

Say each **list word** and write the word on the board. Then, call on volunteers to come to the board, spell each word aloud, and circle the letters that stand for the f sound. For each word, the class can say this sentence, substituting the appropriate word and letter or letters: "In *frightened,* the letter f spells the sound of f."

BONUS WORDS

You may want to suggest that students write a paragraph using all five bonus words, but leave out 3–4 letters per word. Then have partners trade paragraphs and complete each other's words.

Spelling and Writing   **Page 16**

The **Proofreading** exercise will help students pepare to proofread their letters. As students complete the writing activity, encourage them to brainstorm ideas, write a first draft, revise, and proofread their work. To publish their writing, students may want to exchange letters and write replies to each other.

Writer's Corner Students might enjoy reading a book about dolphins, such as *Whales, Dolphins, and Porpoises* by Mark Carwardine. Encourage them to write a review of the book.

Final Test

1. The **atmosphere** contains oxygen and nitrogen.
2. The first **paragraph** should introduce the topic.
3. Is "machine-made" spelled with a **hyphen**?
4. **Dolphins** use clicks to communicate.
5. Did you **suffer** when you broke your wrist?
6. The runner had a great **triumph**.
7. What a magnificent **symphony** this is!
8. This is a **tough** piece to play for the concert.
9. The dog was **frightened** by the thunder.
10. The story was followed by a burst of **laughter**.
11. Nancy has the **autographs** of two presidents.
12. Doctors today seldom see a case of **typhoid**.
13. That diamond is absolutely **flawless**!
14. A **typhoon** is much like a hurricane.
15. Nico's new **telephone** is wireless.
16. Make sure the animals have **enough** water.
17. Please make an **effort** to be on time.
18. Are you studying **photography** in art class?
19. Knowing **geography** helps clarify the news.
20. Ballet requires **physical** and mental energy.

Objective
To spell words in which *kn* or *gn* spells the *n* sound; *wr* or *rr* spells the *r* sound

 Phonics Correlated Phonics Lessons
MCP Phonics, Level E, Lessons 1, 8, 9

Spelling Words in Action   *Page 17*

In this selection, students find out about how pages on the World Wide Web are designed. Ask students if they know people who have their own Web pages and what sort of information can be found there.

Encourage students to look back at the boldfaced words. Ask volunteers to say each word and identify the letters that spell the *n* or *r* sound.

Warm-Up Test
1. Shanelle made a **wreath** from herbs and flowers.
2. Who's the best swimmer you have ever **known**?
3. My parents typed their papers on electric **typewriters**.
4. The poem was **written** by a former student.
5. Will you take the **wrapper** off that bar of soap?
6. Did you shoot the **arrow** into the target?
7. Use proofreading marks to **correct** the sentences.
8. I used a small **mirror** to reflect the sunlight.
9. Gardens **surround** the castle.
10. **Knead** the dough before putting it into the pan.
11. It's not easy to untie a **knotted** rope.
12. Sarah will **resign** as president of the club.
13. Roberto **designed** new uniforms for the team.
14. The coach will **assign** team positions on Monday.
15. David ironed his **wrinkled** shirt.
16. Last year Becky visited a **foreign** country.
17. The Russian **wrestler** won the match.
18. You gave a terrific **campaign** speech!
19. This **cologne** smells just like roses.
20. Grandmother's swollen **knuckles** are painful.

Spelling Practice   *Pages 18–19*

Introduce the spelling rule and have students read the **list words** aloud. Encourage students to look back at their **Warm-Up Tests** and apply the spelling rule to any misspelled words.

As students work through the **Spelling Practice** exercises, remind them to look back at their **list words** or in their dictionaries if they need help.

 for ESL students See Picture Clues, page 15

Spelling Words in Action

What makes a Web page an efficient way to share information?

Web Pages

Computers have almost completely replaced **typewriters** as a way to create **written** messages. By typing on a computer connected to the Internet, a person can share a message with millions of people around the world.

One way to share information using the computer is with a page on the World Wide Web. A Web page can be set up for almost any reason. Many businesses have **designed** Web pages for selling things. Some businesses are big ones that people have **known** about for a long time, while others are brand-new. A Web page can help run a **campaign** for some cause, give helpful instructions, or just share ideas.

Making a Web page takes some knowledge. Some people think learning the computer language for creating Web pages, called HTML, is a lot like learning a **foreign** language. Books and classes can teach people the **correct** way to make a Web page. Of course, there are also Web pages about how to make a Web page! People don't have to **resign** themselves to learning HTML, though. Instead, they can **assign** the job to a Web master, an expert who designs Web pages for a living. For a more inviting Web page, a designer can **surround** the information with art. Adding sound and video can also help to make a Web page fun to visit.

Say each boldfaced word. Listen for the n sound or the r sound. What do you notice about how these sounds are spelled?

17

TIP
The **list** words contain either the n sound you hear in <u>now</u> or the r sound you hear in <u>rip</u>. The n sound can sometimes be spelled **kn** as in known and **gn** as in assign. The r sound can sometimes be spelled **wr** as in written and **rr** as in arrow.

 ## Spelling Practice

LIST WORDS
1. wreath
2. known
3. typewriters
4. written
5. wrapper
6. arrow
7. correct
8. mirror
9. surround
10. knead
11. knotted
12. resign
13. designed
14. assign
15. wrinkled
16. foreign
17. wrestler
18. campaign
19. cologne
20. knuckles

Words with the Sound of n and r

Write each **list word** under the correct heading.

kn spells the sound of n
1. known   2. knead
3. knotted   4. knuckles

gn spells the sound of n
5. resign   6. designed
7. assign   8. foreign
9. campaign   10. cologne

rr spells the sound of r
11. arrow   12. correct
13. mirror   14. surround

wr spells the sound of r
15. wreath
16. typewriters
17. written
18. wrapper
19. wrinkled
20. wrestler

Missing Words

Write the **list word** that best completes each sentence.

1. Carlos designed the scenery for the class play.
2. Aunt Clara will resign from her job.
3. The first foreign country I visited was Denmark.
4. The champion wrestler entered the ring.
5. Robin Hood's arrow hit the center of the target.
6. She was wearing some cologne that smelled like roses.
7. One of Yellowstone National Park's most famous geysers is known as Old Faithful.
8. Mr. Hall will assign the topics for our report.
9. Mrs. Blake saw her reflection in the mirror.
10. The senator ran a successful campaign.
11. Computers have replaced typewriters in many offices.
12. Use the delete key to correct your error.

Rhyming

Write the **list word** that rhymes with each word given.

1. feed knead
2. twinkled wrinkled
3. teeth wreath
4. spotted knotted
5. around surround
6. buckles knuckles
7. bitten written
8. trapper wrapper

Spelling and Writing

Proofreading

The following article has eight mistakes. Use the proofreading marks to fix the mistakes. Then, write the misspelled **list words** correctly on the lines.

Proofreading Marks

- ⬭ spelling mistake
- ⊙ add period

Across the Internet, any kind of writen message can be sent from one computer to another, even to those in forein countries The Internet was originally desiged for the military in the 1960's For years, it was hardly nown outside military and academic circles. Then, in 1989, the invention of the World Wide Web made the Internet useful for many purposes The popularity of the Web depends in part on the use of links to other Web sites. When you're looking for the corect answer to a question, links take you from one site to another with a single click of the mouse.

1. written 2. foreign 3. designed
4. known 5. correct

Writing an Informative Paragraph

Think of a topic for a Web site that would be helpful to others. It could provide directions, information, or a useful idea. Write a paragraph about your Web site. Try to use as many **list words** as you can. Remember to proofread your paragraph and fix any mistakes.

BONUS WORDS

knowledge
align
ferry
wrath
errand

Spelling Strategy

You may want to make two columns on the board: one for the **list words** with the *n* sound spelled *kn* or *gn*, and one for the list words with the *r* sound spelled *rr* or *wr*. (Write the words in a sequence that differs from the one in **Spelling Practice**.) Call on volunteers to come to the board, say each word, and circle the letters that spell the *n* or *r* sound.

BONUS WORDS You may want to suggest that students work with a partner to write a definition for each bonus word. Then, have them look up the words in a dictionary. Ask how many of their definitions are similar to those in the dictionary.

Spelling and Writing **Page 20**

The **Proofreading** exercise will help students prepare to proofread their paragraphs. As students complete the writing activity, encourage them to brainstorm ideas, write a first draft, revise, and proofread their work. To publish their writing, students may want to create a class book with all their ideas.

Writer's Corner Students might enjoy reading *Make Your Own Web Page! A Guide for Kids* by Ted Pedersen or other books about designing a Web page. Suggest that students take notes as they read and then draft the text they would include in a personal Web page.

Final Test

1. Ask your partner to **correct** your work.
2. The ribbon was **knotted** in several places.
3. Computers have replaced **typewriters**.
4. What kind of **cologne** was Aunt Lois wearing?
5. Elephants have gray, **wrinkled** skin.
6. Which architect **designed** that museum?
7. My brother is a **wrestler** on the school team.
8. We made a **wreath** from evergreen branches.
9. Please put the candy **wrapper** in the trash.
10. Tall pine trees **surround** the village.
11. **Knead** the clay with your hands to soften it.
12. The **campaign** workers hung posters.
13. The teacher will **assign** a book report.
14. The **arrow** broke when it hit the big rock.
15. I have **known** Connie for five years.
16. Mario will **resign** as secretary of the math club.
17. Don't break that **mirror**!
18. "Fire and Ice" was **written** by Robert Frost.
19. My **foreign** pen pal lives in Denmark.
20. How did you get that scrape on your **knuckles**?

Words with the Sound of el and l

Objective
To spell words with the final *el* and *l* sounds spelled *le*, *el*, and *al*

Spelling Words in Action — Page 21
Students may be surprised by what they learn in "Pizza Pizzazz." After reading, invite students to tell what kind of pizza they think is best, and why.

Encourage students to look back at the boldfaced words. Ask volunteers to say each word and identify the sound made by *le, el,* or *al.*

Warm-Up Test
1. What was your **final** grade in the class?
2. An egg has an **oval** shape.
3. More **fuel** is used during a cold winter.
4. A half of one-fourth **equals** one-eighth.
5. This **pickle** is so sour it makes my lips pucker.
6. Don't **tickle** the baby!
7. To **double** the recipe, use four eggs instead of two.
8. A **jungle** is a tropical region overgrown with plants.
9. They will **panel** the walls on Saturday.
10. We grabbed our **towels** and ran to the beach.
11. If it rains, we'll **cancel** the picnic.
12. A **plural** noun refers to more than one item.
13. A horse is a **mammal**, but a horsefly is not.
14. Stars **sparkled** in the dark blue sky.
15. Will your dog come when you **whistle**?
16. Denuta found an empty seat next to the **aisle**.
17. Let's **scramble** some eggs for breakfast.
18. On what **channel** is today's baseball game?
19. The football flew through the air in a **spiral**.
20. The sleigh bells **jingle** when the horse moves.

Spelling Practice — Pages 22–23
Introduce the spelling rule and have students read the **list words** aloud. Encourage students to look back at their **Warm-Up Tests** and apply the spelling rule to any misspelled words.

As students work through the **Spelling Practice** exercises, remind them to look back at their **list words** or in their dictionaries if they need help.

See Letter Cards, page 15

26

Words with the Sound of el and l — Lesson 5

Spelling Words in Action

Why is pizza such a popular food?

Pizza Pizzazz

Did you know that Americans eat billions of slices of pizza a year? On average, one person eats 23 pounds of pizza a year. That **equals** almost a half a pound of pizza a week.

Of all age groups in the United States, teenagers and college students eat the most pizza. Maybe they think pizza is the best **fuel** to help them study for **final** exams. Whatever the reason, pizza makers **scramble** to get spots near colleges to set up their shops.

The great thing about pizza is that you can put anything on it. You might like a **pickle** on your pizza or **double** cheese. You can choose whatever will **tickle** your fancy. Some people like broccoli or pineapple on their pizza. If you're like most people, however, you'll ask to **cancel** the anchovies.

Can pizza be improved? What if pizzas were **oval** instead of round? Or, what if pizza makers could twist the toppings, sauce, and crust into a **spiral**? What would you do to make an original pizza? How many toppings would it have? Would it have a thin crust or a thick one? Have a contest with your friends to see who can think of the best new pizza. Yum!

Look back at the boldfaced words. How is the last syllable in each word spelled? Say each word and listen to the sound made by the last syllable.

21

Spelling Practice

TIP
The sounds of el and l can be spelled in different ways. Listen to the sound made by the syllables spelled **le, el,** and **al** in the **list words**. The letters le, el, and al all spell the same sound in the last syllable of words such as pickle, towels, and final.

LIST WORDS
1. final
2. oval
3. fuel
4. equals
5. pickle
6. tickle
7. double
8. jungle
9. panel
10. towels
11. cancel
12. plural
13. mammal
14. sparkled
15. whistle
16. aisle
17. scramble
18. channel
19. spiral
20. jingle

Words with the Sound of el and l
Write each **list word** under the correct heading.

le spells the sound of el or l
1. pickle
2. tickle
3. double
4. jungle
5. sparkled
6. whistle
7. aisle
8. scramble
9. jingle

el spells the sound of el or l
10. fuel
11. panel
12. towels
13. cancel
14. channel

al spells the sound of el or l
15. final
16. oval
17. equals
18. plural
19. mammal
20. spiral

22 Lesson 5 • Words with the Sound of el and l

Definitions

Write a **list word** to match each definition clue. Find the answer to the riddle by reading down the letters in the shaded box.

1. shaped like an egg   o v a l
2. is the same as   e q u a l s
3. walkway between seats   a i s l e
4. last   f i n a l
5. end   c a n c e l
6. twice as much   d o u b l e
7. used for drying   t o w e l s
8. used to supply heat or power   f u e l
9. to cover a wall with wood   p a n e l
10. a noisemaker   w h i s t l e
11. to make ringing sounds   j i n g l e

Riddle: What do most people order in a pizza shop? a slice of pie

Comparing Words

Study the relationship between the first two underlined words. Then, write a **list word** that has the same relationship with the third underlined word.

1. cold is to the Arctic as hot is to a   jungle
2. scream is to scare as laugh is to   tickle
3. pizza is to pepperoni as hamburger is to   pickle
4. fold is to half as twist is to   spiral
5. snake is to reptile as lion is to   mammal
6. cake is to bake as eggs are to   scramble
7. past is to present as single is to   plural
8. radio is to station as TV is to   channel
9. fire is to blazed as diamond is to   sparkled

Spelling and Writing

Proofreading

The following want ad has nine mistakes. Use the proofreading marks to fix the mistakes. Then, write the misspelled **list words** correctly on the lines.

Proofreading Marks
- ⬯ spelling mistake
- ⌃ add something

Are you tired of the workday jungel? Do you feel that life is a constant scamble? Do you have ideas that once sparkeld, but are now dull? Then, you may be the person who fits the job of advertising manager for our pizza products. You will be responsible for writing a new jingel for our television commercials. Does all this tikel your fancy? This is our finel offer! Call 555-1243 to set up an appointment.

1. jungle   2. scramble
3. sparkled   4. jingle
5. tickle   6. final

Writing a Persuasive Paragraph

Think of a favorite healthy snack that you wish your school would serve. Write a paragraph to persuade your school to put the snack on the menu. Use any **list words** that you can. Remember to proofread your paragraph and fix any mistakes.

BONUS WORDS

general

dismal

muscle

noble

easel

Spelling Strategy

Students can work with a partner to practice the **list words**. After one student says a **list word**, the other can hold up a sign labeled with the appropriate letter pair (*al, el,* or *le*) contained in the word.

BONUS WORDS You may want to suggest that students write a question using each bonus word. Then have them ask a partner their questions. Encourage them to answer each one.

Spelling and Writing   *Page 24*

The **Proofreading** exercise will help students prepare to proofread their paragraphs. As students complete the writing activity, encourage them to brainstorm ideas, write a first draft, revise, and proofread their work. To publish their writing, students may want to make a persuasive speech.

Writer's Corner To learn more about pizza, the class can research the subject in the library or by conducting an Internet search. Encourage groups of students to use the information to create a poster that tells the most fascinating pizza facts.

Final Test

1. The **spiral** staircase led to a sunny loft.
2. Will we **panel** the walls in the dining room?
3. Turn the cards over and then **scramble** them.
4. Did you enjoy the **final** chapter of the book?
5. My cat purrs when I **tickle** her under the chin.
6. Coal, oil, and gas are kinds of **fuel**.
7. If you **double** your money, you'll be lucky.
8. Jon wants to sit on the seat next to the **aisle**.
9. The weather **channel** gave the forecast.
10. Most **plural** nouns end in the letter *s*.
11. A whale is a **mammal** that lives in the water.
12. Five times five **equals** twenty-five.
13. Oh, that **pickle** is sour!
14. Tigers can be found in the **jungle** in India.
15. Please hang the wet **towels** on the clothesline.
16. The lifeguard blew a **whistle** to warn the swimmer.
17. José is sick, so we decided to **cancel** the party.
18. When I move, the bells on my bracelet **jingle**.
19. The diamonds in the shop **sparkled** brilliantly.
20. She placed the photo in an **oval** frame.

Lessons 1–5 · Review

Objectives
To review spelling words with the sounds of
k, kw, and *n*; hard and soft *c* and *g*; the
sound of *f*; *kn, gn, wr,* and *rr*; the sounds
of *el* and *l*

Check Your Spelling Notebook
Pages 25–28

Based on your observations, note which words
are giving students the most difficulty and offer
assistance for spelling them correctly. Here are
some frequently misspelled words to watch for:
aches, license, enough, campaign, cologne, cancel, and
whistle.

To give students extra help and practice in
taking standardized tests, you may want to have
them take the **Review Test** for this lesson on pages
30–31. After scoring the tests, return them to
students so that they can record their misspelled
words in their spelling notebooks.

After practicing their troublesome words,
students can work through the exercises for lessons
1–5 and the cumulative review, **Show What You
Know**. Before they begin each exercise, you may
want to go over the spelling rule.

Take It Home

Suggest that students look for the **list words**
from lessons 1–5 in newspapers and magazines.
Students can also use **Take It Home** Master 1 on
pages 32–33 to help them do the activity. (A
complete list of the spelling words is included on
page 32 of the **Take It Home** Master.) At school,
invite students to share their phrases and sentences
that contain **list words**.

Lessons 1–5 · Review

In lessons 1 through 5, you learned different ways to spell words with the sounds k, kw, and n, as well as the sounds f, r, el, and l. You also learned to spell words with the soft and hard sounds for c and g.

Check Your Spelling Notebook

Look at the words in your spelling notebook. Which words for lessons 1 through 5 did you have the most trouble with? Write them here.

Practice writing your troublesome words with a partner. Take turns writing each word as the other slowly spells it aloud.

Lesson 1

 Listen for the kw sound in quarrel. Notice how the k sound is spelled in speaker, mechanic, and jacket. The n sound can be spelled with kn, as in knowing.

Write a **list word** that belongs in each group. Not all the words will be used.

List Words: quiet, orchestra, aches, shake, knocked, jacket, quarter, mechanic, quickly, kneeling, sequence, character

1. events, order, _sequence_
2. fast, rapidly, _quickly_
3. shiver, rattle, _shake_
4. silent, calm, _quiet_
5. nickel, dime, _quarter_
6. plot, setting, _character_
7. pains, sores, _aches_
8. coat, sweater, _jacket_
9. standing, sitting, _kneeling_
10. rapped, tapped, _knocked_

25

Lesson 2

 The letters c and g each have a soft sound and a hard sound. Listen for the sounds of c in certain and coupon. Listen for the sounds of g in gadget.

Write a **list word** that matches each clue. Not all the words will be used.

List Words: concert, sausage, circus, couple, village, celebrate, graduate, gesture, garage, license, dangerous, icicles

1. a sign of winter _icicles_
2. a shelter for a car _garage_
3. finish high school _graduate_
4. have a party _celebrate_
5. band performance _concert_
6. spicy meat _sausage_
7. wave a hand _gesture_
8. a pair _couple_
9. permits driving a car _license_
10. has tents and clowns _circus_

Lesson 3

The f sound can be spelled four ways: f, ff, ph, and gh, as in frightened, suffer, typhoon, and laughter.

Write the **list word** that is a synonym for the word given. Not all the words will be used.

List Words: frightened, effort, autographs, symphony, dolphins, enough, atmosphere, flawless, triumph, laughter, hyphen, tough

1. dash _hyphen_
2. plenty _enough_
3. victory _triumph_
4. signatures _autographs_
5. hard _tough_
6. perfect _flawless_
7. attempt _effort_
8. scared _frightened_
9. air _atmosphere_
10. giggles _laughter_

26 Lesson 6 · Review

28

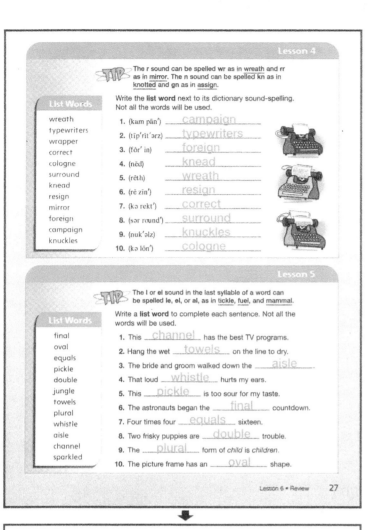

Lesson 4

TIP: The r sound can be spelled wr as in <u>wreath</u> and rr as in <u>mirror</u>. The n sound can be spelled kn as in <u>knotted</u> and gn as in <u>assign</u>.

List Words

wreath
typewriters
wrapper
correct
cologne
surround
knead
resign
mirror
foreign
campaign
knuckles

Write the **list word** next to its dictionary sound-spelling. Not all the words will be used.

1. (kam pān') ___campaign___
2. (tīp'rīt'ərz) ___typewriters___
3. (fôr' in) ___foreign___
4. (nēd) ___knead___
5. (rēth) ___wreath___
6. (rē zin') ___resign___
7. (kə rekt') ___correct___
8. (sər round') ___surround___
9. (nuk'əlz) ___knuckles___
10. (kə lōn') ___cologne___

Lesson 5

TIP: The l or el sound in the last syllable of a word can be spelled le, el, or al, as in <u>tickle</u>, <u>fuel</u>, and <u>mammal</u>.

List Words

final
oval
equals
pickle
double
jungle
towels
plural
whistle
aisle
channel
sparkled

Write a **list word** to complete each sentence. Not all the words will be used.

1. This ___channel___ has the best TV programs.
2. Hang the wet ___towels___ on the line to dry.
3. The bride and groom walked down the ___aisle___.
4. That loud ___whistle___ hurts my ears.
5. This ___pickle___ is too sour for my taste.
6. The astronauts began the ___final___ countdown.
7. Four times four ___equals___ sixteen.
8. Two frisky puppies are ___double___ trouble.
9. The ___plural___ form of *child* is *children*.
10. The picture frame has an ___oval___ shape.

Lesson 6 • Review   27

Show What You Know

Lessons 1–5 Review

One word is misspelled in each set of **list words**. Fill in the circle next to the **list word** that is spelled incorrectly.

#					
1.	aisle	resign	● enoufh	generous	jacket
2.	● wreth	scramble	knuckles	triumph	sausage
3.	quiet	couple	arrow	plural	● gneeling
4.	inquire	garage	physical	● knoted	towels
5.	symphony	quarrel	village	coupon	● photograpy
6.	mirror	tickle	grateful	atmosphere	● wistle
7.	laughter	sparkled	jungle	● duble	correct
8.	● speeker	spiral	channel	questions	shortage
9.	gesture	● orkestra	flawless	surround	pickle
10.	● desined	typhoid	gadget	sequence	aches
11.	concert	effort	● nown	oval	equals
12.	knowing	celebrate	telephone	wrapper	● cansel
13.	knothole	earthquake	● cologn	campaign	mammal
14.	● panle	knead	paragraph	circus	quarter
15.	dolphins	suffer	regular	● lisense	wrinkled
16.	foreign	● typhon	dangerous	knocked	jingle
17.	● restler	hyphen	character	quickly	fuel
18.	written	autographs	credit	mechanic	● finael
19.	● asigne	frightened	certain	icicles	tough
20.	shake	● requir	graduate	geography	typewriters

28 - Lesson 6 • Review

Final Test

1. I'm trying to study, so please be **quiet**.
2. The tickets to the **concert** sold out in an hour.
3. The loud thunder **frightened** the small puppy.
4. Sheila hung a **wreath** on the front door.
5. I will repeat the directions one **final** time.
6. San's knee **aches** whenever it rains.
7. It would be fun to be a **circus** clown.
8. Liz made an **effort** to be more helpful.
9. Computers replaced **typewriters** in our office.
10. The shape of our dining room table is **oval**.
11. If you **shake** the rattle, the baby won't cry.
12. We're going on vacation in a **couple** of weeks.
13. Jen collects **autographs** of sports stars.
14. Please throw the gum **wrapper** in the trash.
15. Thirty-six divided by twelve **equals** three.
16. He **knocked** on the door, but no one answered.
17. Let's **celebrate** your graduation!
18. Three **dolphins** swam beside the boat.
19. Who knows the **correct** answer?
20. Dad put **pickle** slices on his hamburger.
21. Is the zipper on Sam's **jacket** stuck?
22. Carlos will **graduate** from high school in June.
23. There's **enough** food to feed an army!
24. Mr. Yee built a fence to **surround** his garden.
25. The rising dough will **double** in volume.
26. Danielle put a **quarter** in the parking meter.
27. He offered his hand in a **gesture** of friendliness.
28. The **atmosphere** in the auditorium was stuffy.
29. **Knead** the dough until it is smooth and elastic.
30. Use the old **towels** to dry the dog after its bath.
31. If we walk **quickly**, we can catch up with Anne.
32. Jay keeps his bike in the **garage** next to his car.
33. We applauded the **flawless** backflip.
34. Mr. Mann will **resign** as principal of the school.
35. Some words add *es* to form the **plural**.
36. My knees hurt from **kneeling** on the hard floor.
37. Where did Megan get her fishing **license**?
38. The town cheered its team's **triumph**.
39. I think Italian is a beautiful **foreign** language.
40. I heard the **whistle** before I saw the train.
41. Write the events of the story in **sequence**.
42. Skating on thin ice is **dangerous**.
43. Santos has two last names joined by a **hyphen**.
44. The candidates rested after a hard **campaign**.
45. The usher led us down the **aisle** to our seats.
46. The main **character** in this story is an artist.
47. There are **icicles** on the porch roof.
48. The hikers had a **tough** path to follow.
49. I hurt my **knuckles** when I rapped on the door.
50. Which **channel** has the local news?

29

Name _____

Read each set of words. Fill in the circle next to the word that is spelled correctly.

1. (a) sequence   (c) sequents
   (b) sequense   (d) seequence

2. (a) danegerous   (c) dangerous
   (b) dngerus   (d) dangrous

3. (a) triumff   (c) triumph
   (b) triumgh   (d) triumf

4. (a) forign   (c) foureign
   (b) foreign   (d) fureign

5. (a) knealing   (c) neeling
   (b) kneeling   (d) nealing

6. (a) campaign   (c) campagne
   (b) campane   (d) campain

7. (a) coupple   (c) couple
   (b) cupple   (d) coupel

8. (a) atmosfeer   (c) atmospheer
   (b) atmosphere   (d) atmosfere

9. (a) asle   (c) istle
   (b) aistle   (d) aisle

10. (a) hyphen   (c) hyfen
    (b) hiphen   (d) hyphan

11. (a) lisense   (c) liscence
    (b) lisence   (d) license

12. (a) plurral   (c) plural
    (b) plurall   (d) plurale

Name _____

Review Test (Side B)

Read each set of words. Fill in the circle next to the word that is spelled correctly.

13. ⓐ icycles   ⓒ icicels
     ⓑ icecles   ⓓ icicles

14. ⓐ effort   ⓒ efort
     ⓑ ephort   ⓓ effert

15. ⓐ jackett   ⓒ jaket
     ⓑ jakett   ⓓ jacket

16. ⓐ quiett   ⓒ kwiet
     ⓑ quiete   ⓓ quiet

17. ⓐ autographs   ⓒ awtographs
     ⓑ autograffs   ⓓ autograghs

18. ⓐ whistel   ⓒ whistle
     ⓑ wistle   ⓓ whisle

19. ⓐ wrethe   ⓒ reath
     ⓑ wreath   ⓓ wreeth

20. ⓐ garadge   ⓒ garrage
     ⓑ garage   ⓓ garagge

21. ⓐ knuckels   ⓒ knuckles
     ⓑ nuckles   ⓓ nuckels

22. ⓐ ovel   ⓒ ovall
     ⓑ ovle   ⓓ oval

23. ⓐ knocked   ⓒ knoked
     ⓑ knockt   ⓓ nocked

24. ⓐ surrowned   ⓒ surround
     ⓑ suround   ⓓ scuround

25. ⓐ duoble   ⓒ doubel
     ⓑ double   ⓓ dubble

Take It Home

1

Your child has learned to spell many new words and would like to share them with you and your family. Here are some activities that will help your child review the words in lessons 1–5 and provide family fun, too!

Words in Print

Encourage your child to look for spelling words in newspapers and magazines. Have your child copy the phrases and sentences in which the words appear on a sheet of paper, and then highlight the spelling words with a colored marker.

Lesson 1

1. aches
2. character
3. earthquake
4. inquire
5. jacket
6. kneeling
7. knocked
8. knothole
9. knowing
10. mechanic
11. orchestra
12. quarrel
13. quarter
14. questions
15. quickly
16. quiet
17. require
18. sequence
19. shake
20. speaker

Lesson 2

1. celebrate
2. certain
3. circus
4. concert
5. couple
6. coupon
7. credit
8. dangerous
9. gadget
10. garage
11. generous
12. gesture
13. graduate
14. grateful
15. icicles
16. license
17. regular
18. sausage
19. shortage
20. village

Lesson 3

1. atmosphere
2. autographs
3. dolphins
4. effort
5. enough
6. flawless
7. frightened
8. geography
9. hyphen
10. laughter
11. paragraph
12. photography
13. physical
14. suffer
15. symphony
16. telephone
17. tough
18. triumph
19. typhoid
20. typhoon

Lesson 4

1. arrow
2. assign
3. campaign
4. cologne
5. correct
6. designed
7. foreign
8. knead
9. knotted
10. known
11. knuckles
12. mirror
13. resign
14. surround
15. typewriters
16. wrapper
17. wreath
18. wrestler
19. wrinkled
20. written

Lesson 5

1. aisle
2. cancel
3. channel
4. double
5. equals
6. final
7. fuel
8. jingle
9. jungle
10. mammal
11. oval
12. panel
13. pickle
14. plural
15. scramble
16. sparkled
17. spiral
18. tickle
19. towels
20. whistle

Crossword Puzzle for Two

The spelling words in the box will help you and your child solve this crossword puzzle.

suffer	tickle	fuel	equals	quiet
enough	foreign	oval	aisle	surround

ACROSS

2. to feel or have pain
4. coal, gas, oil, and wood
6. a light touch
8. to enclose
10. a narrow passageway

DOWN

1. not noisy
3. of another country
5. the amount needed or wanted
7. is the same amount or size
9. shaped like an egg

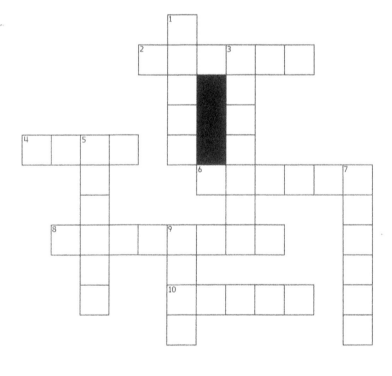

Lesson 7

Vowel Pairs <u>ai</u>, <u>ay</u>, <u>oa</u>, and <u>ow</u>

Objective
To spell words in which vowel pairs *ai*, *ay*, *oa*, and *ow* spell the long *a* and long *o* sounds

 Phonics Correlated Phonics Lessons
MCP Phonics, Level E, Lessons 15, 17

Spelling Words in Action *Page 29*

In "A Sticky Subject," students discover which country has more gum chewers than any other nation in the world. After reading, ask students which part of the selection they liked the best.

Encourage students to look back at the boldfaced words. Ask volunteers to say each word and identify the letters that make the long *a* or long *o* sound.

Warm-Up Test
1. Did you **complain** about the poor service?
2. I will **braid** the ribbons to make a belt.
3. Don't pour grease down **drains**!
4. These pine trees grow mainly along the **coast**.
5. Rosa made a sandwich on **toasted** bread.
6. Too much sugar can cause tooth **decay**.
7. The campers were **roasting** potatoes.
8. Recycle instead of **throwing** objects away.
9. The weather **tomorrow** will be sunny.
10. If you **borrow** something, be sure to return it.
11. Alissa likes to **boast** about how fast she runs.
12. A python **swallows** its food whole.
13. The ocean waves made the water **foamy**.
14. Do you know how to **poach** an egg?
15. Does the recipe call for **cocoa**?
16. He was so shocked that he **fainted**.
17. Dress the **scarecrow** in those old clothes.
18. During the trade, we **gained** a great pitcher.
19. The flying saucer sighting was just a **hoax**.
20. The burn was **painful**, but not serious.

Spelling Practice *Pages 30–31*

Introduce the spelling rule and have students read the **list words** aloud. At this point, you may want to discuss the meanings of unfamiliar words such as *hoax* and *poach*. Then encourage students to look back at their **Warm-Up Tests** and apply the spelling rule to any misspelled words.

As students work through the **Spelling Practice** exercises, remind them to look back at their **list words** or in their dictionaries if they need help.

for ESL students See Spelling Aloud, page 14

34

Vowel Pairs <u>ai</u>, <u>ay</u>, <u>oa</u>, and <u>ow</u> Lesson 7

Spelling Words in Action

What are the pros and cons of bubble gum?

A Sticky Subject

Parents and teachers often **complain** about it. You might hear, "It's bad for your teeth!" or, "If anyone **swallows** it, it might become lodged in the throat!"

In case you haven't guessed, they're talking about chewing gum. You must admit, the complaints are well-founded. Gum is messy, and many people are careless with it. Instead of wrapping it after chewing, some people end up **throwing** it or dropping it. If you blow a bubble big enough to get stuck in your hair, removing the gum can be very **painful**.

Those who say that gum is bad for your teeth are also correct. We all know that too much sugar helps cause tooth **decay**. If you must chew, **borrow** some good advice and make the gum sugarless!

Americans can **boast** of chewing more gum than any other people in the world. The average American chews 300 sticks of gum a year. From **coast** to coast, Americans spend more than $2 billion a year on gum. Just for the record, Susan Montgomery Williams of Fresno, California, **gained** fame in 1979 by blowing the largest bubble ever. Using three pieces of gum, Susan blew a bubble that measured 19 inches in diameter. She went on to break that record three times. In 1994, she blew a 23-inch bubble. If you blew a bubble that big, would you have **fainted**?

Say the boldfaced words in the selection with the vowel pairs ai and ay. How are they alike? Say the boldfaced words with the vowel pairs <u>oa</u> and <u>ow</u>. How are they alike?

29

TIP

A vowel pair is made from two vowels that come together to make one long vowel sound. The first vowel in the pair usually stands for its long sound, and the second is silent. The vowel pairs **ai** and **ay** can spell the long a sound you hear in <u>drains</u> and <u>decay</u>. The vowel pairs **oa** and **ow** can spell the long **o** sound you hear in <u>coast</u> and <u>borrow</u>.

Spelling Practice

LIST WORDS
1. complain
2. braid
3. drains
4. coast
5. toasted
6. decay
7. roasting
8. throwing
9. tomorrow
10. borrow
11. boast
12. swallows
13. foamy
14. poach
15. cocoa
16. fainted
17. scarecrow
18. gained
19. hoax
20. painful

Words with the Sound of Long o and Long a

Write each **list word** under the correct heading.

long o sound
1. coast
2. toasted
3. roasting
4. throwing
5. tomorrow
6. borrow
7. boast
8. swallows
9. foamy
10. poach
11. cocoa
12. scarecrow
13. hoax

long a sound
14. complain
15. braid
16. drains
17. decay
18. fainted
19. gained
20. painful

30 Lesson 7 • Vowel Pairs ai, ay, oa, and **ow**

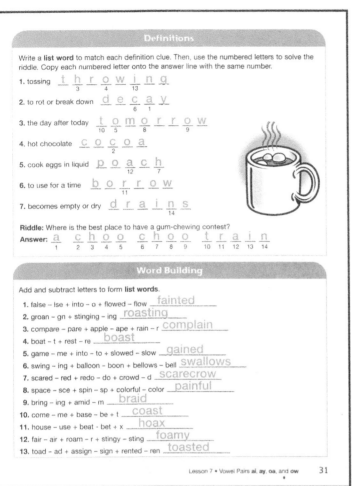

Definitions

Write a **list word** to match each definition clue. Then, use the numbered letters to solve the riddle. Copy each numbered letter onto the answer line with the same number.

1. tossing t h r o w i n g
           3 4   13

2. to rot or break down d e c a y
             6 1

3. the day after today t o m o r r o w
         10 5   8   9

4. hot chocolate c o c o a
           2

5. cook eggs in liquid p o a c h
          12 7

6. to use for a time b o r r o w
           11

7. becomes empty or dry d r a i n s
             14

Riddle: Where is the best place to have a gum-chewing contest?

Answer: a c h o o c h o o t r a i n
     1 2 3 4 5 6 7 8 9 10 11 12 13 14

Word Building

Add and subtract letters to form **list words**.

1. false – lse + into – o + flowed – flow fainted
2. groan – gn + stinging – ing roasting
3. compare – pare + apple – ape + rain – r complain
4. boat – t + rest – re boast
5. game – me + into – to + slowed – slow gained
6. swing – ing + balloon – boon + bellows – bell swallows
7. scared – red + redo – do + crowd – d scarecrow
8. space – sce + spin – sp + colorful – color painful
9. bring – ing + amid – m braid
10. come – me + base – be + t coast
11. house – use + beat - bet + x hoax
12. fair – air + roam – r + stingy – sting foamy
13. toad – ad + assign – sign + rented – ren toasted

Lesson 7 • Vowel Pairs ai, ay, oa, and ow   31

Spelling and Writing

Proofreading

Proofreading Marks
- ⬭ spelling mistake
- ☰ capital letter
- ⌃ add something

The following article has ten mistakes. Use the proofreading marks to fix each mistake. Then, write the misspelled **list words** correctly on the lines.

Where do you think chewing gum came from It came from the dried sap of a jungle tree called sapodilla that was chewed by the aztecs. They called it *chictli*. chewing gum showed up on the east coost of the united States in 1871. Do you know what happened Many people loved the gum, but others began to complayn that chewing drayns moisture from the salivary glands; and if a person swalloes it, the stomach will be upset. It was not until the mid-1900s that people began to worry about tooth decai.

1. coast   2. complain   3. drains
4. swallows   5. decay

Writing a Problem-Solution Essay

Some people think that chewing gum is a bad habit. Do you have any ideas about how a bad habit, such as fingernail biting, might be broken? Write your ideas in a problem-solution essay that describes the problem and presents a possible solution. Use any **list words** that you can. Remember to proofread your paragraph and fix any mistakes.

BONUS WORDS
- sorrow
- stain
- betray
- toadstool
- sparrow

32   Lesson 7 • Vowel Pairs ai, ay, oa, and ow

Spelling Strategy

To help students practice spelling the **list words**, invite them to get together with a partner and take turns writing each **list word** and pronouncing the word. Then have them
- circle the vowel pair *ai*, *ay*, *oa*, or *ow*
- tell the sound the vowel pair stands for.

BONUS WORDS You may want to suggest that students write a story with the bonus words, then erase the bonus words. Have them trade papers with a partner and try to fill in the missing words.

Spelling and Writing   **Page 32**

The **Proofreading** exercise will help students prepare to proofread their writing. As students complete the writing activity, encourage them to brainstorm ideas, write a first draft, revise, and proofread their work. To publish their work, students may want to create a brochure called "Breaking Bad Habits."

Writer's Corner The class can visit the Web site of the National Association of Chewing Gum Manufacturers at http://www.nacgm.org/consumer/consumer.html. Encourage students to take notes as they click around the site to read the story of gum and other fun facts.

Final Test

1. That goat **swallows** anything I give it.
2. What you smell is a **toasted** cheese sandwich.
3. What a **painful** moment that was!
4. They began to **complain** about the bumpy ride.
5. Hot **cocoa** tastes wonderful on cold, rainy days.
6. I helped my little sister **braid** her hair.
7. Do you like the **scarecrow** in the garden?
8. My cat has **gained** too much weight.
9. Don't use the sinks until the **drains** are cleaned.
10. His neighbors were **throwing** out a huge box.
11. Can I **borrow** your social studies notes?
12. It was so hot that a camper **fainted**.
13. Beat the eggs and milk until they are **foamy**.
14. California is a state on the west **coast**.
15. Polite people do not **boast** about themselves.
16. The turkey is **roasting** in the oven right now.
17. This fish will taste better if you **poach** it.
18. Sometimes a **hoax** can even fool the experts.
19. It's wonderful not to have any tooth **decay**!
20. Is your doctor appointment **tomorrow**?

35

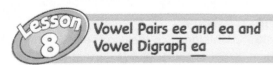

Lesson 8

Vowel Pairs ee and ea and Vowel Digraph ea

Objective
To spell words in which the vowel pair *ee* spells the long *e* sound, vowel pair *ea* spells the long *e* sound, and vowel digraph *ea* spells the short *e* sound

 Correlated Phonics Lessons
MCP Phonics, Level E, Lessons 16, 18

Spelling Words in Action   *Page 33*

In this selection, students read to find out why birds have feathers. Afterward, discuss how feathers help birds survive.

Call on volunteers to say the boldfaced words and identify the letters that spell the long *e* or short *e* sound.

Warm-Up Test

1. The bird had a red tail **feather**.
2. Jim got a blue **sweater** for a birthday present.
3. The cat took a nap **underneath** the chair.
4. The girls came to an **agreement** about the job.
5. In spring, the **meadows** are full of wild flowers.
6. Kathy gave the graduation **speech**.
7. Are there **needles** and thread in that box?
8. The teacher is **keeping** a record of attendance.
9. Does the map show where the **treasure** is?
10. The brightest star shines in the **northeast**.
11. Hai-Sin keeps up a **steady** pace when she jogs.
12. What an unusual sea **creature** that is!
13. It is hard to **breathe** at high altitudes.
14. It was a **pleasure** to meet our new neighbors.
15. It takes hard work to **succeed** in business.
16. Peaches taste **sweeter** to me than apples.
17. A balanced diet will help you stay **healthy**.
18. After the service, he spoke to the **preacher**.
19. Is Arnie's new belt genuine **leather**?
20. **Wealth** does not always bring happiness.

Spelling Practice   *Pages 34–35*

Introduce the spelling rule and have students read the **list words** aloud. You may want to point out that *ea* can be both a vowel pair and a vowel digraph. Encourage students to look back at their **Warm-Up Tests** and apply the spelling rule to any misspelled words.

As students work through the **Spelling Practice** exercises, remind them to look back at their **list words** or in their dictionaries if they need help.

for ESL students **See Picture Clues, page 15**

Spelling Words in Action

Why are feathers a bird's treasure?

On the Wing

It is said that birds of a **feather** flock together. Birds may not be in **agreement** with that statement. That's because no two feathers are exactly the same. Feathers come in a variety of shapes, colors, and sizes. One large bird alone can have as many as 25,000 feathers from head to tail.

Feathers are not only beautiful, but they also help a bird fly. Smaller feathers help streamline the **creature** so that it will not resist air. The larger wing and tail feathers help lift a bird into the sky.

Feathers help birds stay **healthy** by serving like a **sweater** to keep them warm and dry. Each quill has thousands of tiny shafts that lock together, **keeping** the bird dry **underneath**. Water simply rolls off the bird's back. In warmer weather, the feathers act to cool the bird.

The colors of a bird's feathers may be the same as the **meadows** or marshes in which it lives. This helps to protect the bird from enemies. Brightly colored feathers help a bird to **succeed** in finding a mate.

From the great condor to the tiny hummingbird, feathers are a bird's **treasure**.

Say the boldfaced words in the selection. Which vowels together make a long e sound? Which vowels together make a long e sound and a short e sound?

33

⬇

Spelling Practice

TIP
In a vowel pair, the two vowels come together to make one long vowel sound. The vowel pair **ee** has the long e sound you hear in **speech**. The vowel pair **ea** also spells the long e sound, as in **underneath**. The vowels ea can also form a vowel digraph. A vowel digraph is two vowels together that can make a long or short sound, or have a special sound all their own. The vowel digraph **ea** can spell the short e sound, as in **steady**.

LIST WORDS

1. feather
2. sweater
3. underneath
4. agreement
5. meadows
6. speech
7. needles
8. keeping
9. treasure
10. northeast
11. steady
12. creature
13. breathe
14. pleasure
15. succeed
16. sweeter
17. healthy
18. preacher
19. leather
20. wealth

Words with Long and Short e Sounds

Write each **list word** under the correct heading.

ee spells the long e sound
1. agreement   2. speech
3. needles   4. keeping
5. succeed   6. sweeter

ea spells the long e sound
7. underneath
8. northeast
9. creature
10. breathe
11. preacher

ea spells the short e sound
12. feather
13. sweater
14. meadows
15. treasure
16. steady
17. pleasure
18. healthy
19. leather
20. wealth

Complete the Rhyme

Complete each rhyme with a **list word** that contains the vowel pair or digraph that is underlined.

1. The movie was a double feature.

   It starred a monster and a furry __creature__

2. The pirate's map said, "Six feet down, measure.

   There you will find my buried __treasure__ "

3. The sailboat captains got the sails ready, now that

   the wind was strong and __steady__

4. People may wish to be wealthy, but to live a long life

   you must be __healthy__

5. Here's advice you should heed: Always try to __succeed__

6. Birds of a __feather__ fly in all kinds of weather.

Dictionary

Write the **list words** that would be found on dictionary pages between each pair of guide words shown. Be sure to write the **list words** in alphabetical order.

age/northwest	please/wear
1. agreement	1. pleasure
2. breathe	2. preacher
3. creature	3. speech
4. feather	4. steady
5. healthy	5. succeed
6. keeping	6. sweater
7. leather	7. sweeter
8. meadows	8. treasure
9. needles	9. underneath
10. northeast	10. wealth

Lesson 8 • Vowel Pairs **ee** and **ea** and Vowel Digraph **ea**   35

Spelling and Writing

Proofreading

The following story summary has fourteen mistakes. Use the proofreading marks to fix each mistake. Then, write the misspelled **list words** correctly on the lines.

The Greek myth of Daedalus and Icarus tells of a father and son who are held prisoner by a king of great wealt. After the the father sees a bird's fether, he builds two pairs of wings made of feathers and wax. In a speich to his son, Daedalus says they will suced in escaping if they stay steadee and do not fly too close to the sun. At first, they fly over meadows, keping low. Excited by what he sees, Icarus forgets what his father told him. He flies too high over the sea. His wings melt and and he falls into the ocean.

Proofreading Marks

- ◯ spelling mistake
- ⊙ add period
- ꟼ take out something

1. wealth
2. feather
3. speech
4. succeed
5. steady
6. meadows
7. keeping

Writing a Descriptive Paragraph

What is your favorite bird? Write a descriptive paragraph explaining why you like this bird. Be sure to use words that will create vivid images in a reader's mind. Try to use as many **list words** as you can. Remember to proofread your paragraph and fix any mistakes.

BONUS WORDS

measure

heal

peasant

degree

seek

36   Lesson 8 • Vowel Pairs **ee** and **ea** and Vowel Digraph **ea**

Spelling Strategy

To help students associate vowel sounds with their spellings, write *ee*, long *e*; *ea*, long *e*; and *ea*, short *e* in large letters on separate sheets of paper. Tape each sheet in a separate corner of the classroom. Then call out each **list word** and have students point to the appropriate sheet for the word's vowel sound and spelling. Ask a volunteer to write each **list word** on the correct sheet.

BONUS WORDS You may want to suggest that students look up the definitions of the words in a dictionary. Have them write one definition of each word. Then have them trade papers with a partner and see if they can write the correct bonus word for each definition.

Spelling and Writing   *Page 36*

The **Proofreading** exercise will help students prepare to proofread their descriptions. As students complete the writing activity, encourage them to brainstorm ideas, write a first draft, revise, and proofread their work. To publish their writing, students may want to

- compile a book titled *Our Favorite Birds*
- make a bird mural and add their descriptions.

Writer's Corner Students might enjoy reading books about birds, such as *Birds of the World* by Alan Greensmith. Encourage them to write a short poem about the bird that interests them the most.

Final Test

1. If you don't **succeed** right away, keep trying.
2. The two countries signed a peace **agreement**.
3. A peacock's **feather** is colorful and beautiful.
4. The actor achieved **wealth** and fame.
5. The lemonade was **sweeter** after I added sugar.
6. What a fantastic **speech** she gave!
7. Louisa put her knitting **needles** away.
8. I **treasure** Dad's gift.
9. The **preacher** spoke in a clear voice.
10. José has been **keeping** a journal all summer.
11. Did you look **underneath** the porch?
12. Clarice left her **sweater** on the school bus.
13. The wind blew gently across the **meadows**.
14. What cities are **northeast** of us?
15. Exercising makes me feel **healthy**.
16. Tony's soccer shoes are full-grain **leather**.
17. Jen spoke to the crowd in a **steady** voice.
18. Kim plays the part of the wild, weird **creature**.
19. It was such a **pleasure** to stay in bed late today.
20. I love to **breathe** salty beach air.

37

Vowel Digraphs au and aw

Objective
To spell words in which *au* and *aw* spell the *aw* sound

 Correlated Phonics Lesson
MCP Phonics, Level E, Lesson 19

Spelling Words in Action   *Page 37*

Students may enjoy learning about how money is made. Ask students what they might see on a tour of the U.S. Mint in Philadelphia or Denver, or a visit to the Bureau of Engraving and Printing in Washington, D.C. If any students have visited the sites, ask them to share their experiences.

Call on volunteers to say the boldfaced words and identify the letters that make the *aw* sound.

Warm-Up Test

1. Did you see that **hawk** soar across the sky?
2. A dripping **faucet** wastes water.
3. Lynn is the **author** of two mystery novels.
4. After a **pause** for lunch, we continued walking.
5. Have you met Mr. Chun's **daughter**?
6. Alise will **withdraw** from the campaign.
7. The truck **hauled** the heavy load up the hill.
8. Wasn't the pie our class made **awfully** good?
9. Driving through a red light is **unlawful**.
10. Julie wants to be a scientist or a **lawyer**.
11. Fred cut up **strawberries** for his cereal.
12. The frightened chicken began to **squawk**.
13. These **saucers** don't match those teacups.
14. She is a well-known **drawer** of cartoons.
15. Mom used **caution** driving down the icy street.
16. Look at the treasure from the castle's **vault**!
17. The child is **naughty** when he's bored or tired.
18. You may see beavers **gnawing** on branches.
19. That lamp will be an **awkward** shape to wrap.
20. We are beginning to **exhaust** our art supplies.

Spelling Practice   *Pages 38–39*

Introduce the spelling rule and have students read the **list words** aloud. Then encourage students to look back at their **Warm-Up Tests** and apply the spelling rule to any misspelled words.

As students work through the **Spelling Practice** exercises, remind them to look back at their **list words** or in their dictionaries if they need help.

 See Student Dictation, page 14

Spelling Words in Action

Money doesn't grow on trees, but where *does* it come from?

Making Money

A cashier takes a new roll of coins from a **drawer**. You **withdraw** brand-new bills from a bank. Where does the money come from?

The U.S. government makes all of our money. Every year, the U.S. Mint makes 14–20 billion coins. To make the coins, the Mint starts with 1,500-foot-long strips. Round **saucers** called blanks are punched out from the strips. A coining press stamps the designs and words on the coins. Then, the coins are counted, bagged, and stored in a **vault** before being **hauled** by truck to your local bank. After years of use, some money looks as if animals have been **gnawing** on it. No one wants to throw away money, so the U.S. Mint reshapes damaged coins.

To make paper money, the Bureau of Engraving and Printing goes through more than 65 steps. These steps include engraving steel plates by hand and stamping the plates on sheets of paper under 20 tons of pressure. Every bill is checked before it is given another stamp and number to make it official U.S. money.

It is **unlawful** for anyone but the U.S. government to make our money. The process is so complex that it is **awfully** difficult to copy. Even so, **caution** should be used when handling money. People should **pause** to look closely at the bills they receive to make sure the bills are real!

Say the boldfaced words in the selection. What do you notice about the vowel sounds made by the vowel digraphs <u>au</u> and <u>aw</u>?

37

TIP
The vowel digraphs **au** and **aw** sound alike. They spell the **aw** sound you hear in <u>hawk</u> and <u>pause</u>.

Spelling Practice

LIST WORDS

1. hawk
2. faucet
3. author
4. pause
5. daughter
6. withdraw
7. hauled
8. awfully
9. unlawful
10. lawyer
11. strawberries
12. squawk
13. saucers
14. drawer
15. caution
16. vault
17. naughty
18. gnawing
19. awkward
20. exhaust

Words with au and aw

Write each **list word** under the correct heading.

vowel digraph au

1. faucet
2. author
3. pause
4. daughter
5. hauled
6. saucers
7. caution
8. vault
9. naughty
10. exhaust

vowel digraph aw

11. hawk
12. withdraw
13. awfully
14. unlawful
15. lawyer
16. strawberries
17. squawk
18. drawer
19. gnawing
20. awkward

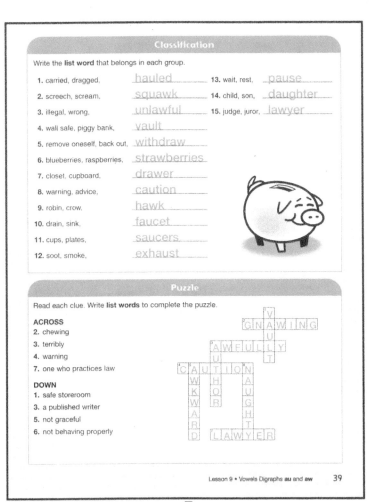

Classification

Write the **list word** that belongs in each group.

1. carried, dragged, hauled
2. screech, scream, squawk
3. illegal, wrong, unlawful
4. wall safe, piggy bank, vault
5. remove oneself, back out, withdraw
6. blueberries, raspberries, strawberries
7. closet, cupboard, drawer
8. warning, advice, caution
9. robin, crow, hawk
10. drain, sink, faucet
11. cups, plates, saucers
12. soot, smoke, exhaust
13. wait, rest, pause
14. child, son, daughter
15. judge, juror, lawyer

Puzzle

Read each clue. Write **list words** to complete the puzzle.

ACROSS
2. chewing
3. terribly
4. warning
7. one who practices law

DOWN
1. safe storeroom
3. a published writer
5. not graceful
6. not behaving properly

Crossword answers: GNAWING, AWFULLY, CAUTION, LAWYER (across); VAULT, AWKWARD, AUTHOR (down)

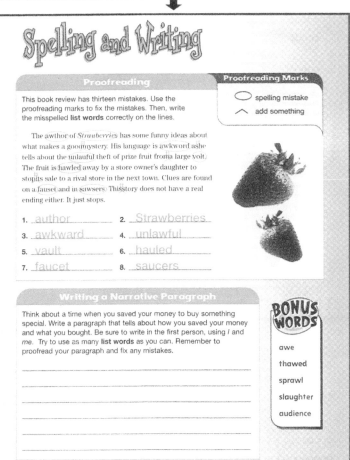

Spelling and Writing

Proofreading

This book review has thirteen mistakes. Use the proofreading marks to fix the mistakes. Then, write the misspelled **list words** correctly on the lines.

Proofreading Marks
◯ spelling mistake
∧ add something

   The awthor of *Strawberries* has some funny ideas about what makes a good mystery. His language is awkword as he tells about the unlawful theft of prize fruit from a large volt. The fruit is hauled away by a store owner's daughter to stop its sale to a rival store in the next town. Clues are found on a faucet and in sawsers. This story does not have a real ending either. It just stops.

1. author
2. Strawberries
3. awkward
4. unlawful
5. vault
6. hauled
7. faucet
8. saucers

Writing a Narrative Paragraph

Think about a time when you saved your money to buy something special. Write a paragraph that tells about how you saved your money and what you bought. Be sure to write in the first person, using *I* and *me*. Try to use as many **list words** as you can. Remember to proofread your paragraph and fix any mistakes.

BONUS WORDS

awe
thawed
sprawl
slaughter
audience

Spelling Strategy

Write each **list word** on the board, minus the digraph *au* or *aw* (f __ cet). For each word have the class ask, "Is it spelled with *au* or *aw*?" Then, call on volunteers to come to the board, name the missing letters, and complete the word. Encourage the class to check each spelling against the **list words** in their books.

BONUS WORDS You may want to suggest that students talk with partners about the meanings of the bonus words. Then have them take turns orally giving each other clues about one of the words. Ask them to try to guess each other's words.

Spelling and Writing   *Page 40*

The **Proofreading** exercise will help students prepare to proofread their paragraphs. As students complete the writing activity, encourage them to brainstorm ideas, write a first draft, revise, and proofread their work. To publish their writing, students may want to send their paragraphs to the letters section of a children's magazine.

Writer's Corner Explain to students that the U.S. Mint is authorized by Congress to strike special coins that celebrate people and events in U.S. history. Suggest that students think of their own ideas for new commemorative coins. Then have them create a flyer describing their coin.

Final Test

1. Our station will **pause** for station identification.
2. The dessert was made with **strawberries**.
3. I wish my little cousin wouldn't be so **naughty**.
4. A **hawk** can see great distances.
5. We must not **exhaust** the Earth's resources.
6. My cat will often **withdraw** from strangers.
7. In many cities, littering is **unlawful** behavior.
8. Put the socks in the top **drawer**.
9. Have you heard that **author** discuss his book?
10. My hamster keeps **gnawing** on wood.
11. It is **awfully** cold outside, so dress warmly.
12. They left their valuables in the **vault**.
13. Usually, the cold-water **faucet** is on the right.
14. The tow truck **hauled** away the wrecked car.
15. Would you like to study to be a **lawyer**?
16. The cups and **saucers** belong on that shelf.
17. His **awkward** movements became graceful.
18. Did you hear the bird **squawk**?
19. Drive with **caution** through a school zone.
20. I have a **daughter** named Jessica.

Lesson 10

Vowel Digraphs ie and e̱i and Vowel Pair e̱i

Objective

To spell words with vowel digraphs *ie* and *ei* and vowel pair *ei*

 Correlated Phonics Lessons
MCP Phonics, Level E,
Lessons 16, 19–20

Spelling Words in Action   *Page 41*

In this selection, students read to find out about art that looks real, but isn't. After reading, ask students to discuss *trompe l'oeil* and tell whether they have ever seen it.

Encourage students to look back at the boldfaced words. Ask volunteers to say each word and tell the order in which *i* and *e* appear.

Warm-Up Test

1. I don't believe they **deceived** us like that!
2. Maya **received** the application in the mail.
3. We only had time for a **brief** conversation.
4. I **believe** that it's time to go now.
5. The batter hit a line drive into the **infield**.
6. Are you ready to **review** what we've learned?
7. We send **freight** by truck, train, ship, or plane.
8. A **vein** carries blood through the human body.
9. Paul wore sunglasses to **shield** his eyes.
10. There are two **pieces** missing from the puzzle.
11. Eight times ten is **eighty**.
12. Dr. Wood has one **niece** and two nephews.
13. The sign told us to **yield** the right of way.
14. You may sit at **either** end of the table.
15. **Neither** Jim nor Alan enjoyed the movie.
16. The king's **deceit** angered the nation.
17. Tears are sometimes a sign of **grief**.
18. The shopkeeper yelled, "Stop that **thief**!"
19. You will soon **achieve** your goal.
20. Who could **conceive** such a crazy idea?

Spelling Practice   *Pages 42–43*

Introduce the spelling rule and have students read the **list words** aloud. Encourage students to look back at their **Warm-Up Tests** and apply the spelling rule to any misspelled words.

As students work through the **Spelling Practice** exercises, remind them to look back at their **list words** or in their dictionaries if they need help.

 for ESL students See Categorizing, page 15

40

Lesson 10
Vowel Digraphs ie and e̱i and Vowel Pair e̱i

Spelling Words in Action

When do you not believe what you see?

Seeing Isn't Believing

Imagine you are walking down a street, and you see a door. You take a **brief** look and reach for the doorknob. You can't get your hand around it. The door won't open. Then, you realize you've been **deceived**! There is no door. There is no doorknob, **either**. It's just a wall painting, or a mural.

A painting this real proves that you can't always **believe** what you see. The French have a name for this kind of art. They call it *trompe l'oeil* (trawmp-loy). These words mean "fool the eye." Trompe l'oeil painting has been around since ancient times. It creates a look of great depth.

Many artists are turning blank walls into **pieces** of trompe l'oeil art. Any scene you could **conceive** of can be created. Three-foot-wide flowers painted on a hotel wall look so bright that you will **shield** your eyes. The Greek columns you see in the photo are actually painted on a university building.

Painter John Pugh worked hard to **achieve** a realistic look, and he certainly succeeded. Someone who saw the mural even complained that the building's wall needed to be fixed! These mural painters also work indoors. A clever artist can turn a boring ceiling into a baseball **infield**. There's no end to the images these artists of **deceit** can create.

> Say the boldfaced words in the selection. What vowel sounds do you hear? What do you notice about the vowel digraphs and vowel pair?

41

TIP

The vowels *ie* and *ei* can be vowel pairs as well as vowel digraphs. Vowel pair *ei* can spell the long e sound, as in the word *deceit*. The vowel digraph *ie* can also spell the long e sound (*believe*). Vowel digraph *ei* can spell the long a sound (*freight*). Here's a helpful rule:
"I before E, except after C, or when *ei* sounds like A, as in *eighty* and *freight*."
The words *either* and *neither* are tricky! They do not follow this rule.

LIST WORDS

1. deceived
2. received
3. brief
4. believe
5. infield
6. review
7. freight
8. vein
9. shield
10. pieces
11. eighty
12. niece
13. yield
14. either
15. neither
16. deceit
17. grief
18. thief
19. achieve
20. conceive

Spelling Practice

Words with ie and ei

Write each **list word** under the correct heading.

ie

1. brief
2. believe
3. infield
4. review
5. shield
6. pieces
7. niece
8. yield
9. grief
10. thief
11. achieve

ei after c

12. deceived
13. received
14. deceit
15. conceive

ei as in freight

16. freight
17. vein
18. eighty

ei in "No Rule" words

19. either
20. neither

42   Lesson 10 • Vowel Digraphs ie and ei and Vowel Pair ei

Complete the Paragraph

Fill in the **list words** that best complete the sentences in the paragraph below.

While watching a baseball game on TV, an ___eighty___ -year-
old woman could not ___believe___ her eyes. The cameras
followed a fly ball over the ___infield___ and into the stands.
Then, to her surprise, her youngest ___niece___, Amy, held up
the ball. She couldn't ___conceive___ how an eight-year-old girl
could catch a fly ball. The woman wondered if her eyes had
___deceived___ her. She called to her husband, who couldn't
believe his eyes ___either___. Then, for a ___brief___
moment, they saw Amy again. This time, they noticed her enormous
baseball mitt. The mitt must have acted like a ___shield___,
blocking others from catching the ball. It was an amazing thing for
an eight year old to ___achieve___.

Word Search

Find these ten **list words** in the puzzle below: deceit, freight, grief, neither, pieces, received, review, thief, vein, yield. The words can go forward or backward, up, down, or diagonally. Then write the words on the lines below.

```
E  G  R  I  F  L  D  E  S  R
L  R  E  N  Q  F  E  I  H  T
S  E  C  E  I  P  R  I  Z  C
F  R  E  I  G  H  T  O  T  I
F  E  I  R  G  Y  P  A  I  H
L  V  V  N  E  I  T  H  E  R
T  R  E  V  I  E  W  I  C  L
N  E  D  I  S  L  B  I  E  Y
E  V  R  L  N  D  N  I  D  Y
```

1. _received_   6. _yield_
2. _review_   7. _thief_
3. _freight_   8. _neither_
4. _vein_   9. _deceit_
5. _pieces_   10. _grief_

Lesson 10 • Vowel Digraphs ie and ei and Vowel Pair ei   43

Spelling and Writing

Proofreading

This article has twelve mistakes. Use the proofreading marks to fix the mistakes. Then, rewrite the misspelled **list words** correctly on the lines.

One of the greatest mural artists to achieeve fame was Diego Rivera. He was born in Guanajuato Mexico, on December 8 1886. A reveiw of his work shows that he had great respect for the common people. He also showed the greef he felt at how poorer people were treated by the government. He did not beleeve that people should yeild to those who wanted to rule them unfairly. His murals appeared on walls of government buildings schools and palaces. He traveled to Detroit New York City and San Francisco to paint. He recieved many honors while he was alive.

Proofreading Marks
○ spelling mistake
∧ add something

1. _achieve_   2. _review_   3. _grief_
4. _believe_   5. _yield_   6. _received_

Writing a Narrative Paragraph

Have you ever thought you saw something that turned out to be something else? Write about your experience or make one up. Try to use as many **list words** as you can. Remember to proofread your paragraph and fix any mistakes.

_____
_____
_____
_____
_____
_____

BONUS WORDS
disbelief
relieved
grieve
eighteen
leisure

44   Lesson 10 • Vowel Digraphs ie and ei and Vowel Pair ei

Spelling Strategy

To help students practice spelling the **list words**, make two columns on the board, one headed with *ie* and the other with *ei*. Call on volunteers to come to the board and say a **list word**, then

- write it in the correct column
- circle the vowels *ie* or *ei*.

BONUS WORDS You may want to suggest that students write a sentence for each bonus word, leaving a blank where the word would be written. Then, have them trade papers with a partner and try to finish each other's sentences.

Spelling and Writing   **Page 44**

The **Proofreading** exercise will help students prepare to proofread their paragraphs. As students complete the writing activity, encourage them to brainstorm ideas, write a first draft, revise, and proofread their work. To publish their writing, students may want to create a book titled *Seeing Is Not Believing*.

Writer's Corner Students might enjoy looking at books of optical illusions. Invite them to draw their favorite illusion on one side of a sheet of paper and write an explanation of it on the back. Students can try out their illusions on one another.

Final Test

1. Let's work together to **conceive** a good plan.
2. Which **vein** carries blood from the lungs to the heart?
3. Can you **believe** what happened today?
4. Dr. Rodriguez has a **niece** named Maria.
5. A lie is an example of **deceit**.
6. We need good catchers in the **infield**.
7. At the corner, **yield** to ongoing traffic.
8. **Shield** your eyes from the bright lights.
9. We were **deceived** by false rumors.
10. My **grief** vanished when my dog came home.
11. **Eighty** people lined up outside the theater.
12. That **freight** train carries grain and cattle.
13. Although her speech was **brief**, it was good.
14. **Neither** Gloria nor Alexis came to the party.
15. I think that actor will **achieve** stardom.
16. A blue jay is a noisy **thief**.
17. We will **either** walk or take the bus.
18. Did you **review** your answers on the test?
19. I finally **received** a letter!
20. Please cut the apple into four **pieces**.

Diphthongs <u>ou</u>, <u>ow</u>, <u>oi</u>, and <u>oy</u>

Objective
To spell words with diphthongs *ou*, *ow*, *oi*, and *oy*

 Correlated Phonics Lessons
MCP Phonics, Level E, Lessons 24–25

Spelling Words in Action   **Page 45**

In "The Big Chill," students discover how the wind can make a cold day feel even colder. Afterward, ask students to share their own experiences with cold, windy weather.

Call on volunteers to say each boldfaced word and identify the sound made by *ou*, *ow*, *oi*, or *oy*.

Warm-Up Test
1. The football stadium was **crowded**.
2. Maura **joined** the science club at her school.
3. Who made the first **voyage** around the world?
4. Bobby **soiled** his shirt while oiling his bike.
5. I find reading very **enjoyable**.
6. They **counted** the money from the garage sale.
7. A bunny's tail looks like a **powder** puff.
8. An **oyster** is a kind of shellfish.
9. The actress displayed great **poise** on stage.
10. A river may serve as a **boundary**.
11. A friend deserves your **loyalty** and support.
12. **Moisture** seeped through the basement walls.
13. Watch out, that's a **poisonous** snake!
14. Much of South America is **mountainous**.
15. Are you **courageous** enough to try skydiving?
16. Everyone enjoyed the songs the **choir** sang.
17. They **toiled** in the factory from dawn to dusk.
18. The chef served **broiled** salmon.
19. Did the car swerve to **avoid** hitting that tree?
20. Your leg bends at the knee **joint**.

Spelling Practice   **Pages 46–47**

Introduce the spelling rule and have students read the **list words** aloud. You may also want to discuss the meaning of *diphthong*: two letters blended together to form one vowel sound. Then encourage students to look back at their **Warm-Up Tests** and apply the spelling rule to any misspelled words.

As students work through the **Spelling Practice** exercises, remind them to look back at their **list words** or in their dictionaries if they need help.

 See Charades/Pantomime, page 15

Spelling Words in Action

How does the wind make a cold day colder?

The Big Chill

How many times have you **counted** on a thermometer to tell you how warmly to dress, then when you got outside it seemed much colder? What was different? Was it the **moisture** in the air? Perhaps, but if the wind was blowing, it was probably the windchill factor.

Does that mean that the wind has **joined** the cold to make things worse? Not really. When the air is still, your body heat forms a shield that acts like a **boundary** between you and the cold air. When the wind blows, however, that shield is broken. As a result, you feel much colder.

Here is a chart to find out what the temperature feels like when there's wind. Check the temperature on a thermometer, then find out the wind speed from a weather report.

Whether you're headed off on an ocean **voyage** or hoping to ski in some fresh **powder** snow falling in a **mountainous** area, consider the wind. Knowing the effect of the windchill could make your trip a lot more **enjoyable**. If you find yourself shivering on the way to school, try walking in **crowded** areas to keep warm. **Avoid** windy streets, and wear that windbreaker!

Windchill Chart

MPH		Temperature								
CALM	35	30	25	20	15	10	5	0	-5	-10
				Equivalent Chill Temperature						
5	30	25	20	15	10	5	0	-5	-10	-15
10	20	15	10	5	0	-10	-15	-20	-25	-35
15	15	10	0	-5	-10	-20	-25	-30	-40	-50
20	10	5	0	-10	-15	-25	-30	-35	-40	-60
25	10	0	-5	-15	-20	-30	-35	-45	-50	-65
30	5	0	-10	-20	-25	-30	-40	-50	-55	-65
35	5	-5	-10	-20	-30	-35	-40	-50	-60	-65
40	0	-5	-15	-20	-30	-35	-45	-55	-60	-70

(Wind Speed — Miles per hour)

> Say the boldfaced words with <u>ou</u> and <u>ow</u> in the selection. What difference is there in the vowel sound you hear in these words? Say the boldfaced words with <u>oi</u> and <u>oy</u> in the selection. What difference is there in the vowel sound you hear in these words?

45

⬇

TIP
A diphthong is two letters blended together to make one vowel sound. The diphthongs *ou* and *ow* spell the *ow* sound you hear in <u>boundary</u> and <u>crowded</u>. The diphthongs *oi* and *oy* spell the *oy* sound you hear in <u>poise</u> and <u>loyalty</u>. Notice that the words <u>choir</u> and <u>courageous</u> and the last syllables in <u>mountainous</u> and <u>poisonous</u> do not have diphthong sounds.

LIST WORDS
1. crowded
2. joined
3. voyage
4. soiled
5. enjoyable
6. counted
7. powder
8. oyster
9. poise
10. boundary
11. loyalty
12. moisture
13. poisonous
14. mountainous
15. courageous
16. choir
17. toiled
18. broiled
19. avoid
20. joint

Spelling Practice

Words with *ou*, *ow*, *oi*, and *oy*

Write each **list word** under the correct heading. You will use some words more than once.

ou and ow spell the sound in <u>loud</u>
1. crowded
2. counted
3. powder
4. boundary
5. mountainous

ou spells the sound in <u>famous</u>
6. poisonous   7. mountainous
8. courageous

oi spells the long i sound
9. choir

oi and oy spell the sound in <u>oil</u>
10. joined   11. voyage
12. soiled   13. enjoyable
14. oyster   15. poise
16. loyalty   17. moisture
18. toiled   19. broiled
20. avoid   21. joint
22. poisonous

Comparing Words

Study the relationship between the first two underlined words or phrases.
Then, write a **list word** that has the same relationship with the third underlined word.

1. <u>patience</u> is to <u>calmness</u> as <u>confidence</u> is to _poise_
2. <u>hive</u> is to <u>bee</u> as <u>shell</u> is to _oyster_
3. <u>went</u> is to <u>returned</u> as <u>separated</u> is to _joined_
4. <u>player</u> is to <u>team</u> as <u>singer</u> is to _choir_
5. <u>soap</u> is to <u>clean</u> as <u>dirt</u> is to _soiled_
6. <u>flying</u> is to <u>flight</u> as <u>sailing</u> is to _voyage_
7. <u>mutual</u> is to <u>common</u> as <u>shared</u> is to _joint_
8. <u>empty</u> is to <u>full</u> as <u>unoccupied</u> is to _crowded_
9. <u>heat</u> is to <u>warmth</u> as <u>water</u> is to _moisture_
10. <u>do</u> is to <u>don't</u> as <u>try</u> is to _avoid_
11. <u>enemy</u> is to <u>treachery</u> as <u>friend</u> is to _loyalty_
12. <u>ladybug</u> is to <u>harmless</u> as <u>rattlesnake</u> is to _poisonous_

Scrambled Words

Unscramble the words below to make eight **list words**. Then, write
each **list word** on the line.

1. I led to — _toiled_
2. aim noun to us — _mountainous_
3. you brand — _boundary_
4. go our cause — _courageous_
5. enable joy — _enjoyable_
6. cot dune — _counted_
7. we drop — _powder_
8. red boil — _broiled_

boundary
broiled
counted
courageous
enjoyable
mountainous
powder
toiled

Spelling and Writing

Proofreading

This science article has eleven mistakes. Use the
proofreading marks to fix the mistakes. Then, write the
misspelled words correctly on the lines.

Proofreading Marks
- ◯ spelling mistake
- ≡ capital letter
- ✓ add apostrophe

Its true that mowtainous areas can affect the weather far
away. they form a bowndary that breaks up clouds and
releases moistchure, as a result, one side might have cool,
enjoiable rains, while the other side is broyled by the sun.
thats why many people live on one side of mountains and
avoud the other side.

1. _mountainous_   2. _boundary_
3. _moisture_   4. _enjoyable_
5. _broiled_   6. _avoid_

Writing a Poem

Has there ever been a time when you felt really cold? Recall or
imagine how you would feel. Then write a short poem about the
experience, using any **list words** that you can. Remember to
proofread your poem and fix any mistakes.

BONUS WORDS
- powerful
- outrageous
- destroyed
- spoiled
- snout

_____
_____
_____
_____
_____
_____
_____
_____

Spelling Strategy

Write one of the **list words** on the board. Then,
have students close their eyes and picture the
word. Erase the word. After students open their
eyes, have them spell the word aloud several
times. Continue, using each of the **list words**.

BONUS WORDS
You may want to suggest that
students work with a partner to write
definitions for each bonus word. Then,
have them compare their definitions to
those in their dictionaries and see how
close they came.

Spelling and Writing   *Page 48*

The **Proofreading** exercise will help students
prepare to proofread their poems. As students
complete the writing activity, encourage them to
brainstorm ideas, write a first draft, revise, and
proofread their work. To publish their work,
students may want to hold a poetry festival and
read their poems aloud.

Writer's Corner To receive one copy of *The
Amateur Weather Forecaster*, the class can write a
letter to the National Oceanic & Atmospheric
Administration: NOAA Office of Public and
Constituent Affairs, Outreach Unit, 1305 East-West
Highway, Room 1W514, Silver Spring, MD 20910.
The letter should indicate the class's grade level.

Final Test
1. He injured his elbow **joint** and can't bend it.
2. The team pledged its **loyalty** to the coach.
3. The astronauts blasted off on their **voyage**.
4. The ballerina showed great **poise** after she fell.
5. The Saccos **joined** us on our summer vacation.
6. What a **courageous** person she is!
7. Did the **choir** practice every day?
8. Early settlers **toiled** hard and long.
9. The juice spilled and **soiled** the tablecloth.
10. **Crowded** places make Juan uncomfortable.
11. The cashier **counted** my change.
12. The oak trees mark the **boundary** of the park.
13. Captain Jenkins served us fresh **oyster** stew.
14. Was this wig whitened with **powder**?
15. We can **avoid** heavy traffic if we leave early.
16. Denver is located in a **mountainous** area.
17. Do you know which mushrooms are **poisonous**?
18. A humidifier adds **moisture** to the air.
19. Did you have an **enjoyable** weekend?
20. The waiter served us **broiled** chicken.

Objectives
To review spelling words with vowel pairs *ai*, *ay*, *oa*, *ow*, *ee*, *ea*, and *ei*; vowel digraphs *ea*, *au*, *aw*, *ie*, and *ei*; and diphthongs *ou*, *ow*, *oi*, and *oy*

Check Your
Spelling Notebook
Pages 49–52

Based on your observations, note which words are giving students the most difficulty and offer assistance for spelling them correctly. Here are some frequently misspelled words to watch for: *breathe*, *succeed*, *awkward*, *received*, *believe*, *mountainous*, and *boundary*.

To give students extra help and practice in taking standardized tests, you may want to have them take the **Review Test** for this lesson on pages 46–47. After scoring the tests, return them to students so that they can record their misspelled words in their spelling notebooks.

After practicing their troublesome words, students can work through the exercises for lessons 7–11 and the cumulative review, **Show What You Know**. Before they begin each exercise, you may want to go over the spelling rule.

Take It Home

Invite students to select several **list words** from lessons 7–11. Students can write the words on a large sheet of paper, tape the paper on a wall at home, and challenge family members to use the words in conversation. Students can also use **Take It Home** Master 2 on pages 48–49 to help them do the activity. (A complete list of the spelling words is included on page 48 of the **Take It Home** Master.) Encourage students to bring in their "wall words" to share with the class.

In lessons 7 through 11, you learned how to spell words with vowels that work together to make one sound. These vowels are called vowel pairs, vowel digraphs, and diphthongs.

Check Your Spelling Notebook

Look at the words in your spelling notebook. Which words for lessons 7 through 11 did you have the most trouble with? Write them here.

_____

_____

Practice writing your troublesome words with a partner. Take turns saying each word and then saying the vowel sound made by the vowel pair, vowel digraph, or diphthong. Write the words.

Lesson 7

TIP A vowel pair is made from two vowels that come together to make one long vowel sound. The vowel pairs **ai** and **ay** can spell the long **a** sound you hear in fainted and decay. The vowel pairs **oa** and **ow** can spell the long **o** sound you hear in cocoa and tomorrow.

Write a **list word** that is a synonym for the word given. Not all the words will be used.

List Words
complain
decay
boast
scarecrow
braid
throwing
foamy
gained
fainted
coast
hoax
painful

1. straw man _scarecrow_
2. increased _gained_
3. sudsy _foamy_
4. aching _painful_
5. brag _boast_
6. grumble _complain_
7. pitching _throwing_
8. rot _decay_
9. trick _hoax_
10. shore _coast_

49

Lesson 8

TIP The vowel pairs **ee** and **ea** make the long **e** sound you hear in the words sweeter and underneath. The vowel digraph **ea** can spell the short **e** sound, as in the word wealth.

List Words
feather
underneath
meadows
speech
needles
northeast
pleasure
healthy
leather
preacher
steady
succeed

Study the relationship between the first two underlined words. Then, write a **list word** that has the same relationship with the third underlined word. Not all the words will be used.

1. concrete is to sidewalks as grass is to _meadows_
2. human is to skin as bird is to _feather_
3. hand is to touch as voice is to _speech_
4. bad is to good as sick is to _healthy_
5. constant is to unchanging as balanced is to _steady_
6. out is to in as above is to _underneath_
7. sadness is to sorrow as joy is to _pleasure_
8. carpentry is to hammers as sewing is to _needles_
9. dress is to fabric as belt is to _leather_
10. New Mexico is to southwest as Maine is to _northeast_

Lesson 9

TIP The vowel digraphs **au** and **aw** both make the same vowel sound. Listen for the same vowel sound in vault and unlawful.

List Words
hawk
withdraw
strawberries
faucet
squawk
author
awkward
exhaust
saucers
pause
unlawful
caution

Write the **list words** that fit each description. Not all the words will be used.

1. What the people do who leave a burning house:
   withdraw with _caution_
2. What small plates of red fruit are: _saucers_ of _strawberries_
3. What an illegal stop is: an _unlawful_ _pause_
4. What a mother bird is when her baby is threatened:
   a _hawk_ that will _squawk_
5. What you call a clumsy writer: an _awkward_ _author_

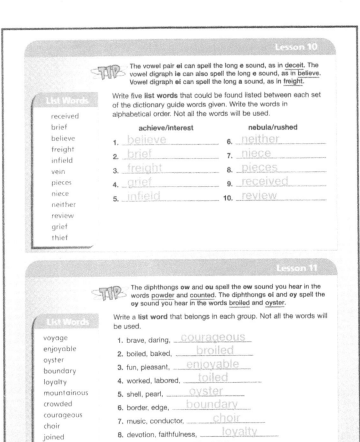

Lesson 10

TIP: The vowel pair **ei** can spell the long e sound, as in deceit. The vowel digraph **ie** can also spell the long e sound, as in believe. Vowel digraph **ei** can spell the long a sound, as in freight.

List Words

received
brief
believe
freight
infield
vein
pieces
niece
neither
review
grief
thief

Write five list words that could be found listed between each set of the dictionary guide words given. Write the words in alphabetical order. Not all the words will be used.

achieve/interest
1. believe
2. brief
3. freight
4. grief
5. infield

nebula/rushed
6. neither
7. niece
8. pieces
9. received
10. review

Lesson 11

TIP: The diphthongs **ow** and **ou** spell the ow sound you hear in the words powder and counted. The diphthongs **oi** and **oy** spell the oy sound you hear in the words broiled and oyster.

List Words

voyage
enjoyable
oyster
boundary
loyalty
mountainous
crowded
courageous
choir
joined
toiled
broiled

Write a list word that belongs in each group. Not all the words will be used.

1. brave, daring, courageous
2. boiled, baked, broiled
3. fun, pleasant, enjoyable
4. worked, labored, toiled
5. shell, pearl, oyster
6. border, edge, boundary
7. music, conductor, choir
8. devotion, faithfulness, loyalty
9. journey, trip, voyage
10. rocky, hilly, mountainous

Lesson 12 • Review   51

Show What You Know

Lessons 7–11 Review

One word is misspelled in each set of **list words**. Fill in the circle next to the **list word** that is spelled incorrectly.

1.	complain	meadows	lawyer	neither	● tosted
2.	joint	braid	speech	● straberries	northeast
3.	deceit	● croded	draws	keeping	caution
4.	saucers	thief	joined	coast	● conceve
5.	treasure	drawer	● achive	voyage	soiled
6.	decay	● stedy	vault	deceived	enjoyable
7.	roasting	creature	● naghty	received	counted
8.	powder	brief	● gnaing	breathe	throwing
9.	● tomorow	boast	pleasure	sweeter	awkward
10.	hawk	believe	review	oyster	● bondary
11.	poise	● infeeld	exhaust	succeed	borrow
12.	swallows	grief	poach	● squak	loyalty
13.	● freit	vein	faucet	author	healthy
14.	preacher	● lether	pause	shield	moisture
15.	poisonous	mountainous	pieces	eighty	● fomy
16.	scarecrow	wealth	feather	● daghter	withdraw
17.	hauled	niece	● coragcous	cocoa	fainted
18.	gained	sweater	awfully	unlawful	● yeld
19.	choir	toiled	either	needles	● underneth
20.	hoax	painful	agreement	● avoyd	broiled

52   Lesson 12 • Review

Final Test

1. He will **complain** to the landlord about the leak.
2. This gray **feather** is from a gull.
3. We watched the **hawk** soar above the trees.
4. Salim **received** a college scholarship.
5. Columbus made more than one **voyage**.
6. The dentist discussed tooth **decay**.
7. Joe found his math book **underneath** his bed.
8. Why did Pam have to **withdraw** from the race?
9. We were sorry that their visit was so **brief**.
10. Did you find that an **enjoyable** book?
11. We can **boast** about completing the marathon.
12. Sheep grazed in the grassy **meadows**.
13. I love to put fresh **strawberries** on my cereal.
14. Do you **believe** the Earth is getting warmer?
15. They found a pearl inside the **oyster**.
16. The **scarecrow** will keep the crows away.
17. Speak clearly when you make a **speech**.
18. The birds will **squawk** if you disturb their nest.
19. Trucks haul **freight** across the country.
20. A wire fence forms the **boundary**.
21. He's **throwing** the ball for the dog to fetch.
22. Pine trees have **needles** instead of leaves.
23. My teacher is the **author** of three books.
24. The nurse drew blood from a **vein** in my arm.
25. The king earned the **loyalty** of all his subjects.
26. The baby loves splashing the **foamy** bubbles.
27. Pepe walked in a **northeast** direction.
28. Angelita was **awfully** sorry she couldn't come.
29. One of the puzzle **pieces** is missing.
30. Kansas is flat, but Colorado is **mountainous**.
31. Last year I grew taller and **gained** weight.
32. What a **pleasure** it was to see you today!
33. Put the cats' dinner in those **saucers**.
34. Is that girl Mrs. Olson's **niece**?
35. The **courageous** woman risked her life.
36. Dad wants to sail down the **coast** this summer.
37. To stay **healthy**, exercise and eat wisely.
38. After a short **pause**, the show continued.
39. **Neither** of the girls wants to see the movie.
40. Mr. Gabriel asked Joan to sing in the **choir**.
41. The story turned out to be a **hoax**.
42. His mother invited the new **preacher** to dinner.
43. Isn't it **unlawful** to litter?
44. The actress wailed to show her **grief**.
45. The workers **toiled** in the fields.
46. A bad sprain can be extremely **painful**.
47. Amanda wants **leather** boots for her birthday.
48. They will explore the cave with **caution**.
49. The police are chasing that **thief**!
50. Dan served **broiled** swordfish to his guests.

Review Test (Side A)

Read each set of phrases. Fill in the circle next to the
phrase with an underlined word that is spelled correctly.

1. ⓐ broyled steak   ⓒ broyld haddock
   ⓑ broild chicken   ⓓ broiled salmon

2. ⓐ a painful toothache   ⓒ a painfull headache
   ⓑ a peinful condition   ⓓ paneful arthritis

3. ⓐ hard to beleave   ⓒ unable to believe
   ⓑ beleive the newst   ⓓ to beleve in

4. ⓐ an oisterr shell   ⓒ a fresh oister
   ⓑ a raw oyster   ⓓ a live oysterr

5. ⓐ fomy bath bubbles   ⓒ the foamy waves
   ⓑ fomey laundry suds   ⓓ phomey shampoo

6. ⓐ the curageous lifeguard   ⓒ the corageous firefighters
   ⓑ a courageous explorer   ⓓ these couragous astronauts

7. ⓐ feather of a swan   ⓒ fether of an albatross
   ⓑ pheather of a crane   ⓓ phether of a pheasant

8. ⓐ frozen strauberries   ⓒ gigantic straberrys
   ⓑ juicy strawberrys   ⓓ scrumptious strawberries

9. ⓐ a straw scarecrow   ⓒ clothing for the skarecrow
   ⓑ the farmer's scaircrow   ⓓ shadow of a scarecroe

10. ⓐ the foolish theef   ⓒ a malicious theaf
    ⓑ a young theif   ⓓ an imprisoned thief

11. ⓐ a mountainous view   ⓒ this mountinous trail
    ⓑ a mountanous route   ⓓ the mountainus scenery

12. ⓐ a healthey employee   ⓒ his helthy diet
    ⓑ this healthy baby   ⓓ her helthe lifestyle

Name _____

Read each set of phrases. Fill in the circle next to the
phrase with an underlined word that is spelled correctly.

13. (a) comeplain in writing   (c) to complain often
    (b) to complane about   (d) to complein publicly

14. (a) an anonymous author   (c) the novel's awthor
    (b) the book's auther   (d) the famous awther

15. (a) niether of them   (c) neether opinion
    (b) neather partner   (d) neither she nor I

16. (a) his moving speeche   (c) the graduate's speache
    (b) a persuasive speech   (d) a political speach

17. (a) aufuly lonely   (c) awfuly long
    (b) awfully tired   (d) aufuly dark

18. (a) toward the northeaste   (c) the fertile northeast
    (b) the flight nourtheast   (d) from the nourtheaste

19. (a) Maine's coast   (c) the coste of California
    (b) the southern coest   (d) France's coaste

20. (a) the boundry line   (c) the only boundery
    (b) the state boundarry   (d) the natural boundary

21. (a) broken peaces   (c) pieces of pie
    (b) peices of yarn   (d) all the peeces

22. (a) a lethur belt   (c) her leather purse
    (b) that lether wallet   (d) his leathur cowboy boots

23. (a) sausers for teacups   (c) cups and sawcers
    (b) flying saucers   (d) chipped sawsers

24. (a) this kwyer music   (c) youth kwoir practice
    (b) the choir loft   (d) these chuir melodies

25. (a) a breef report   (c) the breaf meeting
    (b) the breif version   (d) a brief stay

Take It Home 2

Your child has learned to spell many new words and would enjoy sharing them with you and your family. Here are some ideas that will make reviewing the words in lessons 7–11 fun.

Words in Print

Help your child write several spelling words on a large sheet of paper. Then tape the sheet on a wall in your home where everyone will see it. Challenge family members to use as many of the spelling words as they can in conversations. Encourage your child to make a checkmark beside a word each time it is used.

Lesson 7
1. boast
2. borrow
3. braid
4. coast
5. cocoa
6. complain
7. decay
8. drains
9. fainted
10. foamy
11. gained
12. hoax
13. painful
14. poach
15. roasting
16. scarecrow
17. swallows
18. throwing
19. toasted
20. tomorrow

Lesson 8
1. agreement
2. breathe
3. creature
4. feather
5. healthy
6. keeping
7. leather
8. meadows
9. needles
10. northeast
11. pleasure
12. preacher
13. speech
14. steady
15. succeed
16. sweater
17. sweeter
18. treasure
19. underneath
20. wealth

Lesson 9
1. author
2. awfully
3. awkward
4. caution
5. daughter
6. drawer
7. exhaust
8. faucet
9. gnawing
10. hauled
11. hawk
12. lawyer
13. naughty
14. pause
15. saucers
16. squawk
17. strawberries
18. unlawful
19. vault
20. withdraw

Lesson 10
1. achieve
2. believe
3. brief
4. conceive
5. deceit
6. deceived
7. eighty
8. either
9. freight
10. grief
11. infield
12. neither
13. niece
14. pieces
15. received
16. review
17. shield
18. thief
19. vein
20. yield

Lesson 11
1. avoid
2. boundary
3. broiled
4. choir
5. counted
6. courageous
7. crowded
8. enjoyable
9. joined
10. joint
11. loyalty
12. moisture
13. mountainous
14. oyster
15. poise
16. poisonous
17. powder
18. soiled
19. toiled
20. voyage

What's Cooking?

See how many spelling words you and your child can use as you make up your own silly recipe. Remember, recipes need both ingredients and steps telling what to do.

Prefixes <u>un</u>, <u>in</u>, <u>dis</u>, and <u>trans</u>

Objective
To spell words with the prefixes *un*, *in*, *dis*, and *trans*

 Phonics Correlated Phonics Lessons
MCP Phonics, Level E, Lessons 30–31

Spelling Words in Action   **Page 53**

In "Bird People," students read about the sport of hang gliding. Invite students to tell why they would or would not enjoy hang gliding.

Call on volunteers to say each boldfaced word and identify its prefix.

Warm-Up Test

1. Huge tankers **transport** oil across the ocean.
2. We will take a bus and then **transfer** to a train.
3. Reading helps you **increase** your knowledge.
4. A dishonest ruler brings **disgrace** to a nation.
5. The food will spoil if it is left **uncovered**.
6. Did they **discontinue** their broadcasts?
7. Many people prefer to eat carrots **uncooked**.
8. He is the one who **discovered** the cure.
9. Does the bill **include** the waiter's tip?
10. If you exercise hard, you **inhale** more deeply.
11. The sign on the door said, "Do not **disturb**."
12. Without an ending, a story is **incomplete**.
13. Jefferson felt the British taxes were **unjust**.
14. **Transplant** the fern to a larger pot.
15. What an **unusual** animal the kangaroo is!
16. The **unselfish** woman does volunteer work.
17. The puppy felt **insecure** when it was left alone.
18. What is the **distance** between Dayton and Akron?
19. Does music **inspire** you to dance?
20. The **inexpensive** shoes were a real bargain.

Spelling Practice   **Pages 54–55**

Introduce the spelling rule and have students read the **list words** aloud. Encourage students to look back at their **Warm-Up Tests** and apply the spelling rule to any misspelled words.

As students work through the **Spelling Practice** exercises, remind them to look back at their **list words** or in their dictionaries if they need help. You may want to point out that some words, such as *transplant*, have a base word *(plant)*, while others, such as *transport*, have a root *(port,* from the Latin word *portare*, meaning "to carry").

 for ESL students See Comparing/Contrasting, page 15

50

Prefixes un, in, dis, and trans

Spelling Words in Action

How can a person fly without using any kind of an engine?

Bird People

Many people have discovered the **unusual** sport of hang gliding. Perhaps it's the birds that **inspire** people to strap themselves to giant wings and soar with the wind. "Sometimes we fly in formation with the eagles and hawks," one pilot said. One might think that this would **disturb** the birds, but the pilot insisted that the birds don't mind.

A pilot holds on to the frame of a hang glider. On a day with 5 to 20 miles-per-hour winds, a pilot can run down a steep, open slope and launch into the air. To fly up, a pilot looks for areas where air rises to **transport** a glider upwards. To steer, a pilot shifts from one side of a glider to the other. The **transfer** of weight makes a hang glider turn toward that side. To end a flight, any flat, open area that a pilot has **discovered** can serve as a landing pad.

How high can a hang glider fly? Heights of 20,000 feet above the Earth have been reported. People who fly at such chilly altitudes don't want to leave their hands or head **uncovered**. These "high fliers" also **include** a parachute— just in case. How far do hang gliders go? Pilots often fly a **distance** of 100 miles or more.

Anyone just starting out in the sport should take lessons from a certified teacher. Students can **increase** their skill level by taking more lessons. For experienced and well-trained pilots, the sky's the limit!

Say the boldfaced words in the selection. These words have word parts called prefixes. Prefixes are added to the front of base words or roots to make new words. What prefixes can you find in the boldfaced words?

53

TIP
A prefix is a word part that is added to the beginning of a base word or a root to make a new word. The prefix **trans** means *across* or *over*, as in *transplant*. The prefixes **un** and **dis** mean *not*, as in *unselfish* and *disgrace*. The prefix **dis** can also mean *away* or *opposite of*, as in *distance* and *discovered*. The prefix **in** can mean *into* or *not*, as in *inexpensive*. It can also mean to *cause to become*, as in *increase*.

LIST WORDS
1. transport
2. transfer
3. increase
4. disgrace
5. uncovered
6. discontinue
7. uncooked
8. discovered
9. include
10. inhale
11. disturb
12. incomplete
13. unjust
14. transplant
15. unusual
16. unselfish
17. insecure
18. distance
19. inspire
20. inexpensive

Words with in, dis, trans, or un

Write each **list word** under the correct heading.

words with the prefix in
1. increase   2. include
3. inhale   4. incomplete
5. insecure   6. inspire
7. inexpensive

words with the prefix dis
8. disgrace
9. discontinue
10. discovered
11. disturb
12. distance

words with the prefix trans
13. transport
14. transfer
15. transplant

words with the prefix un
16. uncovered   17. uncooked
18. unjust   19. unusual
20. unselfish

54   Lesson 13 • Prefixes un, in, dis, and trans

Antonyms

Write the **list word** that is an antonym for each word given.

1. complete ___incomplete___   2. secure ___insecure___
3. usual ___unusual___   4. continue ___discontinue___
5. expensive ___inexpensive___   6. decrease ___increase___
7. just ___unjust___   8. selfish ___unselfish___
9. cooked ___uncooked___

Definitions

Write a **list word** to match each definition clue. Then, use the numbered letters to solve the riddle. Copy each numbered letter onto the line below with same number.

1. to change from one
   bus or train to another   t r a n s f e r
                                        3

2. to cause or influence to do something   i n s p i r e
                                            1

3. contain   i n c l u d e
                       4

4. came upon; found out about   d i s c o v e r e d
                                          6

5. carry from one place to another   t r a n s p o r t
                                                   5

6. loss of honor   d i s g r a c e
                      12   10

7. to plant in another place   t r a n s p l a n t
                                              8

8. exposed to view   u n c o v e r e d
                        7   13

9. amount of separation between two points   d i s t a n c e
                                                       11

10. breathe in   i n h a l e
                       9

11. bother   d i s t u r b
                    2

Riddle: Where is the hang glider going next?

Answer: I t ' s   u p   i n   t h e   a i r .
            1 2 3   4 5   6 7   8 9 10   11 12 13

Proofreading

Proofreading Marks

⬭ spelling mistake
⌃ add something

The following editorial has twelve mistakes. Use the proofreading marks to fix the mistakes. Then, write the misspelled **list words** correctly on the lines.

The way some dune-buggy riders treat the land is a dissgrase Why dothey have to ride such a great destance through the desert Don't they realize they disturb avery fragile environment? I don't mean to be unjust tothose riders who are careful. However, in the past few weeks, people have diskovered greatareas of wild land torn up by dune buggies and noted an incresse in noise. The reports are incompleete now, but there will soon be enough evidence to take action. Isn't it time to inspyre others to help protect our land

1. ___disgrace___   2. ___distance___   3. ___discovered___
4. ___increase___   5. ___incomplete___   6. ___inspire___

Writing an Advertisement

Think of an exciting or unusual sport. Write copy for a poster that advertises the sport. Use any **list words** that you can. Remember to proofread your advertising copy and fix any mistakes.

_____
_____
_____
_____
_____
_____
_____

BONUS WORDS

transparent
transmit
display
unavailable
invisible

Spelling Strategy

Write *un*, *in*, *dis*, and *trans* and their meanings on the board. Then, call out each **list word** without its prefix. Ask volunteers to
- come to the board and point to the prefix that goes with the root or base word
- say and spell the complete word aloud
- tell the word's meaning.

BONUS WORDS You may want to suggest that students write a sentence for each word, mixing up the bonus words so they are in the wrong sentences. Then, have them trade papers and correct each sentence.

Spelling and Writing   *Page 56*

The **Proofreading** exercise will help students prepare to proofread their writing. As students complete the writing activity, encourage them to brainstorm ideas, write a first draft, revise, and proofread their work. To publish their writing, students may want to use their advertising copy to create illustrated posters.

Writer's Corner Students might enjoy reading about hang gliding or other outdoor sports in books such as *Hang Gliding* by Norman Barrett. Ask them to pretend that they participated in the sport they read about and to write a description of what they experienced.

Final Test

1. Books about explorers **inspire** me to travel.
2. Salads are made with **uncooked** vegetables.
3. Has there been an **increase** in sales this year?
4. The hammering may **disturb** our neighbors.
5. Francine is always ready to try **unusual** foods.
6. Write a list word in the **incomplete** sentence.
7. The meals at that restaurant are **inexpensive**.
8. **Unselfish** people share their time and ideas.
9. The horse thief brought **disgrace** to his family.
10. Salk **discovered** a vaccine to prevent polio.
11. Be sure to **include** a good ending to your story.
12. Will they **transport** the cattle by train?
13. If left **uncovered**, the cheese will dry out.
14. These new taxes are really **unjust**!
15. The **insecure** little calf hid behind its mother.
16. Kareem traveled a great **distance** to visit me.
17. We **inhale** air to give our bodies oxygen.
18. He will **transplant** the daisies to the garden.
19. Will Joanna have to **transfer** to a new school?
20. Did the factory **discontinue** that radio model?

Prefixes <u>en</u>, <u>im</u>, and <u>mis</u>

Objective
To spell words with the prefixes *en*, *im*, and *mis*

Correlated Phonics Lessons
MCP Phonics, Level E, Lessons 30–32

Spelling Words in Action   *Page 57*

In this selection, students learn about rules of etiquette observed by George Washington. Afterward, ask students how those rules compare to manners they observe in modern times.

Encourage students to look back at the boldfaced words. Ask volunteers to say each word and identify its prefix.

Warm-Up Test

1. Do not **engage** in such a loud conversation.
2. We will **encourage** them to do a good job.
3. Don't be so **impolite**!
4. How can I **improve** my speaking skills?
5. A scholarship will **enable** Dawn to go to college.
6. The police officer's job is to **enforce** the laws.
7. It's **improper** to contradict the umpire.
8. It's easy to **misjudge** a distance across water.
9. If you **mistrust** your memory, write a note.
10. Is there a spelling **mistake** in her sentence?
11. Dennis is looking for the book he **misplaced**.
12. Climbing the cliff could **endanger** your life.
13. What an **impossible** task this is!
14. No one will **misunderstand** if you explain thoroughly.
15. The bus driver hoped no one would **misbehave**.
16. A strong friendship may **endure** for a lifetime.
17. **Immerse** the craft paper in the water.
18. Rosa was **immobile** when her leg was in a cast.
19. I **mistook** one twin for the other.
20. What words do you always **mispronounce**?

Spelling Practice   *Pages 58–59*

Introduce the spelling rule and have students read the **list words** aloud. Encourage students to look back at their **Warm-Up Tests** and apply the spelling rule to any misspelled words.

As students work through the **Spelling Practice** exercises, remind them to look back at their **list words** or in their dictionaries if they need help.

 See Student Dictation, page 14

Spelling Words in Action

How would your behavior have been regarded in the days of colonial America?

Minding Your Manners

Have you ever listed all the behaviors you've been told are **impolite** or **improper**? George Washington did. As a teenager, he wrote out a list of over 100 rules that describe how not to **misbehave**.

It must have been **impossible** to behave in colonial times! Here are just a few of the rules George wrote:

* Do not sit when others are standing.
* Do not **encourage** your friends to discover a secret.
* When around others, do not **engage** in singing or humming to yourself. Also, do not drum your fingers or feet.
* When you sit down, keep your feet **immobile** and flat on the floor. Do not put one foot on the other.
* It is a **mistake** either to run or to move too slowly in the streets. Do not walk with your mouth open.
* Think before you speak, and do not **mispronounce** your words.
* If you must criticize someone, do it as sweetly as you can.

Do you think you could **endure** these rules?

> Say the boldfaced words in the selection. These words are made up of a base word or a root and a prefix. What prefixes do you find in the boldfaced words?

57

Spelling Practice

TIP
The prefix **en** usually means cause to be or make, as in <u>en</u>able. The prefix **im** usually means not, as in <u>im</u>possible. The prefix **im** can also mean more, as in <u>im</u>prove. The prefix **mis** usually means wrong or wrongly, as in <u>mis</u>judge. The prefix **mis** can also mean bad or badly, as in <u>mis</u>behave.

LIST WORDS

1. engage
2. encourage
3. impolite
4. improve
5. enable
6. enforce
7. improper
8. misjudge
9. mistrust
10. mistake
11. misplaced
12. endanger
13. impossible
14. misunderstand
15. misbehave
16. endure
17. immerse
18. immobile
19. mistook
20. mispronounce

Words with en, im, or mis

Write each **list word** under the correct heading.

words with the prefix en

1. engage   2. encourage
3. enable   4. enforce
5. endanger   6. endure

words with the prefix im

7. impolite   8. improve
9. improper   10. impossible
11. immerse   12. immobile

words with the prefix mis

13. misjudge
14. mistrust
15. mistake
16. misplaced
17. misunderstand
18. misbehave
19. mistook
20. mispronounce

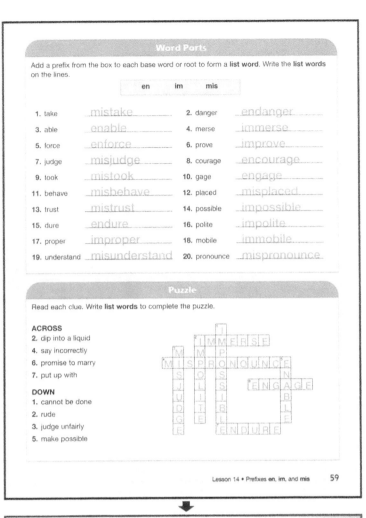

Word Parts

Add a prefix from the box to each base word or root to form a **list word**. Write the **list words** on the lines.

en	im	mis

1. take _mistake_
2. danger _endanger_
3. able _enable_
4. merse _immerse_
5. force _enforce_
6. prove _improve_
7. judge _misjudge_
8. courage _encourage_
9. took _mistook_
10. gage _engage_
11. behave _misbehave_
12. placed _misplaced_
13. trust _mistrust_
14. possible _impossible_
15. dure _endure_
16. polite _impolite_
17. proper _improper_
18. mobile _immobile_
19. understand _misunderstand_
20. pronounce _mispronounce_

Puzzle

Read each clue. Write **list words** to complete the puzzle.

ACROSS
2. dip into a liquid
4. say incorrectly
6. promise to marry
7. put up with

DOWN
1. cannot be done
2. rude
3. judge unfairly
5. make possible

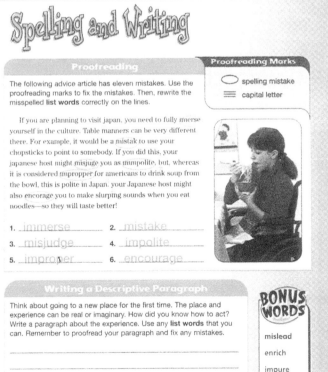

Spelling and Writing

Proofreading

The following advice article has eleven mistakes. Use the proofreading marks to fix the mistakes. Then, rewrite the misspelled **list words** correctly on the lines.

Proofreading Marks
○ spelling mistake
≡ capital letter

If you are planning to visit japan, you need to fully merse yourself in the culture. Table manners can be very different there. For example, it would be a mistak to use your chopsticks to point to somebody. If you did this, your japanese host might misjuge you as immpolite, but, whereas it is considered improper for americans to drink soup from the bowl, this is polite in Japan. your Japanese host might also encorage you to make slurping sounds when you eat noodles—so they will taste better!

1. _immerse_   2. _mistake_
3. _misjudge_   4. _impolite_
5. _improper_   6. _encourage_

Writing a Descriptive Paragraph

Think about going to a new place for the first time. The place and experience can be real or imaginary. How did you know how to act? Write a paragraph about the experience. Use any **list words** that you can. Remember to proofread your paragraph and fix any mistakes.

_____
_____
_____
_____
_____

BONUS WORDS

mislead
enrich
impure
misfortune
impose

Spelling Strategy

Point out to students that when a prefix ends with the same letter that a base word or root begins with, both letters are used (*im* + *mobile* = *immobile*). Then, have students work with a partner to write each **list word** as a word equation (*mis* + *judge* = *misjudge*).

BONUS WORDS You may want to suggest that students write a sentence for each word, and then erase the prefix. Ask them to trade papers with a partner, and add the correct prefix to the words so they make sense.

Spelling and Writing   **Page 60**

The **Proofreading** exercise will help students prepare to proofread their work. As students complete the writing activity, encourage them to brainstorm ideas, write a first draft, revise, and proofread their work. To publish their writing, students may want to use their paragraphs to create a travel brochure.

Writer's Corner Ask students to think of a situation in which a certain behavior is expected, such as talking on the phone or eating dinner. Have them research the etiquette involved, using either the Internet or the library. Encourage students to take notes as they research.

Final Test

1. Be careful not to **mispronounce** her name.
2. Does studying **engage** much of your time?
3. I **mistook** Ed for his brother.
4. Did you **encourage** Mike to do that?
5. When he heard the news, he was **immobile**.
6. It is **impolite** to put your elbows on the table.
7. Don't **immerse** the electric coffeepot in water.
8. The colonists had to **endure** many hardships.
9. My coach helped me **improve** my swing.
10. Those children will not **misbehave**.
11. Did Pat **misunderstand** the directions?
12. The hall monitor will **enforce** the school rules.
13. Landing on the moon is not **impossible**.
14. You're wearing **improper** shoes for hiking.
15. Did she **misjudge** how much time she needed?
16. Burning brush here could **endanger** our lives.
17. We sometimes **mistrust** people.
18. Dan made a careless **mistake** on the test.
19. Machines **enable** us to work more quickly.
20. Danielle **misplaced** her science notebook.

Lesson 15

Prefixes <u>pre</u>, <u>pro</u>, <u>re</u>, and <u>ex</u>

Objective
To spell words with the prefixes *pre*, *pro*, *re*, and *ex*

Correlated Phonics Lessons
MCP Phonics, Level E, Lessons 33, 35

Spelling Words in Action   *Page 61*

Students may enjoy reading about Jackie Robinson's accomplishments. After reading, ask students what qualities of Robinson's helped him to succeed as the first African-American major league baseball player.

Encourage students to look back at the boldfaced words. Ask volunteers to say each word and identify its prefix.

Warm-Up Test
1. Can you **explain** the rules of the game?
2. Drive **exactly** 1.5 miles before you turn right.
3. When the snow is gone, the grass will **reappear**.
4. Sam likes to **pretend** he is an astronaut.
5. What a nice **reward** he got for finding the cat!
6. Are you **returning** those library books?
7. Please don't **exchange** papers yet.
8. We **export** wheat and import bananas.
9. Tina will **provide** hamburgers for the picnic.
10. The ad tried to **promote** a new toothpaste.
11. Did the players **protest** the umpire's decision?
12. We should all **preserve** our natural resources.
13. Wilma will **prepare** sandwiches for all of us.
14. How does a mirror **reflect** an image?
15. A paid athlete is considered a **professional**.
16. Let's **rearrange** the desks to make wider aisles.
17. How long can camels **exist** without water?
18. Did she **exclaim** when she opened the box?
19. Boiling water will **produce** steam.
20. At the meeting, I will **propose** some new rules.

Spelling Practice   *Pages 62–63*

Introduce the spelling rule and have students read the **list words** aloud. You may also want to discuss the multiple meanings of *reflect* ("to show an image; to give thought to") and *promote* ("to encourage; to move a student forward a grade"). Then, encourage students to look back at their **Warm-Up Tests** and apply the spelling rule to any misspelled words.

As students work through the **Spelling Practice** exercises, remind them to look back at their **list words** or in their dictionaries if they need help.

 See Words in Context, page 14

54

Prefixes <u>pre</u>, <u>pro</u>, <u>re</u>, and <u>ex</u>   Lesson 15

Spelling Words in Action

How were baseball teams before 1947 different from sports teams today?

Jackie Robinson, an American Hero

Today, African-American athletes are the stars of many **professional** sports teams. However, before 1947, integration did not **exist** in major-league baseball. Then, the Brooklyn Dodgers hired a ballplayer named Jackie Robinson.

Known for his hitting, his fielding, and his stolen bases, Robinson quickly proved himself to be a great player. He was named Rookie of the Year in 1947, a great **reward** for his playing. Two years later, he was the National League's Most Valuable Player. Despite Robinson's record, there were people who would **protest** loudly that an African-American should not play on a team with white players. At first, Robinson had to **pretend** that he did not hear their insults.

The Dodgers' manager, Branch Rickey, was often asked to **explain** why he hired Robinson. Rickey believed that Robinson would **prepare** the way for other African-Americans in the major leagues. Rickey also wanted the best team possible. Teams had to rely on ticket sales to **provide** money. Rickey thought Robinson could help him **produce** the best and most profitable team.

After Robinson's ten-year career with the Dodgers, he would **reappear** in the news as an active member of organizations known to **promote** the rights of African-Americans. He was a great civil rights leader as well as one of the best athletes baseball has ever seen.

> Look at the boldfaced words in the selection. How many different prefixes can you find? What do you notice about the meaning of the base words or roots when a prefix is added?

61

TIP
The prefix **pre** usually means before, as in prepare.
The prefix **pro** usually means for, in favor of, or forward, as in propose.
The prefix **re** usually means again or back, as in returning.
The prefix **ex** usually means out of or from, as in export.

Spelling Practice

LIST WORDS
1. explain
2. exactly
3. reappear
4. pretend
5. reward
6. returning
7. exchange
8. export
9. provide
10. promote
11. protest
12. preserve
13. prepare
14. reflect
15. professional
16. rearrange
17. exist
18. exclaim
19. produce
20. propose

Words with pre, pro, re, and ex

Write each **list word** under the correct heading.

words with the prefix ex
1. explain   2. exactly
3. exchange   4. export
5. exist   6. exclaim

words with the prefix pro
7. provide   8. promote
9. protest   10. professional
11. produce   12. propose

words with the prefix pre
13. pretend
14. preserve
15. prepare

words with the prefix re
16. reappear
17. reward
18. returning
19. reflect
20. rearrange

62   Lesson 15 • Prefixes pre, pro, re, and ex

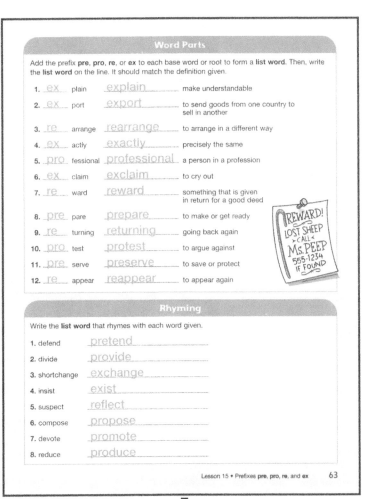

Word Parts

Add the prefix **pre, pro, re,** or **ex** to each base word or root to form a **list word**. Then, write the **list word** on the line. It should match the definition given.

1. ___ex___ plain ___explain___ — make understandable
2. ___ex___ port ___export___ — to send goods from one country to sell in another
3. ___re___ arrange ___rearrange___ — to arrange in a different way
4. ___ex___ actly ___exactly___ — precisely the same
5. ___pro___ fessional ___professional___ — a person in a profession
6. ___ex___ claim ___exclaim___ — to cry out
7. ___re___ ward ___reward___ — something that is given in return for a good deed
8. ___pre___ pare ___prepare___ — to make or get ready
9. ___re___ turning ___returning___ — going back again
10. ___pro___ test ___protest___ — to argue against
11. ___pre___ serve ___preserve___ — to save or protect
12. ___re___ appear ___reappear___ — to appear again

REWARD!
LOST SHEEP
→ CALL →
Ms. PEEP
555-1234
IF FOUND

Rhyming

Write the **list word** that rhymes with each word given.

1. defend ___pretend___
2. divide ___provide___
3. shortchange ___exchange___
4. insist ___exist___
5. suspect ___reflect___
6. compose ___propose___
7. devote ___promote___
8. reduce ___produce___

Spelling and Writing

Proofreading

This biographical article has eleven mistakes. Use the proofreading marks to fix the mistakes. Then, write the misspelled **list words** correctly on the lines.

Proofreading Marks

⬭ spelling mistake
⊙ add period
⤺ take out something

Sammy Sosa gained his fame a as a profesional ballplayer in 1998 by hitting the second highest number of home runs in one season. For his 66 homers, he was named the National League's Most Valuable Player in 1998. His greatest rewward, though, was the opportunity he had to provide relief to the his home country, the Dominican Republic, after it suffered a devastating hurricane in September of 1998. After the storm, money from fans and major-league baseball came pouring into the Sammy Sosa Foundation. With this, Sosa was able to esport food and medicine to give the people of his country the relief they needed. Upon retering to his his homeland, Sosa received a great hero's welcome.

1. ___professional___
2. ___reward___
3. ___provide___
4. ___export___
5. ___returning___

Writing a Letter

Think of someone you admire because of what he or she has accomplished. Write a letter to this person telling why you admire him or her. Use any **list words** that you can. Remember to proofread your letter and fix any mistakes.

BONUS WORDS

prevent
proceed
reprint
extend
exceed

Spelling Strategy

Write the definitions of the prefixes *pre, pro, re,* and *ex* on the board as separate column headings. Then, call out each **list word** and have the class tell you which column it belongs in, based on its meaning. Ask a volunteer to write a word in that column and to give the meaning.

BONUS WORDS

Suggest that students work with a partner to look up the words in a dictionary and write definitions. Ask the students to label each definition with the wrong bonus word. Then, have teams trade papers and try to match words and definitions correctly.

Spelling and Writing   Page 64

The **Proofreading** exercise will help students prepare to proofread their letters. As students complete the writing activity, encourage them to brainstorm ideas, write a first draft, revise, and proofread their work. To publish their writing, students may want to
• read their letters aloud
• send their letters to the person they admire.

Writer's Corner Invite students to read a biography of or an autobiography by a sports figure they admire. Ask them to create a sports card (like a baseball card) that gives important and interesting facts about that person. Encourage students to share or trade their cards with one another.

Final Test

1. When is Halley's comet going to **reappear** next?
2. Please help me **rearrange** the furniture in here.
3. Conservation laws help **preserve** wetlands.
4. My little sister likes to **pretend** she's an astronaut.
5. Mr. Reardon will **explain** what the symbols mean.
6. Did Heather **propose** a better plan?
7. Many life forms **exist** in this one pond.
8. Sheep **provide** us with both food and clothing.
9. What a huge **reward** he received!
10. The hall mirrors **reflect** the outside light.
11. How much cotton do we **export**?
12. This machine can **produce** many cans an hour.
13. Make sure the wall is **exactly** ten feet high.
14. What a storm of **protest** the new law caused!
15. Did Marco **exchange** the red cap for a blue one?
16. I heard Jack **exclaim** when we yelled, "Surprise!"
17. Emily's mother is a **professional** photographer.
18. On weekends, the two boys **prepare** breakfast.
19. Nature films can **promote** a love of animals.
20. Next week we're **returning** the camper we rented.

Objective
To spell words with the prefixes *fore*, *post*, *over*, *co*, *com*, and *con*

Correlated Phonics Lessons
MCP Phonics, Level E, Lessons 36–38

Spelling Words in Action   **Page 65**

In "Spinning Out of Control," students learn some facts about tornadoes. Ask students what they would do if they heard that a tornado warning had been issued in your area.

Call on volunteers to say each boldfaced word and identify its prefix.

Warm-Up Test

1. If it rains, we will have to **postpone** the game.
2. Many jobs were available in the **postwar** period.
3. She **overlooked** a spelling mistake in her report.
4. Throw the anchor **overboard** to moor the boat.
5. The weather **forecast** calls for more sunny days.
6. The baseball player sprained his right **forearm**.
7. Do you **overreact** when you don't get your way?
8. To **conserve** energy, turn off unnecessary lights.
9. What dangerous road **conditions** these are!
10. Ruth **consoled** Tim when he lost the race.
11. Will our school **compete** in the drama festival?
12. A seismograph helps **forewarn** us about earthquakes.
13. Friends can help you **overcome** your worries.
14. Robert and Emilio started a computer **company**.
15. Every team member must **cooperate**.
16. Mountain climbers must **conquer** great heights.
17. I **foresee** great success in your future.
18. She is always willing to **contribute** to the team.
19. I **commend** you for your hard work.
20. The dance **committee** met Tuesday afternoon.

Spelling Practice   **Pages 66–67**

Introduce the spelling rule and have students read the **list words** aloud. Encourage students to look back at their **Warm-Up Tests** and apply the spelling rule to any misspelled words.

As students work through the **Spelling Practice** exercises, remind them to look back at their **list words** or in their dictionaries if they need help. You may want to discuss the meanings of the prefixes and review the concept of base words and roots, using *forearm* (base word *arm*) and *postpone* (root *pone*, from the Latin word *ponere*, meaning "to put").

 See Picture Clues, page 15

56

Spelling Words in Action

How does anyone know when a tornado is about to hit?

Spinning Out of Control

Tornadoes are considered the most violent storms on Earth. They create the fastest winds, which can exceed 300 miles per hour. Tornadoes can move across the land at speeds up to 70 miles per hour. Unfortunately, it's hard to **foresee** exactly when and where a tornado will hit.

Tornadoes form in particular weather **conditions**. Most form where air that is cold and dry meets air that is warm and moist. These air masses **compete** with each other. The cold, dry air pushes up the warm, moist air. This causes strong updrafts and spiraling winds that become tornadoes. The dust and debris picked up off the ground by tornadoes **contribute** to their gray or brown color.

Storm spotters help to **forewarn** people of tornadoes. Storm spotters are people who form a **committee** in a place where tornadoes occur. They look for warning signs such as a greenish sky or hail. Local radio and television news stations **cooperate** with the storm spotters to broadcast tornado warnings quickly.

Some people **overreact** in fearing tornadoes. What can people do to **overcome** their fears? Most importantly, they should be alert. When storms approach, people should tune into a weather **forecast**. If a tornado warning has been issued, they should **postpone** whatever they are doing and get to a safe shelter right away.

Everyone should **commend** the work of storm spotters. In the last fifty years, storm spotters and advanced technology have reduced the number of people killed by tornadoes.

> Look at the boldfaced words. How are their prefixes alike? What do you notice about the word parts in **overreact**?

65

TIP
The prefix **fore** means in front of or before, as in *forewarn*. The prefix **post** means after, as in *postwar*. The prefix **over** means above or too much, as in *overreact*. The prefixes **co**, **com**, and **con** mean with or together, as in *cooperate*.

Spelling Practice

Words with fore, post, over, co, com, and con

For each **list word**, find the meaning of its prefix. Write the **list word** under the correct heading.

LIST WORDS

1. postpone
2. postwar
3. overlooked
4. overboard
5. forecast
6. forearm
7. overreact
8. conserve
9. conditions
10. consoled
11. compete
12. forewarn
13. overcome
14. company
15. cooperate
16. conquer
17. foresee
18. contribute
19. commend
20. committee

above or too much

1. overlooked   2. overboard
3. overreact   4. overcome

after

5. postpone   6. postwar

in front of or before

7. forecast   8. forearm
9. forewarn   10. foresee

with or together

11. conserve
12. conditions
13. consoled
14. compete
15. company
16. cooperate
17. conquer
18. contribute
19. commend
20. committee

Replace the Words

Choose the **list word** that best replaces the underlined word or words.

1. During the hot, dry summer, people were asked to <u>save</u> water. __conserve__
2. He could not <u>put off</u> his chores any longer. __postpone__
3. When working with a group, it's important to <u>get along</u> with the others. __cooperate__
4. Sally could not be <u>comforted</u> after the death of her hamster. __consoled__
5. In overtime, the Warriors were finally able to <u>defeat</u> the Panthers. __conquer__
6. People often <u>give</u> copies of their favorite books to libraries. __contribute__
7. The sailors wore life vests to protect themselves just in case anyone went <u>into the water</u>. __overboard__
8. The mistakes in the story were <u>not noticed</u> because the writer proofread it too quickly. __overlooked__
9. Some people <u>get over</u> their fear of water by taking swimming lessons. __overcome__
10. We had to clean the house before <u>a group of friends</u> arrived. __company__

Word Building

Add and subtract letters to form **list words**.

1. comedy – edy + petal – al + e __compete__
2. before – be + armor – or __forearm__
3. discover – disc + rest – st + faced – fed + t __overreact__
4. foam – am + rewarding – ding + nail – ail __forewarn__
5. become – bee + meal – al + lend – le __commend__
6. posting – ing + warring – ring __postwar__
7. combed – bed + mitten – ten + tease – as __committee__
8. cone – e + dire – re + time – me + ons __conditions__
9. forest – rest + restore – store + seem – m __foresee__
10. face – ace + lore – l + casting – ing __forecast__

Spelling and Writing

Proofreading

The following weather report has ten mistakes. Use the proofreading marks to fix the mistakes. Then, write the misspelled **list words** correctly on the lines.

The forecast for the weekend does not look promising Extremely windy and wet conditions will exist for the next two days. a cold front moving in from the north will bring lots of moisture. Gale-force winds may contribut to air-traffic delays A warning has been issued for sailors to postpone their plans for the weekend. people may be concoled, however, by knowing that we foresey a warming trend by the middle of the week.

Proofreading Marks
- ⬭ spelling mistake
- ≡ capital letter
- ⊙ add period

1. __forecast__   2. __conditions__
3. __contribute__   4. __postpone__
5. __consoled__   6. __foresee__

Writing a Descriptive Paragraph

Remember or imagine a day with extreme weather conditions, such as a blizzard, a flood, or a really hot day. Write a paragraph describing that day's weather. Try to use as many **list words** as you can. Remember to proofread your paragraph and fix any mistakes.

_____

_____

_____

_____

_____

BONUS WORDS

postgame

connect

foresight

overdue

commence

Spelling Strategy

Write two columns on the board, one containing the prefixes in this order: *post, co, over, con, fore, com,* and the other containing these base words and roots: *operate, see, mittee, pone, quer, board.* Then, invite students to work with a partner to
- copy the columns
- draw connecting lines to make **list words**
- take turns writing each **list word**, telling its meaning, and using it in a sentence.

BONUS WORDS You may want to suggest that students work with a partner to write definitions for each bonus word. Then, have them compare the definitions to those in their dictionary.

Spelling and Writing   **Page 68**

The **Proofreading** exercise will help students prepare to proofread their work. As students complete the writing activity, encourage them to brainstorm ideas, write a first draft, revise, and proofread their work. To publish their writing, students may want to
- create a class book titled *Extreme Weather*
- use their work to give dramatic readings.

Writer's Corner Students might enjoy reading more about tornadoes in a book such as *Eyewitness: Hurricane and Tornado* by Jack Challoner. Encourage them to write a book review and read it to the class.

Final Test

1. I can't believe we **overlooked** that clue!
2. Today, we will **compete** against the Bulldogs.
3. Some people **overreact** to small problems.
4. We **commend** Dr. Kikuchi for her contributions.
5. If we all **cooperate**, the job will be easy.
6. Weather forecasters **forewarn** us of storms.
7. He worked hard to **conquer** his fear of snakes.
8. Fran was elected treasurer of the **committee**.
9. We must **conserve** water now!
10. The skin divers jumped **overboard**.
11. The kitten scratched Felipe's **forearm**.
12. During the **postwar** period, England flourished.
13. Friends **consoled** me when I lost the election.
14. When did Pat start her own **company**?
15. He'll **contribute** funds to the research project.
16. Kathy's illness made her **postpone** the project.
17. I **foresee** a happy ending to the story.
18. How soon will their **conditions** improve?
19. The **forecast** promises sunny spring weather.
20. I must **overcome** my fear of spiders.

...

Lesson 17

Prefixes <u>sub</u>, <u>mid</u>, <u>bi</u>, and <u>tri</u>

Objective
To spell words with the prefixes *sub*, *mid*, *bi*, and *tri*

Correlated Phonics Lessons
MCP Phonics, Level E, Lessons 39–40

Spelling Words in Action *Page 69*

In this selection, students read about the exciting sport called BMX. After reading, ask students to read aloud the part of the selection they liked the best.

Call on volunteers to say each boldfaced word and identify its prefix.

Warm-Up Test

1. The three friends formed a new **trio**.
2. Is Amy's favorite **subject** history?
3. We usually have a lot of snow in **midwinter**.
4. Please **submit** all reports by Friday.
5. The birthday party ended at **midnight**.
6. A **triangle** has three sides and three angles.
7. The two canoes passed each other **midstream**.
8. They sold the land for **triple** the original price.
9. Will Chris speed up in the **middle** of the race?
10. The three girls rode their **bicycles** to school.
11. If you **bisect** an apple, you'll have two halves.
12. Sam wants to **subscribe** to that magazine, too.
13. The pilot just avoided a **midair** collision!
14. The waiter had to **substitute** haddock for cod.
15. Can you **subtract** large numbers in your head?
16. Lenny lifts weights to develop his **biceps**.
17. A **tripod** will hold your camera steady.
18. The sun is at its highest point around **midday**.
19. Was Kelly able to **subdue** the wild horse?
20. The storm must **subside** before we can sail.

Spelling Practice *Pages 70–71*

Introduce the spelling rule and have students read the **list words** aloud. Encourage students to look back at their **Warm-Up Tests** and apply the spelling rule to any misspelled words.

As students work through the **Spelling Practice** exercises, remind them to look back at their **list words** or in their dictionaries if they need help. You may also want to discuss the meanings of unfamiliar words as well as the multiple meanings of *subject* ("a person under another's control; a course of study").

 See Words in Context, page 14

58

Prefixes <u>sub</u>, <u>mid</u>, <u>bi</u>, and <u>tri</u> — Lesson 17

Spelling Words in Action

What do you get when you combine a bicycle with a motorcycle?

BMX

To some bikers, **bicycles** are for flying. They call their sport BMX. The letters stand for Bicycle Motocross. A motocross is a race for motorcycles, but BMX racers **substitute** bicycles for motorcycles.

A BMX race takes place on a dirt track. Riders pedal around steep, banked turns. They make double and **triple** jumps. A good jump can send a rider into **midair**! It's important for racers to get a good start out of the gate. It's easy for them to crash when they are in the **middle** of a crowd.

Besides racing, BMX riders do freestyle tricks. "Dirt riders" focus on jumping over obstacles in dirt trails. "Flatlanders" stay on the ground. Their tricks include different ways of riding the bike without touching the pedals. "Street riders" are **subject** to the most danger. They jump gaps in roads and sidewalks. With so many variations in the sport, interest in BMX is not likely to **subside** anytime soon.

BMX riders have to **submit** to hard training and perhaps a few bumps and bruises. While bicycle racers usually have strong leg muscles, BMX riders also need strong **biceps** to pull the bike into the air. The sport can be dangerous, so riders reduce risks by wearing helmets and checking that their bikes are in safe condition. If you think you're interested in BMX riding, watch a BMX race or **subscribe** to a magazine to learn more first.

Look at the boldfaced words in the selection. How many different prefixes can you find? How do the base words or roots change meaning when the prefixes are added?

69

 TIP

The prefix **sub** usually means <u>under</u>, <u>below</u>, or <u>not quite</u>, as in subside.
The prefix **mid** means <u>in the middle part</u>, as in midday.
The prefix **bi** usually means <u>two</u>, as in bisect.
The prefix **tri** usually means <u>three</u>, as in tripod.

Spelling Practice

LIST WORDS

1. trio
2. subject
3. midwinter
4. submit
5. midnight
6. triangle
7. midstream
8. triple
9. middle
10. bicycles
11. bisect
12. subscribe
13. midair
14. substitute
15. subtract
16. biceps
17. tripod
18. midday
19. subdue
20. subside

Words with <u>sub</u>, <u>mid</u>, <u>bi</u>, and <u>tri</u>

Write each **list word** under the correct heading.

words with the prefix tri

1. trio
2. triangle
3. triple
4. tripod

words with the prefix mid

5. midwinter
6. midnight
7. midstream
8. middle
9. midair
10. midday

words with the prefix bi

11. bicycles
12. bisect
13. biceps

words with the prefix sub

14. subject
15. submit
16. subscribe
17. subsitute
18. subtract
19. subdue
20. subside

70   Lesson 17 • Prefixes sub, mid, bi, and tri

Definitions

Write a **list word** to match each definition clue.

1. take away — subtract
2. three times as much — triple
3. three-sided figure — triangle
4. arm muscles — biceps
5. 12:00 A.M. — midnight
6. middle of the winter — midwinter
7. three people who play music — trio
8. 12:00 P.M. — midday
9. a course of study — subject
10. to conquer or overcome — subdue
11. the center — middle
12. person or thing that replaces another — substitute

Riddles

Answer each pair of riddles with a **list word**. Write the word on the line.

1. My prefix usually means <u>three</u>. Peas grow in my base word. — tripod
2. You could order my prefix in a deli, but it also means <u>not quite</u>. My root is something that a triangle has three of. — subside
3. My prefix can mean <u>under</u>. My root rhymes with <u>tribe</u>. — subscribe
4. My prefix usually means <u>two</u>. My root means <u>wheels</u>. — bicycles
5. My prefix means <u>two</u>. My root can be found in the word <u>section</u>. — bisect
6. My prefix can mean <u>below</u>. My root sounds like another name for a baseball glove. — submit
7. My prefix means <u>in the middle part</u>. My base word means a <u>small river</u>. — midstream
8. My prefix rhymes with <u>bid</u>. You breathe my base word. — midair

Lesson 17 • Prefixes **sub**, **mid**, **bi**, and **tri**   71

Spelling and Writing

Proofreading

This article has twelve mistakes. Use the proofreading marks to fix the mistakes. Then, write the misspelled **list words** correctly on the lines.

Proofreading Marks
- ⬭ spelling mistake
- ⤸ add apostrophe
- ⌄ add something

In 1896 bicickles filled Americas streets. People were quick to subskribe to the new craze and substitue horses with two-wheeled vehicles. Young people enjoyed midaye rides in the country while others rode to work. Orville and Wilbur Wrights bicycle shop was busy. However new ideas would subdoo the craze. The automobile would become the subjek of great interest, and the Wright brothers would soon be flying in middair in an airplane.

1. bicycles   2. subscribe   3. substitute
4. midday   5. subdue   6. subject
7. midair

Writing a Poem

People use all kinds of wheels to get around. Bicycles, wheelchairs, and in-line skates are just a few examples. Recall an experience you have had on wheels. Then, write a poem about the experience and your feelings. Use any **list words** that you can. Remember to proofread your poem and fix any mistakes.

BONUS WORDS

submarine
midway
bifocals
triplets
submerge

Spelling Strategy

Divide the class into four groups and assign each group a different prefix from the lesson: *sub*, *mid*, *bi*, or *tri*. Invite the groups to write all the **list words** that contain their assigned prefix, then

- circle the prefix and discuss its meaning
- list other words that have the same prefix
- share their list with another group.

BONUS WORDS You may want to suggest that students work with partners to write the bonus words on slips of paper. Have them put the slips in an envelope and take turns pantomiming and guessing the words.

Spelling and Writing   *Page 72*

The **Proofreading** exercise will help students to prepare to proofread their poems. As students complete the writing activity, encourage them to brainstorm ideas, write a first draft, revise, and proofread their work. To publish their writing, students may want to

- read their poems aloud to the class
- create a book of poems titled *Flying on the Ground.*

Writer's Corner Suggest that students use the library or the Internet to research bicycle-helmet safety laws and facts. Have them put their findings together in a pamphlet to give to your school library.

Final Test

1. The photographer carried a folding **tripod**.
2. My favorite **subject** is geography.
3. Now fold the **triangle** in half.
4. Do you **subscribe** to that newspaper?
5. We can't return home until the waters **subside**.
6. Jade is the third singer in the **trio**.
7. You can make telephone calls in **midair**.
8. The pond did not freeze solid until **midwinter**.
9. The trainer knew how to **subdue** the tiger.
10. At **midstream**, the water is four feet deep.
11. Here's how to **bisect** a piece of rope quickly.
12. You must **submit** the application by Tuesday.
13. Your **biceps** are muscles on your upper arms.
14. If you land on a red box, you **triple** your score.
15. A **substitute** teacher filled in for Mr. Cohen.
16. Do you want to rent **bicycles** at the lake?
17. At **midnight** they shouted, "Happy New Year!"
18. My **midday** meal is usually my largest one.
19. We learn how to **subtract** after learning to add.
20. His teacher left in the **middle** of the year.

Lessons 13–17 · Review

Objectives
To review spelling words with the prefixes *un, in, dis, trans, en, im, mis, pre, pro, re, ex, fore, post, over, co, com, con, sub, mid, bi,* and *tri*

Check Your Spelling Notebook
Pages 73–76

Based on your observations, note which words are giving students the most difficulty and offer assistance for spelling them correctly. Here are some frequently misspelled words to watch for: *unusual, pretend, prepare, cooperate, committee, transfer,* and *bicycles.*

To give students extra help and practice in taking standardized tests, you may want to have them take the **Review Test** for this lesson on pages 62–63. After scoring the tests, return them to students so that they can record their misspelled words in their spelling notebooks.

After practicing their troublesome words, students can work through the exercises for lessons 13–17 and the cumulative review, **Show What You Know**. Before they begin each exercise, you may want to go over the spelling rule.

Take It Home

Invite students to locate and circle the **list words** from lessons 13–17 in junk mail their family receives at home. Students can also use **Take It Home Master 3** on pages 64–65 to help them do the activity. (A complete list of the spelling words is included on page 64 of the **Take It Home** Master.) Have students bring in their mail to share with the class.

60

Lessons 13–17 · Review

In lessons 13 through 17, you learned that a prefix is added to a base word or root to make a new word. Look again at the **list words**. Think about what the prefixes mean.

Check Your Spelling Notebook

Look at the words in your spelling notebook. Which words for lessons 13 through 17 did you have the most trouble with? Write them here.

_____

_____

_____

With a partner, write each prefix on a slip of paper. Take turns writing a prefix, giving its meaning, and writing a word with the prefix.

Lesson 13

TIP in = not, into, or to cause to be   dis = not, away, or opposite of
un = not   trans = across or over

List Words
- transport
- transfer
- increase
- discontinue
- discovered
- disturb
- incomplete
- uncooked
- unjust
- unusual
- insecure
- disgrace

Write the **list word** that completes each sentence. Not all the words will be used.

1. The office building had an ___unusual___ design.
2. Flatbed trucks are used to ___transport___ heavy lumber.
3. With only eleven eggs, the dozen was ___incomplete___.
4. Don't ___disturb___ her when she's concentrating.
5. If the medicine causes a rash, ___discontinue___ its use.
6. Buy these on sale, before they ___increase___ the price.
7. Let's encourage him; he's feeling somewhat ___insecure___.
8. Some students feel that certain rules are ___unjust___.
9. More ruins have been ___discovered___ in Peru.
10. Take the train and then ___transfer___ to the bus.

73

↓

Lesson 14

TIP en = cause to be or make, as in encourage
im = not, as in impolite; more, as in improve
mis = bad or badly, as in misbehave; wrong or wrongly, as in mistake

List Words
- encourage
- impolite
- improve
- enable
- endanger
- improper
- mistrust
- misplaced
- impossible
- misbehave
- immobile
- endure

Write a **list word** that is an antonym for each word given. Not all the words will be used.

1. obey — ___misbehave___
2. ruin — ___improve___
3. likely — ___impossible___
4. mannerly — ___impolite___
5. located — ___misplaced___
6. believe — ___mistrust___
7. prevent — ___enable___
8. discourage — ___encourage___
9. movable — ___immobile___
10. correct — ___improper___

Lesson 15

TIP pre = before, as in prepare   re = again or back, as in rearrange
pro = for, as in promote   ex = out of or from, as in export

List Words
- explain
- returning
- protest
- exchange
- preserve
- exist
- exactly
- reappear
- pretend
- reward
- promote
- professional

Write a **list word** to complete each sentence. Not all the words will be used.

1. If it doesn't fit, ___exchange___ it for another.
2. If she does well, we'll ___promote___ her to manager.
3. If you want to be seen again, you ___reappear___.
4. If you live, you ___exist___.
5. If he's coming back, he's ___returning___.
6. If you like to make-believe, you ___pretend___.
7. If it's complicated, ___explain___ it.
8. If you think it's unfair, you should ___protest___.
9. If you want to save it, ___preserve___ it.
10. If he finds the dog, give him a ___reward___.

74   Lesson 18 • Review

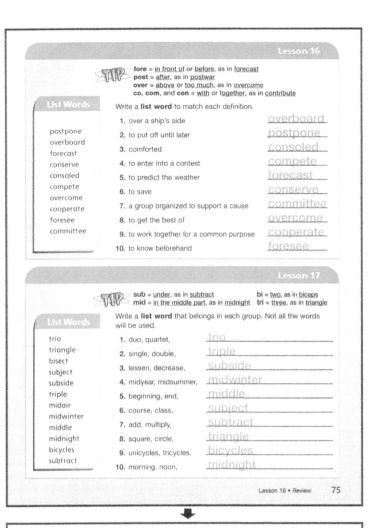

Lesson 16

TIP fore = in front of or before, as in forecast
post = after, as in postwar
over = above or too much, as in overcome
co, com, and con = with or together, as in contribute

List Words

postpone
overboard
forecast
conserve
consoled
compete
overcome
cooperate
foresee
committee

Write a **list word** to match each definition.

1. over a ship's side — overboard
2. to put off until later — postpone
3. comforted — consoled
4. to enter into a contest — compete
5. to predict the weather — forecast
6. to save — conserve
7. a group organized to support a cause — committee
8. to get the best of — overcome
9. to work together for a common purpose — cooperate
10. to know beforehand — foresee

Lesson 17

TIP sub = under, as in subtract   bi = two, as in biceps
mid = in the middle part, as in midnight   tri = three, as in triangle

List Words

trio
triangle
bisect
subject
subside
triple
midair
midwinter
middle
midnight
bicycles
subtract

Write a **list word** that belongs in each group. Not all the words will be used.

1. duo, quartet, — trio
2. single, double, — triple
3. lessen, decrease, — subside
4. midyear, midsummer, — midwinter
5. beginning, end, — middle
6. course, class, — subject
7. add, multiply, — subtract
8. square, circle, — triangle
9. unicycles, tricycles, — bicycles
10. morning, noon, — midnight

Lesson 18 • Review   75

Show What You Know

Lessons 13–17 Review

One word is misspelled in each set of **list words**. Fill in the circle next to the **list word** that is spelled incorrectly.

1. coperate / prepare / discontinue / trio / endanger
2. transport / protest / condisions / submit / rearrange
3. endure / uncooked / midnight / compete / inexpencive
4. inspire / imposible / preserve / substitute / conserve
5. enhale / improper / subscribe / middle / disturb
6. mistake / provide / miday / tripod / postwar
7. reappear / promote / misjudge / discovered / forarm
8. bicycles / consolled / company / exist / immerse
9. immobile / forewarn / bisect / overcome / disgrase
10. impolite / explain / overreact / misplaced / midstreem
11. midair / conquer / mistook / exclame / include
12. incompleat / improve / returning / subtract / produce
13. mispronounce / transpher / increase / foresee / biceps
14. reflect / misunderstand / transplant / exaktly / enable
15. uncovered / triple / subgect / subdue / unjust
16. unusual / misbehave / professional / reward / engaige
17. postpone / unselfish / insecure / triangel / exchange
18. forecast / inforce / midwinter / distance / propose
19. pretend / encourage / subside / comend / mistrust
20. committee / export / overboerd / overlooked / contribute

76   Lesson 18 • Review

Final Test

1. Refrigerated trucks **transport** fruit.
2. It's good to **encourage** people to try harder.
3. You had better **explain** why you are so late.
4. We have to **postpone** the meeting.
5. Tim, Julie, and Ruby like to sing as a **trio**.
6. We will **transfer** your records today.
7. It is **impolite** to leave without saying goodbye.
8. The boat is **returning** to the island.
9. Don't rock the boat, or we'll all fall **overboard**!
10. Please draw a square, a circle, and a **triangle**.
11. You'll **increase** your strength by lifting weights.
12. **Improve** your story by adding more details.
13. Did they **protest** paying the higher fees?
14. The weather **forecast** for tomorrow is rainy.
15. The **subject** Ellen enjoys most is science.
16. The company will **discontinue** its comic books.
17. Telescopes **enable** astronomers to study stars.
18. Will I be able to **exchange** this shirt?
19. To **conserve** resources, recycle containers.
20. The photographer's camera sat on a **tripod**.
21. Who **discovered** this secret passage?
22. It was **improper** for Sally to shout at them.
23. We should **preserve** natural resources.
24. Lee **consoled** his sister after she lost the race.
25. Jason picked **triple** the number of apples Sam picked.
26. Don't **disturb** Dad when he's working.
27. I **mistrust** ads that don't present all the facts.
28. Do you know when dinosaurs ceased to **exist**?
29. Kathy will **compete** against Matt in the match.
30. The sky divers joined hands in **midair**.
31. They sent back the **incomplete** form.
32. Gena can't find the notebook she **misplaced**.
33. The magician made the rabbit **reappear**.
34. The settlers had to **overcome** many hardships.
35. The **middle** of the story was unclear.
36. The people revolted against the **unjust** laws.
37. What an **impossible** task this is!
38. Julio likes to **pretend** he's a robot.
39. Please **cooperate** with the director.
40. At **midnight** we celebrated the new year.
41. What an **unusual** but lovely sweater!
42. Obedient children seldom **misbehave**.
43. Mr. Santos offered a **reward** for finding his cat.
44. He could not **foresee** the change.
45. The twins rode **bicycles** to school each day.
46. Todd felt nervous and **insecure**.
47. I sat **immobile** when he drew my portrait.
48. We will **promote** our best workers.
49. Who is on the **committee** to save the park?
50. If you **subtract** 10 from 30, you get 20.

61

Name _____

Review Test (Side A)

Read each sentence and set of words. Fill in the circle next to the word that is spelled correctly to complete the sentence.

1. Advertising is used to _____ new products.
   - ⓐ promoat
   - ⓑ promote
   - ⓒ pramote
   - ⓓ pramoat

2. My teacher does not accept _____ worksheets.
   - ⓐ incomplete
   - ⓑ incompleet
   - ⓒ imcomeplete
   - ⓓ incomepleat

3. The gymnast performed a _____ flip on the trampoline.
   - ⓐ tripple
   - ⓑ tripal
   - ⓒ trippel
   - ⓓ triple

4. Many countries _____ in the Olympics.
   - ⓐ compeat
   - ⓑ comepete
   - ⓒ compete
   - ⓓ comepeat

5. The preschoolers will _____ that they are royalty.
   - ⓐ preetend
   - ⓑ pretend
   - ⓒ pretenned
   - ⓓ prettend

6. The photographer uses a _____ to steady her camera.
   - ⓐ trippod
   - ⓑ trypod
   - ⓒ tripod
   - ⓓ trypodd

7. _____ are made in a variety of sizes.
   - ⓐ Bicicles
   - ⓑ Bycicles
   - ⓒ Bicycels
   - ⓓ Bicycles

8. The archaeologist _____ some ancient artifacts.
   - ⓐ discoverd
   - ⓑ discovered
   - ⓒ discuvered
   - ⓓ discovored

Review Test (Side B)

Read each sentence and set of words. Fill in the circle next to the word that is spelled correctly to complete the sentence.

9. The purpose of this cast is to make your ankle _____.
   - ⓐ immobil
   - ⓒ immobile
   - ⓑ imobile
   - ⓓ imobbile

10. Decades ago, space travel was thought to be _____.
    - ⓐ impossibel
    - ⓒ impossible
    - ⓑ imposible
    - ⓓ impossable

11. Interrupting someone's conversation is _____.
    - ⓐ impoliet
    - ⓒ impollite
    - ⓑ impolite
    - ⓓ impoalite

12. The meteorologist reports a favorable weather _____.
    - ⓐ forecast
    - ⓒ forecaste
    - ⓑ forrcast
    - ⓓ forcast

13. The magician will now make the rabbit _____!
    - ⓐ reaper
    - ⓒ reappere
    - ⓑ reappear
    - ⓓ reapperare

14. Snow in May is highly _____ in Kansas.
    - ⓐ unusuall
    - ⓒ unushuel
    - ⓑ unushual
    - ⓓ unusual

15. The school _____ meets weekly.
    - ⓐ committe
    - ⓒ commitee
    - ⓑ committee
    - ⓓ comittee

Take It Home 3

Your child has learned to spell many new words and would like to share them with you and your family. Here are some activity ideas that will help your child review the words in lessons 13–17 and provide family entertainment, too.

Word Watch

Just junk mail? Not anymore! Have your child search for spelling words in your junk mail. Encourage your child to circle the words that are found and share them with your family.

Lesson 13

1. discontinue
2. discovered
3. disgrace
4. distance
5. disturb
6. include
7. incomplete
8. increase
9. inexpensive
10. inhale
11. insecure
12. inspire
13. transfer
14. transplant
15. transport
16. uncooked
17. uncovered
18. unjust
19. unselfish
20. unusual

Lesson 14

1. enable
2. encourage
3. endangered
4. endure
5. enforce
6. engage
7. immerse
8. immobile
9. impolite
10. impossible
11. improper
12. improve
13. misbehave
14. misjudge
15. misplaced
16. mispronounce
17. mistake
18. mistook
19. mistrust
20. misunderstand

Lesson 15

1. exactly
2. exchange
3. exclaim
4. exist
5. explain
6. export
7. prepare
8. preserve
9. pretend
10. produce
11. professional
12. promote
13. propose
14. protest
15. provide
16. reappear
17. rearrange
18. reflect
19. returning
20. reward

Lesson 16

1. commend
2. committee
3. company
4. compete
5. conditions
6. conquer
7. conserve
8. consoled
9. contribute
10. cooperate
11. forearm
12. forecast
13. foresee
14. forewarn
15. overboard
16. overcome
17. overlooked
18. overreact
19. postpone
20. postwar

Lesson 17

1. biceps
2. bicycles
3. bisect
4. midair
5. midday
6. middle
7. midnight
8. midstream
9. midwinter
10. subdue
11. subject
12. submit
13. subscribe
14. subside
15. substitute
16. subtract
17. triangle
18. trio
19. triple
20. tripod

Weather or Not!

You and your child can write a weather report describing an impossible weather event. Perhaps you are advising listeners to <u>postpone</u> plans because it's snowing popcorn! See how many spelling words you can use in your report.

_____

_____

_____

_____

_____

_____

_____

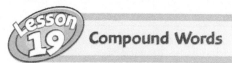

Compound Words

Objective
To spell compound words

 Phonics Correlated Phonics Lesson
MCP Phonics, Level E, Lesson 46

Spelling Words in Action   *Page 77*

In this selection, students learn what it is like to tour the area below Niagara Falls. Afterward, ask students what it might feel like to come so close to Niagara Falls.

Encourage students to look back at the boldfaced words. Ask volunteers to say each word and name the two words that form the compound word.

Warm-Up Test

1. Ryan's **shoelaces** were tied in knots.
2. Susan is reading a **paperback** book.
3. Carlos plans to get a **haircut** on Tuesday.
4. Watch out for **jellyfish** if you swim in the sea.
5. The largest **underwater** animal is the whale.
6. Divers explored the ancient **shipwreck**.
7. We hope there will be **sunshine** for our picnic.
8. Dad hit his **fingernail** with a hammer.
9. Jaclyn made **cornbread** to serve with the stew.
10. The car was buried in a huge **snowdrift**.
11. Hang the campaign posters in the **hallway**.
12. A hockey player wears a pad on each **kneecap**.
13. Do you like blueberry **pancakes** for breakfast?
14. What causes **rainbows** to appear after storms?
15. Kathy saw a beautiful **blue-green** parrot.
16. Staying on a diet requires **self-control**.
17. We were **spellbound** by the brilliant sunset.
18. How exciting it was to listen to the **countdown**!
19. **Grapefruit** grow in the state of Florida.
20. There are **forty-six** musicians in the band.

Spelling Practice   *Pages 78–79*

Introduce the spelling rule and have students read the **list words** aloud. Ask them to think about the meanings of the two words that form each compound. Then encourage students to look back at their **Warm-Up Tests** and apply the spelling rule to any misspelled words.

As students work through the **Spelling Practice** exercises, remind them to look back at their **list words** or in their dictionaries if they need help.

 for ESL students See Charades/Pantomime, page 15

Spelling Words in Action

Why is Mary-Jo's boat ride both fun and scary?

Yours Till Niagara Falls

Dear Amy,

Guess what? I'm writing to you from the bottom of Niagara Falls! The falls are on the border of Canada and New York State in the United States. I'm on a boat that tours the gorge below the falls.

It's so exciting! I've chewed away at least one **fingernail**. I can feel one **kneecap** hit the other as I look nervously over the side of the boat. I need all my **self-control** not to pull back when we approach the roaring water. It seems as if we'll end up as a **shipwreck** for divers to find **underwater** someday. I shouldn't worry, though. Boats like this one have been making this cruise for over 150 years.

I bought the **paperback** book you suggested, but I am too **spellbound** by the view to read. The **sunshine** through the mist makes the most beautiful **rainbows**, and the water has an unusual **blue-green** color. The mist comes from the water breaking over the crest of the waterfall and dropping over 100 feet to the gorge. Our tour guide told us that more than 6 million cubic feet of water go over the crest every minute.

We had a big breakfast of **grapefruit** and **pancakes** at the hotel this morning. Still, I know I'll be hungry again soon after this!

Your friend,
Mary-Jo

Say the boldfaced words in the selection. What do you notice about the way these words are formed?

77

Spelling Practice

TIP
A compound word is made up of two or more words.
shoe + laces = shoelaces
Some compound words have a hyphen between the word.
forty + six = forty-six
self + control = self-control
A helpful rule: When dividing compound words into syllables, first divide the compound words between the words that form them.
finger • nail   blue • green

LIST WORDS
1. shoelaces
2. paperback
3. haircut
4. jellyfish
5. underwater
6. shipwreck
7. sunshine
8. fingernail
9. cornbread
10. snowdrift
11. hallway
12. kneecap
13. pancakes
14. rainbows
15. blue-green
16. self-control
17. spellbound
18. countdown
19. grapefruit
20. forty-six

Compound Words

Write the **list words** on the lines below. Make sure you remember to use hyphens correctly. Then, circle the words that make each compound word.

1. (shoe)(laces)
2. (paper)(back)
3. (hair)(cut)
4. (jelly)(fish)
5. (under)(water)
6. (ship)(wreck)
7. (sun)(shine)
8. (finger)(nail)
9. (corn)(bread)
10. (snow)(drift)
11. (hall)(way)
12. (knee)(cap)
13. (pan)(cakes)
14. (rain)(bows)
15. (blue)(green)
16. (self)(control)
17. (spell)(bound)
18. (count)(down)
19. (grape)(fruit)
20. (forty)(six)

Missing Words

Write the **list word** that completes each sentence.

1. The astronauts anxiously awaited the __countdown__ before the launch.
2. The ocean turns a beautiful shade of __blue-green__ in the sunshine.
3. It takes __self-control__ to practice an instrument regularly.
4. The divers searched the __shipwreck__ in hopes of finding lost treasure.
5. A __grapefruit__ is rich in vitamin C.
6. She needs a __haircut__ to keep her hair out of her eyes.
7. During the blizzard, Mom's car was stuck in a __snowdrift__.
8. If you don't tie your __shoelaces__, you could trip and fall.
9. My favorite breakfast is __pancakes__ with maple syrup.
10. We celebrated the fact that Dad had turned __forty-six__.
11. At the campout, we made __cornbread__ with cornmeal.
12. The movie was so interesting that we were __spellbound__ by it.

Riddles

Answer each riddle with a **list word**.

1. What kind of a nail should you never pound? a __fingernail__
2. What's a whale's favorite kind of sandwich? peanut butter and __jellyfish__
3. Which way will take you from your classroom to the gym? the __hallway__
4. What kind of cap do you always take with you but can never put on your head?
   a __kneecap__
5. Name a book that's often read but never found between hard covers. a __paperback__
6. Why are goldfish orange? They get rusty __underwater__.
7. What did the leprechaun wear in her hair? a __rainbow__
8. What does a mother star call her son? __sunshine__

Spelling and Writing

Proofreading

Proofreading Marks
○ spelling mistake
⌃ add something

The following story has eleven mistakes. Fix the mistakes by using the proofreading marks. Then, write the misspelled **list words** correctly on the lines.

Our canoe trip began with a bang We watched the splash of the blugreap water make raynbows in the sunshine. When we saw the huge rock underwater it was too late. What a crash It was an instant shipwreck. Our corn-bred and my paprebak book fell into the water. My kneecap was scraped and one fingernail was torn. What a mess However, we still had enough food to make some pancakes.

1. blue-green   2. rainbows
3. shipwreck   4. cornbread
5. paperback   6. kneecap

Writing a Descriptive Paragraph

Have you ever seen or heard about a shipwreck? Recall what you saw or imagine what you might see. Describe or make up how the accident might have occurred. Use any **list words** that you can. Remember to proofread your paragraph and fix any mistakes.

_____

_____

_____

_____

_____

_____

BONUS WORDS

undersea

broadcast

railway

self-preservation

sixty-four

Spelling Strategy

Have students write each two-syllable **list word** on the board. Then, ask volunteers to pronounce each word, name the vowel sounds they hear, draw a line between the syllables, and identify the two words that form the compound word.

BONUS WORDS You may want to suggest that students write a sentence for each bonus word, then erase just the first half or the second half of the compound word. Have them trade papers with a partner and fill in the other half of the word.

Spelling and Writing   *Page 80*

The **Proofreading** exercise will help students prepare to proofread their descriptions. As students complete the writing activity, encourage them to brainstorm ideas, write a first draft, revise, and proofread their work. To publish their writing, students may want to

- read their descriptions as radio broadcasts
- trade descriptions and illustrate each other's work.

Writer's Corner Students might enjoy reading sea stories or tales about shipwrecks in books such as *Eyewitness: Shipwreck* by Richard Platt. Invite the class to have a storytelling session and retell the tales to one another.

Final Test

1. Training for a race requires great **self-control**.
2. Is Uncle Jeff **forty-six** years old?
3. Stacy had a splinter under her **fingernail**.
4. Some **jellyfish** are a beautiful shade of pink.
5. Jim bruised his left **kneecap** when he fell.
6. Open the curtains and let in the **sunshine**.
7. Mrs. Kelly made an appointment for a **haircut**.
8. There is a new rug in our **hallway**.
9. The sun sparkled on the **blue-green** water.
10. Sometimes **grapefruit** tastes very bitter.
11. We were **spellbound** by the beauty of the castle.
12. Do you like jam or syrup on your **pancakes**?
13. The submarine is an **underwater** ship.
14. Tie your **shoelaces** so that you won't trip.
15. Dry corn is ground into flour for **cornbread**.
16. I always take a **paperback** book to the beach.
17. The girls dug a tunnel through the **snowdrift**.
18. Look at that beautiful **rainbow**!
19. Did you watch the rocket-launch **countdown**?
20. The divers searched the **shipwreck** for treasure.

Lesson 20 — Possessives and Contractions

Objective
To spell singular and plural possessive nouns and contractions

 Phonics — Correlated Phonics Lessons
MCP Phonics, Level E, Lessons 47–48

Spelling Words in Action   Page 81

In "Kudzu," students learn about a vine that is a real threat to the South. Afterward, ask students to tell what they would do if kudzu began to "swallow" their house.

Call on volunteers to say each boldfaced word and tell where the apostrophe is located.

Warm-Up Test

1. **Georgia's** peach trees bloom in the spring.
2. Our **class's** project is finally finished!
3. **America's** best resource is its people.
4. **Canada's** Thanksgiving holiday is in October.
5. Is there anyone **who'll** be there to let us in?
6. The **champion's** brother hugged her.
7. **Japan's** speedy trains are called "bullet trains."
8. The **women's** track meet is tomorrow.
9. You need a **parent's** signature on that.
10. The **farmers'** vegetables are sold at the market.
11. This **college's** football team is undefeated.
12. **You'd** be surprised by Teri's story.
13. **Kansas'** state flower is the sunflower.
14. **Montreal's** weather is cooler than Boston's.
15. The **governor's** mansion is being redecorated.
16. The **senator's** vote was unpopular.
17. Do you know where the **mayor's** office is?
18. **Mexico's** capital is Mexico City.
19. **They've** helped many people in need.
20. **Texas'** residents are proud of their state.

Spelling Practice   Pages 82–83

Introduce the spelling rule and have students read the **list words** aloud. Encourage students to look back at their **Warm-Up Tests** and apply the spelling rule to any misspelled words.

As students work through the **Spelling Practice** exercises, remind them to look back at their **list words** or in their dictionaries if they need help. You may want to emphasize the placement of the apostrophe in singular and plural possessive nouns.

 for ESL students — See Questions/Answers, page 15

68

Possessives and Contractions — Lesson 20

Spelling Words in Action

Why is controlling kudzu so important?

Kudzu

The vine that Americans call kudzu was originally one of **Japan's** and China's native plants. In the 1930s, the U.S. government began planting kudzu to keep topsoil in place. Then, things got a little out of hand.

It seems that the plant liked the climate of the American South, especially Alabama's and **Georgia's** warmth. It began to grow and grow, spreading at the rate of as much as a foot a day. It spread across thousands of acres, covering **farmers'** land. The strong vines pulled down telephone wires. In fact, **they've** completely covered forests. Kudzu isn't just in the South, either. Though it hasn't yet reached **Canada's** borders, the plant can be found as far north as Connecticut.

It has become some men and **women's** goal to find uses for kudzu. There are some people who make baskets from the vine and others **who'll** make deep-fried kudzu leaves. A **class's** task might be to study ways to use the kudzu that surrounds them.

Kudzu is a very real concern. It now covers about 7 million acres of land in **America's** Southeast. Anyone who could find a safe way to control the growth of kudzu would surely receive a **champion's** reward. In the meantime, southerners hold kudzu festivals to celebrate the "plant that ate the South."

Look back at the boldfaced words in the selection. Each word is spelled with an apostrophe. How are the words alike? How are they different?

81

 TIP

To show possession:
add **'s** to a singular noun, as in **Japan's**
add **'s** to a plural noun not ending in **s**, as in **women's**
add **'** to a plural noun ending in s, as in **farmers'**
add **'** to some proper nouns ending with the s sound, as in **Texas'**
In a contraction, an apostrophe stands for the missing letter or letters as in **who'll**.

Spelling Practice

LIST WORDS
1. Georgia's
2. class's
3. America's
4. Canada's
5. who'll
6. champion's
7. Japan's
8. women's
9. parent's
10. farmers'
11. college's
12. you'd
13. Kansas'
14. Montreal's
15. governor's
16. senator's
17. mayor's
18. Mexico's
19. they've
20. Texas'

Possessives and Contractions

Write each **list word** under the correct heading. You will write two words more than once.

singular possessives
1. Georgia's
2. class's
3. America's
4. Canada's
5. champion's
6. Japan's
7. parent's
8. college's
9. Kansas'
10. Montreal's
11. governor's
12. senator's
13. mayor's
14. Mexico's
15. Texas'

plural possessives
16. women's
17. farmers'

contractions
18. who'll
19. you'd
20. they've

Write the two **list words** that add only an apostrophe to form their singular possessives.

21. Kansas'
22. Texas'

82   Lesson 20 • Possessives and Contractions

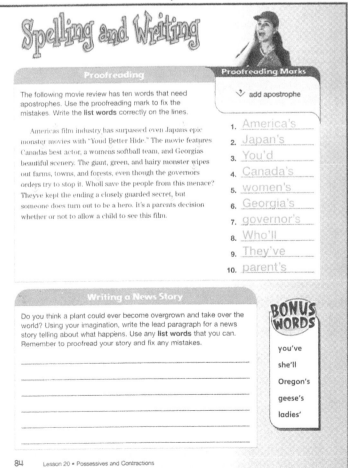

Missing Words

Write the **list word** that best completes each sentence.

1. The trophy of the champion is the __champion's__ trophy.
2. The stories of the women are the __women's__ stories.
3. The peaches of Georgia are __Georgia's__ peaches.
4. They have means the same as the contraction __they've__.
5. You would means the same as the contraction __you'd__.
6. The history of Mexico is __Mexico's__ history.
7. The vote of the senator is the __senator's__ vote.
8. The mansion of the governor is the __governor's__ mansion.
9. The hockey players of Canada are __Canada's__ hockey players.
10. The flag of Texas is __Texas'__ flag.
11. The citizens of Japan are __Japan's__ citizens.
12. The cornfields of Kansas are __Kansas'__ cornfields.

Move the Words

Each underlined **list word** in the sentences below must be moved to a different sentence to make sense. Write the correct **list word** in the blank at the end of the sentence.

1. Have you seen the size of some of the who'll potatoes this season? __farmers'__
2. It's a Montreal's purpose to continue educating students after high school. __college's__
3. Mayor's take a turn passing out papers next? __Who'll__
4. It's a America's job to take care of a town. __mayor's__
5. Parent's winter festival is filled with beautiful ice sculptures. __Montreal's__
6. Our farmer's art projects are on display in the hallway. __class's__
7. My college's name is Mrs. Rita Lewis. __parent's__
8. Class's flag is red, white, and blue. __America's__

Lesson 20 • Possessives and Contractions   83

Spelling and Writing

Proofreading

The following movie review has ten words that need apostrophes. Use the proofreading mark to fix the mistakes. Write the **list words** correctly on the lines.

Americas film industry has surpassed even Japans epic monster movies with "Youd Better Hide." The movie features Canadas best actor, a womens softball team, and Georgias beautiful scenery. The giant, green, and hairy monster wipes out farms, towns, and forests, even though the governors orders try to stop it. Wholl save the people from this menace? Theyve kept the ending a closely guarded secret, but someone does turn out to be a hero. It's a parents decision whether or not to allow a child to see this film.

Proofreading Marks

ˇ add apostrophe

1. America's
2. Japan's
3. You'd
4. Canada's
5. women's
6. Georgia's
7. governor's
8. Who'll
9. They've
10. parent's

Writing a News Story

Do you think a plant could ever become overgrown and take over the world? Using your imagination, write the lead paragraph for a news story telling about what happens. Use any **list words** that you can. Remember to proofread your story and fix any mistakes.

_____
_____
_____
_____
_____
_____

BONUS WORDS

you've
she'll
Oregon's
geese's
ladies'

Spelling Strategy

Write sentences similar to this on the board: "The fields of the farmers are plowed." With a partner, students can look at the noun that names the person or group who possesses something, then

• decide whether that word is singular or plural
• use that information to help rewrite the sentence, using an apostrophe.

BONUS WORDS

You may want to suggest that students work in pairs to write a paragraph about the same subject using the bonus words. One partner uses the long form of each word (*you have; of Oregon*). The other uses the bonus words. Have partners compare their versions.

Spelling and Writing   Page 84

The **Proofreading** exercise will help students prepare to proofread their news stories. As students complete the writing activity, encourage them to brainstorm ideas, write a first draft, revise, and proofread their work. To publish their writing, students may want to read their stories aloud as news broadcasts.

Writer's Corner Suggest that students invite a local plant expert to talk about plant pests found in your region. Encourage students to jot down the information they find the most interesting.

Final Test

1. I don't think **you'd** enjoy that movie.
2. The **mayor's** children stood proudly beside her.
3. **Mexico's** flag is green, red, and white.
4. **Canada's** flag has a red maple leaf.
5. **They've** finally returned from the store!
6. The **senator's** limousine has arrived.
7. Can you predict **who'll** win the race?
8. Atlanta is **Georgia's** capital.
9. Corn is one of **Kansas'** major farm crops.
10. The **class's** picture is in the newspaper.
11. Did you remember to get a **parent's** signature?
12. **Japan's** basic unit of money is the yen.
13. The **women's** shoe department is upstairs.
14. Estelle is our **college's** best tennis player.
15. **Texas'** nickname is the "Lone Star State."
16. The **farmers'** families helped in the fields.
17. **America's** capital is Washington, D.C.
18. The **champion's** victory speech was inspiring.
19. Did you get the **governor's** autograph?
20. We saw **Montreal's** historic section.

Objective
To spell words, recognizing syllables

 Correlated Phonics Lessons
MCP Phonics, Level E,
Lessons 49, 70–71

Spelling Words in Action   *Page 85*

In "Mush!," students read about a kind of race in which the competitors are dogs. Ask students what qualities they think a good sled dog should have.

Encourage students to look back at the boldfaced words. Ask volunteers to say each word and identify the vowel sound in each syllable.

Warm-Up Test
1. Rain is **normal** at this time of year.
2. Did Michelle solve the third math **problem**?
3. The children waded across the **shallow** stream.
4. Customs and **manners** vary around the world.
5. The dove is a worldwide **symbol** of peace.
6. We will **perform** our song during the show.
7. I **suggest** you meet us after school.
8. Gary found a leaf **fossil** in one of the rocks.
9. The clerk passed the can over the **scanner**.
10. Everyone thinks Mark is an **expert** golfer.
11. Both cousins **collect** unusual postcards.
12. Math games are a great **mental** exercise.
13. The park signs **forbid** walking on the grass.
14. The coach gave the **signal** to begin the race.
15. When I give the **command**, start marching.
16. Where is the **cassette** that you recorded?
17. Did Maria **rescue** the cat from the tree?
18. What a **challenge** the contest was!
19. My **partner** and I won the tennis match.
20. Which candidate do you **support**?

Spelling Practice   *Pages 86–87*

Introduce the spelling rule and have students read the **list words** aloud. Encourage students to look back at their **Warm-Up Tests** and apply the spelling rule to any misspelled words.

As students work through the **Spelling Practice** exercises, remind them to look back at their **list words** or in their dictionaries if they need help. You may want to point out that *partner* has three consonants between two vowels. It is divided between the second and third consonants.

 See Spelling Aloud, page 14

70

In what kind of race do dogs compete?

Mush!

It's the day of the big race. The competitors are outside in the snow, jumping about . . . and barking. These competitors are sled dogs, trained to pull sleds in races over the snow. They can't wait to **perform**. It is a **challenge** for the trainers to hold them at the starting line. Then, the **signal** is given. The teams, groups of muscle-bound dogs, pull together. This race is a short sprint, but the most famous dogsled race, Alaska's Iditarod, is over 1,000 miles long.

A **normal** sled-racing team has from four to ten dogs. The most intelligent, alert dog is the "lead." He or she is considered the **expert** racer. In a "double lead," a dog and a **partner** lead the team side by side. Though several breeds are popular in dogsled racing, the Siberian husky is probably the best-known **symbol** of a sled dog.

The driver uses a few basic **command** words. *Gee* means "turn right," and *haw* means "left." It's rare for a driver to shout "mush!" to his team. It's too hard to **forbid** the excited crowds on the sidelines from yelling out "mush!" as the racing team passes. The lead dog could get confused, causing a **problem**. The sled drivers do use one form of the word, though. They call themselves "mushers."

Say the boldfaced words in the selection slowly. Notice how many separate sounds make up each word. Do the words have as many vowel sounds as they do syllables?

85

 TIP

Words have as many syllables as they do vowel sounds. When you spell a word, think about how each syllable is spelled. When two consonants come between two vowels in a word, the word is usually divided between the two consonants: sug•gest per•form

Spelling Practice

LIST WORDS
1. normal
2. problem
3. shallow
4. manners
5. symbol
6. perform
7. suggest
8. fossil
9. scanner
10. expert
11. collect
12. mental
13. forbid
14. signal
15. command
16. cassette
17. rescue
18. challenge
19. partner
20. support

Syllables

Write the **list words** on the lines. Put a • between the two syllables in each word. Look in your dictionary if you need help.

1. nor • mal   2. prob • lem
3. shal • low   4. man • ners
5. sym • bol   6. per • form
7. sug • gest   8. fos • sil
9. scan • ner   10. ex • pert
11. col • lect   12. men • tal
13. for • bid   14. sig • nal
15. com • mand 16. cas • sette
17. res • cue   18. chal • lenge
19. part • ner   20. sup • port

86   Lesson 21 • Syllables

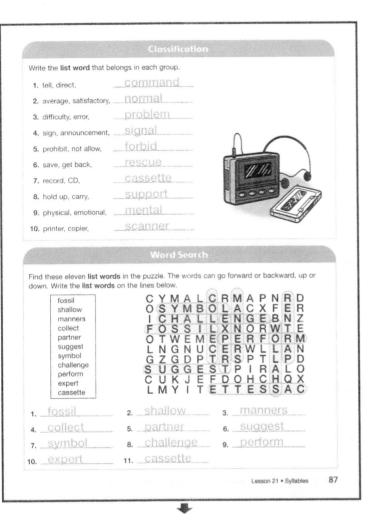

Classification

Write the **list word** that belongs in each group.

1. tell, direct, __command__
2. average, satisfactory, __normal__
3. difficulty, error, __problem__
4. sign, announcement, __signal__
5. prohibit, not allow, __forbid__
6. save, get back, __rescue__
7. record, CD, __cassette__
8. hold up, carry, __support__
9. physical, emotional, __mental__
10. printer, copier, __scanner__

Word Search

Find these eleven **list words** in the puzzle. The words can go forward or backward, up or down. Write the **list words** on the lines below.

| fossil |
| shallow |
| manners |
| collect |
| partner |
| suggest |
| symbol |
| challenge |
| perform |
| expert |
| cassette |

```
C Y M A L C R M A P N R D
O S Y M B O L A C X F E R
I C H A L L E N G E B N Z
F O S S I L X N O R W T E
O T W E M E P E R F O R M
L N G N U C E R W L L A N
G Z G D P T R S P T L P D
S U G G E S T P I R A L O
C U K J E F D O H C H Q X
L M Y I T E T T E S S A C
```

1. _fossil_   2. _shallow_   3. _manners_
4. _collect_   5. _partner_   6. _suggest_
7. _symbol_   8. _challenge_   9. _perform_
10. _expert_   11. _cassette_

Lesson 21 • Syllables   87

Spelling and Writing

Proofreading

The following article has thirteen mistakes. Use the proofreading marks to fix the mistakes. Then, write the misspelled **list words** correctly on the lines.

Proofreading Marks
- ◯ spelling mistake
- ☰ capital letter
- ⌔ take out something

The great sled dogs are a cymbol of the far far north. Some of of the breeds who meet the chalenge are the alaskan malamute and the siberian husky. in the past, these dogs worked with a human parner to rezcue people and and collect supplies. Sled dogs respond well to every comand and and signal. It's wonderful to watch them purform.

1. _symbol_   2. _challenge_
3. _partner_   4. _rescue_
5. _command_   6. _perform_

Writing a Letter

Think about a personal challenge that you have experienced. What aspects of the experience made it seem difficult? Write a letter to a friend describing the challenge. Try to use as many **list words** as you can. Remember to proofread your letter and fix any mistakes.

_____
_____
_____
_____
_____
_____
_____

BONUS WORDS

guilty
advance
sherbet
adhere
mammoth

88   Lesson 21 • Syllables

Spelling Strategy

With a partner, students can
- write each **list word** and underline the two consonants between which they think the word should be divided
- say the word and decide whether the pause that occurs naturally when they speak matches their division
- check their syllabication in their dictionaries.

BONUS WORDS You may want to suggest that students write two definitions for each bonus word, making one definition incorrect. Have them trade papers with a partner and write the bonus word next to the correct definition.

Spelling and Writing   *Page 88*

The **Proofreading** exercise will help students prepare to proofread their letters. As students complete the writing activity, encourage them to brainstorm ideas, write a first draft, revise, and proofread their work. To publish their writing, students may want to
- share their letters with the person they wrote to
- discuss their challenge with a group.

Writer's Corner Students might enjoy reading stories about sled dog racing in books such as *Susan Butcher and the Iditarod Trail* by Ellen M. Dolan. Encourage students to create a bulletin board that includes interesting facts they've learned.

Final Test

1. Ms. Lewis is my dad's business **partner**.
2. What a dangerous **rescue** attempt that was!
3. He is a **normal** height for a ten-year-old boy.
4. My younger brothers **collect** baseball cards.
5. Write the solution to the word **problem**.
6. I **challenge** you to another game of checkers.
7. It's good **manners** to wait your turn to talk.
8. The magician will **perform** a card trick.
9. When was that **fossil** discovered?
10. The traffic **signal** was flashing yellow.
11. Can you **suggest** a good book to read?
12. A light bulb is used as the **symbol** for an idea.
13. Mrs. Woo is an **expert** musician.
14. Can you form a **mental** image of a sunset?
15. The clerk explained how the **scanner** works.
16. Does the river become **shallow** every summer?
17. My dog will obey the **command** "Roll over."
18. Here is a **cassette** recording of the story.
19. The sign said, "**Support** your local library."
20. Conservation laws **forbid** dumping chemicals.

Lesson 22 — Syllables

Objective
To spell words using rules of syllabication

Correlated Phonics Lessons
MCP Phonics, Level E,
Lessons 12, 49, 71

Spelling Words in Action   **Page 89**

In "Achoo!," students find out what makes people sneeze. Afterward, ask students what they learned and invite them to share what they already know about allergies.

Encourage students to look back at the boldfaced words. Ask volunteers to say each word and spell the syllables.

Warm-Up Test

1. A pound is a **unit** used to measure weight.
2. My roller skates have **plastic** wheels.
3. I always wear a **helmet** when I ride my bike.
4. The spy's **mission** was to carry the film safely.
5. The earthquake turned the building into **rubble**.
6. What **splendid** costumes the dancers wore!
7. **Cover** the table with paper before you paint.
8. My mother gave me money to buy a **dozen** eggs.
9. This weekend we will clean out the hall **closet**.
10. The coach will **divide** the class into two teams.
11. What was the **major** topic you discussed?
12. Using a computer is a **modern** skill.
13. My **grandparents** own their own business.
14. Adam's favorite fruit is **watermelon**.
15. Our **fingerprints** can be used to identify us.
16. Good **posture** helps you look and feel better.
17. Everyone listened in **silence** to the song.
18. Recycling paper helps **reduce** litter.
19. Did you get all the **answers** right on the test?
20. The show was a tremendous **success**!

Spelling Practice   **Pages 90–91**

Introduce the spelling rule and have students read the **list words** aloud. Encourage students to look back at their **Warm-Up Tests** and apply the spelling rule to any misspelled words.

As students work through the **Spelling Practice** exercises, remind them to look back at their **list words** or in their dictionaries if they need help. You may want to review the syllabication rule that when two consonants come between two vowels, the word is usually divided between the two consonants.

 See Rhymes and Songs, page 14

72

Syllables — Lesson 22

Spelling Words in Action

Why do people sneeze?

achOO!

There's nothing like a sneeze to break a **silence**. Some people don't like to sneeze, because their **posture** might become contorted. Long ago, though, a sneeze was considered a **splendid** thing. Ancient Greeks believed that a person couldn't sneeze if he or she was lying.

Modern science looks at a sneeze as a reflex action. When a person's nose has an irritant of some sort, the body responds with a sneeze. A single sneeze doesn't contain just a **dozen** or so germs. One sneeze can send 100,000 bacteria into the air. If people **cover** their noses and mouths, they spread fewer germs.

One of the **major** causes of sneezing is hay fever. People with hay fever often use medication to **reduce** the amount of sneezing. Hay fever sufferers are allergic to the pollen produced by grasses, trees, and weeds. One of the most common pollen-producing weeds is ragweed. Some communities have tried to come up with **answers** as to how to get rid of ragweed. However, because the wind can carry pollen great distances, removing ragweed has not been a **success**.

Hay fever isn't the only thing that causes sneezing. Some people sneeze when they are in bright sunlight. Others sneeze after they eat a big meal!

Say the boldfaced words in the selection. Each word has two syllables. How many vowel sounds do you hear in each syllable? Which group of letters form each syllable?

89

Spelling Practice

TIP
When a single consonant comes between two vowels in a word, the word is usually divided after the consonant if the first vowel is short, and before the consonant if the vowel is long.
short first vowel: mod • em
long first vowel: ma • jor
There are exceptions to the rule, as in wa • ter.
Divide a compound word into two words before dividing it into syllables.

LIST WORDS
1. unit
2. plastic
3. helmet
4. mission
5. rubble
6. splendid
7. cover
8. dozen
9. closet
10. divide
11. major
12. modern
13. grandparents
14. watermelon
15. fingerprints
16. posture
17. silence
18. reduce
19. answers
20. success

Syllables

Write each **list word** under the correct heading. Put a • between the syllables in each word. Use your dictionary for help. Two words will be used more than once.

more than one consonant between two vowels
1. plas•tic
2. hel•met
3. mis•sion
4. rub•ble
5. splen•did
6. grand•par•ents
7. wa•ter•mel•on
8. fin•ger•prints
9. pos•ture
10. an•swers
11. suc•cess

single consonant between two vowels
12. u•nit
13. co•ver
14. do•zen
15. clo•set
16. di•vide
17. ma•jor
18. mod•ern
19. grand•par•ents
20. wa•ter•mel•on
21. si•lence
22. re•duce

90   Lesson 22 • Syllables

Answer the Questions

Write the **list word** that answers each question. Write the **list word** on the line.

1. What material might a shower curtain or a soda bottle be made of? __plastic__
2. Where are clothes and shoes kept? __closet__
3. Who are your parents' parents? your __grandparents__
4. What do detectives hope to find when trying to solve a crime? __fingerprints__
5. What's left when there's no sound? __silence__
6. What must a bike rider wear on his or her head? __helmet__
7. What does a big earthquake leave behind? __rubble__
8. What's a large fruit that's green on the outside and pink and juicy on the inside?
   __watermelon__
9. What usually follows questions? __answers__
10. What's the opposite of failure? __success__

Mixed-Up Syllables

The syllables in the nonsense words below have become mixed up. Put them back in their proper order to form **list words**. Write the words on the lines below.

1. u · sion	mis · nit	unit	mission
2. ma · zen	do · jor	major	dozen
3. splen · vide	di · did	splendid	divide
4. mod · ture	pos · ern	modern	posture
5. re · ver	co · duce	reduce	cover

Lesson 22 • Syllables 91

Spelling and Writing

Proofreading

This script for an allergy medicine ad has ten mistakes. Use the proofreading marks to fix the mistakes. Then, write the misspelled **list words** correctly on the lines.

Proofreading Marks
- ◯ spelling mistake
- ⌃ add something
- ⊙ add period

Sniffles: Achoo! Doctor, is there a cure for my allergies. I sneeze more than a dozen times in an hour My parents and grandparents all have the same problem.

Doctor: Please, covere your mouth Yours is a magor problem, indeed. Unfortunately, there is no cure for your allergies, but medicine might reduse the problem and silents some of your sneezes.

Sniffles: Oh, I hope so! Achoo!

1. __dozen__   2. __grandparents__   3. __cover__
4. __major__   5. __reduce__   6. __silence__

Writing an Advertisement

Write an advertisement for a new cure for hay fever. The ad could be a script for TV or radio, or a print ad for a newspaper or magazine. Use any **list words** that you can. Remember to proofread your ad and fix any mistakes.

_____
_____
_____
_____
_____
_____

BONUS WORDS

radar
granite
satin
bookkeeper
spoken

92   Lesson 22 • Syllables

Spelling Strategy

To help students practice syllabication of words in which the first vowel is short, you may want to write such words (*cover, dozen, closet, divide, modern*) on the board. Call on volunteers to say each word, emphasizing the initial short-vowel sound. Have the volunteers tell where the word should be divided, and why.

BONUS WORDS You may want to suggest that students write clues for the bonus words, then trade papers with a partner. Ask them to write the word for each clue, then compare their clues and see if they are similar.

Spelling and Writing   **Page 92**

The **Proofreading** exercise will help students prepare to proofread their ads. As students complete the writing activity, encourage them to brainstorm ideas, write a first draft, revise, and proofread their work. To publish their writing, students may want to
- create a newspaper or magazine spread with the ad
- read their ads aloud as radio or TV broadcasts.

Writer's Corner Have students use the library or the Internet to research common allergies such as hay fever, pets, wheat, milk, or peanuts. Encourage them to use the information to create a brochure on preventing and treating allergies.

Final Test

1. I bought this **watermelon** for the picnic.
2. What a **splendid** meal Granddad prepared!
3. Bring a **plastic** tablecloth for the picnic.
4. Our fund-raising car wash was a great **success**.
5. Oil is a **major** source of energy in this country.
6. The rocket's **mission** was to photograph Mars.
7. Good **posture** makes people look taller.
8. We bought a **dozen** roses for ten dollars.
9. An inch is a **unit** used to measure length.
10. The book supplied the **answers** to our questions.
11. Can you think of five **modern** inventions?
12. The landslide left **rubble** all over the road.
13. **Silence** fell when she appeared on stage.
14. My brother wears a **helmet** to play football.
15. How can we **reduce** the distance we drive?
16. The burglar left **fingerprints** on the safe.
17. Whose picture is on the magazine **cover**?
18. Let's **divide** the pizza into ten pieces.
19. I like to spend the night with my **grandparents**.
20. Please put your boots and coat in the **closet**.

Objective
To spell words using syllabication rules

 Correlated Phonics Lesson
MCP Phonics, Level E, Lesson 71

Spelling Words in Action   *Page 93*

In this selection, students find out about a game that Alice (in *Alice in Wonderland*) played with the Queen of Hearts. After reading, ask students to compare croquet to miniature golf.

Encourage students to look back at the boldfaced words. Ask volunteers to say each word and identify the syllables.

Warm-Up Test

1. Stephanie is researching the **history** of our town.
2. It is **unlikely** that it will rain tomorrow.
3. Did you **remember** to bring an extra pencil?
4. If you like sports, join the **athletic** club.
5. William Penn believed in freedom of **religion**.
6. My grandfather was a **citizen** of Poland.
7. The tiger is a beautiful **animal**.
8. This **magazine** article is about hang gliding.
9. The most **popular** game at school is basketball.
10. Everyone in her family has **artistic** talents.
11. Was **yesterday** the first day of spring?
12. The football fans streamed into the **stadium**.
13. Wasn't that a **horrible** storm last night?
14. What a **beautiful** poem Megan wrote!
15. Is Jorge **serious** about entering the contest?
16. Our town bought a new snow removal **vehicle**.
17. Let's cross to the **opposite** side of the street.
18. My new neighbor made a good first **impression**.
19. Is your family's stove **electric** or gas?
20. I prefer plain milk to **chocolate** milk.

Spelling Practice   *Pages 94–95*

Introduce the spelling rule and have students read the **list words** aloud. Encourage students to look back at their **Warm-Up Tests** and apply the spelling rule to any misspelled words.

As students work through the **Spelling Practice** exercises, remind them to look back at their **list words** or in their dictionaries if they need help. Students may also find it helpful to review previously learned syllabication rules.

 See Tape Recording, page 15

74

Spelling Words in Action

What game did Alice play with the Queen of Hearts in *Alice in Wonderland*?

Don't Lose Your Head!

If you have ever read Lewis Carroll's *Alice in Wonderland*, you may **remember** Alice playing croquet with the **horrible** Queen of Hearts. Poor Alice had to put up with flamingos for mallets, hedgehogs for croquet balls, and a queen who kept crying, "Off with her head!" In spite of Caroll's **unlikely** portrayal, croquet has been a **popular** game throughout its **history**.

The game is thought to have begun in France. It was enjoyed in England and Ireland during the 1800s, and was probably brought to the United States around 1870. To play, you need two competing sides with one or two players each, a lawn, and, of course, a croquet set. A croquet set contains mallets, balls, and narrow wire arches called wickets. The object is to knock the ball in a course through the wickets. You must knock your ball to the **opposite** side of the course and back in as few "strokes" as possible. Sound too easy? With **serious** players, the game can be very hard. One of the rules allows a player to knock another player's ball off course!

Some people have the **impression** that croquet is a game for the wealthy. However, it can be enjoyed by anyone. It's a game that people of different **athletic** abilities can play as equals. Playing on **beautiful** lawns adds to its appeal!

Say the boldfaced words in the selection. Say each syllable slowly. What do you notice about the spelling of each syllable?

93

Spelling Practice

TIP
When a vowel is sounded alone in a word, it usually forms a syllable by itself, as in an • i • mal. When a word ends in a consonant + le, divide the word before that consonant, as in ve • hi • cle. These syllabication rules, and those you have already learned, will help you to spell and pronounce the **list words**.

LIST WORDS

1. history
2. unlikely
3. remember
4. athletic
5. religion
6. citizen
7. animal
8. magazine
9. popular
10. artistic
11. yesterday
12. stadium
13. horrible
14. beautiful
15. serious
16. vehicle
17. opposite
18. impression
19. electric
20. chocolate

Syllables

Write the **list words** on the lines. Put a • between the syllables, as in hol • i • day. Look in your dictionary if you need help.

1. his•to•ry
2. un•like•ly
3. re•mem•ber
4. ath•let•ic
5. re•li•gion
6. cit•i•zen
7. an•i•mal
8. mag•a•zine
9. pop•u•lar
10. ar•tis•tic
11. yes•ter•day
12. sta•di•um
13. hor•ri•ble
14. beau•ti•ful
15. se•ri•ous
16. ve•hi•cle
17. op•po•site
18. im•pres•sion
19. e•lec•tric
20. choc•o•late

94   Lesson 23 • Syllables

Classification

Write the **list word** that belongs in each group.

1. vanilla, strawberry, ___chocolate___
2. voter, taxpayer, ___citizen___
3. newspaper, book, ___magazine___
4. dog, cat, ___animal___
5. car, truck, ___vehicle___
6. strong, active, ___athletic___
7. gym, field, ___stadium___
8. biology, math, ___history___
9. today, tomorrow, ___yesterday___
10. pretty, stunning, ___beautiful___

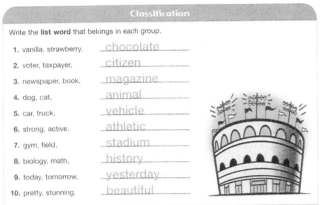

Missing Syllables

A syllable has escaped from each of the following **list words**. Capture the syllable and put it in the blank. Then, write the words on the lines.

1. ___ser___ • i • ous
   ___serious___
2. re • ___mem___ • ber
   ___remember___
3. un • like • ___ly___
   ___unlikely___
4. pop • ___u___ • lar
   ___popular___
5. re • ___li___ • gion
   ___religion___
6. ___ar___ • tis • tic
   ___artistic___
7. op • ___po___ • site
   ___opposite___
8. hor • ___ri___ • ble
   ___horrible___
9. im • ___pres___ • sion
   ___impression___
10. ___e___ • lec • tric
    ___electric___

ser
ri   e
mem
ar   li
po   ly
u
pres

Spelling and Writing

Proofreading

The following poem has ten mistakes. Use the proofreading marks to fix the mistakes. Then, write the misspelled **list words** correctly on the lines.

Isnt its beutiful day,
To stroll on the lawn and play croquet?
Its really quite artistik.
To see a ball go through a wicket.
You can feel the electrik force,
As you hit your opponents ball off course.
All the players look so serius,
While the spectators look so curious.
Another game is about tostart—
Remember, the game of croquet is an art!

Proofreading Marks

◯ spelling mistake
∧ add something
∨ add apostrophe

1. ___beautiful___   2. ___artistic___   3. ___electric___
4. ___serious___   5. ___remember___

Writing a Poster

A croquet tournament can be an enjoyable event. Create a poster for an upcoming tournament. Use attention-getting headlines and copy to get people to come. Try to use as many **list words** as you can. Remember to proofread your poster and fix any mistakes.

_____
_____
_____
_____
_____

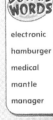

BONUS WORDS

electronic
hamburger
medical
mantle
manager

Spelling Strategy

Ask the class to name all the **list words** in which a single vowel forms a syllable (*citizen, animal, magazine, popular, electric, chocolate*). Write the words on the board, dividing them into syllables, and call on volunteers to name other words that are examples of the syllabication rule.

BONUS WORDS

You may want to suggest that students work with a partner to decide how each bonus word should be divided into syllables. Have them trade papers with another team and correct their syllabication using a dictionary, then write a sentence for each word.

Spelling and Writing   **Page 96**

The **Proofreading** exercise will help students prepare to proofread their posters. As students complete the writing activity, encourage them to brainstorm ideas, write a first draft, revise, and proofread their work. To publish their writing, students may want to use their posters to make a classroom display.

Writer's Corner Suggest that students research croquet rules either in the library or on the Internet. The rules can be found online at the U.S. Croquet Association's Web site: http://www.croquetamerica.com/gams-rls.asp. Encourage the students to take notes as they research.

Final Test

1. Can you **remember** your dreams?
2. **Yesterday** we climbed to the top of the hill.
3. I saw an **animal** in your vegetable garden.
4. Miguel likes to play with his **electric** trains.
5. A smile can brighten a **serious** face.
6. In **history** class, we studied the Civil War.
7. **Religion** is important in many people's lives.
8. Stand **opposite** your dance partner.
9. The brave knight had to fight a **horrible** battle.
10. Chicken is a **popular** food in my family.
11. Each **citizen** should remember to vote.
12. It's **unlikely** that anyone will fail the test.
13. Use your **artistic** talent to make a clay statue.
14. Make a good **impression** by being polite.
15. Did you see her **beautiful** flower garden?
16. The school hired a new **athletic** coach.
17. The **stadium** will seat 30,000 spectators.
18. The tank is an armored **vehicle**.
19. Is there a **magazine** for hikers and campers?
20. What delicious **chocolate** pudding this is!

Lessons 19–23 · Review

Objectives

To review compound words; possessives and contractions; syllables

Check Your
Spelling Notebook   *Pages 97–100*

Based on your observations, note which words are giving students the most difficulty and offer assistance for spelling them correctly. Here are some frequently misspelled words to watch for: *answers*, *divide*, *success*, *athletic*, *chocolate*, and *opposite*.

To give students extra help and practice in taking standardized tests, you may want to have them take the **Review Test** for this lesson on pages 78–79. After scoring the tests, return them to students so that they can record their misspelled words in their spelling notebooks.

After practicing their troublesome words, students can work through the exercises for Lessons 19–23 and the cumulative review, **Show What You Know**. Before they begin each exercise, you may want to go over the spelling rule.

Take It Home

Invite students to select **list words** from lessons 19–23 and to draw a picture clue for each one. Have students ask family members to guess which word goes with each clue. Students can also use **Take It Home** Master 4 on pages 80–81 to help them do the activity. (A complete list of the spelling words is included on page 80 of the **Take It Home** Master.) Invite students to share their work in class.

Lessons 19–23 · Review

In lessons 19 through 23, you learned how to form compound words, how to divide words into syllables, and how to use an apostrophe to write possessive nouns and contractions.

Check Your Spelling Notebook

Look at the words in your spelling notebook. Which words for lessons 19 through 23 did you have the most trouble with? Write them here.

_____

_____

Practice writing your troublesome words with a partner. Take turns dividing the words into syllables as the other spells them aloud.

Lesson 19

 Compound words are made by combining two words, as in <u>snowdrift</u> (<u>snow</u> + <u>drift</u>) and <u>self-control</u> (<u>self</u> + <u>control</u>).

List Words
paperback
haircut
jellyfish
shipwreck
cornbread
sunshine
snowdrift
hallway
self-control
blue-green
countdown
forty-six

Two words in each sentence below form a compound **list word**. Circle the words, and write the compound word on the line. Not all the words will be used.

1. He will cut my hair.   haircut
2. The paper is at the back door.   paperback
3. Show me the way to the hall.   hallway
4. Six waiters served forty people. forty-six
5. Tiny fish swam in the jelly jar. jellyfish
6. Snow will drift in the wind.   snowdrift
7. The sun will shine tomorrow.   sunshine
8. The house is blue and green.   blue-green
9. A storm could wreck the ship.   shipwreck
10. Sit down and count to ten.   countdown

97

Lesson 20

To form a singular or plural possessive, add '**s**; to form the possessive of a plural noun ending in **s**, just add '. Only add ' if adding '**s** to a proper noun ending with the **s** sound makes the word difficult to pronounce, as in **Texas**' or **Kansas**'. Use an apostrophe to stand for letters left out of contractions.

List Words
America's
Canada's
who'll
Japan's
women's
champion's
farmers'
you'd
Kansas'
senator's
Mexico's
class's

Write a **list word** to complete each sentence. Not all the words will be used.

1. The people of Japan are Japan's people.
2. The farms of Kansas are Kansas' farms.
3. Who will can also be written who'll.
4. The flag of America is America's flag.
5. The letter of the senator is the senator's letter.
6. The food of Mexico is Mexico's food.
7. You would can also be written you'd.
8. The ideas of women are women's ideas.
9. The rivers of Canada are Canada's rivers.
10. The crops of the farmers are the farmers' crops.

Lesson 21

When two consonants come between two vowels in a word, the word is usually divided between the two consonants, as in <u>scan</u> • <u>ner</u>.

List Words
problem
command
perform
suggest
expert
collect
forbid
normal
cassette
challenge
partner
support

Combine two syllables from the box to make a **list word**. Write the words on the lines. Not all the words will be used.

sug	form	for	gest	col	sette	sup	lenge	prob	ner
chal	lem	part	pert	per	lect	cas	port	ex	bid

1. suggest   2. challenge
3. forbid   4. partner
5. collect   6. perform
7. support   8. cassette
9. problem   10. expert

TIP When a single consonant comes between two vowels in a word, usually divide the word after the consonant if the first vowel is short, as in cov • er. Usually divide before the consonant if the vowel is long, as in re • duce. There are exceptions, as in wa • ter.

List Words

helmet
rubble
dozen
cover
closet
major
unit
watermelon
fingerprints
silence
answers
success

Write a **list word** to match each clue. Not all the words will be used.

1. result of hard work — success
2. left by an earthquake — rubble
3. opposite of minor — major
4. a juicy fruit — watermelon
5. opposite of noise — silence
6. protects your head — helmet
7. useful to a detective — fingerprints
8. where you put your coat — closet
9. result of questions — answers
10. top of a jar — cover

TIP A vowel can form its own syllable in a word, as in pop • u • lar. When le precedes the last consonant in a word, the word is divided before that consonant, as in hor • ri • ble.

List Words

history
unlikely
remember
athletic
beautiful
animal
artistic
yesterday
serious
horrible
vehicle
chocolate

Write the **list words** that fit each description. Two of the words will not be used.

1. What people do who recall the day before today: remember yesterday
2. What a jogger who paints is: athletic and artistic
3. What a peacock is: a beautiful animal
4. What the story of cocoa is: chocolate history
5. What a car with wings is: an unlikely vehicle

Lesson 24 • Review   99

Show What You Know

One word is misspelled in each set of **list words**. Fill in the circle next to the **list word** that is spelled incorrectly.

1. popular	Canada's	divide	● cornbred	snowdrift
2. ● fosil	history	unit	normal	you'd
3. rainbows	● silense	closet	shoelaces	partner
4. spellbound	parent's	yesterday	● moddern	fingerprints
5. pancakes	mental	reduce	● choclate	major
6. Kansas'	hallway	shallow	grandparents	● religon
7. ● covver	scanner	countdown	answers	Texas'
8. Georgia's	citizen	collect	● watermellon	grapefruit
9. electric	● harcut	animal	manners	helmet
10. class's	● atheletic	mission	stadium	success
11. remember	rubble	suggest	rescue	● forty six
12. Japan's	artistic	women's	plastic	● cassett
13. blue-green	● jelly-fish	perform	serious	posture
14. champion's	college's	support	splendid	● neecap
15. self-control	mayor's	● veicle	farmers'	magazine
16. ● dozzen	command	signal	Montreal's	shipwreck
17. sunshine	forbid	horrible	Mexico's	● impresion
18. ● unlikley	problem	underwater	beautiful	challenge
19. ● simbol	paperback	fingernail	opposite	governor's
20. they've	expert	senator's	● wholl	America's

100   Lesson 24 • Review

Final Test

1. Does this store sell only **paperback** books?
2. The last test **problem** was worth ten points.
3. The bicyclist wore a yellow **helmet**.
4. Kyla is recording an oral **history** of her family.
5. **America's** birthday is celebrated on July 4th.
6. Ramon got a **haircut** at my uncle's barbershop.
7. Tina and Linda will **perform** a comedy skit.
8. They searched the **rubble** for their belongings.
9. It's **unlikely** that there is life on Mars.
10. The sting of a **jellyfish** is extremely painful.
11. Can you **suggest** a good place to eat?
12. We forgot to **cover** the hamster cage.
13. Mary can't **remember** Tonio's phone number.
14. **Canada's** hockey team won the championship.
15. The divers searched the sunken **shipwreck**.
16. He is an **expert** runner who wins many races.
17. Your baseball cap is on the shelf in the **closet**.
18. The coach recognized Suzi's **athletic** ability.
19. I think I know **who'll** get the lead in the play.
20. The **sunshine** was welcome after so much rain.
21. After the bell, Paula will **collect** the test papers.
22. The **major** portion of the money was donated.
23. The cheetah is the fastest four-legged **animal**.
24. The **women's** cars are parked near the house.
25. An eight-foot **snowdrift** blocked the driveway.
26. State laws **forbid** littering on the highways.
27. Kara bit into a juicy slice of **watermelon**.
28. What amazing **artistic** talent Mark has!
29. All of the **farmers'** children helped at the fair.
30. They passed in the **hallway** but did not speak.
31. Do you have a tape **cassette** of that song?
32. Each person has a unique set of **fingerprints**.
33. We went to the library **yesterday**.
34. I was worried that **you'd** never arrive!
35. Al looked out at the **blue-green** sea.
36. Did you **challenge** Claire to a chess game?
37. I want **silence** in this room during the exam.
38. That **horrible** creature is a Komodo dragon.
39. **Kansas'** state bird is the western meadowlark.
40. After the **countdown**, the rocket was launched.
41. My **partner** and I will do a Mexican folk dance.
42. We'll review the test **answers** on Tuesday.
43. What **vehicle** is best for driving in sand?
44. I'll introduce you to the **senator's** son.
45. All **forty-six** seats on the bus were taken.
46. The candidate asked for the voters' **support**.
47. He owes his **success** to hard work.
48. Semi-sweet **chocolate** has a slightly bitter taste.
49. **Mexico's** official language is Spanish.
50. Is **Japan's** largest city Tokyo?

77

Name _____

Read each set of words. Fill in the circle next to the word that is spelled correctly.

1. ⓐ vehacle   ⓒ vehickle
   ⓑ vehicle   ⓓ veicle

2. ⓐ challendge   ⓒ challenge
   ⓑ challege   ⓓ challange

3. ⓐ snowdrift   ⓒ snaudrift
   ⓑ snoedrift   ⓓ snodrift

4. ⓐ histry   ⓒ historey
   ⓑ histery   ⓓ history

5. ⓐ perform   ⓒ purform
   ⓑ perfourm   ⓓ perfurm

6. ⓐ casette   ⓒ cassette
   ⓑ cassete   ⓓ casetet

7. ⓐ watermellon   ⓒ wattermelon
   ⓑ watermelon   ⓓ watermelen

8. ⓐ who'l   ⓒ who'lle
   ⓑ who'le   ⓓ who'll

9. ⓐ forty-six   ⓒ fortyesix
   ⓑ fourty-six   ⓓ fourtysix

10. ⓐ Canadas   ⓒ Canada's
    ⓑ Cana'das   ⓓ Canadda's

11. ⓐ collect   ⓒ colect
    ⓑ callect   ⓓ collectt

12. ⓐ sucess   ⓒ success
    ⓑ succes   ⓓ sucese

Name _____

Read each set of words. Fill in the circle next to the word that is spelled correctly.

13. ⓐ bluegreen   ⓒ bluegrean
    ⓑ blue-green   ⓓ blue-grean

14. ⓐ ansers   ⓒ answers
    ⓑ anwsers   ⓓ awnsers

15. ⓐ forbid   ⓒ fourbid
    ⓑ forebid   ⓓ forbide

16. ⓐ mayjor   ⓒ majer
    ⓑ majir   ⓓ major

17. ⓐ shipwreck   ⓒ shiprewck
    ⓑ shipeck   ⓓ shipreck

18. ⓐ chocalit   ⓒ chocolote
    ⓑ chocolate   ⓓ choclate

19. ⓐ silense   ⓒ silence
    ⓑ silance   ⓓ sillence

20. ⓐ animal   ⓒ aminal
    ⓑ animall   ⓓ annimal

21. ⓐ jelly-fish   ⓒ jelyfish
    ⓑ jellyfish   ⓓ jelliefish

22. ⓐ Kansas'   ⓒ Kansas'se
    ⓑ Kansa's   ⓓ Kansas'es

23. ⓐ horiblle   ⓒ horrible
    ⓑ horible   ⓓ horibele

24. ⓐ you'ld   ⓒ youd
    ⓑ you'de   ⓓ you'd

25. ⓐ womans   ⓒ women's
    ⓑ womens'   ⓓ womens

Take It Home 4

Your child has learned to spell many new words and would enjoy sharing them with you and your family. Here are some ideas your child can use to review the words in lessons 19–23.

See and Spell

You and your child can "draw" on your imaginations to create picture clues for spelling words. When you are ready to unveil your work, invite family members to guess the word that goes with each clue. Challenge them to make up some picture clues of their own.

Lesson 19

1. blue-green
2. cornbread
3. countdown
4. fingernail
5. forty-six
6. grapefruit
7. haircut
8. hallway
9. jellyfish
10. kneecap
11. pancakes
12. paperback
13. rainbows
14. self-control
15. shipwreck
16. shoelaces
17. snowdrift
18. spellbound
19. sunshine
20. underwater

Lesson 20

1. America's
2. Canada's
3. champion's
4. class's
5. college's
6. farmers'
7. Georgia's
8. governor's
9. Japan's
10. Kansas'
11. mayor's
12. Mexico's
13. Montreal's
14. parent's
15. senator's
16. Texas'
17. they've
18. who'll
19. women's
20. you'd

Lesson 21

1. cassette
2. challenge
3. collect
4. command
5. expert
6. forbid
7. fossil
8. manners
9. mental
10. normal
11. partner
12. perform
13. problem
14. rescue
15. scanner
16. shallow
17. signal
18. suggest
19. support
20. symbol

Lesson 22

1. answers
2. closet
3. cover
4. divide
5. dozen
6. fingerprints
7. grandparents
8. helmet
9. major
10. mission
11. modern
12. plastic
13. posture
14. reduce
15. rubble
16. silence
17. splendid
18. success
19. unit
20. watermelon

Lesson 23

1. animal
2. artistic
3. athletic
4. beautiful
5. chocolate
6. citizen
7. electric
8. history
9. horrible
10. impression
11. magazine
12. opposite
13. popular
14. religion
15. remember
16. serious
17. stadium
18. unlikely
19. vehicle
20. yesterday

As Easy As Pie!

With your child, draw a line to the spelling word that best completes each simile.

as flat as	silence
as sour as a	fossil
as warm as	pancakes
as old as a	success
as smart as an	grapefruit
as unique as	fingerprints
as quiet as	rainbows
as white as a	sunshine
as colorful as	snowdrift
as rewarding as	expert

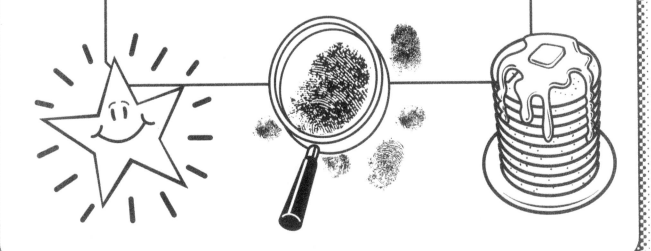

Lesson 25 Suffixes <u>er</u>, <u>est</u>, <u>or</u>, and <u>ist</u>

Objective
To spell words with the suffixes *er*, *est*, *or*, and *ist*

 Correlated Phonics Lessons
MCP Phonics, Level E,
Lessons 52–53

Spelling Words in Action   *Page 101*
In this selection, students learn some ideas that can help them to choose a future career. Afterward, ask students which careers they might want to consider.

Call on volunteers to say each boldfaced word and identify its suffix.

Warm-Up Test
1. The speaker had to talk **louder** to be heard.
2. A **scientist** tries to test all theories.
3. Alexander the Great was a famous **warrior**.
4. The movie's **director** won an award.
5. That is the **scariest** movie I've ever seen!
6. I wake up if anyone makes the **slightest** noise.
7. The butterfly was a **prisoner** in the net.
8. Run the **sweeper** over the rug.
9. We met the **novelist** who wrote the book.
10. The runner wants a **greater** challenge.
11. The **emperor** ruled all the people of China.
12. What is the **busiest** time of year for gardeners?
13. The **tourist** enjoyed visiting the museums.
14. Nothing is **drearier** than a cold, rainy day.
15. The doctor used an **interpreter** to translate.
16. I feel **hungrier** now than I did before lunch.
17. Jenny's **counselor** helped her choose classes.
18. An **inspector** checked our house for termites.
19. Which **cartoonist** draws the comic strip?
20. The **vocalist** sang seven songs in a row.

Spelling Practice   *Pages 102–103*
Introduce the spelling rule and have students read the **list words** aloud. Discuss base words that had spelling changes before the suffixes were added, such as *busy* in *busiest*, in which the final *y* was changed to *i*. Then encourage students to look back at their **Warm-Up Tests** and apply the spelling rule to any misspelled words.

As students work through the **Spelling Practice** exercises, remind them to look back at their **list words** or in their dictionaries if they need help.

 See Change or No Change, page 15

82

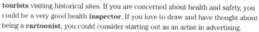

Suffixes <u>er</u>, <u>est</u>, <u>or</u>, and <u>ist</u> Lesson 25

Spelling Words in Action

What kind of a job would you like to have when you're an adult?

Choosing a Career

Some people know exactly what career they want to choose. Others don't have the **slightest** idea. Choosing a career doesn't have to be your **scariest** experience. Thinking about your personal interests and learning about different jobs will help you figure out a good career choice.

For instance, if you love both science and the ocean, you could consider a career as a **scientist** in the field of marine biology. A love of science and writing, on the other hand, could lead to a career as a science-fiction **novelist**. If you love to sing but don't like to perform onstage, you could consider being a **vocalist** for radio advertisements. If you enjoy history and foreign languages, you might want to work as an **interpreter** for **tourists** visiting historical sites. If you are concerned about health and safety, you could be a very good health **inspector**. If you love to draw and have thought about being a **cartoonist**, you could consider starting out as an artist in advertising.

A lot of schools have a career day. That's a day when adults working in different careers visit the school to tell students about their jobs. Many high schools and colleges have a career **counselor** to help students choose a career. Someone who knows about a lot of careers and who likes working with people would be a great career counselor!

Say the boldfaced words in the selection. What suffixes do you find at the end of the words? How are they different?

101

Spelling Practice

TIP A suffix is a word part added to the end of a word. The suffixes **er**, **or**, and **ist** mean *something or someone who does something*.
sweeper   director   tourist
The suffixes **er** and **est** can be used with adjectives to show comparison. The suffix **er** means *more*, as in greater. The suffix **est** means *most*, as in busiest.

LIST WORDS
1. louder
2. scientist
3. warrior
4. director
5. scariest
6. slightest
7. prisoner
8. sweeper
9. novelist
10. greater
11. emperor
12. busiest
13. tourist
14. drearier
15. interpreter
16. hungrier
17. counselor
18. inspector
19. cartoonist
20. vocalist

Words with Suffixes
Write each **list word** under the correct heading.

suffix shows comparison
1. louder
2. scariest
3. slightest
4. greater
5. busiest
6. drearier
7. hungrier

suffix means something or someone who does something
8. scientist
9. warrior
10. director
11. prisoner
12. sweeper
13. novelist
14. emperor
15. tourist
16. interpreter
17. counselor
18. inspector
19. cartoonist
20. vocalist

102   Lesson 25 • Suffixes er, est, or, and ist

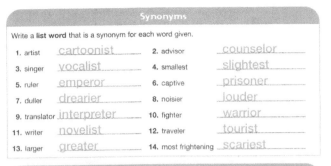

Synonyms

Write a **list word** that is a synonym for each word given.

1. artist __cartoonist__
2. advisor __counselor__
3. singer __vocalist__
4. smallest __slightest__
5. ruler __emperor__
6. captive __prisoner__
7. duller __drearier__
8. noisier __louder__
9. translator __interpreter__
10. fighter __warrior__
11. writer __novelist__
12. traveler __tourist__
13. larger __greater__
14. most frightening __scariest__

Definitions

Write a **list word** to match each definition clue. Then, use the numbered letters to solve the riddle. Copy each numbered letter onto the line below with the same number.

1. person who directs d i r e c t o r
                        15   1   7

2. one who sweeps s w e e p e r
                   3 8   16

3. most active b u s i e s t
                      14 12

4. detective i n s p e c t o r
                          2

5. least s l i g h t e s t
          9   13 5

6. more in need of food h u n g r i e r
                         6   10 11

7. expert in science s c i e n t i s t
                      4   17

Riddle: Why did the girl sleep with a ruler next to her bed?

Answer: She wanted t o   s e e   h o w   l o n g
                        1 2   3 4 5   6 7 8   9 2 10 11
s h e   s l e p t.
12 13 14 12 9 15 16 17

Lesson 25 • Suffixes er, est, or, and ist   103

Spelling and Writing

Proofreading

The poster below has ten mistakes. Use the proofreading marks to fix the mistakes. Then, write the misspelled **list words** correctly on the lines.

Proofreading Marks
- ⬭ spelling mistake
- ≡ capital letter
- ⊙ add period

Career Day Fair
April 12th
9:00–12:00 in the Cafeteria

Come meet a movie (director,) a (cartonist,) a nuclear (sientist) and more. whether you know exactly what you want to do as a career, or don't have the (slightist) idea, there's no (greator) opportunity to learn about different career choices ⊙

this exciting day may leave you (hungryer) than usual, so a special lunch is planned for immediately after the fair ⊙

1. __director__
2. __cartoonist__
3. __scientist__
4. __slightest__
5. __greater__
6. __hungrier__

Writing an Interview

Imagine that you're a reporter for a local TV news show. Your assignment is to interview people who are speaking at a school's career day. Write a list of questions that you would ask. Use any **list words** that you can. Remember to proofread your interview and fix any mistakes.

BONUS WORDS
- realist
- aviator
- fanciest
- harsher
- voter

104   Lesson 25 • Suffixes er, est, or, and ist

Spelling Strategy

Write several **list words** on the board without their endings. Then, ask students which ending (*er*, *est*, *or*, or *ist*) goes with each root or base word to spell a **list word**. Ask a student to write the entire word. Discuss base words that had spelling changes before the suffixes were added.

BONUS WORDS   You may want to suggest that students create crossword puzzles that contain the bonus words. Have them trade puzzles with a partner and try to solve each other's puzzles.

Spelling and Writing   **Page 104**

The **Proofreading** exercise will help students prepare to proofread their questions. As students complete the writing activity, encourage them to brainstorm ideas, write a first draft, revise, and proofread their work. To publish their writing, students may want to get together with a partner and role-play an interview.

Writer's Corner You might want to invite a school counselor to speak to the students about career planning. Encourage students to take notes as they listen to the speaker.

Final Test

1. Each **scientist** studied a different form of life.
2. My school **counselor** suggested that I take art.
3. The shopkeeper helped the **tourist** find the road.
4. At night, a **sweeper** cleans the streets.
5. Is his brother a **vocalist** in the band?
6. Will turning that dial make the radio **louder**?
7. The **interpreter** translated the broadcast.
8. Each **warrior** carried a spear and a shield.
9. Saturday morning is our **busiest** time.
10. The **inspector** made sure the fruit was ripe.
11. The **director** suggested the actors change places.
12. The **novelist** writes a new book every year.
13. In the story, the **emperor** ruled a vast kingdom.
14. The **cartoonist** created two comic strips.
15. Do you get **hungrier** when you exercise?
16. The snow made me a **prisoner** in my house.
17. That was the **scariest** story you ever told!
18. The cabin looked **drearier** than I'd expected.
19. Was this year's rainfall **greater** than usual?
20. My dog barks at the **slightest** sound.

Lesson 26

Suffixes <u>ee</u>, <u>eer</u>, <u>ent</u>, and <u>ant</u>

Objective
To spell words with the suffixes *ee*, *eer*, *ent*, and *ant*

Correlated Phonics Lesson
MCP Phonics, Level E, Lesson 54

Spelling Words in Action   Page 105

Students may enjoy reading about sleight of hand in "Abracadabra." Ask them if they have ever seen a magician's act and if they know how any tricks are performed.

Encourage students to look back at the boldfaced words. Ask volunteers to say the words and identify the different suffixes.

Warm-Up Test

1. Aunt Lisa is an **employee** at the chair factory.
2. The **mountaineer** was a wonderful guide.
3. He voted by an **absentee** ballot.
4. If you practice, you'll be an **excellent** skater.
5. The children are **reliant** upon adults for help.
6. Diego is a **volunteer** at a local hospital.
7. Did the **puppeteer** make or buy his puppets?
8. Uncle Tim is an **engineer** who designs bridges.
9. The **payee** is the person who receives the pay.
10. Was Jorge a **participant** in the game?
11. Carla is now a **resident** of Dallas, Texas.
12. What a **pleasant** day we had at the park!
13. Mr. Ryan is very **competent** at his job.
14. I don't like movies that are **violent**.
15. Sarah is the **assistant** director for the play.
16. My mother works as an **accountant**.
17. How awful that bug **repellent** smells!
18. The **abundant** rains helped the crops grow.
19. What is the **dominant** theme of the play?
20. The **applicant** was called for a job interview.

Spelling Practice   Pages 106–107

Introduce the spelling rule, explaining that nouns ending in *ent* and *ant* usually mean "one who" and that adjectives ending in *ent* and *ant* mean "that which." Then have students read the **list words** aloud. Encourage them to look back at their **Warm-Up Tests** and apply the spelling rule to any misspelled words.

As students work through the **Spelling Practice** exercises, remind them to look back at their **list words** or in their dictionaries if they need help.

 See Questions/Answers, page 15

84

Spelling Words in Action

What is the secret of magic?

Abracadabra

The **dominant** theme in magic is the idea of creating an illusion. In other words, magicians want to make people think they are watching something happen that really isn't taking place. If you're interested in learning magic tricks, a book on the subject is an **excellent** place to begin.

Know what card a person chose from a deck and people will think you're a genius. Make an object disappear and reappear and people won't believe their eyes. Of course, the secret to your magic tricks is fast work with your hands. It also helps if you can distract the audience by talking as you perform your tricks.

It usually takes a magician **abundant** practice in order to appear **competent**. Once you feel that you've mastered a few tricks, try putting on a magic show. You could become the first **resident** magician in your neighborhood. Some magicians are **reliant** on an **assistant**. You can have a friend do the show with you, or you can choose a **pleasant** volunteer from the audience to be a **participant** in your tricks. Wear a top hat and a cape to look like a real professional!

> Say the boldfaced words in the selection. How many suffixes can you find? What pattern do you see in the way words end?

105

Spelling Practice

TIP

The suffixes **ee**, **eer**, **ent**, and **ant** usually mean *one who*. For example:
absentee means *one who is absent*;
mountaineer means *one who climbs mountains*;
resident means *one who resides*;
assistant means *one who assists*.

The suffixes **ent** and **ant** can also mean *that which*. For example:
excellent means *that which excels*;
abundant means *that which abounds*.

LIST WORDS

1. employee
2. mountaineer
3. absentee
4. excellent
5. reliant
6. volunteer
7. puppeteer
8. engineer
9. payee
10. participant
11. resident
12. pleasant
13. competent
14. violent
15. assistant
16. accountant
17. repellent
18. abundant
19. dominant
20. applicant

Words with Suffixes

Write each **list word** under the correct heading.

words with the suffix ee

1. employee
2. absentee
3. payee

words with the suffix eer

9. mountaineer
10. volunteer
11. puppeteer
12. engineer

words with the suffix ent

4. excellent
5. resident
6. competent
7. violent
8. repellent

words with the suffix ant

13. reliant
14. participant
15. pleasant
16. assistant
17. accountant
18. abundant
19. dominant
20. applicant

106   Lesson 26 • Suffixes ee, eer, ent, and ant

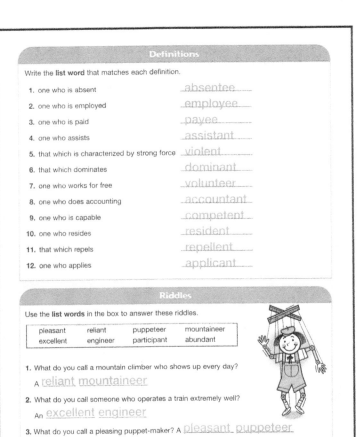

Definitions

Write the **list word** that matches each definition.

1. one who is absent — absentee
2. one who is employed — employee
3. one who is paid — payee
4. one who assists — assistant
5. that which is characterized by strong force — violent
6. that which dominates — dominant
7. one who works for free — volunteer
8. one who does accounting — accountant
9. one who is capable — competent
10. one who resides — resident
11. that which repels — repellent
12. one who applies — applicant

Riddles

Use the **list words** in the box to answer these riddles.

| pleasant | reliant | puppeteer | mountaineer |
| excellent | engineer | participant | abundant |

1. What do you call a mountain climber who shows up every day?
   A reliant mountaineer

2. What do you call someone who operates a train extremely well?
   An excellent engineer

3. What do you call a pleasing puppet-maker? A pleasant puppeteer

4. What do you call a student who loves to take part in every school activity?
   An abundant participant

Lesson 26 • Suffixes ee, eer, ent, and ant   107

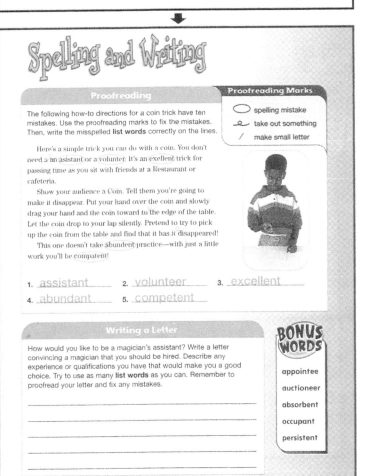

Spelling and Writing

Proofreading

The following how-to directions for a coin trick have ten mistakes. Use the proofreading marks to fix the mistakes. Then, write the misspelled **list words** correctly on the lines.

Proofreading Marks
- ◯ spelling mistake
- ے take out something
- / make small letter

Here's a simple trick you can do with a coin. You don't need a an assistant or a volunteer. It's an excellent trick for passing time as you sit with friends at a Restaurant or cafeteria.

Show your audience a Coin. Tell them you're going to make it disappear. Put your hand over the coin and slowly drag your hand and the coin toward to the edge of the table. Let the coin drop to your lap silently. Pretend to try to pick up the coin from the table and find that it has it disappeared!

This one doesn't take abundent practice—with just a little work you'll be competant!

1. assistant   2. volunteer   3. excellent
4. abundant   5. competent

Writing a Letter

How would you like to be a magician's assistant? Write a letter convincing a magician that you should be hired. Describe any experience or qualifications you have that would make you a good choice. Try to use as many **list words** as you can. Remember to proofread your letter and fix any mistakes.

BONUS WORDS
- appointee
- auctioneer
- absorbent
- occupant
- persistent

108   Lesson 26 • Suffixes ee, eer, ent, and ant

Spelling Strategy

Write the suffixes *ee, eer, ent,* and *ant* on the board as separate column headings. Then tell students a root or base word (contained in a **list word**) and ask which suffix they would add to it to form a **list word**. Call on a volunteer to write the complete word on the board in the appropriate column. Continue this procedure until all the **list words** have been written.

BONUS WORDS You may want to suggest that students work with a partner to divide the words. Have them write both a real and a fake definition for each word. Ask them to trade papers and circle the meanings they think are correct.

Spelling and Writing   *Page 108*

The **Proofreading** exercise will help students prepare to proofread their letters. As students complete the writing activity, encourage them to brainstorm ideas, write a first draft, revise, and proofread their work. To publish their writing, students may want to trade letters and write responses to one another.

Writer's Corner Suggest that students invite a local magician to talk about and demonstrate a few magic tricks. Encourage students to write thank-you notes to the guest speaker.

Final Test

1. The **puppeteer** put on a great show.
2. My uncle is a **resident** of Washington, D.C.
3. Is there an **assistant** teacher in your classroom?
4. The **dominant** color in the picture is orange.
5. The teacher sent work home to the **absentee**.
6. An **accountant** can help you fill out these forms.
7. Is she the first **applicant** to be interviewed?
8. The garden is so **pleasant** to look at!
9. The **engineer** presented his building plans.
10. Wasn't that an **excellent** restaurant?
11. Our farm produces **abundant** vegetables.
12. I'd like to be a **participant** in that event.
13. What a **violent** storm that was!
14. Do you work as a **volunteer** at the library?
15. The **mountaineer** lives in a log cabin.
16. Who is the most **competent** person for the job?
17. Insect **repellent** may protect the children.
18. She is a strong, **reliant** person.
19. Martha is an **employee** of a large hotel.
20. The **payee** was grateful to receive the check.

Lesson 27

Suffixes <u>ward</u>, <u>en</u>, <u>ize</u>, <u>ful</u>, and <u>ness</u>

Objective
To spell words with the suffixes *ward*, *en*, *ize*, *ful*, and *ness*

 Phonics **Correlated Phonics Lessons**
MCP Phonics, **Level E,**
Lessons 52, 55

Spelling Words in Action   *Page 109*

In "Shy Guy," students read about the octopus. After reading, invite students to tell how they would react if they met an octopus.

Encourage students to look back at the boldfaced words. Ask volunteers to say the words and identify the five different suffixes.

Warm-Up Test

1. His **shyness** keeps him from giving speeches.
2. The countryside is **peaceful** in the morning.
3. We look **forward** to going to the skating rink.
4. Everyone was **cheerful** on the trip.
5. Do you plan to return home **afterward**?
6. As night approaches, the sky begins to **darken**.
7. Is wildlife **plentiful** in your region?
8. The **loudness** of that music hurts my ears.
9. We counted **backward** from one hundred.
10. Did you **tighten** the bolts on the new bicycle?
11. We were impressed by Tony's **politeness**.
12. I will **sharpen** the scissors.
13. The class was given a poem to **memorize**.
14. What **wonderful** ideas Pat always has!
15. I think I **recognize** that girl.
16. It's **shameful** how much food we waste.
17. Their **friendliness** surprised the stranger.
18. Please **alphabetize** this list of names.
19. What a **delightful** show that was!
20. Sounds in the **wilderness** can be frightening.

Spelling Practice   *Pages 110–111*

Introduce the spelling rule and have students read the **list words** aloud. Encourage them to look back at their **Warm-Up Tests** and apply the spelling rule to any misspelled words.

As students work through the **Spelling Practice** exercises, remind them to look back at their **list words** or in their dictionaries if they need help. You may want to point out the words in which the spelling of the base word was changed in order to add the suffix.

for ESL students See Spelling Aloud, page 14

86

Suffixes <u>ward</u>, <u>en</u>, <u>ize</u>, <u>ful</u>, and <u>ness</u>   Lesson 27

Spelling Words in Action

Which animal is the shyest animal in the ocean?

Shy Guy

The octopus is thought of as the most bashful inhabitant of the ocean **wilderness**. The octopus's **shyness** shows. When an octopus spies another animal—even another octopus—it hides. When frightened, it will squirt a cloud of ink to confuse its enemy. **Afterward**, it will scoot away to some dark place. It might even **darken** or lighten its color, or camouflage itself, so that no animal can **recognize** it.

An octopus is a **delightful** animal to watch— if you can get a glimpse of one! Rather than swimming **forward** like most fish, it can swim **backward** in a very unusual manner. First, it draws water into its body. Then, it forces the water out in a strong gush.

An octopus has eight strong arms called tentacles. Each tentacle has two **plentiful** rows of suckers. With these suckers, the octopus can pull itself along the ocean floor. It also uses the suckers to catch its food, such as crabs, clams, and snails.

An octopus is very smart. Tests have shown that an octopus can **memorize** the solution to a problem it has figured out. It can even remove a cork from a jar to get food!

Say the boldfaced words in the selection. Notice how each word ends. Can you find the five different suffixes? How are they different?

109

Spelling Practice

TIP

The suffix **ward** means in the direction of, as in forward. The suffixes **en** and **ize** can mean to make, to become, or to cause to be, as in darken or alphabetize. The suffix **ful** means full of or having a tendency to, as in peaceful. The suffix **ness** means the quality or condition of being, as in politeness.

LIST WORDS

1. shyness
2. peaceful
3. forward
4. cheerful
5. afterward
6. darken
7. plentiful
8. loudness
9. backward
10. lighten
11. politeness
12. sharpen
13. memorize
14. wonderful
15. recognize
16. shameful
17. friendliness
18. alphabetize
19. delightful
20. wilderness

Words with Suffixes

Write each **list word** under the correct heading.

words with the suffix ward

1. forward
2. afterward
3. backward

words with the suffix en

4. darken
5. tighten
6. sharpen

words with the suffix ize

7. memorize
8. recognize
9. alphabetize

words with the suffix ful

10. peaceful
11. cheerful
12. plentiful
13. wonderful
14. shameful
15. delightful

words with the suffix ness

16. shyness
17. loudness
18. politeness
19. friendliness
20. wilderness

110   Lesson 27 • Suffixes ward, en, ize, ful, and ness

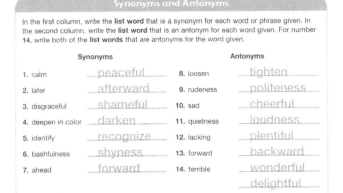

Synonyms and Antonyms

In the first column, write the **list word** that is a synonym for each word or phrase given. In the second column, write the **list word** that is an antonym for each word given. For number 14, write both of the **list words** that are antonyms for the word given.

Synonyms		Antonyms	
1. calm	peaceful	8. loosen	tighten
2. later	afterward	9. rudeness	politeness
3. disgraceful	shameful	10. sad	cheerful
4. deepen in color	darken	11. quietness	loudness
5. identify	recognize	12. lacking	plentiful
6. bashfulness	shyness	13. forward	backward
7. ahead	forward	14. terrible	wonderful
			delightful

Puzzle

Read each clue. Write **list words** to complete the puzzle.

Across
4. full of pleasure
5. a wild region
7. meekness
8. remember

Down
1. kindness
2. noisiness
3. to put in A,B,C order
6. put an edge on

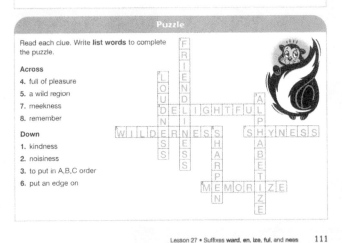

Lesson 27 • Suffixes **ward, en, ize, ful,** and **ness**   111

⬇

Spelling and Writing

Proofreading

The following TV listing has ten mistakes. Use the proofreading marks to fix the mistakes. Then, write the misspelled **list words** correctly on the lines.

Proofreading Marks

◯ spelling mistake
/ make a small letter

8:00 P.M. Channel 89: Wonnarfull Ocean Willderniss
The Host, Shirley Chin, takes a delitefull underwater tour suitable for the whole family. Time-lapse Photography lets the viewer see some unusual sights. You can actually see how a Shark's reserve teeth move foreword to replace lost ones. You'll see a starfish lose an arm, and afterword, grow a new one. You'll watch camouflage in action as Fish darkin their colors to blend in with their backgrounds.

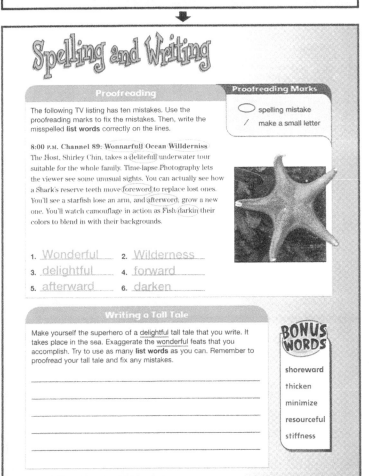

1. Wonderful   2. Wilderness
3. delightful   4. forward
5. afterward   6. darken

Writing a Tall Tale

Make yourself the superhero of a delightful tall tale that you write. It takes place in the sea. Exaggerate the wonderful feats that you accomplish. Try to use as many **list words** as you can. Remember to proofread your tall tale and fix any mistakes.

_____
_____
_____
_____
_____
_____

BONUS WORDS

shoreward
thicken
minimize
resourceful
stiffness

112   Lesson 27 • Suffixes ward, en, ize, ful, and ness

Spelling Strategy

Write several sentences containing **list words** on the board, but leave blanks for the suffixes. For example: "The sea is calm and peace___." Then, invite the class to read each sentence aloud, completing the **list word**. Ask a volunteer to come to the board and fill in the missing suffix.

BONUS WORDS You may want to suggest that students work with partners to list at least one synonym or antonym for each bonus word. Then have them use a thesaurus or dictionary to check their work and see how many additional synonyms or antonyms they can find.

Spelling and Writing   *Page 112*

The **Proofreading** exercise will help students prepare to proofread their tall tales. As students complete the writing activity, encourage them to brainstorm ideas, write a first draft, revise, and proofread their work. To publish their writing, students may want to record their tales on audiotape.

Writer's Corner Students may enjoy reading a book about creatures that live deep under the ocean such as *Beneath Blue Waters: Meetings With Remarkable Creatures* by D. Kovacs and K. Madin. Afterward, suggest that they use the information they learned to create a bulletin board.

Final Test

1. Brave pioneers settled in the **wilderness**.
2. Jason worked hard to overcome his **shyness**.
3. That baby girl has a **delightful** smile.
4. We had a picnic by a **peaceful** brook.
5. Did you **alphabetize** the names?
6. We looked **forward** to our vacation all winter.
7. Chan's **friendliness** helped everyone relax.
8. Michelle is happy and **cheerful** every day.
9. It is **shameful** that people litter the highways.
10. We will eat, and **afterward** we will rest.
11. I didn't **recognize** Ed in his clown costume.
12. When the lights **darken**, the play will begin.
13. What a **wonderful** singing voice Nicole has!
14. The apples will be **plentiful** this fall.
15. Did you **memorize** your speech?
16. The **loudness** of the band made it hard to talk.
17. Paul will **sharpen** the ax blade.
18. Did you put the tape in **backward**?
19. **Politeness** is always appreciated by others.
20. Maria should **tighten** the laces on her skates.

Objective

To spell words with the suffixes *hood*, *ship*, *ment*, *able*, and *ible*

Correlated Phonics Lessons
MCP Phonics, Level E,
Lessons 56–57

Spelling Words in Action   *Page 113*

In "A Juggling Act," students discover how people can learn to juggle. Afterward, ask students whether juggling is a good hobby.

Encourage students to look back at the boldfaced words. Ask volunteers to say the words and identify the five different suffixes.

Warm-Up Test

1. It's **possible** that we'll have rain later today.
2. What was all that **excitement** in the street?
3. What a **terrible** flood we had last spring!
4. Our **neighborhood** has a party every summer.
5. Dan took on the **leadership** of the club.
6. **Membership** in the club is open to everyone.
7. The football team was issued new **equipment**.
8. Is their bike repair business **profitable**?
9. Who claimed **ownership** of the bike?
10. That story was a complete **falsehood**!
11. Our swim team will try for the **championship**.
12. The principal made an important **statement**.
13. My brother is very **sensible** about what he eats.
14. **Motherhood** certainly agrees with Mrs. Caspar.
15. My **dependable** dog meets my bus every day.
16. This is an incredibly **comfortable** chair!
17. The bridge is barely **visible** through the fog.
18. What is the **likelihood** of your going to camp?
19. If you're **agreeable**, we'll go to the movies.
20. A **durable** fabric lasts through many washings.

Spelling Practice   *Pages 114–115*

Introduce the spelling rule and explain that *hood*, *ship*, and *ment* form nouns; *able* and *ible* form adjectives. Then, have students read the **list words** aloud. Encourage them to look back at their **Warm-Up Tests** and apply the spelling rule to any misspelled words.

As students work through the **Spelling Practice** exercises, remind them to look back at their **list words** or in their dictionaries if they need help.

 for ESL students   See Change or No Change, page 15

88

Suffixes <u>hood</u>, <u>ship</u>, <u>ment</u>, <u>able</u>, and <u>ible</u>   **Lesson 28**

Spelling Words in Action

Why is it so fun to watch someone juggle?

A Juggling Act

Did you know that it's **possible** to learn to juggle in just a few easy steps? Most beginners start by juggling balls. It helps if they are **dependable** and **durable**.

You begin with one ball in each hand. First, you toss the ball in your right hand in an arc toward the left hand. When this ball is at the high point of its arc, that's the signal to throw the second ball from your left hand to the right. First, you catch the ball heading toward your left hand. Then, you catch the ball heading toward your right hand. When you are **comfortable** with this, repeat the exercise, but start by tossing the ball in your left hand toward the right. Eventually, you will add a third ball to begin juggling.

Experienced jugglers may juggle rings, clubs, or other objects and might use four or five objects at a time. For a first-time juggler, however, learning to juggle just three balls is more **sensible** and will give you a greater **likelihood** of success. If juggling is **agreeable** to you, you might consider **membership** in a juggling club.

There are lots of clubs in towns and cities across the country for all different ages. Even if you don't win a championship, you can create a lot of **excitement** by putting on your own **neighborhood** juggling act.

> Say the boldfaced words in the selection. Notice how each word ends. Can you find the five different suffixes? How are they different?

113

Spelling Practice

TIP

The suffixes, **hood**, **ship**, and **ment** mean the state or condition of being, as in motherhood, leadership, and statement.
The suffixes **able** and **ible** usually mean able to be or full of, as in agreeable and sensible.

LIST WORDS

1. possible
2. excitement
3. terrible
4. neighborhood
5. leadership
6. membership
7. equipment
8. profitable
9. ownership
10. falsehood
11. championship
12. statement
13. sensible
14. motherhood
15. dependable
16. comfortable
17. visible
18. likelihood
19. agreeable
20. durable

Words with Suffixes

Write each **list word** under the correct heading. Then, circle the suffix in each word.

words with the suffixes **able** or **ible**	words with the suffixes **hood, ship,** or **ment**
1. poss(ible)	10. excite(ment)
2. terr(ible)	11. neighbor(hood)
3. profit(able)	12. leader(ship)
4. sens(ible)	13. member(ship)
5. depend(able)	14. equip(ment)
6. comfort(able)	15. owner(ship)
7. vis(ible)	16. false(hood)
8. agree(able)	17. champion(ship)
9. dur(able)	18. state(ment)
	19. mother(hood)
	20. likeli(hood)

114   Lesson 28 • Suffixes hood, ship, ment, able, and ible

Definitions

Write the **list word** that matches each definition.

1. lasting in spite of hard wear __durable__
2. able to be seen __visible__
3. fearful; frightful; dreadful __terrible__
4. legal right of possession __ownership__
5. the position of being the one who guides or shows the way __leadership__
6. at ease in body or mind __comfortable__
7. having or showing sound judgment __sensible__
8. able to happen or be done __possible__
9. all the things needed for some purpose __equipment__
10. chance of something happening __likelihood__

Mixed-Up Suffixes

The words below have mixed-up suffixes. Draw a line from the word on the left that goes with a word on the right. Put the suffixes back in place to form two **list words**. Then, write the correct pair of words on the lines. One line has been drawn for you.

excitehood — dependment
neighborship — agreehood
profitship — falsement
stateable — memberable
motherable — championhood

agreeable
championship
dependable
excitement
falsehood
membership
motherhood
neighborhood
profitable
statement

1. __statement__ __dependable__
2. __excitement__ __falsehood__
3. __neighborhood__ __championship__
4. __profitable__ __membership__
5. __motherhood__ __agreeable__

Spelling and Writing

Proofreading

The following Web site's home page about a juggling festival has eleven mistakes. Use the proofreading marks to fix the mistakes. Then, write the misspelled **list words** correctly on the lines.

Proofreading Marks
◯ spelling mistake
⌃ add something

Martinsville Juggling Festival—February 28th
Join the exitement!
Watch championship jugglers, and learn their tricks.
Buy new equiptment—balls rings, batons, and more.
Consider membershipp in our clubs for children, teenagers, and adults. Ledership positions are always available for those who want to take charge of a club.
Wear comfotable clothes, and plan to spend the day.

1. __excitement__ 2. __championship__
3. __equipment__ 4. __membership__
5. __Leadership__ 6. __comfortable__

Writing a Journal Entry

Think of a sport or hobby that you enjoy. Write a brief journal entry describing a day that you spent pursuing your sport or hobby. Use any **list words** that you can. Remember to proofread your journal and fix any mistakes.

_____
_____
_____
_____
_____

BONUS WORDS
brotherhood
scholarship
settlement
washable
legible

Spelling Strategy

Write these base words on the board in one column in this order: *state, agree, member, terror, likely*. In a second column, write this sequence of suffixes: *ible, ment, hood, able, ship*. Have students work with a partner to copy the columns and draw connecting lines to form **list words**. Point out to students that they will have to change two of the base words in order to add the suffix. Repeat this procedure with other groups of base words contained in the **list words**.

BONUS WORDS
You may want to suggest that students write a question for each bonus word. Then, have them trade questions with a partner and write the answers, being sure to include the bonus words.

Spelling and Writing   Page 116

The **Proofreading** exercise will help students prepare to proofread their journal entries. As students complete the writing activity, encourage them to brainstorm ideas, write a first draft, revise, and proofread their work. To publish their writing, students may want to use their journal entries to create a bulletin board display.

Writer's Corner   Rent a video that teaches juggling from a video store. Before you show the video, suggest that students jot down questions that they have about learning how to juggle.

Final Test

1. Was everyone **agreeable** to the plan?
2. The whole city is **visible** from the tower.
3. Jessie is a **dependable** employee.
4. Diana follows a **sensible** exercise program.
5. The **championship** team celebrated its victory.
6. No one claimed **ownership** of the jacket.
7. Paco must get the **equipment** to the field.
8. Amy exhibits outstanding **leadership** qualities.
9. There was a **terrible** crash of thunder.
10. Is it **possible** for everyone to ride in one car?
11. Mom bought a **durable** pair of hiking boots.
12. There is a good **likelihood** of snow tonight.
13. What **comfortable** shoes these are!
14. **Motherhood** is a difficult and challenging job.
15. The chairperson will make a **statement**.
16. Did you spot the **falsehood** in his story?
17. Babysitting can be a **profitable** business.
18. Does she enjoy her **membership** in the club?
19. Our **neighborhood** is very friendly.
20. **Excitement** spread through the crowd.

Lesson 29

Suffixes ion, tion, ance, ence, ity, and ive

Objective
To spell words with the suffixes *ion*, *tion*, *ance*, *ence*, *ity*, and *ive*

Correlated Phonics Lessons
MCP Phonics, Level E, Lessons 58–59

Spelling Words in Action   **Page 117**

In this selection, students discover what is unique about skiers who belong to a group called BOLD. Afterward, invite students to read aloud the part they liked the best.

Encourage students to look back at the boldfaced words. Ask volunteers to say each word and identify its suffix.

Warm-Up Test
1. I pointed in the **direction** of the stadium.
2. For **protection** from rain, wear a raincoat.
3. Gary's parents increased his weekly **allowance**.
4. Laws guarantee **equality** for American citizens.
5. Are you **selective** in your television viewing?
6. The **population** of the town has increased.
7. During the storm, a **massive** tree fell down.
8. The lightning bugs were held **captive** in the jar.
9. Last summer the **humidity** was awful!
10. We will take a **vacation** in the mountains.
11. Clean water is of **importance** to everyone.
12. In your **opinion**, which book is better?
13. Everyone's going to vote in the class **election**.
14. They showed great **humanity** by helping us.
15. What is your **objection** to my plan?
16. With **confidence**, you can achieve many things.
17. Are there **imitation** flavorings in the cake mix?
18. Our teacher records class **attendance**.
19. The writer showed **originality** in the script.
20. Our country fought hard for **independence**.

Spelling Practice   **Pages 118–119**

Introduce the spelling rule and have students read the **list words** aloud. Discuss unfamiliar meanings and call attention to any spelling changes that were made to a base word when a suffix was added. Then, encourage students to look back at their **Warm-Up Tests** and apply the spelling rule to any misspelled words.

As students work through the **Spelling Practice** exercises, remind them to look back at their **list words** or in their dictionaries if they need help.

for ESL students **See Tape Recording, page 15**

90

Suffixes ion, tion, ance, ence, ity, and ive   Lesson 29

Spelling Words in Action

What would it be like to be blind and go skiing?

Brave and Bold

A ski instructor is describing snow conditions to a student. "The surface is powdery, and it's a wide, easy slope with no bumps. Try to get up some speed. Go for it!" The student reaches the bottom of the hill, beaming over her demonstration of **independence**.

These two skiers are part of a group called BOLD. The letters stand for "Blind Outdoor Leisure Development." The young instructor is a volunteer. It's his job to help the blind student experience the thrill of skiing on her winter **vacation**. Guides are carefully trained to give each **direction** clearly. For **protection**, they also ski closely to the students. They know the **importance** of winning a student's **confidence**.

BOLD was begun by Jean Eymere, who learned to ski again after he became blind. He realized that other blind people could also learn to ski. He believed that a program such as BOLD would help the blind **population** to be less **selective** about sports in which they participate.

What is a blind skier's **opinion** of the program? Participants in BOLD feel an **equality** with other athletes. In addition, they discover they can do something they never thought was possible.

Look back at the boldfaced words in the selection. Notice how each word ends. How are the suffixes alike? How are they different?

117

Spelling Practice

TIP
The suffixes *ion* and *tion* usually mean the act of or the condition of being, as in protection. The suffixes *ance*, *ence*, and *ity* usually mean the quality or state of being, as in importance and equality. The suffix *ive* usually means likely or having to do with, as in selective.

LIST WORDS
1. direction
2. protection
3. allowance
4. equality
5. selective
6. population
7. massive
8. captive
9. humidity
10. vacation
11. importance
12. opinion
13. election
14. humanity
15. objection
16. confidence
17. imitation
18. attendance
19. originality
20. independence

Words with Suffixes

Write each **list word** under the correct heading.

words with the suffix **ive**
1. selective
2. massive
3. captive

words with the suffix **tion or ion**
4. direction
5. protection
6. population
7. vacation
8. opinion
9. election
10. objection
11. imitation

words with the suffix **ence**
12. confidence
13. independence

words with the suffix **ity**
14. equality
15. humidity
16. humanity
17. originality

words with the suffix **ance**
18. allowance
19. importance
20. attendance

118   Lesson 29 • Suffixes ion, tion, ance, ence, ity, and ive

Missing Words

Write the **list word** that best completes each sentence.

1. People who are not dependent show _independence_.
2. People who select carefully are _selective_.
3. People who direct give a lot of _direction_.
4. A person who objects has an _objection_.
5. People who protect give _protection_.
6. If you confide, or trust, in people, you have _confidence_ in them.
7. People who elect officials vote in an _election_.
8. A person who opines, or thinks, has an _opinion_.
9. People who are equal have _equality_.
10. People are humans and are part of _humanity_.
11. People call objects that are large and have a lot of mass _massive_.
12. People who are original and creative show _originality_.
13. People vacate, or leave, home to go on a _vacation_.
14. What people notice about humid, or damp, weather is the _humidity_.
15. A person who imitates shows an _imitation_.

VOTE HERE TODAY

Hidden Words

Each word in the box is hidden in a **list word**. Pull a word out of the box. On the lines, write the hidden word and the **list word** that contains it.

cap	pin
pop	confide
mass	allow
man	tend
port	depend

1. _cap_ _captive_
2. _pop_ _population_
3. _pin_ _opinion_
4. _mass_ _massive_
5. _allow_ _allowance_
6. _depend_ _independence_
7. _port_ _importance_
8. _tend_ _attendance_
9. _man_ _humanity_
10. _confide_ _confidence_

Spelling and Writing

Proofreading

The certificate below honoring a local BOLD organization has ten mistakes. Use the proofreading marks to fix the mistakes. Then, write the misspelled **list words** correctly on the lines.

Proofreading Marks

◯ spelling mistake
≡ capital letter

The Mayor's Helping Huminaty Award

Under the direcshion of capable volunteers, our local chapter of BOLD has helped further the indipendanse and confidance of others. our citizens recognize the importice of one person reaching out to help another, and, therefore, the city of lynbrook awards this certificate. in our upinion, BOLD instructors are heroes.
mayor Juan Daquino

1. _Humanity_
2. _direction_
3. _independence_
4. _confidence_
5. _importance_
6. _opinion_

Writing a Dialogue

Imagine that you are an instructor trying to convince a student to try a new sport. Write the dialogue that might take place between you and that student. Use any **list words** that you can. Remember to proofread your dialogue and fix any mistakes.

BONUS WORDS

adoption
violence
acceptance
sincerity
relative

Spelling Strategy

You may want to write the definitions in the Tip box on the board and ask students to name the suffix or suffixes that go with each definition. Then challenge students to
- name **list words** for each suffix
- define each word based on the suffix's meaning
- spell each word.

BONUS WORDS You may want to suggest that students write one definition for each bonus word, then check their work using a dictionary. Have them circle the suffix in each bonus word and place a star next to any words that have more than one meaning.

Spelling and Writing   *Page 120*

The **Proofreading** exercise will help students prepare to proofread their dialogues. As students complete the writing activity, encourage them to brainstorm ideas, write a first draft, revise, and proofread their work. To publish their writing, students may want to
- record their dialogues with a partner
- use their dialogues to create a storyboard.

Writer's Corner Students might enjoy reading the entries in a sports encyclopedia for young people such as *Eyewitness: Sports* by Tim Hammond. Encourage students to write a book review and read it to the class.

Final Test

1. Do you have **confidence** that you will succeed?
2. You can only ask four people, so be **selective**.
3. Ted was not sure in which **direction** to travel.
4. America celebrates its **independence**.
5. The principal has no **objection** to a class picnic.
6. Moving all these books is a **massive** job!
7. Sadako became class president in that **election**.
8. Padding gives players **protection** from injuries.
9. The poem won praise for its **originality**.
10. Many tropical plants require **humidity**.
11. School **attendance** has been quite stable.
12. He possesses a strong sense of **humanity**.
13. Some traps do not harm **captive** animals at all.
14. My parents give me an **allowance** every Friday.
15. Do not state an **opinion** as if it were a fact.
16. Is that coat made from **imitation** leather?
17. In many nations, people only dream of **equality**.
18. During summer **vacation**, I go camping.
19. Every year, the world's **population** increases.
20. Dentists stress the **importance** of regular care.

Objectives
To review spelling words with the suffixes *er, est, or, ist, ee, eer, ent, ant, ward, en, ize, ful, ness, hood, ship, ment, able, ible, ion, tion, ance, ence, ity,* and *ive*

Check Your
Spelling Notebook   *Pages 121–124*
Based on your observations, note which words are giving students the most difficulty and offer assistance for spelling them correctly. Here are some frequently misspelled words to watch for: *prisoner, forward, friendliness, equipment, durable,* and *attendance.*

To give students extra help and practice in taking standardized tests, you may want to have them take the **Review Test** for this lesson on pages 94–95. After scoring the tests, return them to students so that they can record their misspelled words in their spelling notebooks.

After practicing their troublesome words, students can work through the exercises for lessons 25–29 and the cumulative review, **Show What You Know**. Before they begin each exercise, you may want to go over the spelling rule.

Take It Home
Invite students to locate the **list words** from lessons 25–29 in newspapers and magazines at home. Students can also use **Take It Home** Master 5 on pages 96–97 to help them do the activity. (A complete list of the spelling words is included on page 96 of the **Take It Home** Master.) Invite students to bring in their clippings to share with the class.

Lessons 25–29 · Review

In lessons 25 through 29, you learned about suffixes and their meanings. Look again at the suffixes in these lessons. How do they change the meaning of base words and roots?

Check Your Spelling Notebook
Look at the words in your spelling notebook. Which words for lessons 25 through 29 did you have the most trouble with? Write them here.

_____

_____

_____

Practice writing your troublesome words with a partner. Circle the suffix in each word and tell its meaning.

Lesson 25
TIP The suffixes **er, or,** and **ist** mean something or someone who does something, as in counselor. The suffixes **er** and **est** can be added to adjectives to show comparison, as in hungrier and scariest.

List Words

louder
warrior
scariest
slightest
novelist
greater
sweeper
emperor
busiest
tourist
inspector
vocalist

Write the two **list words** that fit each description. Not all the words will be used.

1. a better writer of books:
   the ____greater____ ____novelist____
2. the detective with the most to do:
   the ____busiest____ ____inspector____
3. the most frightening fighter:
   the ____scariest____ ____warrior____
4. the least important ruler:
   the ____slightest____ ____emperor____
5. the singer who can be heard farther away:
   the ____louder____ ____vocalist____

121

Lesson 26
TIP ee, eer, ent, and ant = one who
ent and ant = that which

List Words

employee
mountaineer
engineer
participant
resident
competent
violent
assistant
accountant
repellent
abundant
puppeteer

Write the **list word** that relates best to the word or words given. Not all the words will be used.

1. helper — ____assistant____
2. occupant — ____resident____
3. conductor — ____engineer____
4. hiker — ____mountaineer____
5. member — ____participant____
6. bug spray — ____repellent____
7. capable — ____competent____
8. plenty — ____abundant____
9. counting — ____accountant____
10. worker — ____employee____

Lesson 27
TIP ward = in the direction of
en and ize = to make, to become, to cause to be
ful = full of or having a tendency to
ness = the quality or condition of being

List Words

peaceful
forward
shyness
cheerful
afterward
darken
plentiful
loudness
politeness
sharpen
memorize
recognize

Write a **list word** to complete each sentence. Not all the words will be used.

1. You ____recognize____ a friend you know.
2. You ____sharpen____ a pencil.
3. You ____memorize____ a poem to recite it.
4. You are ____peaceful____ when you sleep.
5. You arrive ____afterward____ when you're late.
6. You are ____cheerful____ when you're happy.
7. You ____darken____ the room to go to sleep.
8. Your ____politeness____ shows you have manners.
9. You move ____forward____ to get ahead.
10. You cover your ears because of the band's ____loudness____

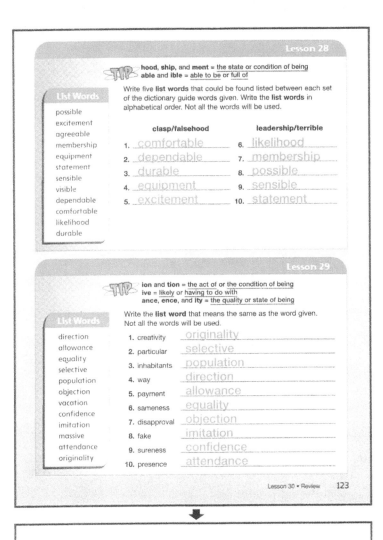

Lesson 28

TIP hood, ship, and ment = the state or condition of being
able and ible = able to be or full of

List Words

possible
excitement
agreeable
membership
equipment
statement
sensible
visible
dependable
comfortable
likelihood
durable

Write five list words that could be found listed between each set of the dictionary guide words given. Write the list words in alphabetical order. Not all the words will be used.

clasp/falsehood
1. comfortable
2. dependable
3. durable
4. equipment
5. excitement

leadership/terrible
6. likelihood
7. membership
8. possible
9. sensible
10. statement

Lesson 29

TIP ion and tion = the act of or the condition of being
ive = likely or having to do with
ance, ence, and ity = the quality or state of being

List Words

direction
allowance
equality
selective
population
objection
vacation
confidence
imitation
massive
attendance
originality

Write the list word that means the same as the word given. Not all the words will be used.

1. creativity — originality
2. particular — selective
3. inhabitants — population
4. way — direction
5. payment — allowance
6. sameness — equality
7. disapproval — objection
8. fake — imitation
9. sureness — confidence
10. presence — attendance

Lesson 30 • Review   123

Show What You Know

Lessons 25–29 Review

One word is misspelled in each set of list words. Fill in the circle next to the list word that is spelled incorrectly.

1.	profitable	● elektion	backward	payee	greater
2.	drearier	direction	● politness	falsehood	pleasant
3.	● reliunt	cartoonist	wonderful	imitation	engineer
4.	terrible	novelist	peaceful	● mountaneer	captive
5.	darken	prisoner	louder	● humannity	visible
6.	possible	loudness	hungrier	● puppeter	scariest
7.	cheerful	● asisstant	tighten	massive	statement
8.	importance	participant	motherhood	equality	● warior
9.	likelihood	● attendence	repellent	sharpen	objection
10.	busiest	● absentie	allowance	humidity	plentiful
11.	● abundent	ownership	emperor	vacation	durable
12.	selective	population	employee	● shiness	protection
13.	● independance	wilderness	agreeable	applicant	vocalist
14.	scientist	● exellent	forward	excitement	opinion
15.	confidence	● neghborhood	afterward	resident	director
16.	inspector	slightest	competent	● dornminant	delightful
17.	originality	● councelor	accountant	alphabetize	comfortable
18.	● sweaper	leadership	memorize	violent	tourist
19.	interpreter	recognize	● shamefull	friendliness	membership
20.	● equiptment	championship	sensible	dependable	volunteer

124   Lesson 30 • Review

Final Test

1. Daryl turned the music up **louder**.
2. Melba is an outstanding **employee**.
3. We enjoyed a **peaceful** picnic in the park.
4. I didn't think it was **possible** to run that fast.
5. We went in the wrong **direction**.
6. In ancient days, a great **warrior** was a hero.
7. The **mountaineer** wrote a book about climbing.
8. They're looking **forward** to summer vacation.
9. The crowd showed its **excitement** by cheering.
10. Teresa receives a weekly five-dollar **allowance**.
11. That was the **scariest** monster I've ever seen!
12. The **engineer** drove the train into the station.
13. What a **cheerful** person Chris is!
14. Do you have a **membership** at the museum?
15. The employer promised **equality** to the workers.
16. The baby wakes up at the **slightest** sound.
17. Who was the most enthusiastic **participant**?
18. We will celebrate our victory **afterward**.
19. Can you carry all the **equipment** by yourself?
20. Mom is very **selective** when shopping for fruit.
21. Her dad is a **novelist** who writes mysteries.
22. He has been a **resident** of the town for a year.
23. Before the storm hit, the sky began to **darken**.
24. We need a **statement** about company policies.
25. How much has the **population** grown?
26. Which of the two buildings is **greater** in size?
27. What a **competent** babysitter Keri is!
28. Can you hear over the **loudness** of the music?
29. Julie is **sensible** and will avoid danger.
30. If there's no **objection**, I will end the meeting.
31. The **emperor** wore a gold crown.
32. The carpenter's **assistant** carried the beams.
33. Her **politeness** was welcome.
34. Pedro is a **dependable** friend.
35. He has the **confidence** to perform.
36. The farmers are **busiest** at harvest time.
37. The **accountant** figured out how much we owe.
38. Miko asked if she could **sharpen** her pencil.
39. She looked so **comfortable** resting on the sofa.
40. I hate the taste of **imitation** ice cream!
41. The **inspector** looked carefully for clues.
42. Bug **repellent** kept the mosquitoes from biting.
43. I have to **memorize** this poem by tomorrow.
44. The **likelihood** of your getting a raise is good.
45. School **attendance** was down last year.
46. Ask the **vocalist** to sing Mom's favorite song.
47. Good weather produced an **abundant** crop.
48. We could hardly **recognize** the town.
49. My grandfather builds **durable** furniture.
50. Her artwork shows creativity and **originality**.

93

Name _____

Read each set of phrases. Fill in the circle next to the phrase with an underlined word that is spelled correctly.

1. ⓐ the <u>busiest</u> teacher   ⓒ the <u>bussiest</u> student
    ⓑ the <u>busyest</u> intersection   ⓓ the <u>bussest</u> team

2. ⓐ <u>likelehood</u> of a storm   ⓒ <u>likelyhood</u> of success
    ⓑ <u>likelihood</u> of that happening ⓓ <u>liklyhood</u> of winning

3. ⓐ <u>imitayshun</u> flavor   ⓒ a clever <u>imitation</u>
    ⓑ the <u>imitasion</u> crabmeat   ⓓ <u>imitiaton</u> diamonds

4. ⓐ drive in the <u>direcktion</u>   ⓒ the right <u>dirrection</u>
    ⓑ under her <u>direction</u>   ⓓ in need of <u>directon</u>

5. ⓐ a greedy <u>emporor</u>   ⓒ the kingdom's <u>empererr</u>
    ⓑ a fair <u>empirer</u>   ⓓ the ruling <u>emperor</u>

6. ⓐ her nephew's <u>polightness</u>   ⓒ showing <u>politeness</u>
    ⓑ treat with <u>polliteness</u>   ⓓ spoke with <u>politteness</u>

7. ⓐ increased <u>population</u>   ⓒ the total <u>poppulation</u>
    ⓑ survey the <u>poplation</u>   ⓓ the town's <u>popullation</u>

8. ⓐ the <u>slighest</u> breeze   ⓒ the <u>slaghtist</u> change
    ⓑ the <u>slitest</u> movement   ⓓ the <u>slightest</u> noise

9. ⓐ <u>sherpen</u> this blade   ⓒ to <u>sharppen</u> pencils
    ⓑ to <u>sharpen</u> a knive   ⓓ <u>sharrpen</u> an ax

10. ⓐ take <u>attendance</u>   ⓒ <u>atendance</u> chart
    ⓑ daily <u>attendence</u>   ⓓ <u>atendence</u> records

11. ⓐ a longtime <u>emploee</u>   ⓒ a trusted <u>employee</u>
    ⓑ <u>imployee</u> of a company   ⓓ an admired <u>employe</u>

12. ⓐ <u>comfortble</u> sleeping bag   ⓒ the <u>comftorble</u> shoes
    ⓑ <u>comfortible</u> chair   ⓓ <u>comfortable</u> clothing

Name _____

Review Test (Side B)

Lesson 30

Read each set of phrases. Fill in the circle next to the phrase with an underlined word that is spelled correctly.

13.   ⓐ a famous novalist   © the retired novalist
      ⓑ my favorite novellist   ⓓ a mystery novelist

14.   ⓐ share the excitement   © cause of the exsitement
      ⓑ the crowd's exitement   ⓓ in all the exsitment

15.   ⓐ a rugged mountainneer   © a young mountainaer
      ⓑ the brave mountaineer   ⓓ the confident mountainere

16.   ⓐ to lunge foreward   © couldn't go forewerd
      ⓑ looking forwad to it   ⓓ slowly moving forward

17.   ⓐ peaceful and calm   © a peacefull day
      ⓑ a peacful agreement   ⓓ peaseful setting

18.   ⓐ get the repelant   © some insect repellent
      ⓑ a repellante idea   ⓓ the repelant spray

19.   ⓐ dapendable reference book   © dependable babysitter
      ⓑ dependible workers   ⓓ dapendible friend

20.   ⓐ see you afterward   © takes place aftorward
      ⓑ will follow afterword   ⓓ ate dinner afterwerd

21.   ⓐ a factory inspeckter   © the experienced inspecter
      ⓑ a careful inspectur   ⓓ the house inspector

22.   ⓐ reckonize my work   © recagnize the house
      ⓑ difficult to recognise   ⓓ recognize his voice

23.   ⓐ camera equipmant   © their soccer equiptment
      ⓑ my football equipment   ⓓ forgot her equippment

24.   ⓐ be very salective   © not selective enough
      ⓑ have selecktive tastes   ⓓ the sellective consumer

25.   ⓐ an abundant feast   © abundent resources
      ⓑ an abundaent harvest   ⓓ abundante good humor

Take It Home 5

Your child has learned to spell many new words and would like to share them with you and your family. Here are some activities for reviewing the words in lessons 25–29.

Paging All Words!

How many spelling words can you find in newspapers and magazines? Have your child circle the words, cut out the pages on which they appear, and share them at school.

Lesson 25

1. busiest
2. cartoonist
3. counselor
4. director
5. drearier
6. emperor
7. greater
8. hungrier
9. inspector
10. interpreter
11. louder
12. novelist
13. prisoner
14. scariest
15. scientist
16. slightest
17. sweeper
18. tourist
19. vocalist
20. warrior

Lesson 26

1. absentee
2. abundant
3. accountant
4. applicant
5. assistant
6. competent
7. dominant
8. employee
9. engineer
10. excellent
11. mountaineer
12. participant
13. payee
14. pleasant
15. puppeteer
16. reliant
17. repellent
18 resident
19. violent
20. volunteer

Lesson 27

1. afterward
2. alphabetize
3. backward
4. cheerful
5. darken
6. delightful
7. forward
8. friendliness
9. loudness
10. memorize
11. peaceful
12. plentiful
13. politeness
14. recognize
15. shameful
16. sharpen
17. shyness
18. tighten
19. wilderness
20. wonderful

Lesson 28

1. agreeable
2. championship
3. comfortable
4. dependable
5. durable
6. equipment
7. excitement
8. falsehood
9. leadership
10. likelihood
11. membership
12. motherhood
13. neighborhood
14. ownership
15. possible
16. profitable
17. sensible
18. statement
19. terrible
20. visible

Lesson 29

1. allowance
2. attendance
3. captive
4. confidence
5. direction
6. election
7. equality
8. humanity
9. humidity
10. imitation
11. importance
12. independence
13. massive
14. objection
15. opinion
16. originality
17. population
18. protection
19. selective
20. vacation

What's My Line?

Can you complete the building directory shown below? With your child, fill in the directory using the spelling words in the box.

interpreter	mountaineer	puppeteer	counselor
novelist	vocalist	inspector	director
scientist	accountant	cartoonist	engineer

I. Wright, _____novelist_____ Room 428

Sgt. Luke Clue, _____ Room 834

Punch N. Judy, _____ Room 901

Dr. I. N. Vent, _____ Room 681

Num Burr, _____ Room 723

Hugh Morous, _____ Room 445

Upton Hill, _____ Room 333

Movie Mann, _____ Room 523

R.R. Track, _____ Room 991

Minnie Languages, _____ Room 345

Lis N. Ur, _____ Room 401

Ima Singer, _____ Room 783

Objective
To spell words in which the final consonant is doubled, or the final _e_ is dropped, before a suffix is added

Correlated Phonics Lessons
MCP Phonics, Level E, Lessons 62–63

Spelling Words in Action   Page 125

In "The Race to the North Pole," students learn about the controversies over the discovery of the North Pole. After reading, ask students how an important discovery might be proved or disproved today.

Encourage students to look back at the boldfaced words. Ask volunteers to say each word and tell how the base word changed when the suffix was added.

Warm-Up Test
1. Has Joyce **shredded** the lettuce for the salad?
2. We had **planned** to go skating this afternoon.
3. She **pledged** to contribute money to the fund.
4. Brandon woke up with a **throbbing** headache.
5. The child played with a **spinning** top.
6. José was **hoping** to make some new friends.
7. Kathy **decided** that it was a good plan.
8. That's the **strangest** creature I've ever seen!
9. He is **shipping** the furniture by truck.
10. Is that a **usable** computer or is it damaged?
11. These old plates are very **valuable**.
12. Do you find this fragrance **pleasing**?
13. Dad is **scraping** the old wallpaper off the wall.
14. His bicycle tires **skidded** on the wet pavement.
15. Joan has a vivid **imagination**.
16. She will be **introducing** us to her new friend.
17. The librarian **disapproved** of the noise.
18. Did James find the insult **unforgivable**?
19. Tom **persuaded** us to help him paint the fence.
20. What an **amazing** robot Kenji built!

Spelling Practice   Pages 126–127

Introduce the spelling rule and have students read the **list words** aloud. Encourage students to look back at their **Warm-Up Tests** and apply the spelling rule to any misspelled words.

As students work through the **Spelling Practice** exercises, remind them to look back at their **list words** or in their dictionaries if they need help.

 See Comparing/Contrasting, page 15

98

Spelling Words in Action

Who really discovered the North Pole?

The Race to the North Pole

In September 1909, an American doctor and explorer named Frederick Cook made an **amazing** announcement. He said that in 1908, he had discovered the North Pole! Bad weather had prevented him from returning any earlier. There was just one problem. A few days later, explorer Robert E. Peary returned from the Arctic and said _he_ had discovered the North Pole in April 1909.

The North Pole had long captured the world's **imagination**. Peary had been **hoping** to find it on two previous trips that he had **planned**. However, the trip to the far north by ship and dogsled was a very difficult one.

A bitter argument arose. Photographs, diaries, and records of navigation methods were the only proof available. Eventually, people became **persuaded** that Cook never reached the pole. But had Peary reached his goal? Some said yes and some said no.

In 1989, the National Geographic Society **pledged** to settle the question. They looked at every **usable** clue, even analyzing the shadows cast by the people in Peary's photos. They **decided** that the pictures were taken "very close" to the pole—within about five miles. The news was **pleasing** to supporters of Peary. The argument has been settled—unless modern science invents even more **valuable** ways to unlock the secrets of the past.

Robert E. Peary

Frederick Cook

Look back at the boldfaced words in the selection. Find the base word in each boldfaced word. What happened to the base word when the suffixes were added?

125

Spelling Practice

TIP
Some short-vowel words end in a single consonant. If you add a suffix or ending beginning with a vowel to them, first double the final consonant:
spin + **ing** = spinning;
shred + **ed** = shredded.
Some words end in a silent _e_. If you add a suffix or ending beginning with a vowel to them, first drop the silent _e_: imagine + **ation** = imagination.

LIST WORDS
1. shredded
2. planned
3. pledged
4. throbbing
5. spinning
6. hoping
7. decided
8. strangest
9. shipping
10. usable
11. valuable
12. pleasing
13. scraping
14. skidded
15. imagination
16. introducing
17. disapproved
18. unforgivable
19. persuaded
20. amazing

Adding Suffixes, Endings, and Prefixes

Add a suffix or ending, or a prefix and a suffix or ending, to each word given to make a **list word**.

1. amaze amazing	2. value valuable
3. strange strangest	4. skid skidded
5. forgive unforgivable	6. plan planned
7. approve disapproved	8. ship shipping
9. decide decided	10. hope hoping
11. imagine imagination	12. throb throbbing
13. introduce introducing	14. spin spinning
15. persuade persuaded	16. shred shredded
17. please pleasing	18. scrape scraping
19. use usable	20. pledge pledged

Replace the Words

Find the **list word** that best replaces the underlined word or words in each sentence. Write the **list word** on the line.

1. The company plans on sending its merchandise overseas. _shipping_
2. The car slipped on the snowy road. _skidded_
3. My teacher did not accept my project choice. _disapproved_
4. The witness promised to be honest when answering questions. _pledged_
5. My friends convinced me to try mountain-bike riding. _persuaded_
6. I saw an astonishing movie on television last night. _amazing_
7. My friend wore the weirdest costume for Halloween. _strangest_
8. I wonder if the old coin I found is worth a lot. _valuable_
9. I was anticipating that the turn-out for the show would be good. _hoping_
10. Artists are known for their creativity. _imagination_
11. Thank you for presenting us to our new neighbors. _introducing_
12. Handing in the assignment a month late is inexcusable. _unforgivable_

Rhyming Words

Fill in the blank with the **list word** that makes sense in the sentence and rhymes with the underlined word.

1. As the roller coaster was weaving and bobbing, I could feel my head _throbbing_.
2. We went to hear the band, just as we had _planned_.
3. The hole was gaping where the dog had been _scraping_.
4. It will be inexcusable if that train ticket is not _usable_.
5. To hear my cat sneezing was not at all _pleasing_.
6. The skater with the best chance of winning was the one who did the most _spinning_.
7. It was the sight I had dreaded: my homework had been _shredded_.
8. Because the votes were divided, nothing could be _decided_.

Spelling and Writing

Proofreading

The following biography of explorer Matthew Henson has eight mistakes. Use the proofreading marks to correct them. Then, write the **list words** correctly on the lines.

Proofreading Marks
- ◯ spelling mistake
- ˇ add apostrophe

Matthew Hensons life was truly amazeing. He was orphaned at an early age and went to sea when he was twelve. Henson became an expert sailor and mapmaker. By the stranjest coincidence, he met Robert Peary. Impressed with Hensons skills, Peary disided to bring him on his expeditions. On Pearys 1909 trip to the North Pole, it was Henson who made friends with the Inuit guides and learned their ways of survival. Henson, who was an African American, experienced racism during his lifetime, and it took many years for the public to recognize his valable achievements. Today, he is known as one of Americas true heroes.

1. _amazing_
2. _strangest_
3. _decided_
4. _valuable_

Writing an Editorial

Write a short editorial to convince readers that one of your personal heroes deserves a medal. Give examples to support your argument. Use as many **list words** as you can. Remember to proofread your editorial and fix any mistakes.

_____
_____
_____
_____
_____
_____

Spelling Strategy

To help students avoid confusion between *hoping* and *hopping*, write both words on the board and ask students to name and define their base words (*hope* and *hop*). Then, explain that when you add a suffix beginning with a vowel
- to *hope*, you must drop the final *e*
- to *hop*, you must double the final consonant because *hop* is a short-vowel word that ends in a single consonant.

BONUS WORDS
You may want to suggest that students write a sentence for each word, writing the base word instead of the bonus word. Then, have them trade papers with a partner, add the suffixes, and write each bonus word.

Spelling and Writing   *Page 128*

The **Proofreading** exercise will help students prepare to proofread their editorials. As they complete the writing activity, encourage them to brainstorm ideas, write a first draft, revise, and proofread their work. To publish their writing, students may want to trade editorials with a partner.

Writer's Corner Invite students to brainstorm and write a list of the supplies they would bring on a trek to the Pole. Remind them that they must prepare for subzero temperatures and care for their dog team.

Final Test
1. Alice **persuaded** us to vote for Jorge.
2. Use your **imagination** to picture this scene.
3. He **pledged** that he would work harder.
4. My uncle collects **valuable** stamps and coins.
5. Rebecca **decided** to attend the program.
6. The truck **skidded** to a stop on the icy road.
7. Cruelty to animals is an **unforgivable** crime.
8. This car will be **usable** after the engine is fixed.
9. We **planned** to take a trip to Vermont.
10. Are you **hoping** for a high score on the test?
11. This recipe calls for **shredded** coconut.
12. They watched the **spinning** top.
13. The committee **disapproved** of the plan.
14. When will you be **shipping** the trunk?
15. They are **scraping** loose paint off the house.
16. After the exercise, our hearts were **throbbing**.
17. The garden room has a **pleasing** appearance.
18. We will be **introducing** the winner shortly.
19. What **amazing** stunts the acrobats performed!
20. Did she win the prize for the **strangest** costume?

Lesson 32

Adding Suffixes and Endings to Words Ending in y

Objective
To spell words ending in y that have suffixes or endings added

Correlated Phonics Lesson
MCP Phonics, **Level E, Lesson 65**

Spelling Words in Action   *Page 129*

In this selection, students learn some tips on making a good speech. Afterward, ask students what they might do differently the next time they have to make an oral presentation.

Encourage students to look back at the boldfaced words. Ask volunteers to say each word and tell whether or not the base word changed when the suffix or ending was added.

Warm-Up Test

1. Nicole **envied** her friend's success in school.
2. Stop **worrying** about things!
3. The dog was **friendlier** after I patted it.
4. I make sure the players are **obeying** the rules.
5. Our kitchen is the **sunniest** room in the house.
6. I **readily** accepted the invitation.
7. This is the **stickiest** glue I have ever used!
8. Martin heard the bell and **hastily** left the room.
9. This box is **heavier** than the last one I carried.
10. The children raced **noisily** down the hallway.
11. Please make those shelves a little **sturdier**.
12. I eyed the food **greedily**, because I was hungry.
13. That puppy is the **sleepiest** animal.
14. The clown skipped **merrily** through the crowd.
15. Who is **occupying** that seat?
16. Our class is **supplying** the cups for the picnic.
17. A whale is **classified** as a mammal.
18. A **magnifying** glass will help you read this.
19. "Stop that!" Ryan said **angrily**.
20. Birds sang **cheerily** in the treetops.

Spelling Practice   *Pages 130–131*

Introduce the spelling rule and have students read the **list words** aloud. Encourage students to look back at their **Warm-Up Tests** and apply the spelling rule to any misspelled words.

As students work through the **Spelling Practice** exercises, remind them to look back at their **list words** or in their dictionaries if they need help. You may want to point out that a y changed to i is not part of the suffix or ending.

for ESL students. **See Words in Context, page 14**

100

Spelling Words in Action

Why do some speeches capture an audience's attention better than others?

Stand and Deliver

How do you feel about making a speech? Do you approach the task **angrily** or **merrily**? Do you spend the night before **worrying** about what you'll say? Perhaps, like a lot of people, you've **envied** those who seem to make a speech as easily as they talk to a friend. **Obeying** a few helpful rules can help you make great speeches.

A common concern is being heard. Think about the size of the room and practice in it if you can to judge how loudly you need to speak. Speak slowly and clearly, not **hastily**. It's also a good idea to vary your tone of voice. The speeches that can make listeners the **sleepiest** are those in which the speaker has used the same tone throughout! Look over your speech for places where a **friendlier** tone or a more serious one might be appropriate. Think about **magnifying** your voice when you reach the most important parts.

Most importantly, be sure you are **supplying** your audience with news, entertainment, or information about something that matters to them. You're **occupying** their time, so you want them to feel it's worthwhile to listen carefully. If you're like most people, you'll find that the more speeches you give, the easier they become!

Look back at the boldfaced words in the selection. Say the base word for each boldfaced word. What happens to base words that end in y when a suffix is added?

129

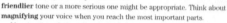

Spelling Practice

TIP

When a final y follows a consonant, change the y to i before adding a suffix or ending, *unless* adding the ending ing.
worry   worried   worrier   worrying

When a final y follows a vowel, just add the suffix or ending.
obey   obeyed   obeying

LIST WORDS

1. envied
2. worrying
3. friendlier
4. obeying
5. sunniest
6. readily
7. stickiest
8. hastily
9. heavier
10. noisily
11. sturdier
12. greedily
13. sleepiest
14. merrily
15. occupying
16. supplying
17. classified
18. magnifying
19. angrily
20. cheerily

Adding Suffixes and Endings

Write each **list word** below its base word. Circle the suffix or ending in each **list word**.

1. greedy	2. angry
greed(ily)	angr(ily)
3. sunny	**4. sturdy**
sunn(iest)	sturd(ier)
5. noisy	**6. ready**
nois(ily)	read(ily)
7. envy	**8. worry**
env(ied)	worry(ing)
9. cheery	**10. supply**
cheer(ily)	supply(ing)
11. sticky	**12. heavy**
stick(iest)	heav(ier)
13. magnify	**14. merry**
magnify(ing)	merr(ily)
15. hasty	**16. obey**
hast(ily)	obey(ing)
17. friendly	**18. classify**
friendl(ier)	classif(ied)
19. sleepy	**20. occupy**
sleep(iest)	occupy(ing)

Missing Words

Write a **list word** to complete each sentence.

1. Job seekers read the _classified_ ads in the newspaper.
2. This plant needs sun, so place it in the _sunniest_ spot.
3. The hungry dog gobbled the food _greedily_.
4. A _magnifying_ glass will allow you to see small objects in more detail.
5. He was in a hurry and wrote the word so _hastily_ that he made a spelling mistake.
6. Alex won the spelling bee by quickly _supplying_ one correct answer after another.
7. Rather than trying to figure out a solution, I spent the day _worrying_ about my problem.
8. Since the bags were _heavier_ than I thought, I needed help carrying them up the stairs.
9. As a political candidate, her past experience as mayor was _envied_ by others.
10. Melted ice cream can make one of the _stickiest_ messes.

Word Building

Add and subtract letters to form **list words**. Write the **list words** on the line.

1. fries – es + end + l + funnier – funn _friendlier_
2. slam – am + keep – k + tie – t + best – be _sleepiest_
3. no + ion – on + silly – l _noisily_
4. mane – me + grace – ace + busily – bus _angrily_
5. me + starry – stay + ill – l + y _merrily_
6. rob – r + hey – h + staring – star _obeying_
7. stare – are + tour – to + dice – ice + flier – fl _sturdier_
8. occupant – pant + spying – sing + hearing – hear _occupying_
9. ache – a + ear – a + messily – mess _cheerily_
10. red – d + had – h + chill – chl + y _readily_

Lesson 32 • Adding Suffixes and Endings to Words Ending in y   131

Spelling and Writing

Proofreading

The following speech has nine mistakes. Use the proofreading marks to correct them. Then, write the misspelled **list words** correctly on the lines.

Proofreading Marks
◯ spelling mistake
≡ capital letter

I envyed my brother's baseball-card collection until I started my own stamp collection. My uncle, who lives in london and travels a lot, is always supplyng me with interesting stamps on the letters he sends. I have classyfied my stamps by country. I can usually peel a stamp off the envelope without tearing it. For the stickyest ones, though, i cut the envelope around the stamp. with a magnifing lens, I can see designs within the pictures on the stamps. I like to learn about each of the people or symbols on stamps. I find my collection occuping a lot of my free time, but it's lots of fun.

1. _envied_
2. _supplying_
3. _classified_
4. _stickiest_
5. _magnifying_
6. _occupying_

Writing a Speech

Think about something you enjoy collecting. Write a short speech to tell people about your collection. Use any **list words** that you can. Remember to proofread your speech and fix any mistakes.

BONUS WORDS

modified
levying
surveying
tardiest
displayed

132   Lesson 32 • Adding Suffixes and Endings to Words Ending in y

---

Spelling Strategy

With a partner, students can take turns saying a **list word** aloud and telling which rule was followed when a suffix or ending was added. You may want to observe students as they work and offer assistance as needed.

BONUS WORDS You may want to suggest that students create a newspaper headline for each bonus word, leaving a blank line where the word belongs. Encourage them to use a dictionary if necessary. Have them trade papers with a partner and fill in the missing words.

Spelling and Writing   **Page 132**

The **Proofreading** exercise will help students prepare to proofread their speeches. As students complete the writing activity, encourage them to brainstorm ideas, write a first draft, revise, and proofread their work. To publish their writing, students may want to deliver their speeches.

Writer's Corner Collect comic strips and mask out the dialogue. Distribute copies to students and ask them to use the characters' body language and facial expressions to create new dialogue. Encourage students to read their strips aloud.

Final Test

1. When he boarded the bus, Raul waved **cheerily**.
2. The dog **greedily** gulped down all the food.
3. Put the plant in your **sunniest** window.
4. They came inside **noisily**, slamming the door.
5. I have always **envied** your ability to sing.
6. This is the **stickiest** mess I've ever cleaned!
7. He's **magnifying** the problem by fretting so much.
8. Before leaving, Sara **hastily** made a sandwich.
9. Everyone's **friendlier** at my new school.
10. The child who was the **sleepiest** went to bed.
11. What made you speak so **angrily** to Ashley?
12. The brown chair is **sturdier** than the black one.
13. Quit **worrying** about tomorrow's race!
14. When she asked for help, I volunteered **readily**.
15. The Parents' Association is **supplying** cookies.
16. This suitcase is **heavier** than it looks.
17. Everyone on the bus was singing **merrily**.
18. Leave your coat on the chair you're **occupying**.
19. Which players are not **obeying** the rules?
20. An apple is **classified** as a fruit.

Lesson 33

Plurals of Words Ending in y

Objective
To spell plurals of words ending in *y*

Correlated Phonics Lesson
MCP Phonics, Level E, Lesson 65

Spelling Words in Action   *Page 133*

In this selection, students find out what life was like for immigrants in the early 1900s. After reading, invite students to share any stories they know or have read about the immigration experience.

Encourage students to look back at the boldfaced words. Ask volunteers to say the words and tell how the endings differ.

Warm-Up Test

1. The Egyptian pyramids have stood for **centuries**.
2. Brandon went to the store to buy **groceries**.
3. Italy and China are **countries** I want to visit.
4. After several **journeys** by land, they went by air.
5. How many **families** participated in the yard sale?
6. The travel **delays** were caused by flooding.
7. Not everyone is born with two **kidneys**.
8. Those duck **decoys** don't look very real.
9. Both **bakeries** sell herbed breads.
10. Many **libraries** lend movies as well as books.
11. The dentist said I have three **cavities**.
12. Hans used the **cranberries** to make juice.
13. What suspenseful **mysteries** these are!
14. Mrs. Cruz schedules the after-school **activities**.
15. In accidents, seat belts reduce **injuries**.
16. Please accept my **apologies** for being late.
17. We honored the **secretaries** for their hard work.
18. Many art **authorities** said the painting was old.
19. How many **victories** has your team won?
20. Every grade had four runners in the **relays**.

Spelling Practice   *Pages 134–135*

Introduce the spelling rules and have students read the **list words** aloud. You may want to point out that *relays* has several meanings. Then encourage students to look back at their **Warm-Up Tests** and apply the spelling rules to any misspelled words.

As students work through the **Spelling Practice** exercises, remind them to look back at their **list words** or in their dictionaries if they need help.

 See Picture Clues, page 15

Spelling Words in Action

Why do people leave their homelands to live in America?

In Search of a Better Life

July 26, 1910
New York, New York

Dear Michael,

I'm writing to let you know that our younger sister, Rose, arrived safely here in New York after her Atlantic crossing. Doesn't it seem as if **centuries** have passed since we last saw her in Ireland?

I must say, our **journeys** to this country were easier than Rose's. She experienced such a fearful storm at sea that she lost her footing on a stairway, experiencing some minor **injuries**. Sleeping quarters were cramped, and the passengers sorely missed fresh **groceries**. When she reached Ellis Island, the **authorities** said there might be a problem with Rose's **kidneys**, and they kept her for a full week. Finally they released her into my care.

Rose is enjoying many small **victories** as she begins to learn her way around New York. She has already visited some of the city's **libraries** and **bakeries**. She has also applied for a position as a cook with several **families** who seem quite kind. You will be glad to know that she embraces her new country's customs, just as we do.

Your loving brother,
John

Look back at the boldfaced words in the selection. How are the words alike? What do you notice about their spellings?

133

↓

 TIP

Follow these rules to write the plural form of words ending in *y*:
• If the letter before the **y** is a consonant, change the y to i and add **es**, as in <u>victories</u>.
• If the letter before the **y** is a vowel, just add s, as in <u>relays</u>.

LIST WORDS

1. centuries
2. groceries
3. countries
4. journeys
5. families
6. delays
7. kidneys
8. decoys
9. bakeries
10. libraries
11. cavities
12. cranberries
13. mysteries
14. activities
15. injuries
16. apologies
17. secretaries
18. authorities
19. victories
20. relays

Spelling Practice

Writing the Plural Form of Words

Write each **list word** below its singular form.

1. victory	2. injury
victories	injuries
3. apology	4. journey
apologies	journeys
5. country	6. delay
countries	delays
7. grocery	8. authority
groceries	authorities
9. mystery	10. activity
mysteries	activities
11. relay	12. decoy
relays	decoys
13. century	14. secretary
centuries	secretaries
15. family	16. kidney
families	kidneys
17. library	18. cranberry
libraries	cranberries
19. cavity	20. bakery
cavities	bakeries

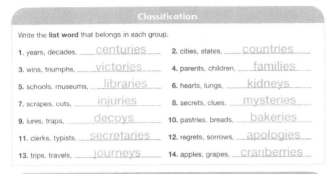

Classification

Write the **list word** that belongs in each group.

1. years, decades, __centuries__
2. cities, states, __countries__
3. wins, triumphs, __victories__
4. parents, children, __families__
5. schools, museums, __libraries__
6. hearts, lungs, __kidneys__
7. scrapes, cuts, __injuries__
8. secrets, clues, __mysteries__
9. lures, traps, __decoys__
10. pastries, breads, __bakeries__
11. clerks, typists, __secretaries__
12. regrets, sorrows, __apologies__
13. trips, travels, __journeys__
14. apples, grapes, __cranberries__

Definitions

Write a **list word** to match each definition clue. Then, use the numbered letters to solve the riddle. Copy each numbered letter on the line with the same number.

1. long waits d e l a y s
            7
2. decay in teeth c a v i t i e s
               3
3. actions, movements a c t i v i t i e s
                    4
4. groups of related people f a m i l i e s
             6
5. Sorry! Sorry! Sorry! a p o l o g i e s
           5   10
6. those who enforce laws a u t h o r i t i e s
             9 11 2
7. kinds of races r e l a y s
         1
8. food and supplies g r o c e r i e s
           8

Riddle: What do you need before you can own a dozen bakeries?

Answer: L o t s   o f   d o u g h
    1 2 3 4   5 6   7 8 9 10 11

Lesson 33 • Plurals of Words Ending in y   135

Spelling and Writing

Proofreading

The following article has eleven mistakes. Use the proofreading marks to correct them. Then, write the misspelled **list words** correctly on the lines.

Proofreading Marks
⬭ spelling mistake
≡ capital letter
∧ add something

    Ellis Island opened as an immigration center on january 1, 1892. On its first day, it welcomed over 2000 people after their difficult journys from faraway contries. A fifteen-year-old irish girl named Annie Moore was the first official immigrant. There were special activites to celebrate the opening of Ellis island. Annie was given a ten-dollar gold piece by the authorites of the center. Examinations for injuries and illnesses caused a few more delayes. Finally, Annie and her brothers joined their parents.

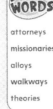

1. __journeys__
2. __countries__
3. __activities__
4. __authorities__
5. __injuries__
6. __delays__

Writing a Letter

Imagine you are traveling on a ship as an immigrant to America. Write a letter to a friend at home about your thoughts and hopes on the journey. Try to use as many **list words** as you can. Remember to proofread your letter and fix any mistakes.

_____
_____
_____
_____
_____
_____
_____

BONUS WORDS

attorneys
missionaries
alloys
walkways
theories

Spelling Strategy

Write *consonant + y* on one side of the board and *vowel + y* on the other. Say the singular of each **list word** and have a volunteer
- point to the side of the board that applies to the last two letters in the word
- spell the plural of the word aloud, and write the plural form on the correct side.

BONUS WORDS
You may want to suggest that students write a sentence for each bonus word, then trade papers with a partner. Have them take turns telling which spelling rule was used to form the plural words.

Spelling and Writing   *Page 136*

The **Proofreading** exercise will help students prepare to proofread their letters. As students complete the writing activity, encourage them to brainstorm ideas, write a first draft, revise, and proofread their work. To publish their writing, students may want to create a display called "Many Voices, Many Journeys."

Writer's Corner Invite students to research Ellis Island in the library or on the Internet (the Ellis Island Museum's Web site can be found at http://www.ellisisland.com). Suggest that they use the information they have learned to write a short poem from the viewpoint of an immigrant arriving at Ellis Island.

Final Test

1. Our team has had three **victories** this season.
2. My friend accepted my **apologies**.
3. The students' **families** came to an open house.
4. I helped Mrs. Adams carry her **groceries** inside.
5. I like to read **mysteries** and westerns.
6. The runners in the **relays** must cooperate.
7. How many **centuries** ago was this house built?
8. I collect stamps from many **countries**.
9. My brother's college has two **libraries**.
10. The dentist said I had no **cavities** this time.
11. Luckily, the player's **injuries** were not serious.
12. Do migrating birds make long **journeys**?
13. Because of two **delays**, our bus was late.
14. The speakers are **authorities** on bicycle races.
15. Our school offers many afternoon **activities**.
16. In this office, the **secretaries** leave at 4:00.
17. Who carved those duck **decoys**?
18. **Kidneys** are very complicated organs.
19. What delicious **cranberries** these are!
20. Both of the **bakeries** sell Italian rolls.

Objective
To spell irregular plural nouns

 Correlated Phonics Lessons
MCP Phonics, Level E, Lessons 67–69

Spelling Words in Action   *Page 137*

In "Adaptable Animals," students learn fascinating facts about some interesting animals. Invite students to share additional information they may know about animals that adapt to a harsh climate.

Encourage students to look back at the boldfaced words. Ask volunteers to say each word and compare the singular and plural spellings.

Warm-Up Test

1. We saw three **moose** by the stream.
2. I think rainbow **trout** are beautiful fish.
3. Some **salmon** can weigh up to eighty pounds.
4. How many **wolves** did she count in the pack?
5. Two little **calves** grazed in the meadow.
6. Please cut the apple into equal **halves**.
7. These are my favorite **scarves**.
8. Grandma steamed the carrots and **broccoli**.
9. What fantastic **spaghetti** Houng makes!
10. Most cars have **radios** in them.
11. We'll put two big **tomatoes** in the salad.
12. The **sheriffs** led the parade on horseback.
13. The **cuffs** on this old shirt are badly frayed.
14. Will you help me mash the **potatoes**?
15. Your **beliefs** may be different from mine.
16. The **chiefs** were present at the council meeting.
17. How many **volcanoes** erupted on the island?
18. There are many **species** of mammals.
19. The snow **igloos** kept out the wind and cold.
20. **Tornadoes** are extremely dangerous storms.

Spelling Practice   *Pages 138–139*

Introduce the spelling rule and have students read the **list words** aloud. Encourage students to look back at their **Warm-Up Tests** and apply the spelling rule to any misspelled words.

.As students work through the **Spelling Practice** exercises, remind them to look back at their **list words** or in their dictionaries if they need help.

 **See Student Dictation, page 14**

104

Spelling Words in Action

How do animals adapt to a harsh climate?

Adaptable Animals

Around the world, animals can be found living in extreme climates. How do they adapt?

The gila monster is an animal that has adapted well to desert life. The gila monster can store fat in its tail and abdomen to use in times when food is scarce. The animal is one of only two **species** of lizards that are venomous.

The caribou is a good example of an Arctic survivor. Like **moose** and elks, it is a member of the deer family. The caribou has no **scarves** or mittens to protect it from the bitter cold, but it does have a long coat! Dense hairs trap air and help to keep the caribou warm. Because both humans and **wolves** hunt caribou, its newborn **calves** must be able to keep up with the herd. The calves can run soon after birth.

A tide pool is another extreme place for animals to live. The periwinkle protects itself from the waves with its hard, round shell. Mussels protect themselves by living very close to one another. A mussel's shell has two **halves**, like a clam's.

There is one threat that some animals cannot adapt to: humans. The use of river water for irrigation, for instance, has threatened some types of **salmon** and **trout**. However, people's **beliefs** can also help animals. In one part of Florida, for example, **sheriffs** patrol the waters to keep speedboats away from slow-moving manatees.

Look back at the boldfaced words in the selection. Say the singular form of each plural word. What do you notice about the spellings of some plural forms of words?

137

TIP
Some singular nouns, like <u>moose</u>, do not change when they become plurals. When singular nouns end in **f** or **fe**, usually change the **f** or **fe** to **v** and add **es**: <u>calf</u> → <u>calves</u>. Some words are exceptions to this rule, such as <u>chiefs</u>. Words that end in **ff** also form the plural by adding **s**: <u>cuff</u> → <u>cuffs</u>. When singular nouns end in **o**, add **s** to form the plural: <u>radio</u> → <u>radios</u>. Some nouns that end in **o** take **es** to form the plural: <u>potato</u> → <u>potatoes</u>.

LIST WORDS

1. *moose*
2. *trout*
3. *salmon*
4. *wolves*
5. *calves*
6. *halves*
7. *scarves*
8. *broccoli*
9. *spaghetti*
10. *radios*
11. *tomatoes*
12. *sheriffs*
13. *cuffs*
14. *potatoes*
15. *beliefs*
16. *chiefs*
17. *volcanoes*
18. *species*
19. *igloos*
20. *tornadoes*

Spelling Practice

Writing the Plural Form of Words

Write each **list word** below its singular form.

1. volcano — volcanoes
2. cuff — cuffs
3. spaghetti — spaghetti
4. trout — trout
5. tomato — tomatoes
6. calf — calves
7. tornado — tornadoes
8. chief — chiefs
9. broccoli — broccoli
10. radio — radios
11. sheriff — sheriffs
12. igloo — igloos
13. potato — potatoes
14. half — halves
15. salmon — salmon
16. wolf — wolves
17. belief — beliefs
18. species — species
19. scarf — scarves
20. moose — moose

138   Lesson 34 • Irregular Plurals

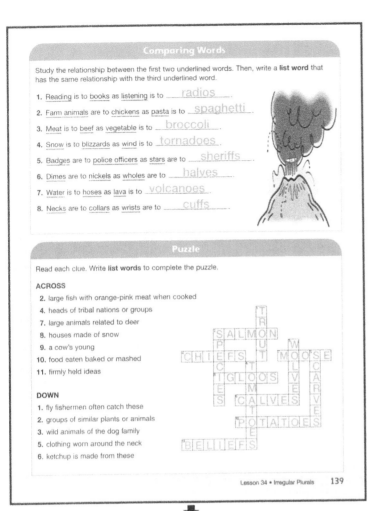

Comparing Words

Study the relationship between the first two underlined words. Then, write a **list word** that has the same relationship with the third underlined word.

1. Reading is to books as listening is to ___radios___.
2. Farm animals are to chickens as pasta is to ___spaghetti___.
3. Meat is to beef as vegetable is to ___broccoli___.
4. Snow is to blizzards as wind is to ___tornadoes___.
5. Badges are to police officers as stars are to ___sheriffs___.
6. Dimes are to nickels as wholes are to ___halves___.
7. Water is to hoses as lava is to ___volcanoes___.
8. Necks are to collars as wrists are to ___cuffs___.

Puzzle

Read each clue. Write **list words** to complete the puzzle.

ACROSS
2. large fish with orange-pink meat when cooked
4. heads of tribal nations or groups
7. large animals related to deer
8. houses made of snow
9. a cow's young
10. food eaten baked or mashed
11. firmly held ideas

DOWN
1. fly fishermen often catch these
2. groups of similar plants or animals
3. wild animals of the dog family
5. clothing worn around the neck
6. ketchup is made from these

Crossword answers: SALMON, CHIEFS, MOOSE, IGLOOS, CALVES, POTATOES, BELIEFS (with TROUT, SPECIES, WOLVES, SCARVES, TOMATOES)

Lesson 34 • Irregular Plurals   139

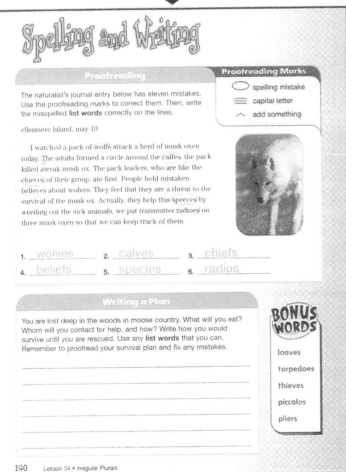

Spelling and Writing

Proofreading

The naturalist's journal entry below has eleven mistakes. Use the proofreading marks to correct them. Then, write the misspelled **list words** correctly on the lines.

Proofreading Marks
◯ spelling mistake
≡ capital letter
⌃ add something

ellesmere Island, may 19

   I watched a pack of wolfs attack a herd of musk oxen today. The adults formed a circle around the calfes, the pack killed a weak musk ox. The pack leaders, who are like the chieves of their group, ate first. People hold mistaken believes about wolves. They feel that they are a threat to the survival of the musk ox. Actually, they help this speeces by weeding out the sick animals. we put transmitter radioes on three musk oxen so that we can keep track of them.

1. ___wolves___ 2. ___calves___ 3. ___chiefs___
4. ___beliefs___ 5. ___species___ 6. ___radios___

Writing a Plan

You are lost deep in the woods in moose country. What will you eat? Whom will you contact for help, and how? Write how you would survive until you are rescued. Use any **list words** that you can. Remember to proofread your survival plan and fix any mistakes.

BONUS WORDS
loaves
torpedoes
thieves
piccolos
pliers

Spelling Strategy

Write each of these pairs of words on the board at the top of a column: *fish* (*fish*), *elf* (*elves*), *roof* (*roofs*), *auto* (*autos*), *mosquito* (*mosquitoes*). For each pair, ask a volunteer to name the singular and plural forms of a **list word** that follows the same rule to form its plural. Have the volunteer write both forms of the word in the correct column.

BONUS WORDS You may want to suggest that students create a simple sketch for each bonus word. Then, have them trade drawings with a partner and try to write the word that matches each picture clue.

Spelling and Writing   *Page 140*

The **Proofreading** exercise will help students prepare to proofread their plans. As students complete the writing activity, encourage them to brainstorm ideas, write a first draft, revise, and proofread their work. To publish their writing, students may want to create a pamphlet on wilderness survival.

Writer's Corner Students might enjoy reading about other "adaptable animals" in books such as *Eyewitness: Natural World* by Steve Parker. Encourage them to write a short story about their favorite wild animal and to share it with the class.

Final Test
1. In the Old West, **sheriffs** wore big silver stars.
2. Do **tornadoes** threaten your state?
3. The **chiefs** of all the tribes agreed to cooperate.
4. **Wolves** are often villains in folk tales.
5. We grew a row of twelve **broccoli** plants.
6. I heard the far-off calls of a herd of **moose**.
7. Let's have **spaghetti** for dinner tonight.
8. The little **calves** huddled next to their mothers.
9. Are there many **volcanoes** in the United States?
10. Roll up the **cuffs** of your sleeves.
11. We caught five big **salmon** yesterday.
12. What beautiful silk **scarves** these are!
13. We made two model **igloos** out of ice cubes.
14. Our **beliefs** affect our behavior.
15. Aunt Sue picked fresh **tomatoes**.
16. Do both of the ships have ship-to-shore **radios**?
17. Mother cut the large cantaloupe into **halves**.
18. Many **trout** have been caught in this stream.
19. The plant kingdom includes many **species**.
20. I peeled the **potatoes** for the fish chowder.

Challenging Words

Objective
To spell words that do not follow usual spelling rules

Spelling Words in Action   *Page 141*

Students may enjoy reading about the world's most famous portrait. Afterward, ask students what they would like their own portrait to look like if they had it painted.

Encourage students to look back at the boldfaced words. Ask volunteers to say each word and tell why it might be difficult to spell.

Warm-Up Test
1. The recipe calls for the **yolk** of one egg.
2. That new student looks very **familiar** to me.
3. Do not **separate** the pages of the newspaper.
4. The noises coming from that old house are **weird**!
5. Juanita's birthday is in **February**.
6. Please **choose** three items from the first **column**.
7. Did they have any **surprises** for you at the party?
8. At dawn, the sailors discovered the **islands**.
9. David found two **misspelled** words.
10. Did you buy the tickets to the **ballet**?
11. Some colors never seem to go out of **fashion**.
12. Your **stomach** feels full after a big meal.
13. I **recommend** Mrs. Kopek for the job.
14. The man who is speaking is a **famous** actor.
15. My ancestors crossed the **prairie** by wagon.
16. Follow the rules or **forfeit** the prize.
17. We saw the **wisdom** in the teacher's decision.
18. Lola was the first one **chosen** for the team.
19. What spectacular **weather** we're having today!
20. Make sure you use correct **punctuation**.

Spelling Practice   *Pages 142–143*

Introduce the information in the Tip box and have students read the **list words** aloud. After each word, invite students to discuss what is odd or difficult about its spelling.

As students work through the **Spelling Practice** exercises, remind them to look back at their **list words** or in their dictionaries if they need help.

 See Charades/Pantomime, page 15

106

Right column (Student page)

Challenging Words   Lesson 35

Spelling Words in Action

Why is the *Mona Lisa* the world's most famous portrait?

Lisa's Smile

In the 1500s, a woman named Lisa del Giocondo lived in Florence, Italy. Today, this woman's face is **familiar** the world over because of a portrait painted by the **famous** artist Leonardo da Vinci. He called his painting *La Gioconda*, a name that is often **misspelled**. We know it as the *Mona Lisa*.

The *Mona Lisa* is probably the best-known painting in the world. What makes it so special? Most people agree that it's Lisa's mysterious smile. Leonardo used a technique that shaded the corners of his subject's mouth and eyes. The woman seems to change before the viewer's eyes.

There are **weird** facts about this portrait. Until Leonardo did this work, no artist had **chosen** to portray a subject from the head down to the **stomach**. The **fashion** was to show only a subject's head. The painting was also stolen in 1911. Luckily, it was found again.

With the **wisdom** of modern technology, a scientist used a computer to put a self-portrait of Leonardo over Lisa's face. She found some **surprises**. The two **separate** portraits almost seem to merge into one face. This may be another clue to the puzzle of *La Gioconda*.

Look back at the boldfaced words in the selection. Say the words. Do you notice anything unusual about their spellings?

141

Spelling Practice

TIP
Some words don't follow the usual spelling rules. The best way to become familiar with these unexpected spellings is to practice using them as often as you can.
yolk   stomach   forfeit

LIST WORDS
1. yolk
2. familiar
3. separate
4. weird
5. February
6. column
7. surprises
8. islands
9. misspelled
10. ballet
11. fashion
12. stomach
13. recommend
14. famous
15. prairie
16. forfeit
17. wisdom
18. chosen
19. weather
20. punctuation

Words with Unexpected Spellings

Write each **list word** below the unexpected spelling it contains.

1. fei **forfeit**	2. ose **chosen**
3. liar **familiar**	4. par **separate**
5. rpr **surprises**	6. umn **column**
7. ach **stomach**	8. wis **wisdom**
9. wea **weather**	10. let **ballet**
11. wei **weird**	12. rair **prairie**
13. punc **punctuation**	14. isl **islands**
15. lk **yolk**	16. hion **fashion**
17. mous **famous**	18. mmen **recommend**
19. sspe **misspelled**	20. bru **February**

142   Lesson 35 • Challenging Words

Complete the Paragraph

Write the **list word** that best completes each sentence of the paragraph.

Megan loved to dance and had taken ___ballet___ lessons for four years. She was willing to work hard at it, even to ___forfeit___ time with friends. Daily practice kept the muscles in her legs, arms, back, and ___stomach___ strong and limber. Megan was ___familiar___ with all the famous ballets. Her favorite was "Coppélia," though she ___misspelled___ the title the first time she wrote it down. Her ballet school had a performance scheduled for ___February___. Megan hoped to be ___chosen___ for a lead role. She even hoped to be a ___famous___ ballerina some day. Megan would ___recommend___ ballet lessons for any person who enjoyed dance and was willing to work hard.

Word Search

Find these eleven **list words** in the puzzle below: column, fashion, islands, prairie, punctuation, separate, surprises, weird, weather, wisdom, yolk. The words can appear forward or backward, horizontally, vertically, or diagonally. Then, write the **list words** on the lines.

```
Z A D O S E P A R A T E
H Q N M U L O C L N F T
R M E I R S D U W O X J
L S A K P R A I R I E B
K N L C R M N S I T P I
M O D S I W C L B A S R
Y I X M S E R A J U B S
F H Q D E A D N N T O R
E S E L S T A D I C G L
G A P Q W H C S L N T U
L F M F X E E K I U O H
Z C W E I R D S V P J D
```

1. separate
2. weather
3. column
4. islands
5. prairie
6. wisdom
7. yolk
8. surprises
9. punctuation
10. fashion
11. weird

Proofreading

The following biography has ten mistakes. Use the proofreading marks to fix the mistakes. Then, write the misspelled **list words** correctly on the lines.

Proofreading Marks
- ◯ spelling mistake
- ⊙ add period
- ⤶ take out something

Leonardo da Vinci (1452–1519) created several notebooks filled with with suprizes. At first glance, the writing looks wierd That's because Leonardo had had chozen to write backward. His famus books can only be read with a mirror. Many of the drawings in the notebooks will look familiar to us today. They include sketches of a parachute and a simple helicopter. Despite his great wizdum, his designs for flying machines are not workable. They all have flapping wings that require too much effort to be effective.

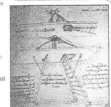

1. surprises
2. weird
3. chosen
4. famous
5. familiar
6. wisdom

Writing a Dialogue

Write a dialogue that might have taken place between Lisa del Giocondo and Leonardo da Vinci. Did they know that someday they would both be <u>famous</u>? Use any **list words** that you can. Remember to proofread your dialogue and fix any mistakes.

_____
_____
_____
_____
_____

BONUS WORDS

eerie

seize

orchid

conscience

basically

Spelling Strategy

Have students get together with a partner and take turns calling out the **list words**. The partner who is listening repeats each word, spells it aloud, and then writes it. Have students check the spellings of the words and rewrite any that are incorrect. Suggest that they note the errors they made in the misspelled words.

BONUS WORDS
You may want to suggest that students create an exclamatory sentence using each bonus word, then erase a few letters of each word. Have them trade sentences with a partner and fill in the missing letters.

Spelling and Writing   Page 144

The **Proofreading** exercise will help students prepare to proofread their dialogues. As students complete the writing activity, encourage them to brainstorm ideas, write a first draft, revise, and proofread their work. To publish their writing, students may want to
- role-play their dialogues
- use their dialogues to create a cartoon strip.

Writer's Corner You might want to photocopy a brochure from a local museum or an art gallery and give a copy to each student. Invite students to write a paragraph telling what they would be most interested in seeing at the museum or gallery.

Final Test

1. Even in cold **weather**, Peter is always warm.
2. They will **forfeit** the game.
3. **Separate** each English muffin.
4. Ariel's birthday was filled with happy **surprises**.
5. The old shirt won't button over his **stomach**.
6. That **weird** noise came from a screech owl.
7. A sentence ends with a **punctuation** mark.
8. Stir the egg **yolk** in that bowl.
9. Charlie Chaplin was a **famous** comedian.
10. Does **February** seem colder this year?
11. Who was **chosen** to represent our class?
12. The old house looked **familiar**.
13. Add up all the numbers in the first **column**.
14. The king was known for his great **wisdom**.
15. What a wonderful **ballet** we saw!
16. A **prairie** dog is a rodent.
17. There are many small **islands** off the coast.
18. Once, powdered wigs were the **fashion**.
19. The librarian can **recommend** books.
20. My name is rarely **misspelled**.

Objectives
To review spelling rules for doubling final consonants, adding suffixes and endings to words that end with *e*; adding suffixes and endings to words ending in *y*; plurals of words ending in *y*; irregular plurals; and to review challenging words

Check Your Spelling Notebook   *Pages 145–148*

Based on your observations, note which words are giving students the most difficulty and offer assistance for spelling them correctly. Here are some frequently misspelled words to watch for: *persuaded, libraries, sheriffs, forfeit, recommend, weird,* and *weather.*

To give students extra help and practice in taking standardized tests, you may want to have them take the **Review Test** for this lesson on pages 110–111. After scoring the tests, return them to students so that they can record their misspelled words in their spelling notebooks.

After practicing their troublesome words, students can work through the exercises for lessons 31–35 and the cumulative review, **Show What You Know**. Before they begin each exercise, you may want to go over the spelling rule.

Take It Home

Suggest that students look for **list words** from lessons 31–35 on labels and signs they see in stores. Students can also use **Take It Home** Master 6 on pages 112–113 to help them do the activity. (A complete list of the spelling words is included on page 112 of the **Take It Home** Master.) Encourage students to bring their lists to class to compare them with those of their classmates.

In lessons 31 through 35, you learned how to add suffixes and endings to words that end with a single vowel and consonant, and words that end in e or y. You also learned how plurals are formed and how to spell words with unexpected spellings.

Check Your Spelling Notebook

Look at the words in your spelling notebook. Which words for lessons 31 through 35 did you have the most trouble with? Write them here.

_____

_____

Practice writing your troublesome words with a partner. Underline the letters that change when adding a suffix or ending or when forming the plural of the word.

Lesson 31

TIP Before adding a suffix or ending to a word, sometimes you need to double the final consonant, as in <u>shredded</u>, or drop the final e, as in <u>amazing</u>.

List Words
planned
spinning
hoping
shredded
decided
strangest
usable
valuable
skidded
pleasing
imagination
amazing

Add a suffix or ending to each base word to form a **list word**. Write the word on the line. Not all the words will be used.

1. decide + ed ___decided___
2. plan + ed ___planned___
3. skid + ed ___skidded___
4. imagine + ation ___imagination___
5. please + ing ___pleasing___
6. value + able ___valuable___
7. strange + est ___strangest___
8. hope + ing ___hoping___
9. use + able ___usable___
10. spin + ing ___spinning___

145

Lesson 32

TIP Before adding a suffix or ending to a word that ends in y, sometimes you need to change the y to i, as in <u>stickiest</u>.

List Words
sturdier
cheerily
worrying
envied
stickiest
greedily
hastily
sleepiest
heavier
magnifying
sunniest
noisily

Write a **list word** that is an antonym for the word given. Not all the words will be used.

1. reducing ___magnifying___
2. generously ___greedily___
3. weaker ___sturdier___
4. sadly ___cheerily___
5. slowly ___hastily___
6. lighter ___heavier___
7. quietly ___noisily___
8. most awake ___sleepiest___
9. relaxing ___worrying___
10. cloudiest ___sunniest___

Lesson 33

TIP Use the following rules to make words that end in y plural:
• If a consonant precedes the y, change the y to i and add es, as in <u>centuries</u>.
• If a vowel precedes the y, add s, as in <u>decoys</u>.

List Words
delays
cavities
injuries
victories
decoys
kidneys
cranberries
journeys
apologies
bakeries
mysteries
families

Write a **list word** that matches each clue. Not all the words will be used.

1. wounds; harm done to people ___injuries___
2. groups of related people ___families___
3. trips; excursions ___journeys___
4. the opposite of losses ___victories___
5. areas of decay in teeth ___cavities___
6. places to buy baked goods ___bakeries___
7. pair of major body organs ___kidneys___
8. unexplained things; secrets ___mysteries___
9. postponements ___delays___
10. sour, red berries ___cranberries___

146   Lesson 36 • Review

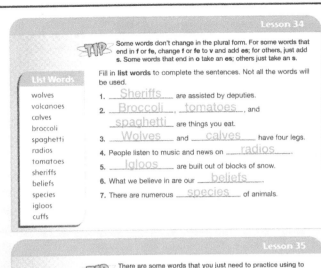

Lesson 34

TIP Some words don't change in the plural form. For some words that end in **f** or **fe**, change **f** or **fe** to **v** and add **es**; for others, just add **s**. Some words that end in **o** take an **es**; others just take an **s**.

List Words

wolves
volcanoes
calves
broccoli
spaghetti
radios
tomatoes
sheriffs
beliefs
species
igloos
cuffs

Fill in **list words** to complete the sentences. Not all the words will be used.

1. _Sheriffs_ are assisted by deputies.
2. _Broccoli_ , _tomatoes_ , and _spaghetti_ are things you eat.
3. _Wolves_ and _calves_ have four legs.
4. People listen to music and news on _radios_ .
5. _Igloos_ are built out of blocks of snow.
6. What we believe in are our _beliefs_ .
7. There are numerous _species_ of animals.

Lesson 35

TIP There are some words that you just need to practice using to become familiar with their spellings.

List Words

famous
yolk
column
stomach
surprises
separate
islands
misspelled
weather
February
ballet
punctuation

Write a **list word** to complete each sentence. Not all the words will be used.

1. A comma is a form of _punctuation_ .
2. A word with letters missing is _misspelled_ .
3. The yellow center of an egg is a _yolk_ .
4. The month after January is _February_ .
5. A dance performed on toes is _ballet_ .
6. Places surrounded by water are _islands_ .
7. A vertical list of numbers is a _column_ .
8. Another word for unattached is _separate_ .
9. Rain and snow are kinds of _weather_ .
10. Food is digested in a person's _stomach_ .

Lesson 36 • Review   147

Show What You Know

Lessons 31—35 Review

One word in misspelled in each set of **list words**. Fill in the circle next to the **list word** that is spelled incorrectly.

1.	sturdyer	kidneys	stomach	valuable	potatoes
2.	famous	spagheti	victories	magnifying	imagination
3.	stickiest	libraries	supplying	broccolli	wisdom
4.	familiar	surprizes	decoys	decided	sunniest
5.	centuries	pleged	moose	apologies	injuries
6.	weird	calves	scraping	families	volcanos
7.	introducing	balet	fashion	heavier	spinning
8.	column	tornadoes	wheather	classified	shipping
9.	separate	sheriffs	noisely	hoping	authorities
10.	Febuary	islands	countries	groceries	yolk
11.	shreaded	planned	envied	journeys	trout
12.	amazing	cheerily	relays	igloos	puntuation
13.	usable	hastily	backeries	radios	tomatoes
14.	chossen	forfeit	species	chiefs	secretaries
15.	unforgivable	disapproved	angrily	occupying	prairy
16.	cavitys	cranberries	strangest	worrying	friendlier
17.	obeying	delays	throbbing	misteries	recommend
18.	activities	salmon	wolfes	pleasing	skidded
19.	readily	greadily	sleepiest	merrily	halves
20.	scarves	cuffs	beliefs	mispelled	persuaded

148   Lesson 36 • Review

Final Test

1. The boys **planned** every detail of their bike trip.
2. This big chair is **sturdier** than the small stool.
3. After two **delays**, the train left the station.
4. The zoologist spent her life studying **wolves**.
5. This jumbo egg has a double **yolk**.
6. When I got off the ride, my head was **spinning**.
7. The happy children sang **cheerily**.
8. Will this new toothpaste prevent **cavities**?
9. At the farm, we saw the new **calves**.
10. She added up the **column** of numbers.
11. I am **hoping** that my essay will win a prize.
12. Stop **worrying** about that test!
13. Marise received minor **injuries** in the accident.
14. Green Grocer Farm sells fresh **broccoli**.
15. When I'm hungry, my **stomach** gurgles.
16. Andy **decided** to try out for the baseball team.
17. The cat **greedily** lapped up the saucer of milk.
18. The team celebrated its three straight **victories**.
19. Mom makes **spaghetti** every Tuesday night.
20. She will **separate** her summer and winter clothes.
21. What is the **strangest** animal you've ever seen?
22. We packed so **hastily** we forgot many things.
23. The **kidneys** filter waste from our blood.
24. This store has good prices on **radios** and TVs.
25. How many **islands** did the boat visit?
26. After it got wet, the paper bag was not **usable**.
27. Tam was the **sleepiest** of all the children.
28. We saw **cranberries** growing in bogs.
29. Ali gave us a bag of **tomatoes** from his garden.
30. You **misspelled** your own name on the test!
31. Anna inherited a **valuable** ring.
32. This chair seems **heavier** than that one.
33. Which of your **journeys** did you enjoy the most?
34. All the **sheriffs** joined in the search.
35. The **weather** forecast for tomorrow is sunny.
36. The quiet music was **pleasing** to hear.
37. Examine the insect with a **magnifying** glass.
38. The town **bakeries** hold a raisin-bread contest.
39. The two friends have similar **beliefs**.
40. Nikita's birthday is **February** twenty-fifth.
41. It took **imagination** to create that story.
42. Today is the **sunniest** day we've had in months.
43. Kate's Bookstore sells only **mysteries**.
44. The botanist discovered a new **species** of roses.
45. Erica's **ballet** recital is on Sunday.
46. What an **amazing** magician Mr. Soo is!
47. They played so **noisily** that people complained.
48. All the **families** on the block attended the party.
49. **Igloos** are made from blocks of snow.
50. Add the correct **punctuation** to the sentence.

Name _____

Review Test (Side A)

Read each sentence and set of words. Fill in the circle next to the word that is spelled correctly to complete the sentence.

1. Sherry loves to read murder _____.
    - ⓐ mysteries
    - ⓑ misteries
    - ⓒ mysteres
    - ⓓ mistyries

2. Artists need a powerful _____ to be successful.
    - ⓐ imageination
    - ⓑ imagination
    - ⓒ imaggination
    - ⓓ imaginasion

3. Her advice _____ in the newspaper was very popular.
    - ⓐ column
    - ⓑ colunm
    - ⓒ colum
    - ⓓ collum

4. I'll need a _____ glass to read this tiny print!
    - ⓐ magnifyeing
    - ⓑ magnefying
    - ⓒ magniffying
    - ⓓ magnifying

5. They used hand-held _____ to communicate.
    - ⓐ radioes
    - ⓑ radios
    - ⓒ raddios
    - ⓓ raddioes

6. The chef hoped his pots were still _____.
    - ⓐ usible
    - ⓑ useible
    - ⓒ usable
    - ⓓ ussable

7. Our friend _____ to have a party this weekend.
    - ⓐ decided
    - ⓑ dacided
    - ⓒ desided
    - ⓓ dasided

8. Please buy some _____ for Thanksgiving dinner.
    - ⓐ cranberies
    - ⓑ cranburies
    - ⓒ cramberries
    - ⓓ cranberries

Lesson 36 Review Test (Side B)

Read each sentence and set of words. Fill in the circle next to the word that is spelled correctly to complete the sentence.

9. This chair is much _____ than that small one.
   - (a) sturder
   - (b) sturdir
   - (c) sturdier
   - (d) sturdyer

10. Many _____ vacation at the shore in the summer.
    - (a) famlies
    - (b) familes
    - (c) famelies
    - (d) families

11. Don't forget to use proper _____ in your essays.
    - (a) punctation
    - (b) puntuation
    - (c) punctuaton
    - (d) punctuation

12. Phil's _____ grumbled because he missed breakfast.
    - (a) stomech
    - (b) stomache
    - (c) stomach
    - (d) stumach

13. Stop _____ and do something about it!
    - (a) worying
    - (b) wirrying
    - (c) woryng
    - (d) worrying

14. Maybe I'll put some _____ in that salad.
    - (a) broccolli
    - (b) brocolli
    - (c) broccoli
    - (d) brocali

15. Our neighbor grows wonderful _____ in the backyard.
    - (a) tomatoes
    - (b) tomatos
    - (c) tomtoes
    - (d) tomaytoes

Take It Home

Your child has learned to spell many new words and would enjoy sharing them with you and your family. You can use the ideas below to help your child review the words in lessons 31–35 and to have some family fun, too!

Shopping for Spelling

Have your child "go shopping" for spelling words the next time you have errands to run. Encourage your child to keep an eye open for labels and signs that contain spelling words, make a list of the words, and share them at home.

Lesson 31

1. amazing
2. decided
3. disapproved
4. hoping
5. imagination
6. introducing
7. persuaded
8. planned
9. pleasing
10. pledged
11. scraping
12. shipping
13. shredded
14. skidded
15. spinning
16. strangest
17. throbbing
18. unforgivable
19. usable
20. valuable

Lesson 32

1. angrily
2. cheerily
3. classified
4. envied
5. friendlier
6. greedily
7. hastily
8. heavier
9. magnifying
10. merrily
11. noisily
12. obeying
13. occupying
14. readily
15. sleepiest
16. stickiest
17. sturdier
18. sunniest
19. supplying
20. worrying

Lesson 33

1. activities
2. apologies
3. authorities
4. bakeries
5. cavities
6. centuries
7. countries
8. cranberries
9. decoys
10. delays
11. families
12. groceries
13. injuries
14. journeys
15. kidneys
16. libraries
17. mysteries
18. relays
19. secretaries
20. victories

Lesson 34

1. beliefs
2. broccoli
3. calves
4. chiefs
5. cuffs
6. halves
7. igloos
8. moose
9. potatoes
10. radios
11. salmon
12. scarves
13. sheriffs
14. spaghetti
15. species
16. tomatoes
17. tornadoes
18. trout
19. volcanoes
20. wolves

Lesson 35

1. ballet
2. chosen
3. column
4. familiar
5. famous
6. fashion
7. February
8. forfeit
9. islands
10. misspelled
11. prairie
12. punctuation
13. recommend
14. separate
15. stomach
16. surprises
17. weather
18. weird
19. wisdom
20. yolk

Imagination That!

With your child, find ten spelling words that each share at least one letter with the word *imagination*. Write the words vertically below. Then put your imagination to work by making up a story that contains all the words.

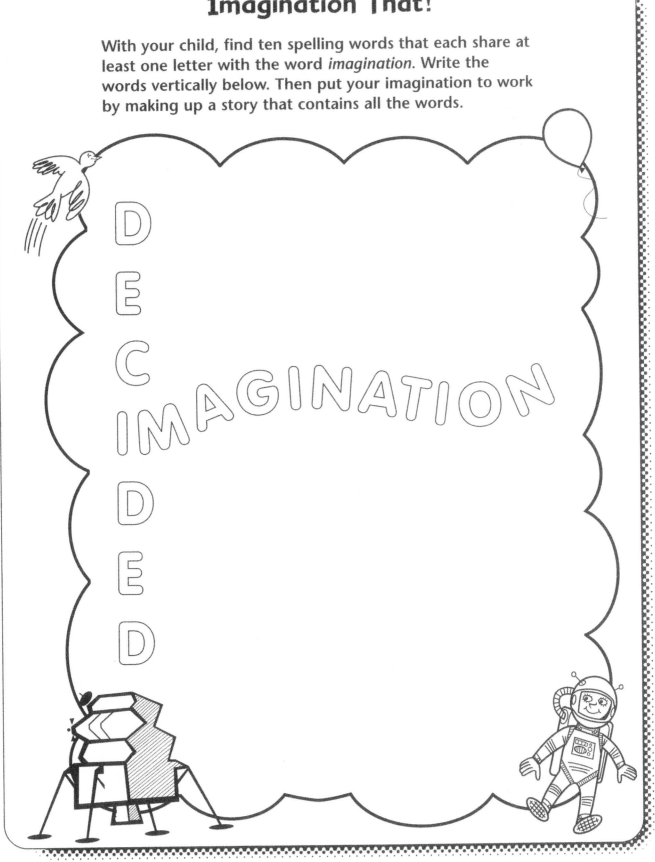

D
E
C
I M A G I N A T I O N
D
E
D

Writing and Proofreading Guide

1. Choose a topic to write about.

2. Write your ideas. Don't worry about mistakes.

3. Now organize your writing so that it makes sense.

4. Proofread your work.

   Use these proofreading marks to make changes.

   ## Proofreading Marks

⬭	spelling mistake
≡	capital letter
⊙	add period
⌃	add something
⌄	add apostrophe
ℓ	take out something
¶	indent paragraph
/	make small letter

   tomorrow well interview the ~~auther~~ of ~~of~~ our favorite Mystery story⊙

5. Write your final copy.

   Tomorrow we'll interview the author of our favorite mystery story.

6. Share your writing.

Using Your Dictionary

The *Spelling Workout* Dictionary shows you many things about your spelling words.

The **entry word** listed in alphabetical order is the word you are looking up.

The **sound-spelling** or **respelling** tells how to pronounce the word.

The **part of speech** is given as an abbreviation.

im·prove (im pro͞ov′) *v.* **1** to make or become better [Business has *improved*.] **2** to make good use of [She *improved* her spare time by reading.] —**im·proved′**, **im·prov′ing**

Sample sentences or **phrases** show how to use the word.

Other **forms** of the word are given.

The **definition** tells what the word means. There may be more than one definition.

Pronunciation Key

SYMBOL	KEY WORDS	SYMBOL	KEY WORDS	SYMBOL	KEY WORDS	SYMBOL	KEY WORDS
a	ask, fat	o͞o	look, pull	b	bed, dub	t	top, hat
ā	ape, date	yo͞o	unite, cure	d	did, had	v	vat, have
ä	car, lot	o͞o	ooze, tool	f	fall, off	w	will, always
		yo͞o	cute, few	g	get, dog	y	yet, yard
e	elf, ten	ou	out, crowd	h	he, ahead	z	zebra, haze
er	berry, care			j	joy, jump		
ē	even, meet	u	up, cut	k	kill, bake	ch	chin, arch
		u	fur, fern	l	let, ball	ŋ	ring, singer
i	is, hit			m	met, trim	sh	she, dash
ir	mirror, here	ə	a in ago	n	not, ton	th	thin, truth
ī	ice, fire		e in agent	p	put, tap	*th*	then, father
			e in father	r	red, dear	zh	s in pleasure
ō	open, go		i in unity	s	sell, pass		
ô	law, horn		o in collect				
oi	oil, point		u in focus				

An Americanism is a word or usage of a word that was born in this country. An open star (☆) before an entry word or definition means that the word or definition is an Americanism.

ab·sen·tee (ab sən tē′) *n.* a person who is absent, as from school, work, etc. ◆ *adj.* living far away from land or a building that one owns [an *absentee* landord]

ab·sorb·ent (ab sôr′bənt *or* ab zôr′bənt) *adj.* able to absorb moisture, light, etc. [*absorbent* cotton]

a·bun·dant (ə bun′dənt) *adj.* **1** very plentiful; more than enough [The farmers had an *abundant* crop of grain last year.] **2** rich; well-supplied [a lake *abundant* in fish]

ac·cept·ance (ak sep′təns) *n.* **1** the act of accepting [the actor's *acceptance* of the award] **2** the condition of being accepted [his *acceptance* as a member of the club] **3** approval or belief [a theory that has the *acceptance* of most scientists]

ac·count·ant (ə kount′nt) *n.* a person whose work is keeping or examining accounts, or business records

ac·cu·mu·late (ə kyōom′yōo lāt′) *v.* to pile up, collect, or gather over a period of time [Junk has *accumulated* in the garage. Our school has *accumulated* a large library.] —**ac·cu′mu·lat·ed, ac·cu′mu·lat·ing**

ache (āk) *v.* **1** to have or give a dull, steady pain [My head *aches*.] **2** to want very much; long; *used only in everyday talk* [She is *aching* to take a trip.] —**ached, ach′ing**

a·chieve (ə chēv′) *v.* **1** to do; succeed in doing, accomplish [He *achieved* very little while he was mayor.] **2** to get or reach by trying hard; gain [She *achieved* her ambition to be a lawyer.] —**a·chieved′, a·chiev′ing**

a·cre (āk′ər) *n.* **1** a measure of land equal to 43,560 square feet **2** acres, —*pl.* lands *or* fields [golden *acres* of grain]

ac·tiv·i·ty (ak tiv′ə tē) *n.* **1** the condition of being active; action; motion [There was not much *activity* in the shopping mall today.] ◆ *v.* **1** normal power of mind or body; liveliness; alertness [His mental *activity* at age eighty was remarkable.] **2** something that one does besides one's regular work [We take part in many *activities* after school.] —*pl.* **ac·tiv′i·ties**

ad·here (ad hir′) *v.* **1** to stick and not come loose; stay attached [This stamp won't *adhere* to the envelope.] **2** to follow closely or faithfully [to *adhere* to a plan] —**ad·her′ing**

ad·min·is·tra·tion (əd min′i strā′shən) *n.* **1** an administering; management; direction **2** *often* Administration, the president and the other people who work in the executive branch of a government [The *Administration* was criticized for its foreign policy.] **3** their term of office [Johnson was vice-president during Kennedy's *administration*.] **4** the people who manage a company, school, or other organization —**ad·min′is·tra′tive adj.**

a·dopt (ə däpt′) *v.* **1** to take into one's family by a legal process [to *adopt* a child] **2** to take and use as one's own [He *adopted* her teaching methods for his own classroom.] **3** to choose or follow [to *adopt* a plan of action] —**a·dop′tion n.**

ad·vance (ad vans′) *v.* **1** to go or bring forward; move ahead [The trail became rougher as we *advanced*.] **2** to make or become higher; increase [Prices continue to *advance*.] —**ad·vanced′, ad·vanc′ing**

af·ter·ward (af′tər wərd) *or* **af·ter·wards** (af′ter werdz) *adv.* at a later time; later [We had dinner and went for a walk *afterward*.]

a·gree·a·ble (ə grē′ə bəl) *adj.* **1** pleasing or pleasant [an *agreeable* odor] **2** willing or ready to say "yes" [The principal was *agreeable* to our plan.] —**a·gree′a·bly adv.**

a·gree·ment (ə grē′mənt) *n.* **1** the fact of agreeing or being similar [The news report was not in *agreement* with the facts.] **2** a fixing of terms between two or more people, countries, etc., as in a treaty [The U.S. has trade *agreements* with many nations.]

aisle (īl) *n.* **1** an open way for passing between sections of seats, as in a theater **2** a part of a church along the inside wall, set off by a row of pews

a·lign (ə līn′) *v.* **1** to put into a straight line [*Align* the chairs along the wall.] —**a·ligned′, a·lign′ing**

al·low·ance (ə lou′əns) *n.* **1** an amount of money, food, etc. given regularly to a child or to anyone who depends on others for support **2** an amount added or taken off to make up for something [We give an *allowance* of $5 on your used tire when you buy a new one.]

al·loy (al′oi) *n.* a metal that is a mixture of two or more metals, or of a metal and something else [Bronze is an *alloy* of copper and tin.]

al·pha·bet·ize (al′fə bə tīz) *v.* to arrange in alphabetical order —**al′pha·bet·ized′, al′pha·bet·iz′ing**

a·maz·ing (ə māz′iŋ) *adj.* causing amazement; astonishing —**a·maz′ing·ly adv.**

A·mer·i·ca (ə mer′ə kə) **1** either North America or South America **2** North America and South America together ☆**3** the United States of America

a	ask, fat
ā	ape, date
ä	car, lot
e	elf, ten
ē	even, meet
i	is, hit
ī	ice, fire
ō	open, go
ô	law, horn
oi	oil, point
oo	look, pull
ōo	ooze, tool
ou	out, crowd
u	up, cut
ʉ	fur, fern
ə	a in ago
	e in agent
	e in father
	i in unity
	o in collect
	u in focus
ch	chin, arch
ŋ	ring, singer
sh	she, dash
th	thin, truth
th	then, father
zh	s in pleasure

an·ces·tor (an′ses tər) *n.* **1** a person who comes before one in a family line, especially someone earlier than a grandparent; forefather [Their *ancestors* came from Poland.] **2** an early kind of animal from which later kinds have developed [The *ancestor* of the elephant was the mammoth.]

an·gri·ly (aŋ′grə lē) *adv.* in an angry manner

an·gry (aŋ′grē) *adj.* **1** feeling or showing anger [*angry* words; an *angry* crowd] **2** wild and stormy [an *angry* sea] —**an′gri·er, an′gri·est**

an·i·mal (an′ə məl) *n.* **1** any living being that can move about by itself, has sense organs, and does not make its own food as plants do from inorganic matter [Insects, snakes, fish, birds, cattle, and people are all *animals*.] **2** any such being other than a human being; especially, any four-footed creature; beast

an·i·mat·ed (an′ə māt′əd) *adj.* vigorous; lively [an *animated* conversation] —**an′i·mat′ed·ly** *adv.*

☆**animated cartoon** *n.* a motion picture made by filming a series of drawings, each changed slightly from the one before: the drawn figures seem to move when the drawings are shown on a screen, one quickly after the other

an·swer (an′sər) *n.* **1** something said, written, or done in return to a question, argument, letter, action, etc.; reply; response [The only *answers* required for the test were "true" or "false." His *answer* to the insult was to turn his back.] **2** a solution to a problem, as in arithmetic ◆*v.* to give an answer; reply or react, as to a question or action

a·pol·o·gy (ə päl′ə jē) *n.* a statement that one is sorry for doing something wrong or being at fault [Please accept my *apology* for sending you the wrong book.] —*pl.* **a·pol′o·gies**

ap·pli·cant (ap′li kənt) *n.* a person who applies or asks for something [*applicants* for a job]

ap·point·ee (ə pɔin tē′) *n.* a person who has been appointed to some position

a·pri·cot (ap′rə kät′ *or* ā′prə kät′) *n.* **1** a pale orange fruit that is a little like a peach, but smaller **2** the tree it grows on ◆*adj.* a pale orange color

ar·e·a (er′ē ə) *n.* **1** the amount or size of a surface, measured in square units [If a floor is 10 meters wide and 20 meters long, its *area* is 200 square meters.] **2** a part of the earth's surface; region [Our family lives mostly in rural *areas*.] **3** a space used for a special purpose [a picnic *area*]

ar·row (er′ō) *n.* **1** a slender rod that is shot from a bow: arrows usually have a point at the front end and feathers at the back end **2** anything that looks or is used like an arrow; especially, a sign (◄—) used to point out a direction or place

ar·ter·y (är′tər ē) *n.* **1** any of the tubes that carry blood from the heart to all parts of the body **2** a main road or channel [a railroad *artery*] —*pl.* **ar′ter·ies**

ar·tis·tic (är tis′tik) *adj.* **1** of art or artists **2** done with skill and a good sense of color, form, design, etc. [an *artistic* job of redecorating] **3** knowing and enjoying what is beautiful —**ar·tis′ti·cal·ly** *adv.*

as·sign (ə sīn′) *v.* **1** to set apart for a special purpose; designate [Let's *assign* a day for the trip.] **2** to place at some task or work [Two pupils were *assigned* to write the report.] **3** to give out as a task; allot [The teacher *assigned* some homework.]

as·sist·ant (ə sis′tənt) *n.* a person who assists or helps another; helper; aid [an *assistant* to the president] ◆*adj.* assisting or helping the person under whom one works [an *assistant* principal]

as·so·ci·ate (ə sō′shē āt′ *or* ə sō′sē āt′) *v.* **1** to connect in one's mind; think of together [We *associate* the taste of something with its smell.] **2** to bring or come together as friends or partners [Don't *associate* with people who gossip.] —**as·so′ci·at·ed, as·so′ci·at·ing** ◆*n.* (ə sō′shē āt *or* ə sō′sē āt) a person with whom one is joined in some way; friend, partner, or fellow worker

ath·let·ic (ath let′ik) *adj.* **1** of or for athletes or athletics **2** like an athlete; physically strong and active —**ath·let′i·cal·ly** *adv.*

at·mos·phere (at′məs fir) *n.* **1** all the air around the earth **2** the gases around any planet or star **3** the air in any particular place

at·tach·ment (ə tach′mənt) *n.* **1** the act of attaching something **2** anything used for attaching; fastening **3** strong liking or love; friendship; affection

at·tend·ance (ə ten′dəns) *n.* **1** the act of attending **2** people present [The *attendance* at the ball game was 36,000.]

at·ti·tude (at′ə tōōd *or* at′ə tyōōd) *n.* **1** the position of the body in doing a particular thing [We knelt in an *attitude* of prayer.] **2** a way of acting or behaving that shows what one is thinking or feeling [a friendly *attitude*]

at·tor·ney (ə tʉr′nē) *n.* a person whose profession is giving advice on law or acting for others in lawsuits —*pl.* **at·tor′neys**

auc·tion·eer (ôk shə nir′ *or* äk shə nir′) *n.* a person whose work is selling things at auctions

au·di·ence (ô′dē əns *or* ä′dē əns) *n.* a group of persons gathered together to hear and see a speaker, a play, or a concert [The *audience* cheered the singer.]

au·thor (ô′thər *or* ä′thər) *n.* **1** a person who writes something, as a book or story [The Brontë sisters were the *authors* of novels.] **2** a person who makes or begins something; creator [the author of a new plan for peace] ◆*v.* to be the author of

au·thor·i·ty (ə thôr′ə tē) *n.* **1** the right to give orders, make decisions, or take action [Do you have the *authority* to spend the money?] **2** a person or agency that has the right to govern or the power to enforce laws [The city *authorities* have approved the plan.] **3** a person, book, etc. that can be trusted to give the right information or advice [an *authority* on rare diseases]
—*pl.* **au·thor′i·ties**

au·to·graph (ôt′ə graf *or* ät′ə graf) *n.* something written in a person's own handwriting, especially that person's name ◆*v.* to write one's name on [Please *autograph* this baseball.]

a·vi·a·tor (ā′ vē āt′ər) *n.* a person who flies airplanes; pilot

a·void (ə void′) *v.* **1** to keep away from; get out of the way of; shun [to *avoid* crowds] **2** to keep from happening [Try to *avoid* spilling the milk.] —**a·void′a·ble** *adj.*
—**a·void′ance** *n.*

awe (ô *or* ä) *n.* deep respect mixed with fear and wonder [The starry sky filled them with *awe*.]

aw·ful·ly (ô′ fəl ē *or* ä′fəl ē) *adv.* **1** in an awful way ☆**2** very; extremely; *used only in everyday talk* [I'm *awfully* glad you came.]

awk·ward (ôk′wərd *or* äk′wərd) *adj.* **1** not having grace or skill; clumsy; bungling [an *awkward* dancer; an *awkward* writing style] **2** hard to use or manage; not convenient [an *awkward* tool] **3** uncomfortable; cramped [sitting in an *awkward* position] **4** embarrassed or embarrassing [an *awkward* remark]
—**awk′ward·ly** *adv.*
—**awk′ward·ness** *n.*

back·ward (bak′wərd) *adv.* **1** toward the back; behind [to look *backward*] **2** with the back toward the front [If a man rides *backward*, he can see where he has been.] **3** in a way opposite to the usual way [Noel is Leon spelled *backward*.]

☆**bak·er·y** (bāk′ər ē) *n.* a place where bread, cakes, etc. are baked or sold
—*pl.* **bak′er·ies**

bal·let (bal′ā *or* ba lā′) *n.* **1** a dance performed on a stage, usually by a group of dancers in costume: it often tells a story by means of its graceful, fixed movements **2** a group of such dancers

bas·i·cal·ly (bā′ sik lē) *adv.* in a basic way

beau·ti·ful (byōo′ti fəl) *adj.* very pleasant to look at or hear; giving delight to the mind [a *beautiful* face] —**beau′ti·ful·ly** *adv.*

be·hav·ior (bē hāv′yər) *n.* the way a person or thing behaves, or acts; conduct or action [His *behavior* at the dance was rude. The Curies studied the *behavior* of radium.]

be·lief (bē lēf′) *n.* **1** a believing or feeling that certain things are true or real; faith [You cannot destroy my *belief* in the honesty of most people.] **2** trust or confidence [I have *belief* in Pat's ability.] **3** anything believed or accepted as true; opinion [What are your religious *beliefs*?]

be·lieve (bē lēv′) *v.* **1** to accept as true or real [Can we *believe* that story?] **2** to have religious faith [to *believe* in life after death] **3** to have trust or confidence [I know you will win; I *believe* in you.] **4** to suppose; guess —**be·lieved′, be·liev′ ing**
—**be·liev′a·ble** *adj.* —**be·liev′er** *n.*

ben·e·fit (ben′ə fit) *n.* **1** help or advantage; also, anything that helps [Speak louder for the *benefit* of those in the rear.] **2** *often* **benefits**, *pl.* money paid by an insurance company, the government, etc. as during old age or sickness, or for death **3** any public event put on to raise money for a certain person, group, or cause [The show is a *benefit* for children.]

be·tray (bē trā′) *v.* to fail to keep a promise, secret, or agreement; be unfaithful [My cousin *betrayed* my trust by wasting my money.] —**be·trayed′, be·tray′ing**

bi·ceps (bī′səps) *n.* the large muscle in the front of the upper arm

bi·cy·cle (bī′si kəl) *n.* a vehicle to ride on that has two wheels, one behind the other: it is moved by foot pedals and steered by a handlebar ◆*v.* to ride a bicycle
—**bi′cy·cled, bi′cy·cling** —**bi·cy·clist** (bī′si klist) *n.*

bi·fo·cals (bī′fō kəlz) *pl.n.* eyeglasses in which each lens has two parts, one for reading and seeing nearby objects and the other for seeing things far away

bi·og·ra·phy (bī äg′rə fē) *n.* the story of a person's life written by another person
—*pl.* **bi·og′ra·phies** —**bi·o·graph·i·cal** (bī′ə graf′i kəl) *adj.*

bi·sect (bī sekt′ *or* bī′sekt) *v.* **1** to cut into two parts [Budapest is *bisected* by the Danube River.] **2** to divide into two equal parts [A circle is *bisected* by its diameter.]

blue (blōō) *adj.* having the color of the clear sky or the deep sea

blue-green (blōō′grēn) *adj.* having a combination of the colors blue and green

boast (bōst) *v.* **1** to talk about with too much pride and pleasure; praise too highly; brag [We're tired of hearing him *boast* of his bravery.] **2** to be proud of having [Our city *boasts* a fine new zoo.] —**boast′ er** *n.*

a	ask, fat
ā	ape, date
ä	car, lot
e	elf, ten
ē	even, meet
i	is, hit
ī	ice, fire
ō	open, go
ô	law, horn
oi	oil, point
oo	look, pull
ōō	ooze, tool
ou	out, crowd
u	up, cut
₩	fur, fern
ə	a in ago
	e in agent
	e in father
	i in unity
	o in collect
	u in focus
ch	chin, arch
ŋ	ring, singer
sh	she, dash
th	thin, truth
th	then, father
zh	s in pleasure

bond (bänd) *n.* **1** anything that binds or ties [Handcuffs or shackles are called *bonds*.] **2** an agreement that binds one, as to pay certain sums or to do or not do certain things **3** a certificate sold by a government or business as a way of raising money: it promises to return the money to the buyer by a certain date, along with interest [The city issued *bonds* to build a subway.]

book·keep·er (book'kēp ər) *n.* a person whose work is to keep accounts for a business

bor·row (bär'ō *or* bôr'ō) *v.* **1** to get to use something for a while by agreeing to return it later [You can *borrow* that book from the library.] **2** to take another's word, idea, etc. and use it as one's own [The Romans *borrowed* many Greek myths.]

bot·a·ny (bät'n ē) *n.* the science that studies plants and how they grow —**bot´a·nist** *n.*

bound·a·ry (boun'drē *or* bou'dər ē) *n.* a line or thing that marks the outside edge or limit [The Delaware River forms the eastern *boundary* of Pennsylvania.] —*pl.* **bound´a·ries**

braid (brād) *v.* **1** to weave together three or more strands of hair, straw, ribbon, etc. **2** to make by weaving such strands [to *braid* a rug] ►*n.* **1** a length of braided hair **2** a band of braided cloth, ribbon, etc. used for trimming or decoration

breathe (brēth) *v.* **1** to take air into the lungs and then let it out **2** to live [While I *breathe*, you are safe.] **3** to speak quietly; whisper [Don't *breathe* a word of it to anyone.] **4** to stop for breath; rest [to *breathe* a horse after a long run] —**breathed, breath´ing**

brief (brēf) *adj.* **1** not lasting very long; short in time [a *brief* visit] **2** using just a few words; concise [a *brief* news report]

broad·cast (brôd'kast) *v.* to send over the air by means of radio or television [to *broadcast* a program] —**broad´cast** or **broad´cast·ed, broad´cast·ing**

broc·co·li (bräk'ə lē) *n.* a vegetable whose tender shoots and loose heads of tiny green buds are cooked for eating

broil (broil) *v.* **1** to cook or be cooked close to a flame or other high heat [to *broil* steaks over charcoal] **2** to make or be very hot [a *broiling* summer day] ►*n.* the act or state of broiling —**broiled**

broth·er·hood (bruth'ər hood) *n.* the tie between brothers or between people who feel they all belong to one big family.

bu·reau (byoor'ō) *n.* ☆**1** a chest of drawers for holding clothes: it usually has a mirror. **2** an office, as for a certain part of a business [an information *bureau*] ☆**3** a department of the government [The *Bureau* of Internal Revenue is in charge of collecting Federal taxes.] —*pl.* **bu´reaus** or **bu·reaux** (byoor'ōz)

bus·y (biz'ē) *adj.* **1** doing something; active; at work; not idle [The students are *busy* at their desks.] **2** full of activity; with much action or motion [a *busy* morning; a *busy* store] —**bus´i·er, bus´i·est** —**bus´ied, bus´y·ing** *v.* —**bus´y·ness** *n.*

cab·i·net (kab'i nət) *n.* **1** a case or cupboard with drawers or shelves for holding or storing things [a china *cabinet*; a medicine *cabinet*] ☆**2** *often* **Cabinet,** a group of officials who act as advisers to the head of a nation: our president's cabinet is made up of the heads of the departments of our government

calf (kaf) *n.* **1** a young cow or bull **2** a young elephant, whale, hippopotamus, seal, etc. —*pl.* **calves**

cam·paign (kam pān') *n.* **1** a series of battles or other military actions having a special goal [Napoleon's Russian *campaign* ended in his defeat.] **2** a series of planned actions for getting something done [a *campaign* to get someone elected] ►*v.* to take part in a campaign —**cam·paign´er** *n.*

Can·a·da (kan'ə də) a country in the northern part of North America

can·cel (kan'səl) *v.* **1** to cross out with lines or mark in some other way [Postage stamps and checks are *canceled* to show that they have been used.] **2** to do away with; wipe out; say that it will no longer be [to *cancel* an order] **3** to balance something so that it has no effect [My gains and losses *cancel* each other.] —**can´celed** or **can´celled, can´cel·ing** or **can´cel·ling**

ca·pac·i·ty (kə pas'ə tē) *n.* **1** the amount of space that can be filled; room for holding [a jar with a *capacity* of 2 quarts; a stadium with a seating *capacity* of 80,000] **2** the ability to be, learn, become, etc.; skill or fitness [the *capacity* to be an actor] **3** position or office [He made the decision in his *capacity* as president.] —*pl.* **ca·pac´i·ties**

cap·il·lar·y (kap'i ler ē) *n.* **1** a tube that is very narrow inside [The ordinary thermometer is a *capillary*.] **2** any of the tiny blood vessels joining the arteries and the veins —*pl.* **cap´il·lar´ies**

☆**cap·tion** (kap'shən) *n.* a title at the head of an article or below a picture, as in a newspaper

cap·tive (kap'tiv) *n.* a person caught and held prisoner, as in war ►*adj.* **1** held as a prisoner ☆**2** forced to listen, whether wanting to or not [a *captive* audience]

carbon dioxide (kär′bən dī äks′īd) *n.* a gas made up of carbon and oxygen, that has no color and no smell and is heavier than air: it is breathed out of the lungs and is taken in by plants, which use it to make their food

ca·reer (kə rir′) *n.* **1** the way one earns one's living; profession or occupation [Have you thought of teaching as a *career*?] **2** one's progress through life or in one's work [a long and successful *career* in politics]

car·toon (kär tōōn′) *n.* **1** a drawing, as in a newspaper or magazine, that shows how the editor or artist feels about some person or thing in the news: it is often a caricature that criticizes or praises **2** a humorous drawing ☆**3** *same as* **comic strip** ☆**4** *same as* **animated cartoon** ☆ ➛*v.* to draw cartoons —**car·toon′ist** *n.*

cas·sette (kə set′) *n.* **1** a case with a roll of film in it, for loading a camera quickly and easily **2** a case with recording tape in it, for quick, easy use in a tape recorder

cas·u·al (kazh′ōō əl) *adj.* **1** happening by chance; not planned [a *casual* visit] **2** for wear at times when dressy clothes are not needed [*casual* sports clothes] —**cas′u·al·ly** *adv.* —**cas′u·al·ness** *n.*

cat·a·log *or* **cat·a·logue** (kat′ə lôg *or* kat′ə läg) *n.* ☆**1** a card file in alphabetical order giving a complete list of things in a collection, as of all the books in a library **2** a book or paper listing all the things for sale or on display ➛*v.* to make a list of or put into a list —**cat′a·loged** *or* **cat′a·logued, cat′a·log·ing** *or* **cat′a·logu·ing**

cau·li·flow·er (kôl′ə flou′ər *or* käl′ə flou′ər) *n.* a kind of cabbage with a head of white, fleshy flower clusters growing tightly together: it is eaten as a vegetable

cau·tion (kô′shən *or* kä′shən) *n.* **1** the act of being careful not to get into danger or make mistakes [Use *caution* in crossing streets.] **2** a warning [Let me give you a word of *caution*.] ➛*v.* to warn; tell of danger [The sign *cautioned* us to slow down.]

cav·i·ty (kav′i tē) *n.* **1** a hollow place, such as the one caused by decay in a tooth **2** a natural hollow space in the body [the chest *cavity*] —*pl.* **cav′i·ties**

cel·e·brate (sel′ə brāt) *v.* **1** to honor a victory, the memory of something, etc. in some special way [to *celebrate* a birthday with a party; to *celebrate* the Fourth of July with fireworks] **2** to honor or praise widely [Aesop's fables have been *celebrated* for centuries.] **3** to perform a ceremony in worshiping [to *celebrate* Mass] **4** to have a good time; used only in everyday talk [Let's *celebrate* when we finish painting the garage.] —**cel′e·brat·ed, cel′e·brat·ing** —**cel′e·bra′tion** *n.*

cen·tu·ry (sen′chər ē) *n.* **1** any of the 100-year periods counted forward or backward from the beginning of the Christian Era [From 500 to 401 B.C. was the fifth *century* B.C. From 1901 to 2000 is the twentieth *century* A.D.] **2** any period of 100 years [Mark Twain was born over a *century* ago.] —*pl.* **cen′tu·ries**

cer·e·mo·ny (ser′ə mō′ nē) *n.* **1** an act or set of acts done in a special way, with all the right details [a wedding *ceremony* in church; the *ceremony* of inaugurating the president.] **2** very polite behavior that follows strict rules; formality [The special dinner was served with great *ceremony*.] —*pl.* **cer′e·mo′nies**

cer·tain (surt′n) *adj.* **1** without any doubt or question; sure; positive [Are you *certain* of your facts?] **2** bound to happen; not failing or missing [to risk *certain* death; the soldier's *certain* aim] **3** not named or described, though perhaps known [It happened in a *certain* town out west.]

cer·tif·i·cate (sur tif′i kət) *n.* a written or printed statement that can be used as proof of something because it is official [A birth *certificate* proves where and when someone was born.]

chal·lenge (chal′ənj) *v.* **1** to question the right or rightness of; refuse to believe unless proof is given [to *challenge* a claim; to *challenge* something said or the person who says it] **2** to call to take part in a fight or contest; dare [He *challenged* her to a game of chess.] **3** to refuse to let pass unless a certain sign is given [The sentry waited for the password after *challenging* the soldier.] **4** to call for skill, effort, or imagination [That puzzle will really *challenge* you.] —**chal′lenged, chal′leng·ing**

cham·pi·on (cham′pē ən) *n.* **1** a person or thing that wins first place or is judged to be best, as in a contest or sport [a spelling *champion*; a tennis *champion*] **2** a person who fights for another or for a cause; defender [a *champion* of the poor]

cham·pi·on·ship (cham′pē ən ship′) *n.* **1** the position or title of a champion; first place **2** the act of championing, or defending

chan·nel (chan′əl) *n.* **1** the bed of a river or stream **2** the deeper part of a river, harbor, etc. **3** a body of water joining two larger bodies of water [The English *Channel* links the Atlantic Ocean to the North Sea.] **4** the band of frequencies on which a single radio or television station sends out its programs —**chan′ neled** *or* **chan′ nelled, chan′ nel·ing** *or* **chan′ nel·ling** *v.*

a	ask, fat
ā	ape, date
ä	car, lot
e	elf, ten
ē	even, meet
i	is, hit
ī	ice, fire
ō	open, go
ô	law, horn
oi	oil, point
ōō	look, pull
ōō	ooze, tool
ou	out, crowd
u	up, cut
ʉ	fur, fern
ə	a in ago
	e in agent
	e in father
	i in unity
	o in collect
	u in focus
ch	chin, arch
ŋ	ring, singer
sh	she, dash
th	thin, truth
th	then, father
zh	s in pleasure

char·ac·ter (kar′ək tər) *n.* **1** all the things that a person does, feels, and thinks by which that person is judged as being good or bad, strong or weak, etc. [That insulting remark showed her true *character*.] **2** all those things that make one person or thing different from others; special quality; nature [The fields and woods around the school gave it a rural *character*.] **3** any letter, figure, or symbol used in writing and printing **4** a person in a story or play

☆**check·book** (chək′book) *n.* a book that holds forms for writing checks

cheer·ful (chir′fəl) *adj.* **1** full of cheer; glad; joyful [a *cheerful* smile] **2** bright and gay [a *cheerful* room] **3** willing; glad to help [a *cheerful* worker] —**cheer′ful·ly** *adv.* —**cheer′ful·ness** *n.*

cheer·y (chir′ē) *adj.* cheerful; lively and happy [They gave us a *cheery* welcome.] —**cheer′i·er, cheer′i·est** —**cheer′i·ly** *adv.* —**cheer′i·ness** *n.*

chem·i·cal (kem′i kəl) *adj.* **1** of or in chemistry [a *chemical* process] **2** made by or used in chemistry [*chemical* compounds] —**chem′i·cal·ly** *adv.*

chief (chēf) *n.* the leader or head of some group [an Indian *chief*; the *chief* of a hospital staff] ◆*adj.* **1** having the highest position [the *chief* foreman] **2** main; most important [Jill's *chief* interest is golf.]

chim·pan·zee (chim′pan zē′ *or* chim pan′zē) *n.* an ape of Africa that is smaller than a gorilla and is a very intelligent animal: *the word is often shortened to* **chimp** (chimp)

chin·chil·la (chin chil′ə) *n.* **1** a small, ratlike animal found in the Andes Mountains in South America **2** a soft, gray fur, which is very expensive **3** a heavy wool cloth with a rough surface, used for making coats

Chi·nese (chī nēz′) *n.* **1** a member of a people whose native country is China —*pl.* **Chi·nese′** **2** the language of China ◆*adj.* of China, its people, language, or culture

choc·o·late (chôk′lət *or* chäk′lət *or* chôk′ə lət *or* chäk′ə lət) *n.* **1** a paste, powder, syrup, or bar made from cacao seeds that have been roasted and ground **2** a drink made of chocolate, sugar, and milk or water **3** a candy made of chocolate or covered with chocolate **4** reddish brown ◆*adj.* made of or flavored with chocolate

choir (kwīr) *n.* **1** a group of people trained to sing together, especially as part of a church service **2** the part of a church where the choir sits or stands

choose (chooz) *v.* **1** to pick out one or more from a number or group [*Choose* a subject from this list.] **2** to make up one's mind; decide or prefer [She *chose* to stay home.] —**chose, cho′sen, choos′ing**

cho·sen (chō′zen) *past participle of* **choose** ◆*adj.* picked out carefully, as for a special purpose [a *chosen* few soldiers formed the king's guard.]

cir·cus (sur′kəs) *n.* **1** a traveling show held in tents or in a hall, with clowns, trained animals, acrobats, etc. ☆**2** a very funny or entertaining person or thing: *used only in everyday talk* **3** a stadium or arena in ancient Rome, where games or races were held

cir·rus (sir′əs) *n.* a kind of cloud that looks like thin strips of woolly curls —*pl.* **cir′rus**

cit·i·zen (sit′i zən) *n.* **1** a person who is a member of a country or state either because of being born there or having been made a member by law: citizens have certain duties to their country and are entitled to certain rights **2** a person who lives in a particular city or town [the *citizens* of Atlanta]

class (klas) *n.* **1** a number of people or things thought of as a group because they are alike in certain ways [Whales belong to the *class* of mammals. She is a member of the working *class*.] ☆**2** a group of students meeting together to be taught; also, a meeting of this kind [My English *class* is held at nine o'clock.] ☆**3** a group of students who are or will be graduating together [the *class* of 1981] **4** a division or grouping according to grade or quality [to travel first *class*]

clas·si·fy (klas′i fī′) *v.* to arrange by putting into classes or groups according to some system [Plants and animals are *classified* into various orders, families, species, etc.] —**clas′si·fied, clas′si·fy·ing**

cli·ent (klī′ənt) *n.* **1** a person or company for whom a lawyer, accountant, etc. is acting **2** a customer

clos·et (kläz′ət *or* klôz′ət) *n.* a small room or cupboard for clothes, linens, supplies, etc. ◆*v.* to shut up in a room for a private talk [The president was *closeted* with his close advisers.]

☆**cloud·burst** (kloud′burst) *n.* a sudden, very heavy rain

coast (kōst) *n.* **1** land along the sea; seashore. ☆**2** a slide or ride downhill, as on a sled ◆*v.* **1** to sail along a coast ☆**2** to ride or slide downhill, as on a sled ☆**3** to keep on moving after the driving power is cut off [We ran out of gas, but the car *coasted* into the gas station.]

co·coa (kō′kō) *n.* **1** a powder made from roasted cacao seeds, used in making chocolate **2** a drink made from this powder by adding sugar and hot water or milk **3** a light, reddish brown

co·co·nut or **co·coa·nut** (kō′kə nut) *n.* the large, round fruit of a tall, tropical palm tree (called the **coconut palm** or **coco palm**): coconuts have a thick, hard, brown shell that has an inside layer of sweet white matter used as a food: the hollow center is filled with a sweet, milky liquid

col·lect (kə lekt′) *v.* **1** to gather in one place; assemble [*Collect* the rubbish and burn it. Water *collects* around the drain.] **2** to gather things as a hobby [She *collects* stamps.] **3** to call for and get money owed [The building manager *collects* the rent.]

col·lege (käl′ij) *n.* **1** a school that one can go to after high school for higher studies: colleges give degrees to students when they graduate; often a part of a university, which may have a number of special colleges, as of law or medicine **2** a school where one can get training in some special work [a business *college*]

co·logne (kə lōn′) *n.* a sweet-smelling liquid like perfume, but not so strong

co·lon (kō′lən) *n.* the main part of the large intestine, that leads to the rectum

col·umn (käl′əm) *n.* **1** a long, generally round, upright support; pillar: columns usually stand in groups to hold up a roof or other part of a building, but they are sometimes used just for decoration **2** any long, upright thing like a column [a *column* of water; the spinal *column*] **3** any of the long sections of print lying side by side on a page and separated by a line or blank space [Each page of this book has two *columns*.] **4** any of the articles by one writer or on a special subject, that appear regularly in a newspaper or magazine [a chess *column*]

com·fort·a·ble (kumf′tər bəl *or* kum′fər tə bəl) *adj.* **1** giving comfort or ease; not giving pain [a *comfortable* pair of shoes] **2** feeling comfort; not uneasy [Are you *comfortable* in that chair?] —**com′fort·a·bly** *adv.*

com·ic (käm′ik) *adj.* **1** having to do with comedy **2** funny or amusing; making one laugh ☆ ◆*n.* **comics**, *pl.* a section of comic strips, as in a newspaper

com·mand (kə mand′) *v.* **1** to give an order to; direct [I *command* you to halt!] **2** to be in control of [Captain Stone *commands* Company B.] **3** to deserve to have [Her courage *commands* our respect.] ◆*n.* **1** an order or direction [He obeyed the queen's *commands*.] **2** the power or ability to control or command; control [Who is in *command* here? He has no *command* of his temper.]

com·mence (kə mens′) *v.* to begin or start [The trial will *commence* at noon.] —**com·menced′, com·menc′ing**

com·mend (kə mend′) *v.* **1** to mention with approval; praise [a ballet company *commended* by all the dance critics] **2** to put in someone's care or keeping; commit —**com·men·da·tion** (kam′ən dā′shən) *n.*

com·mit·tee (kə mit′ē) *n.* a group of people chosen to study some matter or to do a certain thing [a *committee* to plan the party]

com·pan·ion (kəm pan′yən) *n.* **1** a person who goes along with another; especially, one who often shares or supports the other's activities; comrade; associate **2** either one of a pair of matched things [Where is the *companion* to this glove?]

com·pa·ny (kum′pə nē) *n.* **1** a group of people; especially, a group joined together in some work or activity [a *company* of actors; a business *company*] **2** a group of soldiers that is usually under the command of a captain **3** the state of being companions; companionship [We enjoy each other's *company*.] **4** friends or companions [One is judged by the *company* one keeps.] **5** a guest or guests [We've invited *company* for dinner.] —*pl.* **com′pa·nies**

com·pen·sa·tion (käm′pən sā′shən) *n.* **1** the act of compensating **2** something given or done to make up for something else [She was given an expensive gift as extra *compensation* for her services.]

com·pete (kəm pēt′) *v.* to take part in a contest; be a rival for something [Two hundred students *competed* for the scholarship.] —**com·pet′ed, com·pet′ing**

com·pe·tent (käm′pə tənt) *adj.* having enough ability to do what is needed; capable [a *competent* typist] —**com′pe·tent·ly** *adv.*

com·plain (kəm plān′) *v.* **1** to find fault with something or show pain or displeasure [Everyone *complained* about the poor food in the cafeteria.] **2** to make a report about something bad [We *complained* to the police about the noisy party next door.]

con·ceive (kən sēv′) *v.* **1** to form or develop in the mind; think of; imagine [I have *conceived* a plan for making a fortune.] **2** to understand [It is difficult to *conceive* how this motor works.] **3** to become pregnant —**con·ceived′, con·ceiv′ing**

con·cern (kən surn′) *v.* to have a relation to; be important to; involve [This matter *concerns* all of us.] —**con·cerned′, con·cern′ing** ◆*n.* worry or anxiety [He felt great *concern* over his wife's health.]

con·cert (kän′sərt) *n.* a musical program, especially one in which a number of musicians perform together

con·di·tion (kən dish′ən) *n.* **1** the particular way a person or thing is [What is the *condition* of the patient? Weather *conditions* won't allow us to go.] **2** the right or healthy way to be [The whole team is in *condition*.] **3** anything which must be or must happen before something else can take place [Her parents made it a *condition* that she had to do her homework before she could watch TV.]

a	ask, fat
ā	ape, date
ä	car, lot
e	elf, ten
ē	even, meet
i	is, hit
ī	ice, fire
ō	open, go
ô	law, horn
oi	oil, point
o͝o	look, pull
o͞o	ooze, tool
ou	out, crowd
u	up, cut
ʉ	fur, fern
ə	a in ago
	e in agent
	e in father
	i in unity
	o in collect
	u in focus
ch	chin, arch
ŋ	ring, singer
sh	she, dash
th	thin, truth
th	then, father
zh	s in pleasure

con·fi·dence (kän′ fi dəns) *n.* **1** strong belief or trust in someone or something; reliance [They have *confidence* in my skill.] **2** a belief in oneself; self-confidence [I began to play the piano with *confidence*.] **3** trust in another to keep one's secret [She told it to him in strict *confidence*.] **4** a secret [Don't burden me with your *confidences*.]

con·gress (kän′ grəs) *n.* **1** a coming together; meeting; convention ☆**2 Congress**, the group of elected officials that makes the laws: it consists of the Senate and the House of Representatives

con·gru·ent (kän′ gro͞o ənt) *adj.* in agreement or harmony; corresponding

con·nect (kə nekt′) *v.* **1** to join together; unite [Several bridges *connect* Ohio and Kentucky.] **2** to relate in some way; think of together [Do you *connect* his silence with her arrival?] —**con·nect′ed, con·nect′ing**

con·quer (käŋ′ kər) *v.* **1** to get or gain by using force, as by winning a war [The Spaniards *conquered* Mexico.] **2** to overcome by trying hard; get the better of; defeat [She *conquered* her bad habits.] —**con′ quer·or** *n.*

con·science (kän′ shəns) *n.* a sense of right and wrong; feeling that keeps one from doing bad things [My *conscience* bothers me after I tell a lie.]

con·serve (kən sʉrv′) *v.* to keep from being hurt, lost, or wasted [to *conserve* one's energy] —**con·served′**

con·sid·er·ate (kən sid′ər ət) *adj.* thoughtful of other people's feelings; kind [It was *considerate* of you to invite her too.] —**con·sid′ er·ate·ly** *adv.*

con·sole (kən sōl′) *v.* to make less sad or troubled; comfort [A toy *consoled* the lost child.] —**con·soled′, con·sol′ing**

con·sti·tu·tion (kän′sti to͞o′shən *or* kän′sti tyo͞o′shən) *n.* **1** the act of setting up, forming, establishing, etc. **2** the way in which a person or thing is formed; makeup; structure [My strong *constitution* keeps me from catching cold.] **3** the system of basic laws or rules of a government, society, etc. **4** a document in which these laws and rules are written down [The *Constitution* of the U.S. is the supreme law here.]

con·trib·ute (kən trib′yo͞ot) *v.* **1** to give together with others [I *contribute* to my church.] **2** to write an article, poem, etc. as for a magazine or newspaper —**con·trib′ut·ed, con·trib′ut·ing**

con·vex (kän vəks′ *or* kän′vəks) *adj.* curving outward like the outside of a ball [a *convex* lens] —**con·vex′i·ty** *n.* —**con·vex′ly** *adv.*

cook (ko͞ok) *v.* **1** to prepare food by heating; boil, roast, bake, etc. **2** to be cooked [The roast should *cook* longer.]

co·op·er·ate (kō äp′ər āt′) *v.* to work together to get something done [If we all *cooperate*, we can finish sooner.] —**co·op′ er·at·ed, co·op′ er·at·ing** —**co·op′ er·a′ tion** *n.*

☆**corn·bread** (kôrn′ bred) *n.* bread made with cornmeal

cor·rect (kə rekt′) *v.* **1** to make right; get rid of mistakes in [*Correct* your spelling before turning in your papers.] **2** to point out the mistakes of; sometimes, to punish or scold for such mistakes [to *correct* a child's behavior] ◆*adj.* **1** without a mistake; right; true [a *correct* answer] **2** agreeing with what is thought to be proper [*correct* behavior] —**cor·rect′ly** *adv.* —**cor·rect′ness** *n.*

cough (kôf *or* käf) *v.* to force air from the lungs with a sudden, loud noise —**coughed, cough′ing** ◆*n.* the act or sound of coughing [I have a bad *cough*.]

coun·se·lor or **coun·sel·lor** (koun′sə lər) *n.* **1** a person who advises; adviser **2** a lawyer **3** a person in charge of children at a camp

count (kount) *v.* **1** to name numbers in a regular order [I'll *count* to five.] **2** to add up so as to get a total [*Count* the people here.] **3** to take account of; include [There are ten here, *counting* you.] **4** to be taken into account; have importance, value, etc. [Every bit of help *counts*.] —**count′ed**

☆**count·down** (kount′doun) *n.* the schedule of things that take place in planned order just before the firing of a rocket, the setting off of a nuclear explosion, etc.; also, the counting backward in units of time while these things take place

coun·try (kun′ trē) *n.* **1** an area of land; region [wooded *country*] **2** the whole land of a nation [The *country* of Japan is made up of islands.] **3** the people of a nation [The speech was broadcast to the whole *country*.] **4** the nation to which one belongs ["My *country*, 'tis of thee"] —*pl.* **coun′tries**

cou·ple (kup′əl) *n.* **1** two things of the same kind that go together; pair [a *couple* of book ends] **2** a man and woman who are married, engaged, or partners, as in a dance ◆*v.* to join together; unite; connect [to *couple* railroad cars] —**cou′pled, cou′pling**

cou·pon (ko͞o′pän *or* kyo͞o′pän) *n.* **1** a ticket or part of a ticket that gives the holder certain rights [The *coupon* on the cereal box is worth 10¢ toward buying another box.] **2** a part of a bond which is cut off at certain times and turned in for payment of interest **3** a part of a printed advertisement that can be used for ordering goods, samples, etc.

cou·ra·geous (kə rā′ jəs) *adj.* having or showing courage; brave

cour·te·ous (kʉr′tē əs) *adj.* polite and kind; thoughtful of others

cous·in (kuz'ən) **n. 1** the son or daughter of one's uncle or aunt: *also called* **first cousin** [You are a second *cousin* to the children of your parents' first *cousins*, and you are a first *cousin* once removed to the children of your first cousins] **2** a distant relation

cov·er (kuv'ər) **v. 1** to place one thing over another; spread over [*Cover* the bird cage at night. *Cover* the wall with white paint. Water *covered* the fields.] **2** to keep from being seen or known; hide [He tried to *cover* up the scandal.] **3** to protect, as from harm or loss [Are you *covered* by insurance?] **4** to provide for; take care of [Is this case *covered* by the rules?] **5** to have to do with; be about; include [This book *covers* the Civil War.]

cran·ber·ry (kran'ber'ē) **n. 1** a hard, sour, red berry used in sauces and jellies **2** the marsh plant it grows on —*pl.* **cran'ber'ries**

crea·ture (krē'chər) **n.** a living being; any person or animal

cred·it (kred'it) **n. 1** belief; trust [I give little *credit* to what he says.] **2** praise or approval [I give her *credit* for trying.] **3** official recognition in a record [You will receive *credit* for your work on this project.] **4** a person or thing that brings praise [She is a *credit* to the team.] **5** trust that a person will be able and willing to pay later [That store doesn't give *credit*, so you have to pay cash.]

crim·i·nal (krim'i nəl) **adj. 1** being a crime; that is a crime [a *criminal* act] **2** having to do with crime [*criminal* law] ◆*n.* a person guilty of a crime —**crim'i·nal·ly adv.**

crowd (kroud) **n. 1** a large group of people together [*crowds* of Christmas shoppers] **2** the common people; the masses ☆**3** a group of people having something in common; set: *used only in everyday talk* [My brother's *crowd* is too old for me.] ◆*v.* **1** to push or squeeze [Can we all *crowd* into one car?] **2** to come together in a large group [People *crowded* to see the show.] —**crowd'ed**

cu·cum·ber (kyōo'kum bər) **n. 1** a long vegetable with green skin and firm, white flesh: it is used in salads and made into pickles **2** the vine that it grows on —**cool as a cucumber,** calm; not excited

cuff (kuf) **n. 1** a band at the wrist of a sleeve, either fastened to the sleeve or separate **2** a fold turned up at the bottom of a trouser leg **3** a handcuff

cu·mu·lus (kyōom'yə ləs) **n.** a kind of cloud in which round masses are piled up on each other

cur·rant (kur'ənt) **n. 1** a small, sweet, black raisin, used in cooking **2** a small, sour berry used in jams and jellies; also, the bush it grows on

cus·tom·er (kus'tə mər) **n. 1** a person who buys, especially one who buys regularly [I have been a *customer* of that shop for many years.] **2** any person with whom one has dealings: *used only in everyday talk*

dan·ger·ous (dān'jər əs) **adj.** full of danger; likely to cause injury, pain, etc.; unsafe [This shaky old bridge is *dangerous*.] —**dan'ger·ous·ly adv.**

Dan·ube (dan'yōob) a river in southern Europe, flowing from southwestern Germany eastward into the Black Sea

dark (därk) **adj. 1** having little or no light [a *dark* room; a *dark* night] **2** closer to black than to white; deep in shade; not light [*dark* green] **3** hidden; full of mystery [a *dark* secret] **4** gloomy or hopeless [Things look *dark* for Lou.] —**dark'ly adv.** —**dark'ness n.**

dark·en (där'kən) **v.** to make or become dark

daugh·ter (dôt'ər *or* dät'ər) **n. 1** a girl or woman as she is related to a parent or to both parents **2** a girl or woman who is influenced by something in the way that a child is by a parent [a *daughter* of France]

de·cay (dē kā') **v. 1** to become rotten by the action of bacteria [The fallen apples *decayed* on the ground.] **2** to fall into ruins; become no longer sound, powerful, rich, beautiful, etc. [Spain's power *decayed* after its fleet was destroyed.] **3** to break down so that there are fewer radioactive atoms

de·ceit (dē sēt') **n. 1** a deceiving or lying **2** a lie or a dishonest act or acts

de·ceive (dē sēv') **v.** to make someone believe what is not true; fool or trick; mislead [The queen *deceived* Snow White by pretending to be her friend.] —**de·ceived', de·ceiv'ing** —**de·ceiv'er n.**

de·cid·ed (dē sīd'əd) **adj. 1** clear and sharp; definite [a *decided* change in the weather] **2** sure or firm; without doubt [Clem has very *decided* ideas on the subject.] —**de·cid'ed·ly adv.**

de·code (dē kōd') **v.** to figure out the meaning of something written in code —**de·cod'ed, de·cod'ing**

dec·o·ra·tive (dek'ə rə tiv *or* dek'ə rā'tiv) **adj.** that serves to decorate; ornamental

de·coy (dē'koi *or* dē koi') **n. 1** an artificial bird or animal used to attract wild birds or animals to a place where they can be shot or trapped; also, a live bird or animal used in the same way **2** a thing or person used to lure someone into a trap

a	ask, fat
ā	ape, date
ä	car, lot
e	elf, ten
ē	even, meet
i	is, hit
ī	ice, fire
ō	open, go
ô	law, horn
oi	oil, point
ŏŏ	look, pull
ōō	ooze, tool
ou	out, crowd
u	up, cut
ʉ	fur, fern
ə	a in ago
	e in agent
	e in father
	i in unity
	o in collect
	u in focus
ch	chin, arch
ŋ	ring, singer
sh	she, dash
th	thin, truth
th	then, father
zh	s in pleasure

de·gree (dē grē′) *n.* **1** a step in a series; stage in the progress of something [He advanced by *degrees* from office clerk to president.] **2** a unit used in measuring temperature that is shown by the symbol °: the boiling point of water is 100° Celsius or 212° Fahrenheit **3** a unit used in measuring angles and arcs of circles [There are 360 *degrees* in the circumference of a circle.] **4** a rank given by a college to a student who has satisfactorily completed a course of study, or to an outstanding person as an honor [a B.A. *degree*]

de·lay (dē lā′) *v.* **1** to put off to a later time; postpone [The bride's illness will *delay* the wedding.] **2** to make late; hold back; keep from going on [We were *delayed* by the storm.]

de·light·ful (dē līt′fəl) *adj.* giving delight or pleasure; very pleasing [a *delightful* party] —**de·light′·ful·ly** *adv.*

de·part·ment (dē pärt′mənt) *n.* a separate part or branch, as of a government or business [the police *department*; the shipping *department*; the *department* of mathematics in a college] —**de·part·men·tal** (dē′part ment′l) *adj.*

de·pend·a·ble (dē pen′də bəl) *adj.* that can be depended on; reliable [a *dependable* friend] —**de·pend′·a·bil′·i·ty** *n.*

de·pos·it (dē päz′it) *v.* **1** to place for safekeeping, as money in a bank **2** to give as part payment or as a pledge [They *deposited* $500 on a new car.] **3** to lay down [I *deposited* my books on the chair. The river *deposits* tons of mud at its mouth.] ►*n.* **1** something placed for safekeeping, as money in a bank **2** money given as a pledge or part payment

de·scend·ant (dē sen′dənt) *n.* a person who is descended from a certain ancestor

de·sign (dē zīn′) *n.* **1** a drawing or plan to be followed in making something [the *designs* for a house] **2** the arrangement of parts, colors, etc.; pattern or decoration [the *design* in a rug] ►*v.* **1** to think up and draw plans for [to *design* a new model of a car] **2** to arrange the parts, colors, etc. of [Who *designed* this book?] **3** to set apart for a certain use; intend [This chair was not *designed* for hard use.] —**de·signed′**

de·stroy (dē strɔi′) *v.* to put an end to by breaking up, tearing down, ruining, or spoiling [The flood *destroyed* 300 homes.] —**de·stroyed′, de·stroy′ing**

de·tec·tor (dē tek′tər) *n.* a person or thing that detects; especially, a device used to show that something is present

di·am·e·ter (dī am′ət ər) *n.* **1** a straight line passing through the center of a circle or sphere, from one side to the other **2** the length of such a line [The *diameter* of the moon is about 2,160 miles.]

di·a·ry (dī′ə rē) *n.* **1** a record written day by day of some of the things done, seen, or thought by the writer **2** a book for keeping such a record —*pl.* **di′·a·ries**

dic·tion·ar·y (dik′shə ner′ē) *n.* **1** a book in which some or most of the words of a language, or of some special field, are listed in alphabetical order with their meanings, pronunciations, etc. [a school *dictionary*; a medical *dictionary*] **2** a book like this in which words of one language are explained in words of another language [a Spanish-English *dictionary*] —*pl.* **dic′·tion·ar′ies**

dig·it (dij′it) *n.* **1** any number from 0 through 9 **2** a finger or toe

di·plo·ma (di plō′mə) *n.* a certificate given to a student by a school or college to show that the student has completed a required course of study

di·rec·tion (də rek′shən) *n.* **1** a directing or managing; control [The choir is under the *direction* of Ms. Jones.] **2** an order or command **3** *usually* **directions**, *pl.* instructions on how to get to some place or how to do something [*directions* for driving to Omaha; *directions* for building a model boat] **4** the point toward which something faces or the line along which something moves or lies ["North," "up," "forward," and "left" are *directions*.] —**di·rec′·tion·al** *adj.*

di·rec·tor (də rek′tər) *n.* **1** a person who directs or manages the work of others [the *director* of a play, a band, a government bureau] **2** a member of a group chosen to direct the affairs of a business —**di·rec′·tor·ship** *n.*

dis·ap·pear (dis ə pir′) *v.* to stop being seen or to stop existing; vanish [The car *disappeared* around a curve. Dinosaurs *disappeared* millions of years ago.] —**dis′·ap·pear′ance** *n.*

dis·ap·prove (dis ə pr⁻oōv′) *v.* to refuse to approve; have an opinion or feeling against; think to be wrong [The Puritans *disapproved* of dancing.] —**dis·ap·proved′, dis·ap·prov′ing** —**dis′·ap·prov′ing·ly** *adv.*

dis·be·lief (dis bə lēf′) *n.* the state of not believing; lack of belief [The guide stared at me in *disbelief*.]

dis·con·tin·ue (dis′kən tin′y⁻oō) *v.* to stop doing, using, etc; give up [to *discontinue* a subscription to a magazine] —**dis′·con·tin′ued, dis′·con·tin′u·ing**

dis·cov·er (di skuv′ər) *v.* **1** to be the first to find, see, or learn about [Marie and Pierre Curie *discovered* radium.] **2** to come upon, learn, or find out about [I *discovered* my name on the list.] **3** to be the first person who is not a native to come to or see a continent, river, etc. [De Soto *discovered* the Mississippi River.] —**dis·cov′·ered**

dis·grace (dis grās′) *n.* **1** loss of favor, respect, or honor; dishonor; shame [She is in *disgrace* for cheating on the test.] **2** a person or thing bringing shame [Slums are a *disgrace* to a city ►*v.* to bring shame or dishonor upon; hurt the reputation of [My cousin's crime has *disgraced* our family.] —**dis·graced′, dis·grac′ing**

dis·mal (diz′məl) *adj.* **1** causing gloom or misery; sad [a *dismal* story] **2** dark and gloomy [a *dismal* room] —**dis′mal·ly** *adv.*

dis·play (di splā′) *v.* to put or spread out so as to be seen; exhibit [to *display* a collection of stamps] —**dis·played′, dis·play′ing** ◆*n.* something that is displayed [a *display* of jewelry]

dis·tance (dis′təns) *n.* **1** the length of a line between two points [The *distance* between New York and Chicago is 713 miles.] **2** the condition of being far apart in space or time; remoteness ["*Distance* lends charm." There was quite a *distance* between their views.] **3** a place far away [viewing things from a *distance*] —**dis′tanced, dis′tanc·ing** ◆*v.*

dis·turb (dis tʉrb′) *v.* **1** to break up the quiet or calm of [The roar of motorcycles *disturbed* the peace.] **2** to make worried or uneasy; upset [They are *disturbed* by their parents′ divorce.] **3** to put into disorder; mix up [Someone *disturbed* the books on my shelf.]

di·vide (də vīd′) *v.* **1** to separate into parts; split up [a classroom *divided* by a movable wall] **2** to separate into equal parts by arithmetic [If you *divide* 12 by 3, you get 4.] **3** to put into separate groups; classify [Living things are *divided* into plants and animals.] **4** to make separate or keep apart [A stone wall *divides* their farms.]

dol·phin (dôl′fin) *n.* a water animal related to the whale but smaller: the common dolphin has a long snout and many teeth

dom·i·nant (däm′ə nənt) *adj.* most important or most powerful; ruling, controlling [a *dominant* world power]

dou·ble (dub′əl) *adj.* **1** having two parts that are alike [a *double* house; a *double* door; gun with a *double* barrel] **2** being of two kinds [Sometimes a word is used in a joke because it has a *double* meaning and can be understood in two different ways.] **3** twice as much, as many, as great, as fast, etc. [a *double* portion; *double* time] **4** made for two [a *double* bed; a *double* garage] ◆*adv.* two at one time; in a pair [to ride *double* on a bicycle] —**dou′bled, doub′ling** *v.*

doz·en (duz′ən) *n.* a group of twelve. —*pl.* **doz′ens** or, *especially after a number*, **doz′en.**

drain (drān) *v.* **1** to make flow away [*Drain* the water from the potatoes.] **2** to draw off water or other liquid from; make empty [to *drain* a swamp; to *drain* one′s glass] **3** to flow off [Water won′t *drain* from a flat roof.] **4** to become empty or dry [Our bathtub *drains* slowly.] **5** to flow into [The Ohio River *drains* into the Mississippi.]

dra·ma (drä′mə *or* dram′ə) *n.* **1** a story that is written to be acted out, as on a stage; play **2** the art of writing or performing plays **3** a series of interesting or exciting events [the *drama* of the American Revolution]

draw·er (drô′r *or* drôr) *n.* **1** a person or thing that draws **2** a box that slides in and out of a table, chest, desk, etc.

drear·y (drir′ē) *adj.* without happiness or cheer; gloomy, sad, or dull [a long, *dreary* tale] —**drear′i·er, drear′i·est** —**drear′i·ly** *adv.* —**drear′i·ness** *n.*

du·ra·ble (door′ə bəl *or* dʉr′ə bəl) *adj.* lasting in spite of hard wear or much use —**du′ra·bil′i·ty** *n.* —**du′ra·bly** *adv.*

Ee

earth·quake (ʉrth′kwāk) *n.* a shaking or trembling of the ground, caused by the shifting of underground rock or by the action of a volcano

ea·sel (ē′zəl) *n.* a standing frame for holding an artist′s canvas or a picture

ee·rie or **ee·ry** (ir′ē) *adj.* giving a person a feeling of fear or mystery; weird [an *eerie* house that looked haunted]

ef·fort (ef′ərt) *n.* **1** the use of energy to get something done; a trying hard with the mind or body [It took great *effort* to climb the mountain.] **2** a try or attempt [They made no *effort* to be friendly.] **3** something done with effort [My early *efforts* at poetry were not published.]

eight·een (ā′tēn′) *n., adj.* the cardinal number between seventeen and nineteen; 18

eight·y (āt′ē) *n., adj.* eight times ten; the number 80 —*pl.* **eight′ies** —**the eighties,** the numbers or years from 80 through 89

ei·ther (ē′thər *or* ī′thər) *adj.* **1** one or the other of two [Use *either* exit.] **2** both one and the other; each [She had a tool in *either* hand.] ◆*pron.* one or the other of two [*Either* of the suits will fit you.]

e·lec·tion (ē lek′shən) *n.* the act of choosing or the fact of being chosen, especially by voting

e·lec·tric (ē lek′trik) *adj.* **1** of or having to do with electricity [*electric* current; *electric* wire] **2** making or made by electricity [an *electric* generator; *electric* lighting] **3** worked by electricity [an *electric* toothbrush]

e·lec·tron·ic (ē lek′trän′ ik *or* el′ek trän′ik) *adj.* working or produced by the action of electrons [*electronic* equipment]

el·e·va·tion (el′ə vā′shən) *n.* **1** a raising up or being raised up [her *elevation* to the position of principal] **2** a higher place or position [The house is on a slight *elevation*.] **3** height above the surface of the earth or above sea level [The mountain has an *elevation* of 20,000 feet.]

em·per·or (em′pər ər) *n.* a man who rules an empire

a	ask, fat
ā	ape, date
ä	car, lot
e	elf, ten
ē	even, meet
i	is, hit
ī	ice, fire
ō	open, go
ô	law, horn
σi	oil, point
σo	look, pull
σo	ooze, tool
σu	out, crowd
u	up, cut
ʉ	fur, fern
ə	a in ago
	e in agent
	e in father
	i in unity
	o in collect
	u in focus
ch	chin, arch
ŋ	ring, singer
sh	she, dash
th	thin, truth
th	then, father
zh	s in pleasure

em·pire (em′pīr) *n.* **1** a group of countries or territories under the control of one government or ruler [Much of Europe was once a part of the Roman *Empire*.] **2** any government whose ruler has the title of emperor or empress **3** a large business or group of businesses controlled by one person, family, or group

em·ploy·ee or **em·ploy·e** (em plɔi′ē *or* em′plɔi ē′) *n.* a person who works for another in return for pay

en·a·ble (en ā′bəl) *v.* to make able; give the means or power to [A loan *enabled* Lou to go to college.] —**en·a′bled, en·a′bling**

en·cour·age (en kʉr′ij) *v.* to give courage or hope to; make feel more confident [Praise *encouraged* the children to try harder.] —**en·cour′aged, en·cour′′ag·ing**

en·cy·clo·pe·di·a or **en·cy·clo·pae·di·a** (en sī′klə pē′ dē ə) *n.* a book or set of books that gives information on all branches of knowledge or, sometimes, on just one branch of knowledge: it is made up of articles usually in alphabetical order

en·dan·ger (en dān′jər) *v.* to put in danger or peril [to *endanger* one's life]

en·dan·gered species (en dān′jərd) *n.* a species of animal or plant in danger of becoming extinct, or dying off [The whooping crane is an *endangered* species.]

en·dure (en dʊr′ *or* en dyʊr′) *v.* **1** to hold up under pain, weariness, etc.; put up with; bear; stand [to *endure* torture; to *endure* insults] **2** to go on for a long time; last; remain [The Sphinx has *endured* for ages.] —**en·dured′, en·dur′ing** —**en·dur′a·ble** *adj.*

en·force (en fôrs′) *v.* **1** to force people to pay attention to; make people obey [to *enforce* traffic laws] **2** to bring about by using force or being strict [He is unable to *enforce* his views on others.] —**en·forced′, en·forc′ing** —**en·force′ment** *n.*

en·gage (en gāj′) *v.* **1** to promise to marry [Harry is *engaged* to Grace.] **2** to promise or undertake to do something [She *engaged* to tutor the child after school.] **3** to get the right to use something or the services of someone; hire [to *engage* a hotel room; to *engage* a lawyer] **4** to take part or be active [I have no time to *engage* in dramatics.] —**en·gaged′, en·gag′ing**

en·gi·neer (en′jə nir′) *n.* **1** a person who is trained in some branch of engineering **2** a person who runs an engine, as the driver of a railroad locomotive **3** a soldier whose special work is the building or wrecking of roads, bridges, etc.

en·joy·a·ble (en jɔi′ə bəl) *adj.* giving joy or pleasure; delightful [What an *enjoyable* concert!]

e·nough (ē nuf′) *adj.* as much or as many as needed or wanted; sufficient [There is *enough* food for all.] ➤*n.* the amount needed or wanted [I have heard *enough* of that music.] ➤*adv.* as much as needed; to the right amount [Is your steak cooked *enough*?]

en·rich (en rich′) *v.* to make richer in value or quality [Music *enriches* one's life.] —**en·riched′, en·rich′ing**

en·ter·prise (en′tər prīz) *n.* **1** any business or undertaking, especially one that takes daring and energy **2** willingness to undertake new or risky projects [They succeeded because of their *enterprise*.]

en·tire (en tīr′) *adj.* **1** including all the parts; whole; complete [I've read the *entire* book.] **2** not broken, not weakened, not lessened, etc. [We have his *entire* support.] —**en·tire′ly** *adv.*

en·vi·ron·ment (en vī′rən mənt) *n.* the things that surround anything; especially, all the conditions that surround a person, animal, or plant and affect growth, actions, character, etc. [Removing pollution from water and air will improve our *environment*.] —**en·vi·ron·men′tal** *adj.*

en·vy (en′vē) *n.* **1** jealousy and dislike felt toward another having some thing, quality, etc. that one would like to have [He glared at the winner with a look of *envy*.] **2** the person or thing one has such feelings about [Their new car is the *envy* of the neighborhood.] —*pl.* **en′vies** ➤*v.* to feel envy toward or because of [to *envy* a person for her wealth] —**en′vied, en′vy·ing**

e·qual (ē′kwəl) *adj.* **1** of the same amount, size, or value [The horses were of *equal* height.] **2** having the same rights, ability, or position [All persons are *equal* in a court of law in a just society.] ➤*v.* **1** to be equal to; match [His long jump *equaled* the school record. Six minus two *equals* four.] **2** to do or make something equal to [You can *equal* my score easily.] —**e′qualed** or **e′qualled, e′qual·ing** or **e′qual·ling** —**e′qual·ly** *adv.*

e·qual·i·ty (ē kôwl′ə tē) *n.* the condition of being equal, especially of having the same political, social, and economic rights and duties

e·quip·ment (ē kwip′mənt) *n.* **1** the special things needed for some purpose; outfit, supplies, etc. [fishing *equipment*] **2** the act of equipping

er·rand (er′ənd) *n.* a short trip to do a thing, often for someone else [I'm going downtown on an *errand* for my sister.]

e·soph·a·gus (e säf′ə gəs) *n.* the tube through which food passes from the throat to the stomach

e·vap·o·rate (e vap′ə rāt) *v.* **1** to change into vapor [Heat *evaporates* water. The perfume in the bottle has *evaporated*.] **2** to disappear like vapor; vanish [Our courage *evaporated* when we saw the lion.] **3** to make thicker by heating so as to take some of the water from [to *evaporate* milk] —**e·vap′o·rat·ed, e·vap′o·rat·ing** —**e·vap′o·ra′tion** *n.*

ev·i·dence (ev′ə dəns) *n.* something that shows or proves, or that gives reason for believing; proof or indication [The footprint was *evidence* that someone had been there. Clear skin gives *evidence* of a good diet.] ►*v.* to show clearly; make plain [His smile *evidenced* his joy.] —**ev′i·denced, ev′i·denc·ing**

ex·act·ly (eg zakt′lē) *adv.* **1** in an exact way; precisely [That's *exactly* the bike I want.] **2** quite true; I agree: *used as an answer to something said by another*

ex·ceed (ek sēd′) *v.* **1** to go beyond what is allowed [to *exceed* the speed limit] **2** to be more or better than [Her success *exceeded* her own wildest dreams.] —**ex·ceed′ed, ex·ceed′ing**

ex·cel·lent (ek′sə lənt) *adj.* better than others of its kind; very good [Their cakes are fairly good, but their pies are *excellent*.] —**ex′cel·lent·ly** *adv.*

ex·change (eks chānj′) *v.* **1** to give in return for something else; trade [She *exchanged* the bicycle for a larger one.] **2** to give each other similar things [The bride and groom *exchanged* rings during the ceremony.] —**ex·changed′, ex·chang′ing** ►*n.* **1** a giving of one thing in return for another; trade [I'll give you my pen in *exchange* for that book.] **2** a giving to one another of similar things [Our club has a gift *exchange* at Christmas time.]

ex·cite·ment (ek sīt′mənt) *n.* **1** the condition of being excited [The hotel fire caused great *excitement* in the town.] **2** anything that excites

ex·claim (eks klām′) *v.* to speak out suddenly and with strong feeling, as in surprise, anger, etc. ["I won't go!" she *exclaimed*.]

ex·haust (eg zôst′ *or* eg zäst′) *v.* **1** to use up completely [Our drinking water was soon *exhausted*.] **2** to let out the contents of; make completely empty [The leak soon *exhausted* the gas tank.] **3** to use up the strength of; tire out; weaken [They are *exhausted* from playing tennis.] ►*n.* **1** the used steam or gas that comes from the cylinders of an engine; especially, the fumes from the gasoline engine in an automobile

ex·ist (eg zist′) *v.* **1** to be; have actual being [The unicorn never really *existed*.] **2** to occur or be found [Tigers do not *exist* in Africa.] **3** to live [Fish cannot *exist* long out of water.]

ex·pe·di·tion (ek′spə dish′ən) *n.* **1** a long journey or voyage by a group of people, as to explore a region or to take part in a battle **2** the people, ships, etc. making such a trip **3** speed or quickness with little effort or waste [We finished our task with *expedition*.] —**ex′pe·di′tion·ar′y** *adj.*

ex·pe·ri·ence (ek spir′ē əns) *n.* **1** the fact of living through a happening or happenings [*Experience* teaches us many things.] **2** something that one has done or lived through [This trip was an *experience* that I'll never forget.] **3** skill that one gets by training, practice, and work [a lawyer with much *experience*] —**ex·pe′ri·enced, ex·pe′ri·enc·ing** *v.*

ex·pert (eks′pərt *or* ek spurt′) *adj.* **1** having much special knowledge and experience; very skillful [an *expert* golfer] **2** of or from an expert [*expert* advice] ►*n.* (ek′spərt) an expert person; authority [an *expert* in art]

ex·plain (ek splān′) *v.* **1** to make clear or plain; give details of [He *explained* how the engine works.] **2** to give the meaning of [The teacher *explained* the story.] **3** to give reasons for [Can you *explain* your absence?]

ex·port (ek spôrt′) *v.* to send goods from one country for sale in another [Japan *exports* many radios.] ►*n.* (eks′pôrt) **1** the act of exporting [Brazil raises coffee for *export*.] **2** something exported [Oil is Venezuela's chief *export*.] —**ex·por·ta′tion, ex·port′er**

ex·pres·sion (ek spresh′ən) *n.* **1** an expressing, or putting into words [This note is an *expression* of my gratitude.] **2** a way of speaking, singing, or playing something that gives it real meaning or feeling [to read with *expression*] **3** the act of showing how one feels, what one means, etc. [Laughter is an *expression* of joy.]

ex·tend (ek stend′) *v.* **1** to make longer; stretch out [Careful cleaning *extends* the life of a rug.] **2** to lie or stretch [The fence *extends* along the meadow.] **3** to make larger or more complete; enlarge; increase [to *extend* one's power] **4** to offer or give [May I *extend* congratulations to the winner?] —**ex·tend′ed** *adj.*

ex·tinc·tion (ek stiŋk′shən) *n.* **1** the fact of becoming extinct, or dying out [The California condor faces *extinction*.] **2** a putting an end to or wiping out [the *extinction* of all debts] **3** an extinguishing, or putting out [the *extinction* of a fire]

a	ask, fat
ā	ape, date
ä	car, lot
e	elf, ten
ē	even, meet
i	is, hit
ī	ice, fire
ō	open, go
ô	law, horn
oi	oil, point
oo	look, pull
o͞o	ooze, tool
ou	out, crowd
u	up, cut
ʉ	fur, fern
ə	a in ago
	e in agent
	e in father
	i in unity
	o in collect
	u in focus
ch	chin, arch
ŋ	ring, singer
sh	she, dash
th	thin, truth
th	then, father
zh	s in pleasure

faint (fānt) *adj.* **1** weak; not strong or clear; dim or feeble [a *faint* whisper; a *faint* odor; *faint* shadows] **2** weak and dizzy, as if about to swoon **3** not very certain; slight [a *faint* hope] ✦ *n.* a condition in which one becomes unconscious because not enough blood reaches the brain, as in sudden shock ✦ *v.* to fall into a faint; swoon —**faint′ed** —**faint′ly** *adv.*

false·hood (fôls′hood) *n.* a lie or the telling of lies

fa·mil·iar (fə mil′yər) *adj.* **1** friendly; intimate; well-acquainted [a *familiar* face in the crowd] **2** too friendly; intimate in a bold way [We were annoyed by the *familiar* manner of our new neighbor.] **3** knowing about; acquainted with [Are you *familiar* with this book?] **4** well-known; common; ordinary [Car accidents are a *familiar* sight.] ✦ *n.* a close friend

fam·i·ly (fam′ə lē) *n.* **1** a group made up of one or two parents and all of their children **2** the children alone [a widow who raised a large *family*] **3** a group of people who are related by marriage or a common ancestor; relatives; clan **4** a large group of related plants or animals [The robin is a member of the thrush *family*.] —*pl.* **fam′i·lies**

fa·mous (fā′məs) *adj.* much talked about as being outstanding; very well known

fan·cy (fan′sē) *adj.* having much design and decoration; not plain; elaborate [a *fancy* dress] —**fan′ci·er, fan′ci·est**

farm (färm) *n.* **1** a piece of land used to raise crops or animals; also, the house, barn, orchards, etc. on such land **2** any place where certain things are raised [An area of water for raising fish is a fish *farm*.]

farm·er (fär′mər) *n.* a person who owns or works on a farm

fash·ion (fash′ən) *n.* **1** the popular or up-to-date way of dressing, speaking, or behaving; style [It was once the *fashion* to wear powdered wigs.] **2** the way in which a thing is done, made, or formed [tea served in the Japanese *fashion*] ✦ *v.* to make, form, or shape [Bees *fashion* honeycombs out of wax.]

fau·cet (fô′sət *or* fä′sət) *n.* a device with a valve which can be turned on or off to control the flow of a liquid, as from a pipe; tap; cock

feath·er (fe*th*′ər) *n.* **1** any of the parts that grow out of the skin of birds, covering the body and filling out the wings and tail: feathers are soft and light **2** anything like a feather in looks, lightness, etc. **3** the same class or kind [birds of a *feather*] —**feath′er·y** *adj.*

Feb·ru·ar·y (feb′roo er′ ē *or* feb′yoo er′ ē) *n.* the second month of the year: it usually has 28 days but in leap year it has 29 days; abbreviated **Feb.**

fed·er·al (fed′ər əl) *adj.* **1** of or describing a union of states having a central government **2** of such a central government [a *federal* constitution] ☆**3** *usually* **Federal,** of the central government of the U.S. [the *Federal* courts] —**fed′er·al·ist** *adj., n.*

fel·low·ship (fel′ō ship′) *n.* **1** friendship; companionship **2** a group of people having the same activities or interests **3** money given to a student at a university or college to help him or her study for a higher degree

fer·ry (fer′ē) *v.* to take or go across a river or bay in a boat or raft [They *ferried* our cars to the island.] —**fer′ried, fer′ry·ing**

fes·ti·val (fes′tə vəl) *n.* **1** a happy holiday [The Mardi Gras in New Orleans is a colorful *festival*.] **2** a time of special celebration or entertainment [Our town holds a garlic *festival* every spring.]

fierce (firs) *adj.* **1** wild or cruel; violent; raging [a *fierce* dog; a *fierce* wind] **2** very strong or eager [a *fierce* effort] —**fierc′er, fierc′est** —**fierce′ly** *adv.* —**fierce′ness** *n.*

fi·nal (fī′nəl) *adj.* **1** coming at the end; last; concluding [the *final* chapter in a book] **2** allowing no further change; deciding [The decision of the judes is *final*.] ✦ *n.* **1** anything final **2 finals,** *pl.* the last set in a series of games, tests, etc. —**fi′nal·ly** *adv.*

fi·nance (fi nans′ *or* fī′nans) *n.* **1 finances,** *pl.* all the money or income that a government, company, person, etc. has ready for use **2** the managing of money matters [Bankers are often experts in *finance*.] ✦ *v.* to give or get money for [loans to *finance* new business] —**fi·nanced′, fi·nanc′ing**

fin·ger·nail (fiŋ′gər nāl) *n.* the hard, tough cover at the top of each finger tip

fin·ger·print (fiŋ′gər print) *n.* the mark made by pressing the tip of a finger against a flat surface: the fine lines and circles form a pattern that can be used to identify a person ✦ *v.* to take the fingerprints of someone by pressing the finger tips on an inked surface and then on paper

flaw (flô *or* flä) *n.* **1** a break, scratch, crack, etc. that spoils something; blemish [There is a *flaw* in this diamond.] **2** any fault or error [a *flaw* in one's reasoning] —**flaw′less** *adj.* —**flaw′less·ly** *adv.*

flur·ry (flur′ē) *n.* **1** a sudden, short rush of wind, or a sudden, light fall of rain or snow **2** a sudden, brief excitement or confusion —*pl.* **flur′ries** ✦ *v.* to confuse or excite [New drivers get *flurried* when they are in heavy traffic.] —**flur′ried, flur′ry·ing**

foam·y (fōm′ē) *adj.* foaming, full of foam, or like foam [the *foamy* water in the rapids] —**foam′i·er, foam′i·est** —**foam′i·ness** *n.*

for·bid (fər bid′) **v.** to order that something not be done; not allow; prohibit [The law *forbids* you to park your car there. Talking out loud is *forbidden* in the library.] —**for·bade′** or **for·bad′, for·bid′den, for·bid′ding**

fore·arm (fôr′ärm) **v.** to arm beforehand; get ready for trouble before it comes ►*n.* The part of the arm between the elbow and the wrist

fore·cast (fôr′kast) **v.** to tell or try to tell how something will turn out; predict [Rain is *forecast* for tomorrow.] —**fore′cast** or **fore′cast·ed, fore′cast·ing** ►*n.* a telling of what will happen; prediction [a weather *forecast*] —**fore′cast·er n.**

for·eign (fôr′in *or* fär′in) **adj.** **1** that is outside one's own country, region, etc. [a *foreign* land] **2** of, from, or dealing with other countries [*foreign* trade; *foreign* languages; *foreign* policy] **3** not belonging; not a natural or usual part [conduct *foreign* to one's nature; *foreign* matter in the eye]

fore·see (fôr sē′) **v.** to see or know beforehand [to *foresee* the future] —**fore·saw′, fore·seen′, fore·see′ing**

fore·sight (fôr′sīt) **n.** the ability to look ahead and plan for the future [Amy had the *foresight* to bring a snack on our hike.]

fore·warn (fôr wôrn′) **v.** to warn ahead of time [We were *forewarned* we wouldn't get tickets later.]

for·feit (fôr′fit) **v.** to give up or lose something because of what one has done or has failed to do [Because our team was late in arriving, we had to *forfeit* the game.] ►*n.* the thing that is forfeited; penalty

for·giv·a·ble (fər giv′ə bəl) **adj.** deserving to be forgiven; excusable [*forgivable* anger]

for·give (fər giv′) **v.** to give up feeling angry or wanting to punish; show mercy to; excuse or pardon [She *forgave* him for his unkindness to her.] —**for·gave′, for·giv′en, for·giv′ing** —**for·giv′a·ble adj.**

for·ty-six (fôrt′ē siks) **n.** the cardinal number equal to four times ten plus six; 46

for·ward (fôr′wərd) **adj.** **1** at, toward, or of the front **2** ahead of others in ideas, growth, progress, etc.; advanced **3** ready or eager; prompt [She was *forward* in helping.] **4** too bold or free in manners; rude or impudent —**for′ward·ness n.**

fos·sil (fäs′əl) **n.** **1** any hardened remains or prints, as in rocks or bogs, of plants or animals that lived many years ago **2** a person who is very set or old-fashioned in his or her ideas or ways ►*adj.* **1** of or like a fossil **2** taken from the earth [Coal and oil are *fossil* fuels.]

freight (frāt) **n.** **1** a load of goods shipped by train, truck, ship, airplane, etc. **2** the cost of shipping such goods **3** the shipping of goods in this way [Send it by *freight*.]

friend·ly (frend′lē) **adj.** **1** of, like, to, or from a friend; kindly [some *friendly* advice] **2** showing good and peaceful feelings; ready to be a friend [a *friendly* nation] —**friend′li·er, friend′li·est** ►*adv.* in a friendly way [to act *friendly*] —**friend′li·ness n.**

fright·en (frīt′n) **v.** **1** to make or become suddenly afraid; scare **2** to force to do something by making afraid [He was *frightened* into confessing.] —**fright′ened**

frol·ic (fräl′ik) **n.** a lively game or party; merry play ►*v.* to play or romp about in a happy and carefree way —**frol′icked, frol′ick·ing**

fu·el (fyo͞o′əl) **n.** **1** anything that is burned to give heat or power [Coal, gas, oil, and wood are *fuels*.] **2** anything that makes a strong feeling even stronger [Their teasing only added *fuel* to her anger.] ►*v.* **1** to supply with fuel **2** to get fuel —**fu′eled** or **fu′elled, fu′el·ing** or **fu′el·ling**

fund (fund) **n.** **1** an amount of money to be used for a particular purpose [a scholarship *fund*] **2 funds,** *pl.* money on hand, ready for use **3** a supply; stock [a *fund* of good will]

fu·ture (fyo͞o′chər) **adj.** **1** in the time to come; after the present time [a *future* date; my *future* happiness] **2** showing time to come ["Shall" and "will" are used with a verb to express *future* tense.] ►*n.* **1** the time that is to come [We'll buy a new car sometime in the *future*.] **2** what is going to be [We all have some control over the *future*.] **3** chance to succeed [She has a great *future* as a lawyer.] —**fu′tur·is′tic adj.**

gadg·et (gaj′ət) **n.** **1** a small, mechanical thing having some special use [a *gadget* for opening cans] **2** any interesting but not very useful device

gain (gān) **n.** **1** a thing or amount added; increase or addition [a *gain* in weight] **2** *often* **gains,** *pl.* profit or winnings [the *gains* from our business] **3** the act of getting something, especially money [A love of *gain* can make a person greedy.] ►*v.* **1** to get as an increase or advantage [He *gained* ten pounds in two months.] **2** to become better; improve [She *gained* in health.] —**gained, gaining**

gall·blad·der (gôl′blad ər) **n.** a small sac attached to the liver; the gall, or bile, is stored in it

ga·rage (gər äzh′ *or* gər äj′) **n.** **1** a closed place where automobiles are sheltered **2** a place where automobiles are repaired

a	ask, fat
ā	ape, date
ä	car, lot
e	elf, ten
ē	even, meet
i	is, hit
ī	ice, fire
ō	open, go
ô	law, horn
σi	oil, point
σσ	look, pull
o͞o	ooze, tool
ou	out, crowd
u	up, cut
ʉ	fur, fern
ə	a in ago
	e in agent
	e in father
	i in unity
	o in collect
	u in focus
ch	chin, arch
ŋ	ring, singer
sh	she, dash
th	thin, truth
th	then, father
zh	s in pleasure

gen·er·al (jen'ər əl) *adj.* **1** of, for or from the whole or all, not just a part or some [to promote the *general* welfare] **2** widespread or common [The *general* opinion of him is unfavorable.] **3** having to do with the main parts but not with details [the *general* features of a plan] **4** not special or specialized [*general* science; a *general* store] **5** highest in rank; most important [the attorney *general*]

gen·er·a·tion (jen' ər ā'shən) *n.* **1** a single stage in the history of a family [Grandmother, mother, and son are three *generations*.] **2** all the people born at about the same time [Most of his *generation* of men spent time in the army.] **3** the average time between the birth of one generation and the birth of the next, about 30 years

gen·er·ous (jen'ər əs) *adj.* **1** willing to give or share; not selfish or stingy; openhanded **2** large; great in amount [*generous* helpings of dessert] **3** not mean; noble and forgiving [To forgive your enemy is a *generous* act.] —**gen'er·ous·ly** *adv.* —**gen'er·ous·ness** *n.*

ge·og·ra·phy (jē ȯg'rə fē *or* jē ä'grə fē) *n.* **1** the study of the surface of the earth and how it is divided into continents, countries, seas, etc.: geography also deals with the climates, plants, animals, minerals, etc. of the earth **2** the natural features of a certain part of the earth [the *geography* of Ohio] —**ge·og'ra·pher**

ge·ol·o·gy (jē ä'lə jē) *n.* the study of the earth's crust and of the way in which its layers were formed: it includes the study of rocks and fossils —**ge·ol'o·gist**

ge·om·e·try (jē äm'ə trē) *n.* the branch of mathematics that deals with lines, angles, surfaces, and solids, and with their measurement

Geor·gia (jȯr'jə) **1** a state in the southeastern part of the U.S.: abbreviated **Ga., GA 2** a republic southwest of Russia —**Geor'gian** *adj., n.*

ges·ture (jes' chər) *n.* **1** a motion made with some part of the body, especially the hands or arms, to show some idea or feeling **2** anything said or done to show one's feelings; sometimes, something done just for effect, and not really meant [Our neighbor's gift was a *gesture* of friendship.] ✦ *v.* to make a gesture or gestures —**ges'tured, ges'tur·ing**

gi·gan·tic (jī gan'tik) *adj.* like a giant in size; very big; huge; enormous [a gigantic building]

gnaw (nȯ *or* nä) *v.* **1** to bite and wear away bit by bit with the teeth [The rat *gnawed* the rope in two. The dog *gnawed* on the bone.] **2** to make by gnawing [to *gnaw* a hole] **3** to keep on troubling for a long time [Jealousy *gnawed* at her heart.] —**gnawed, gnaw'ing, gnaws**

goose (go͞os) *n.* a swimming bird that is like a duck but has a larger body and a longer neck; especially, the female of this bird: the male is called a *gander* —*pl.* **geese**

gorge (gȯrj) *n.* a narrow pass or valley between steep cliffs or walls ✦ *v.* to stuff with food in a greedy way [to *gorge* oneself with cake] —**gorged, gorg'ing**

☆**go·ril·la** (gə ril'ə) *n.* **1** the largest and strongest of the apes, found in African jungles

gov·er·nor (guv'ər nər) *n.* ☆**1** the person elected to be head of a state of the United States **2** a person appointed to govern a province, territory, etc. **3** any of the people who direct some organization [the board of *governors* of a hospital] **4** a device in an engine, etc. that automatically controls its speed —**gov'er·nor·ship'**

grad·u·ate (gra'jo͞o ət) *n.* a person who has finished a course of study at a school or college and has been given a diploma or degree —**grad'u·a'tion** *n.* ✦ *adj.* **1** that is a graduate [*Graduate* students work for degrees above the bachelor's.] ☆**2** of or for graduates [*graduate* courses] ✦ *v.* (gra'jo͞o āt') **1** to make or become a graduate of a school or college **2** to mark off with small lines for measuring [A thermometer is a tube *graduated* in degrees.] —**grad'u·at·ed, grad'u·at·ing**

grand·par·ent (grand'per ənt) *n.* a grandfather or grandmother

gran·ite (gran'it) *n.* a very hard rock used for buildings and monuments

grape·fruit (grāp'fro͞ot) *n.* a large, round citrus fruit with a yellow rind and a juicy, somewhat sour pulp

grate·ful (grāt'fəl) *adj.* **1** feeling thankful or showing thanks; appreciative **2** pleasing or welcome [a *grateful* blessing] —**grate'ful·ly** *adv.* —**grate'ful·ness** *n.*

great (grāt) *adj.* **1** much above the average in size, degree, power, etc.; big or very big; much or very big [the *Great* Lakes; a *great* distance; *great* pain] **2** very much of a [a *great* reader] **3** very important; noted; remarkable [a *great* composer; a great discovery] **4** older or younger by a generation: *used in words formed with a hyphen* [my *great*-aunt; my *great*-niece] —**great'er, great'est** —**great'ly** *adv.* —**great'ness** *n.*

greed·y (grēd'ē) *adj.* wanting or taking all that one can get with no thought of what others need [The *greedy* girl ate all the cookies.] —**greed'i·er, greed'i·est** —**greed'i·ly** *adv.* —**greed'i·ness** *n.*

green (grēn) *adj.* having the color of grass [*green* peas]

grief (grēf) *n.* **1** deep and painful sorrow, as that caused by someone's death **2** something that causes such sorrow

grieve (grēv) *v.* to feel grief; be sad [She is *grieving* over a lost cat.] —**grieved, griev'ing**

gro·cer·y (grō′sər ē) *n.* ☆**1** a store selling food and household supplies **2 groceries,** *pl.* the goods sold by a grocer

guest (gest) *n.* **1** a person who is visiting another's home, or who is being treated to a meal, etc. by another **2** any paying customer of a hotel or restaurant **3** any person invited to appear on a program

guilt·y (gil′tē) *adj.* **1** having done something wrong; being to blame for something [She is often *guilty* of telling lies.] **2** judged in court to be a wrongdoer [The jury found him *guilty* of robbery.] —**guilt′i·er, guilt′i·est** —**guilt′i·ly** *adv.* —**guilt′i·ness** *n.*

gust (gust) *n.* **1** a strong and sudden rush of air or of something carried by the air [a *gust* of wind; *gusts* of smoke] **2** a sudden outburst of laughter, rage, etc. ◆*v.* to blow in gusts —**gust′y** *adj.*

hab·i·tat (hab′i tat′) *n.* the place where an animal or plant is normally found [Woodland streams are the *habitat* of beavers.]

hair·cut (her′kut) *n.* the act or a style of cutting the hair of the head

half (haf) *n.* **1** either of the two equal parts of something [Five is *half* of ten.] **2** a half hour [It is *half* past two.] **3** either of the two parts of an inning in baseball, or of the two main time periods of a game of football, basketball, etc. —*pl.* **halves**

☆**hall·way** (hôl′wā) *n.* a passageway, as between rooms; corridor

ham·burg·er (ham′bʉrg ər) *n.* **1** ground beef **2** a small patty of ground beef, fried or broiled

ham·mock (ham′ək) *n.* a long piece of netting or canvas that is hung with ropes at each end and is used as a bed or couch

harsh (härsh) *adj.* **1** not pleasing to the senses [*harsh* music] **2** cruel or severe [*harsh* punishment] —**harsh′er, harsh′est**

har·vest (här′vəst) *n.* **1** the act of gathering a crop of grain, fruit, etc. when it becomes ripe **2** the time of the year when a crop is gathered **3** all the grain, fruit, etc. gathered in one season; crop [a large *harvest*] **4** the results of doing something [She reaped a *harvest* of love for all her good works.]

hast·y (hās′tē) *adj.* **1** done or made with haste; hurried [a *hasty* lunch] **2** done or made too quickly, without enough thought; rash [a *hasty* decision] —**hast′i·er, hast′i·est** —**hast′i·ly** *adv.* —**hast′i·ness** *n.*

haul (hôl) *v.* **1** to move by pulling; drag or tug [We *hauled* the boat up on the beach.] **2** to carry by wagon, truck, etc. [He *hauls* steel for a large company.] **3** to change the course of a ship by setting the sails —**hauled**

hawk (hôk *or* häk) *n.* a large bird with a strong, hooked beak and claws, and keen sight: it captures and eats smaller birds and animals ◆*v.* to hunt small game with the help of trained hawks

heal (hēl) *v.* to make or become well, sound, or healthy; cure or be cured [The wound *healed* slowly.] —**healed, heal′ing**

health·y (hel′thē) *adj.* **1** having good health; well [a *healthy* child] **2** showing good health [a *healthy* appetite] **3** good for one's health; healthful [a *healthy* climate] —**health′i·er, health′i·est** —**health′i·ness** *n.*

heav·y (hev′ē) *adj.* **1** hard to lift or move because of its weight; weighing very much [a *heavy* load] **2** weighing more than is usual for its kind [Lead is a *heavy* metal.] **3** larger, deeper, greater, etc. than usual [a *heavy* vote; a *heavy* sleep; a *heavy* blow] **4** full of sorrow; sad [a *heavy* heart] **5** hard to do, bear, etc.; difficult [*heavy* work; *heavy* sorrow] —**heav′i·er, heav′i·est** —**heav′i·ly** *adv.* —**heav′i·ness** *n.*

He·brew (hē′brōō) *n.* **1** a member of the ancient people of the Bible who settled in Canaan; Israelite: the Hebrews were the ancestors of the Jews **2** the ancient language of the Israelites or the modern form of this language, used in Israel today: it is written in a different alphabet from English ◆*adj.* of the Hebrews or of the Hebrew language

hel·met (hel′mət) *n.* a hard covering to protect the head, worn by soldiers, certain athletes, motorcycle riders, etc.

hem·i·sphere (hem′i sfir′) *n.* **1** half of a sphere or globe [The dome of the church was in the shape of a *hemisphere*.] **2** any of the halves into which the earth's surface is divided in geography

his·to·ry (his′tər ē) *n.* **1** what has happened in the life of a people, country, science, art, etc.; also, an account of this [the *history* of medicine; a *history* of England] **2** the record of everything that has happened in the past [Nero was one of the worst tyrants in *history*.] **3** the science or study that keeps a record of past events [How will *history* treat our times?] **4** a story or tale [This hat has a strange *history*.] —*pl.* **his′to·ries**

hoax (hōks) *n.* something that is meant to trick or fool others, especially a practical joke ◆*v.* to play a trick on; fool —**hoax′er** *n.*

hope (hōp) *n.* **1** a feeling that what one wants will happen [We gave up *hope* of being rescued.] **2** the thing that one wants [It is my *hope* to go to college.] **3** a person or thing on which one may base some hope [The 1500-meter run is our last *hope* for a victory.] ◆*v.* **1** to have hope; want and expect [I *hope* to see you soon.] **2** to want to believe [I *hope* I didn't overlook anybody.] —**hoped, hop′ing**

a	ask, fat
ā	ape, date
ä	car, lot
e	elf, ten
ē	even, meet
i	is, hit
ī	ice, fire
ō	open, go
ô	law, horn
oi	oil, point
၀၀	look, pull
o͞o	ooze, tool
ou	out, crowd
u	up, cut
ʉ	fur, fern
ə	a in ago
	e in agent
	e in father
	i in unity
	o in collect
	u in focus
ch	chin, arch
ŋ	ring, singer
sh	she, dash
th	thin, truth
th	then, father
zh	s in pleasure

hor·ri·ble (hôr′ə bəl) *adj.* **1** causing a feeling of horror; terrible; dreadful [a *horrible* accident] **2** very bad, ugly, unpleasant, etc.: *used only in everyday talk* [What a *horrible* color!] —**hor′ri·bly** *adv.*

hu·man·i·ty (hyo͞o man′ə tē) *n.* **1** all human beings; the human race [Could *humanity* survive an atomic war?] **2** kindness or sympathy [She showed her *humanity* by caring for the sick.] **3** the special qualities of all human beings; human nature [It is our common *humanity* to be selfish at one time and unselfish at another.] —*pl.* **hu·man′i·ties** —**the humanities**, studies that deal with human relations and human thought, as literature, philosophy, the fine arts, etc., but not the sciences

hu·mid·i·ty (hyo͞o mid′ə tē) *n.* dampness; especially, the amount of moisture in the air

hu·mor·ous (hyo͞o′mər əs) *adj.* funny or amusing; comical —**hu′mor·ous·ly** *adv.*

Hun·ga·ry (huŋ′gər ē) a country in central Europe —**Hun·gar′i·an** (huŋ ger′ē ən) *adj., n.*

hun·gry (huŋ′grē) *adj.* **1** wanting or needing food [Cold weather makes me *hungry*.] **2** having a strong desire; eager [*hungry* for praise] —**hun′gri·er, hun′gri·est** —**hun′gri·ly** *adv.* —**hun′gri·ness** *n.*

hy·phen (hī′fən) *n.* the mark (-) used between the parts of a compound word (as *court-martial*), or between the parts of a word divided at the end of a line ◆*v.* to hyphenate

ice·berg (īs′bʉrg) *n.* a mass of ice broken off from a glacier and floating in the sea: the larger part of an iceberg is under water

i·ci·cle (ī′sik əl) *n.* a hanging stick of ice formed by water freezing as it drips down

i·den·ti·fi·ca·tion (ī den′tə fi kā′ shən) *n.* **1** anything that identifies a person or thing [Fingerprints are used as *identification*.] **2** an identifying or being identified

ig·loo (ig′lo͞o) *n.* a hut built by Eskimos using blocks of packed snow —*pl.* **ig′loos**

il·lus·trate (il′ə strāt *or* i lus′trāt) *v.* **1** to make clear or explain by giving examples, making comparisons, etc. [Census figures *illustrate* how the city has grown.] **2** to put drawings or pictures in that explain or decorate [an *illustrated* book] —**il′lus·trat·ed, il′lus·trat·ing**

i·mag·i·na·tion (i maj′ i nā′shən) *n.* **1** the act or power of making up pictures or ideas in the mind of what is not present or of how things might be [The flying saucer you thought you saw is just in your *imagination*. It takes great *imagination* to write a play.] **2** the ability to understand and appreciate what others imagine, especially in art and literature [She hasn't enough *imagination* to know what that short story is about.]

im·i·ta·tion (im′ i tā′shən) *n.* **1** the act of imitating or copying [The children danced in *imitation* of swaying trees.] **2** a copy or likeness [These jewels are clever *imitations* of precious gems.] ◆*adj.* made to look like something better; not real [a belt of *imitation* leather]

im·mense (im mens′) *adj.* very large; huge; vast [an *immense* territory] —**im·mense′ly** *adv.*

im·merse (im mʉrs′) *v.* **1** to plunge or dip into a liquid **2** to baptize a person by dipping under water **3** to get or be deeply in; absorb [*immersed* in study; *immersed* in sadness] —**im·mersed′, im·mers′ing** —**im·mer·sion** (im mʉr′shən) *n.*

im·mo·bile (im mō′bəl) *adj.* not moving or changing; without motion [The frightened deer stood *immobile*.] —**im′mo·bil′i·ty** *n.*

im·po·lite (im pə līt′) *adj.* not polite; rude —**im·po·lite′ly** *adv.* —**im·po·lite′ness** *n.*

im·por·tance (im pôrt′ns) *n.* the fact of being important [news of little *importance*]

im·por·tant (im pôrt′nt) *adj.* **1** having much meaning or value [Our wedding anniversary is an *important* date in our lives.] **2** having power of authority, or acting as if one had power [an *important* official] —**im·por′tant·ly** *adv.*

im·pose (im pōz′) *v.* to put on as a duty, burden, or penalty [to *impose* a tax on furs] —**im·posed′, im·pos′ing**

im·pos·si·ble (im päs′ə bəl) *adj.* **1** that cannot be, be done, or happen; not possible [He found it *impossible* to lift the crate.] **2** very unpleasant or hard to put up with [You're always asking *impossible* questions!] —**im·pos′si·bil′i·ty** *n.* —**im·pos′si·bly** *adv.*

im·pres·sion (im presh′ən) *n.* **1** the act of impressing **2** a mark or imprint made by pressing [The police took an *impression* of his fingerprints.] **3** an effect produced on the mind [The play made a great *impression* on us.] **4** the effect produced by some action [Cleaning made no *impression* on the stain.] **5** a vague feeling [I have the *impression* that someone was here.]

im·prop·er (im präp′ər) *adj.* **1** not proper or suitable, unfit [Sandals are *improper* shoes for tennis.] **2** not true; wrong; incorrect [an *improper* street address] **3** not decent; in bad taste [*improper* jokes] —**im·prop′er·ly** *adv.*

im·prove (im pro͞ov′) v. 1 to make or become better [Business has *improved*.] 2 to make good use of [She *improved* her spare time by reading.] —im·proved′, im·prov′ing

im·pure (im pyo͝or′) adj. 1 not clean; dirty [Smoke made the air *impure*.] 2 mixed with things that do not belong [*impure* gold] 3 not decent or proper [*impure* thoughts]

in·clude (in klo͞od′) v. to have or take in as part of a whole; contain [Prices *include* taxes.] —in·clud′ed, in·clud′ing

in·come (in′kum) n. the money that one gets as wages, salary, rent, interest, profit, etc.

in·com·plete (in kəm plēt′) adj. not complete; without all its parts; not whole or finished —in·com·plete′ly adv.

in·crease (in krēs′) v. to make or become greater, larger, etc.; add to or grow [When she *increased* her wealth, her power *increased*.] —in·creased′, in·creas′ing ➧n. (in′krēs) 1 an increasing; addition; growth [an *increase* in population] 2 the amount by which something increases [a population *increase* of 10 percent]

in·de·pend·ence (in′ dē pen′dəns) n. the state of being independent; freedom from the control of another or others

in·ex·pen·sive (in′ ek spen′siv) adj. not expensive; low-priced —in′ex·pen′sive·ly adv.

in·fant (in′fənt) n. a very young child; baby ➧adj. 1 of or for infants [a book on *infant* care] 2 in a very early stage [an *infant* nation]

☆in·field (in′fēld) n. 1 the part of a baseball field enclosed by the four base lines 2 all the infielders

in·for·ma·tion (in′ fər mā′shən) n. 1 an informing or being informed [This is for your *information* only.] 2 something told or facts learned; news or knowledge; data [An encycolopedia gives *information* about many things.] 3 a person or service that answers certain questions [Ask *information* for the location of the shoe department.]

in·hale (in hāl′) v. to breathe in; draw into the lungs, as air or tobacco smoke —in·haled′, in·hal′ing —in·ha·la·tion (in′ hə lā′shən), in·hal′er n.

in·ju·ry (in′jər ē) n. harm or damage done to a person or thing [*injuries* received in a fall; *injury* to one's good name] —pl. in′ju·ries

in·quire (in kwīr′) v. to ask a question; ask about in order to learn [The students *inquired* about their grades. We *inquired* the way home.] —in·quired′, in·quir′ing —in·quir′er n.

in·se·cure (in′ si kyo͝or′) adj. 1 not secure or safe; dangerous; not dependable [an *insecure* mountain ledge; an *insecure* partnership] 2 not feeling safe or confident [A person can feel *insecure* in a new job.] —in′se·cure′ly adv. —in·se·cu·ri·ty (in′si kyo͝or′ ə tē) n.

in·spec·tor (in spek′ tər) n. 1 a person who inspects, as in a factory 2 a police officer who ranks next below a superintendent

in·spire (in spīr′) v. 1 to cause, urge, or influence to do something [The sunset *inspired* her to write a poem.] 2 to cause to have a certain feeling or thought [Praise *inspires* us with confidence.] 3 to arouse or bring about [Your kindness *inspired* his love.] 4 to do or make as if guided by some higher power [That was an *inspired* speech.] —in·spired′, in·spir′ing

in·stant (in′stənt) n. 1 a very short time; moment [Wait just an *instant*.] 2 a particular moment [At that *instant* I fell.] ➧adj. 1 with no delay; immediate [an *instant* response] 2 that can be prepared quickly; as by adding water [*instant* coffee]

in·sti·tu·tion (in′ stə to͞o′shən or in′ stə tyo͞o′shən) n. 1 an instituting or being instituted 2 an established law, custom, practice, etc. [the *institution* of marriage] 3 a school, church, prison, or other organization with a special purpose —in′sti·tu′tion·al adj.

in·ter·pret·er (in tur′prə tər) n. a person who interprets, especially one whose work is translating things said in one language into another language

in·ter·view (in′tər vyo͞o) n. 1 a meeting of one person with another to talk about something [an *interview* with an employer about a job] ☆2 a meeting in which a person is asked about his or her opinions, activities, etc., as by a reporter —in′ter·view·er

in·tes·tine (in tes′tin) n. *usually* intestines, *pl.* the tube through which food passes from the stomach: the long, narrow part with many coils is called the **small intestine**, and the shorter and thicker part is called the **large intestine** [Food is digested in the *intestines* as well as in the stomach.]

in·tro·duce (in trə do͞os′ or in trə dyo͞os′) v. 1 to make known; make acquainted; present [Please *introduce* me to them.] 2 to bring into use; make popular or common [Science has *introduced* many new words.] 3 to make familiar with something [They *introduced* me to the music of Bach.] 4 to bring to the attention of others in a formal way [to *introduce* a bill into Congress] —in·tro·duced′, in·tro·duc′ing

in·ven·to·ry (in′vən tôr′ ē) n. 1 a complete list of goods or property [The store makes an *inventory* of its stock every year.] 2 the stock of goods on hand [Because of fewer sales this year, dealers have large *inventories*.] —pl. in′ven·to′ries ➧v. to make an inventory or list of [to *inventory* our books] —in′ven·to′ried, in′ven·to′ry·ing

in·ves·ti·gate (in ves′tə gāt′) v. to search into so as to learn the facts, examine in detail [to *investigate* an accident] —in·ves′ti·gat′ed, in·ves′ti·gat′ing —in·ves′ti·ga′tion, in·ves′ti·ga′tor n.

a	ask, fat
ā	ape, date
ä	car, lot
e	elf, ten
ē	even, meet
i	is, hit
ī	ice, fire
ō	open, go
ô	law, horn
oi	oil, point
o͝o	look, pull
o͞o	ooze, tool
ou	out, crowd
u	up, cut
ʉ	fur, fern
ə	a in ago
	e in agent
	e in father
	i in unity
	o in collect
	u in focus
ch	chin, arch
ŋ	ring, singer
sh	she, dash
th	thin, truth
th	then, father
zh	s in pleasure

in·vis·i·ble (in viz′ə bəl) *adj.* not able to be seen [The moon was *invisible* behind the clouds.] —**in·vis′i·bly** *adv.*

i·ron (ī′ərn) *n.* **1** a strong metal that is a chemical element: it can be molded or stretched into various shapes after being heated, and is much used in the form of steel **2** a device made of iron or other metal and having a flat, smooth bottom: it is heated and used for pressing clothes, etc. **3 irons,** *pl.* iron shackles or chains

is·land (ī′lənd) *n.* **1** a piece of land smaller than a continent and surrounded by water **2** any place set apart from what surrounds it [The oasis was an *island* of green in the desert.]

I·tal·ian (i tal′yən) *adj.* of Italy, its people, etc. ◆*n.* **1** a person born or living in Italy **2** the language of Italy

jack·et (jak′ət) *n.* **1** a short coat **2** an outer covering, as the skin of a potato, or the paper wrapper for a book ☆**3** a cardboard holder for a phonograph record

Ja·pan (jə pan′) a country east of Korea, made up of many islands

Jap·a·nese (jap ə nēz′) *n.* **1** a member of a people whose native country is Japan —*pl.* **Jap·a·nese′ 2** the language of Japan ◆*adj.* of Japan, its people, language, or culture

Jef·fer·son (jef′er sən), **Thomas** (täm′əs) 1743–1826; the third president of the United States, from 1801–1809

jel·ly·fish (jel′ē fish′) *n.* a sea animal with a body that feels like jelly

jin·gle (jiŋ′ gəl) *v.* **1** to make ringing, tinkling sounds, as bits of metal striking together [The pennies *jingled* in my pocket.] **2** to make jingle [She *jingled* her keys.] **3** to have simple rhymes and a regular rhythm, as some poetry and music —**jin′ gled, jin′gling** *n.* a ringing, tinkling sound

join (join) *v.* **1** to bring together; connect; fasten [We *joined* hands and stood in a circle.] **2** to come together; meet [Where do the Ohio and Mississippi rivers *join*?] **3** to become a part or a member of [Paula has *joined* our club.] **4** to go along with; accompany [*Join* us in a walk.] **5** to take part along with others [*Join* in the game.] —**joined**

joint (joint) *n.* **1** a place where two things or parts are joined [Water leaked from the *joint* in the pipe.] **2** a place or part where two bones are joined, usually so that they can move [the elbow *joint*] **3** a large cut of meat with the bone still in it ◆*v.* **1** to connect by a joint or joints [Bamboo is *jointed*.] **2** to cut at the joints [The butcher *jointed* the chicken.]

jour·ney (jur′nē) *n.* a traveling from one place to another; trip —*pl.* **jour′ neys** ◆*v.* to go on a trip; travel —**jour′ neyed, jour′ ney·ing**

jun·gle (juŋ′gəl) *n.* land thickly covered with trees, vines, etc., as in the tropics: jungles are usually filled with animals that prey on one another

ju·ry (joor′ē *or* jur′ē) *n.* **1** a group of people chosen to listen to the evidence in a law trial, and then to reach a decision, or verdict **2** a group of people chosen to decide the winners in a contest —*pl.* **ju′ries**

jus·tice (jus′tis) *n.* **1** the condition of being just or fair [There is *justice* in their demand.] **2** reward or punishment as deserved [The prisoner asked only for *justice*.] **3** the upholding of what is just or lawful [a court of *justice*] **4** a judge [a *justice* of the Supreme Court]

Kan·sas (kan′zəs) a state in the central part of the U.S.: abbreviated **Kans., KS** —**Kan′ san** *adj.*, *n.*

kar·at (ker′ət) *n.* one 24th part of pure gold [14 *karat* gold is 14 parts pure gold and 10 parts other metal.]

keep·ing (kēp′iŋ) *n.* **1** care or protection [He left his money in her *keeping*.] **2** the observing of a rule, holiday, etc.

kid·ney (kid′nē) *n.* **1** either of a pair of organs in the central part of the body that take water and waste products out of the blood and pass them through the bladder as urine **2** the kidney of an animal, used as food —*pl.* **kid′neys**

kind·ness (kīnd′nəs) *n.* the condition or habit of being kind

knead (nēd) *v.* **1** to keep pressing and squeezing dough, clay, etc. to make it ready for use **2** to rub or press with the hands; massage [to *knead* a muscle]

knee·cap (nē′kap) *n.* the flat, movable bone that forms the front of a person's knee

kneel (nēl) *v.* to rest on a knee or knees [Some people *kneel* when they pray.] —**knelt** or **kneeled, kneel′ ing**

knob (näb) *n.* a handle that is more or less round on a door or drawer

knock (näk) *v.* **1** to hit as with the fist; especially, to rap on a door [Who is *knocking*?] **2** to hit and cause to fall [The dog *knocked* down the papergirl.] **3** to make by hitting [to *knock* a hole in the wall] **4** to make a pounding or tapping noise [An engine *knocks* when the combustion is faulty.] —**knocked**

knot (nät) *n.* **1** a lump, as in a string or ribbon, formed by a loop or a tangle drawn tight **2** a fastening made by tying together parts or pieces of string, rope, etc. [Sailors make a variety of *knots*.] **3** a small group [a *knot* of people] **4** something that joins closely, as the bond of marriage **5** a unit of speed of one nautical mile (1.852 meters, or 6,076.12 feet) an hour [The ship averaged 20 *knots*.] —**knot´ted, knot´ting** *v.*

knot·hole (nät´hōl) *n.* a hole in a board or tree trunk where a knot has fallen out

know (nō) *v.* **1** to be sure of or have the facts about [Do you *know* why grass is green? She *knows* the law.] **2** to be aware of; realize [He suddenly *knew* he would be late.] **3** to have in one's mind or memory [The actress *knows* her lines.] **4** to be acquainted with [I *know* your brother well.] **5** to recognize [I'd *know* that face anywhere.] **6** to be able to tell the difference in [It's not always easy to *know* right from wrong.] —**knew, known, know´ing**

knowl·edge (nä´lij) *n.* **1** the fact or condition of knowing [*Knowledge* of the crime spread through the town.] **2** what is known or learned through study, experience, etc. [a great *knowledge* of history]

known (nōn) *past participle of* **know**

knuck·le (nuk´əl) *n.* **1** a joint of the finger; especially, a joint connecting a finger to the rest of the hand **2** the knee or hock joint of a pig, calf, etc., used as food —**knuck´led, knuck´ling** *v.*

la·bor (lā´bər) *n.* **1** work; toil **2** a piece of work; task [We rested from our *labors*.] **3** workers as a group [an agreement between *labor* and management on wages] **4** the act of giving birth to a child

lab·o·ra·to·ry (lab´rə tôr´ē) *n.* a room or building where scientific work or tests are carried on, or where chemicals, drugs, etc. are prepared —*pl.* **lab´o·ra·to´ries**

la·dies (lā´dēs) *n.* a polite form of address for women in a group ["*Ladies* and gentlemen," the speaker began.]

laugh (laf) *v.* **1** to make a series of quick sounds with the voice that show one is amused or happy or, sometimes, that show scorn: one usually smiles or grins when laughing **2** to bring about, get rid of, etc. by means of laughter [*Laugh* your fears away.] ◆*n.* the act or sound of laughing

laugh·ter (laf´tər) *n.* the act or sound of laughing [He shook with *laughter*.]

law·yer (lô´yər *or* lä´yər) *n.* a person whose profession is giving advice on law or acting for others in lawsuits

lead·er (lēd´ər) *n.* a person or thing that leads, or guides —**lead´er·ship**

leath·er (leth´ər) *n.* a material made from the skin of cows, horses, goats, etc. by cleaning and tanning it ◆*adj.* made of leather

leg·i·ble (lej´ə bəl) *adj.* clear enough to be read easily [*legible* handwriting]

lei·sure (lē´zher *or* lezh´ər) *n.* free time not taken up with work or duty, that a person may use for rest or recreation ◆*adj.* free and not busy; spare [*leisure* time]

lep·re·chaun (lep´rə kôn *or* lep´rə kän) *n.* an elf in Irish folklore who can show a buried crock of gold to anyone who catches him

lev·y (lev´ē) *v.* **1** to order the payment of [to *levy* a tax] **2** to wage; carry on [to *levy* war] —**lev´ied, lev´y·ing**

li·brar·y (lī´brer´ē) *n.* **1** a place where a collection of books is kept for reading or borrowing **2** a collection of books —*pl.* **li´brar´ies**

li·cense (lī´səns) *n.* **1** a paper, card, etc. showing that one is permitted by law to do something [a marriage *license*; driver's *license*] **2** freedom to ignore the usual rules [To take poetic *license* is to ignore, as in a poem, the usual rules of style, logic, etc. in order to gain a special effect.] **3** freedom of action or speech that goes beyond what is right or proper [Booing in a courtroom isn't free speech—it's *license*.] ◆*v.* to give a license to; permit by law [Are they *licensed* to fish?] —**li´censed, li´cens·ing**

like·li·hood (līk´lē hood´) *n.* the fact of being likely to happen; probability [There is a strong *likelihood* he will win.]

Lin·coln (liŋ´kən), **Abraham** (ā´brə ham) 1809–1865; 16th president of the United States, from 1861–1865: he was assassinated

lit·er·a·ture (lit´ər ə chər) *n.* **1** all the writings of a certain time, country, etc.; especially, those that have lasting value because of their beauty, imagination, etc., as fine novels, plays, and poems **2** the work or profession of writing such things; also, the study of such writings **3** all the writings on some subject [medical *literature*]

liv·er (liv´ər) *n.* **1** a large organ of the body, near the stomach: it makes bile and helps break down food into substances that the body can absorb **2** the liver of some animals, used as food

loaf (lōf) *n.* a portion of bread baked in one piece, usually oblong in shape —*pl.* **loaves**

loud (loud) *adj.* **1** strong in sound; not soft or quiet [a *loud* noise; a *loud* bell] **2** noisy [a *loud* party] **3** so strong as to force attention; forceful [*loud* demands] ◆*adv.* in a loud way —**loud´er, loud´est** —**loud´ly** *adv.* —**loud´ness** *n.*

a	ask, fat
ā	ape, date
ä	car, lot
e	elf, ten
ē	even, meet
i	is, hit
ī	ice, fire
ō	open, go
ô	law, horn
oi	oil, point
oo	look, pull
oo	ooze, tool
ou	out, crowd
u	up, cut
u	fur, fern
ə	a in ago
	e in agent
	e in father
	i in unity
	o in collect
	u in focus
ch	chin, arch
ŋ	ring, singer
sh	she, dash
th	thin, truth
th	then, father
zh	s in pleasure

loy·al (loi′əl) *adj.* **1** faithful to one's country [a *loyal* citizen] **2** faithful to one's family, duty, beliefs, etc. [a *loyal* friend; a *loyal* member] —**loy′al·ly** *adv.*

loy·al·ty (loi′əl tē) *n.* the condition of being loyal; faithfulness —*pl.* **loy′al·ties**

lyr·ic (lir′ik) *adj.* **1** of or having to do with poetry that describes the poet's feelings and thoughts [Sonnets and odes are *lyric* poems.] **2** like a song or suitable for singing **3** of or having a high voice that moves lightly and easily from note to note [a *lyric* soprano] ◆*n.* **1** a lyric poem **2** *usually* **lyrics**, *pl.* the words of a song

mag·a·zine (mag ə zēn′ *or* mag′ ə zēn) *n.* **1** a publication that comes out regularly, as weekly or monthly, and contains articles, stories, pictures, etc. **2** a place for storing things, as military supplies **3** a space, as in a warship, for storing explosives

mag·ni·fy (mag′nə fī) *v.* to make look or seem larger or greater than is really so [This lens *magnifies* an object to ten times its size. He *magnified* the seriousness of his illness.] —**mag′ni·fied, mag′ni·fy·ing**

ma·jor (mā′ jər) *adj.* **1** greater in size, importance, amount, etc. [the *major* part of his wealth; a *major* poet] **2** in music, that is separated from the next tone by a full step instead of a half step [a *major* interval] ◆*n.* **1** a military officer ranking just above a captain ☆**2** the main subject that a student is studying [History is my *major*.]

mam·mal (mam′əl) *n.* any animal with glands in the female that produce milk for feeding its young —**mam·ma·li·an** (me mā′ lē ən) *adj., n.*

mam·moth (mam′əth) *n.* a large, extinct elephant with hairy skin and long tusks that curved upward ◆*adj.* very big; huge [a *mammoth* arena]

man·ag·er (man′ij ər) *n.* a person who manages a business

man·ner (man′ər) *n.* **1** a way in which something happens or is done; style [the *manner* in which an artist sketches a scene] **2** a way of acting; behavior [an angry *manner*] **3** **manners**, *pl.* ways of behaving or living, especially polite ways of behaving [It is good *manners* to say "Thank you."] **4** kind; sort [What *manner* of man is he?]

man·tle (man′təl) *n.* a loose cloak without sleeves; cape

mas·sive (mas′iv) *adj.* large, solid, heavy, etc. [a *massive* statue] —**mas′sive·ly** *adv.* —**mas′sive·ness** *n.*

may·or (mā′ ər) *n.* the head of the government of a city or town

mead·ow (med′ō) *n.* **1** a piece of land where grass is grown for hay **2** low, level grassland near a stream or lake

meas·ure (mezh′ər) *v.* to find out the size, amount, or extent of something, often by comparing with something else [*Measure* the child's height with a yardstick.] —**meas′ured, meas′ur·ing** ◆*n.* the size amount, or extent of something, found out by measuring [The *measure* of the bucket is 15 liters.]

me·chan·ic (mə kan′ik) *n.* a worker skilled in using tools or in making, repairing, and using machinery

me·di·a (mē′ de ə) *n.* a plural of medium

med·i·cal (med′i kəl) *adj.* having to do with the practice or study of medicine [*medical* care]

me·di·um (mē′ dē əm) any way by which something is done; especially, a way of communicating with the general public, as TV or newspapers: *in this meaning the plural* **media** *is sometimes used as a singular noun* [The *media* is covering the president's inauguration.]

mem·ber·ship (mem′bər ship) *n.* **1** the condition of being a member **2** all the members of a group **3** the number of members

☆**mem·o·rize** (mem′ə rīz) *v.* to fix in one's memory exactly or word for word; learn by heart —**mem′o·rized, mem′o·riz·ing** —**mem′o·ri·za′tion** *n.*

men·tal (ment′l) *adj.* **1** of, for, by, or in the mind [*mental* ability; *mental* arithmetic] **2** sick in mind [a *mental* patient] **3** for the sick in mind [a *mental* hospital]

mer·ry (mer′ē) *adj.* filled with fun and laughter; lively and cheerful [a *merry* party] —**mer′ri·er, mer′ri·est** —**make merry,** to have fun —**mer′ri·ly** *adv.* —**mer′ri·ness** *n.*

Mex·i·co (mek′sī kō) a country in North America, south of the U.S.

mid·air (mid er′) *n.* any point in space, not touching the ground or other surface

mid·day (mid′dā) *n., adj. another word for* **noon**

mid·dle (mid′əl) *n.* the point or part that is halfway between the ends or that is in the center [the *middle* of the morning; an island in the *middle* of the lake] ◆*adj.* being in the middle or center [the *middle* toe]

mid·night (mid′nīt) *n.* twelve o'clock at night; the middle of the night ◆*adj.* **1** of or at midnight [a *midnight* ride] **2** like midnight; very dark [*midnight* blue]

mid·stream (mid′strēm) *n.* the middle of a stream

mid·way (mid′wā *or* mid wā′) *adj., adv.* in the middle; halfway ◆*n.* (mid′wā) the part of a fair, circus, or amusement park where sideshows or rides are located

mid·win·ter (mid′win′tər) *n.* **1** the middle of the winter **2** the period around December 22

min·i·mize (min′ə mīz) *v.* to make as small as possible; reduce to a minimum [Safe storage of gas will *minimize* the danger of fire.] —**min′·i·mized, min′·i·miz·ing**

mir·ror (mir′ər) *n.* 1 a smooth surface that reflects light; especially, a piece of glass coated with silver on the back; looking glass 2 anything that gives a true description [A good novel is a *mirror* of life.] ◆*v.* to reflect as in a mirror [The moon was *mirrored* in the lake.]

mis·be·have (mis′bē hāv′) *v.* to behave in a bad way; do what one is not supposed to do —**mis′be·haved′, mis′be·hav′ing** —**mis·be·hav·ior** (mis′bi hāv′yər) *n.*

mis·for·tune (mis fôr′chən) *n.* bad luck; trouble

mis·judge (mis juj′) *v.* to judge unfairly or wrongly —**mis·judged′, mis·judg′ing**

mis·lead (mis lēd′) *v.* 1 to lead in a wrong direction [That old road map will *mislead* you.] 2 to cause to believe what is not true; deceive [She *misled* us into thinking she would help.] —**mis·led′, mis·lead′ing**

mis·place (mis plās′) *v.* 1 to put in a wrong place [He *misplaced* the book of poems in the art section.] 2 to give trust, love, etc. to one who does not deserve it [I *misplaced* my confidence in you.] —**mis·placed′, mis·plac′ing**

mis·pro·nounce (mis prə nouns′) *v.* to pronounce in a wrong way [Some people *mispronounce* "cavalry" as "calvary."] —**mis·pro·nounced′, mis·pro·nounc′ing** —**mis·pro·nun·ci·a·tion** (mis′prə nun′sē ā′ shən) *n.*

mis·sion (mish′ən) *n.* 1 the special duty or errand that a person or group is sent out to do, as by a church, government, air force, etc. [a *mission* to gain converts; a *mission* to increase trade; a *mission* to bomb a factory] 2 a group of missionaries, or the place where they live, work, etc. [the foreign *missions* of a church] 3 a group of persons sent to a foreign government to carry on dealings, as for trade, a treaty, etc.

mis·sion·ar·y (mish′ən er′ē) *n.* a person sent out by a church to spread its religion in a foreign country —*pl.* **mis′sion·ar′ies**

mis·spell (mis spel′) *v.* to spell incorrectly —**mis·spelled′or mis·spelt′, mis·spell′ing**

mis·take (mi stāk′) *n.* an idea, answer, act, etc. that is wrong; error or blunder ◆*v.* 1 to get a wrong idea of; misunderstand [You *mistake* his real purpose.] 2 to think that someone or something is some other person or thing [to *mistake* one twin for the other.] —**mis·took′, mis·tak′en, mis·tak′ing**

mis·trust (mis trust′) *n.* a lack of trust or confidence; suspicion; doubt [He felt *mistrust* of the stranger.] ◆*v.* to have no trust or confidence in; doubt —**mis·trust′ful** *adj.*

mis·un·der·stand (mis′ un dər stand′) *v.* to understand in a way that is wrong; give a wrong meaning to —**mis·un·der·stood** (mis′ un dər stood′), —**mis′·un·der·stand′ing**

mod·ern (mäd′ərn) *adj.* 1 of or having to do with the present time or the period we live in [a *modern* poet] 2 of the period after about 1450 [the *modern* history of Europe] 3 of or having to do with the latest styles, methods, or ideas; up-to-date [He travels the *modern* way, by jet airplane.] ◆*n.* a person who lives in modern times or has up-to-date ideas

mod·i·fy (mäd′ə fī) *v.* 1 to make a small or partial change in [Exploration has *modified* our maps of Antarctica.] 2 in grammar, to limit the meaning of; describe or qualify [In the phrase "old man" the adjective "old" *modifies* the noun "man."] —**mod′i·fied, mod′i·fy·ing**

mois·ture (mois′chər) *n.* liquid causing a dampness, such as fine drops of water in the air

mois·tur·ize (mois′chər īz) *v.* to add, supply, or restore moisture to the skin, the air, etc. —**mois′tur·ized, mois′tur·iz·ing** —**mois′tur·iz·er** *n.*

Mont·re·al (män′trē ôl′) a city in southern Quebec, Canada, on an island in the St. Lawrence River

mon·u·ment (män′yoo mənt) *n.* 1 something put up in memory of a person or happening, as a statue, building, etc. 2 something great or famous, especially from long ago [Shakespeare's plays are *monuments* of English culture.]

☆**moose** (moos) *n.* a large animal related to the deer, of the northern U.S. and Canada: the male has broad antlers with many points —*pl.* **moose**

mort·gage (môr′gij) *n.* 1 an agreement in which a person borrowing money gives the lender a claim to property as a pledge that the debt will be paid [The bank holds a *mortgage* of $15,000 on our house.] 2 the legal paper by which such a claim is given ◆*v.* to pledge by a mortgage in order to borrow money [to *mortgage* a home] —**mort′gaged, mort′gag·ing**

moth·er (muth′ər) *n.* 1 a woman as she is related to her child or children; a female parent 2 the origin, source, or cause of something [Virginia is the state known as the *mother* of presidents.] 3 a nun who is the head of a convent, school, etc.: *the full name is* **mother superior** ◆*adj.* of, like, or as if from a mother [*mother* love; one's *mother* tongue] ◆*v.* to care for as a mother does —**moth′er·hood** *n.* —**moth′er·less** *adj.*

mo·ti·vate (mōt′ə vāt) *v.* to give a motive to or be a motive for [Love *motivated* my actions.] —**mo′ti·vat·ed, mo′ti·vat·ing** —**mo′ti·va′tion** *n.*

a	ask, fat
ā	ape, date
ä	car, lot
e	elf, ten
ē	even, meet
i	is, hit
ī	ice, fire
ō	open, go
ô	law, horn
oi	oil, point
oo	look, pull
oo	ooze, tool
ou	out, crowd
u	up, cut
u	fur, fern
ə	a in ago
	e in agent
	e in father
	i in unity
	o in collect
	u in focus
ch	chin, arch
ŋ	ring, singer
sh	she, dash
th	thin, truth
th	then, father
zh	s in pleasure

moun·tain·eer (mount'n ir') *n.* **1** a person who lives in a region of mountains **2** a person who climbs mountains ◆*v.* to climb mountains, as for sport

moun·tain·ous (mount'n əs) *adj.* **1** full of mountains **2** very large [a *mountainous* debt]

move·ment (mo͞ov'mənt) *n.* **1** the act of moving or a way of moving [a *movement* of the branches; the regular *movement* of the stars] **2** a working together to bring about some result [the *movement* for world peace]

mus·cle (mus'əl) *n.* the tissue in the body that is made up of bundles of long cells or fibers that can be stretched or squeezed together to move parts of the body [Eating protein helps build *muscle*.]

mys·ter·y (mis'tər ē *or* mis'trē) *n.* **1** something that is not known or explained, or that is kept secret [the *mystery* of life] **2** anything that remains unexplained or is so secret that it makes people curious [That murder is still a *mystery*.] **3** a story or play about such a happening —*pl.* **mys'ter·ies**

nar·row (ner'ō) *adj.* **1** small in width; less wide than usual [a *narrow* road] **2** small or limited in size, amount, or degree [I was the winner by a *narrow* majority.] **3** with barely enough space, time, means, etc.; close [a *narrow* escape] —**nar'row·ly** *adv.* —**nar'row·ness** *n.*

nat·u·ral (nach'ər əl) *adj.* **1** produced by nature; not made by man [*natural* resources; *natural* curls] **2** of or dealing with nature [Biology and chemistry are *natural* sciences.] **3** that is part of one from birth; native [He has a *natural* ability in music.] **4** free and easy; not forced or artificial [a *natural* laugh] —**nat'u·ral·ness** *n.*

naugh·ty (nôt'ē *or* nät'ē) *adj.* **1** not behaving; bad, disobedient, mischievous, etc. [*naughty* children] **2** not nice or proper [*naughty* words] —**naugh'ti·er, naught'ti·est** —**naugh'ti·ly** *adv.* —**naugh'ti·ness** *n.*

nec·tar (nek'tər) *n.* **1** the sweet liquid in many flowers, made into honey by bees **2** the drink of the gods in Greek myths

nec·tar·ine (nek tə rēn') *n.* a kind of peach that has a smooth skin

nee·dle (nēd'əl) *n.* **1** a small, slender piece of steel with a sharp point and a hole for thread, used for sewing **2** a slender rod of steel, bone, plastic, etc., used in knitting or crocheting **3** a short, slender piece of metal, often tipped with diamond, that moves in the grooves of a phonograph record to pick up the vibrations **4** the pointer of a compass, gauge, meter, etc. —**nee'dled, nee'dling** *v.*

neg·a·tive (neg'ə tiv) *adj.* **1** saying that something is not so or refusing; answering "no" [a *negative* reply] **2** that does not help, improve, etc. [*negative* criticism] **3** opposite to or lacking something that is positive [He always takes a *negative* attitude and expects the worst.] **4** showing that a certain disease, condition, etc is not present [The reaction to her allergy test was *negative*.] —**neg'a·tive·ly** *adv.*

neigh·bor·hood (nā'bər ho͝od) *n.* **1** a small part or district of a city, town, etc. [an old *neighborhood*] **2** the people in such a district [The whole *neighborhood* helped.]

nei·ther (nē'thər *or* nī'thər) *adj., pron.* not one or the other of two; not either (*Neither* boy went. *Neither* of them was invited.] ◆*conj.* not either; nor yet

news·pa·per (no͞oz'pā pər *or* nyo͞oz'pā pər) *n.* a daily or weekly publication printed on large, folded sheets of paper and containing news, opinions, advertisements, etc.

niece (nēs) *n.* **1** the daughter of one's brother or sister **2** the daughter of one's brother-in-law or sister-in-law

no·ble (nō'bəl) *adj.* **1** having or showing a very good character or high morals; lofty [*noble* ideals] **2** of or having a high rank or title; aristocratic [a *noble* family]

nois·y (noi'zē) *adj.* **1** making noise [a *noisy* bell] **2** full of noise [a *noisy* theater] —**nois'i·er, nois'i·est** —**nois'i·ly** *adv.* —**nois'i·ness** *n.*

noon (no͞on) *n.* twelve o'clock in the daytime: also **noon'day, noon'tide, noon'time**

nor·mal (nôr'məl) *adj.* **1** agreeing with a standard or norm; natural; usual; regular; average [It is *normal* to make a mistake sometimes.] **2** in good health; not ill or diseased

north·east (nôrth ēst' *or* nôr ēst') *n.* **1** the direction halfway between north and east **2** a place or region in or toward this direction

nov·el (näv'əl) *adj.* new and unusual [In the year 1920, flying was still a *novel* way of travel.] ◆*n.* a long story, usually a complete book about imaginary people and happenings

nov·el·ist (näv'əl ist) *n.* a person who writes novels

☆**ny·lon** (nī'län) *n.* **1** a very strong, elastic material made from chemicals and used for thread, bristles, etc. **2 nylons,** *pl.* stockings made of nylon yarn

Oo

o·bey (ō bā′) **v.** **1** to carry out the orders of [Soldiers must *obey* their officers.] **2** to do as one is told [My dog always *obeys*.]
—**o·beyed′, o·bey′ing, o·beys′**
—**o·bey′er n.**

ob·jec·tion (äb jek′shən) **n.** **1** a feeling of dislike or disapproval; protest [I have no *objection* to that plan.] **2** a reason for disliking or disapproving [My main *objection* to this climate is its dampness.]

ob·ser·va·tion (äb zər vā′shən) **n.** the act or power of seeing or noticing [It's a good night for *observation* of the stars.] ◆**adj.** for observing [an *observation* tower]

oc·cu·pant (äk′yo͞o pənt) **n.** a person who occupies land, a house, or a position [a former *occupant* of the White House]

oc·cu·py (äk′yo͞o pī′) **v.** **1** to take possession of a place by capturing it or settling in it [The Germans *occupied* much of France during World War II. Pioneers *occupied* the wilderness.] **2** to have or hold [She *occupies* an important post in the government.] **3** to live in [to *occupy* a house] **4** to keep busy; employ [Many activities *occupy* his time.] —**oc′cu·pied′, oc′cu·py′ing**

o·pin·ion (ə pin′yən) **n.** **1** a belief that is not based on what is certain, but on what one thinks to be true or likely [In my *opinion*, it will rain before dark.] **2** what one thinks about how good or valuable something is [What is your *opinion* of that painting?] **3** a judgment made by an expert [It would be better to get several medical *opinions*.]

op·por·tu·ni·ty (äp′ ər to͞o′nə tē *or* äp′ ər tyo͞o′nə tē) **n.** a time or occasion that is right for doing something; good chance [You will have an *opportunity* to ask questions after the talk.]
—*pl.* **op′por·tu′ni·ties**

op·po·site (äp′ə zit) **adj.** **1** different in every way; exactly reverse or in contrast [Up is *opposite* to down.] **2** at the other end or side; directly facing or back to back [the *opposite* end of a table; the *opposite* side of a coin] ◆**n.** anything opposite or opposed [Love is the *opposite* of hate.] ◆**prep.** across from; facing [We sat *opposite* each other.] —**op′po·site·ly adv.**

op·ti·cal (äp′ti kəl) **adj.** **1** of the sense of sight; visual [an *optical* illusion] **2** made to give help in seeing [Lenses are *optical* instruments.] —**op′ti·cal·ly adv.**

o·rang·u·tan (ô raŋ′ə tan′) **n.** a large ape with very long arms and shaggy, reddish hair, found in Borneo and Sumatra: *also* **o·rang·ou·tang** (o raŋ′ə taŋ′)

or·ches·tra (ôr′kəs trə) **n.** **1** a group of musicians playing together, especially with some stringed instruments **2** the instruments of such a group —**or·ches·tral** (ôr kəs′trəl) **adj.**

or·chid (ôr′kid) **n.** a plant with flowers having three petals: the middle petal is larger than the others and has the shape of a lip

Or·e·gon (ôr′ə gən *or* ôr′ə gän) a state in the northwestern part of the U.S.: abbreviated **Oreg., OR**

o·rig·i·nal (ə rij′ə nəl) **adj.** **1** having to do with an origin; first or earliest [the *original* settlers of North America] **2** that has never been before; not copied; fresh; new [an *original* idea; *original* music] **3** able to think of new things; inventive [Edison had an *original* mind.] **4** being the one of which there are copies [the *original* letter and three carbon copies] —**o·rig·i·nal·i·ty** (ə rij′ə nal′ ə tē) **n.**

out·ra·geous (o͞ut rā′jəs) **adj.** doing great injury or wrong [*outrageous* crimes] —**out·ra′geous·ly adv.**

o·val (ō′vəl) **adj.** shaped like an egg or like an ellipse ◆**n.** anything with such a shape

o·ver·board (ō′vər bôrd) **adv.** from a ship into the water [He fell *overboard*.]

o·ver·come (ō vər kum′) **v.** **1** to get the better of; defeat; master [to *overcome* an enemy; to *overcome* a problem] **2** to make weak or helpless [We were *overcome* by laughter.] **3** to be victorious; win —**o·ver·came′, o·ver·come′, o·ver·com′ing**

o·ver·due (ō vər do͞o′ *or* ō vər dyo͞o′) **adj.** **1** not paid by the time set for payment [an *overdue* bill] **2** delayed past the arrival time; late [Her bus was long *overdue*.]

o·ver·look (ō vər lo͝ok′) **v.** **1** to give a view of from above; look down on [Your room *overlooks* the sea.] **2** to fail to notice [I *overlooked* no detail.] **3** to pay no attention to; excuse [I can *overlook* her rudeness.] —**o·ver·looked′**

o·ver·re·act (ō′ vər rē akt′) **v.** to respond to something with greater feeling or force than seems necessary

own·er·ship (ōn′ər ship) **n.** the condition of being an owner; possession

ox·y·gen (äks′i jən) **n.** a gas that has no color, taste, or odor and is a chemical element: it makes up almost one fifth of the air and combines with nearly all other elements: all living things need oxygen

oys·ter (ois′tər) **n.** a shellfish with a soft body enclosed in two rough shells hinged together: some are used as food, and pearls are formed inside others

o·zone (ō′zōn) **n.** a pale-blue gas that is a form of oxygen with a sharp smell: it is formed by an electrical discharge in the air and is used as a bleach, water purifier, etc.

a	ask, fat
ā	ape, date
ä	car, lot
e	elf, ten
ē	even, meet
i	is, hit
ī	ice, fire
ō	open, go
ô	law, horn
oi	oil, point
o͝o	look, pull
o͞o	ooze, tool
ou	out, crowd
u	up, cut
ᵾ	fur, fern
ə	a in ago
	e in agent
	e in father
	i in unity
	o in collect
	u in focus
ch	chin, arch
ŋ	ring, singer
sh	she, dash
th	thin, truth
th	then, father
zh	s in pleasure

pack·age (pak′ ij) *n.* **1** a thing or things wrapped or tied up, as in a box or in wrapping paper; parcel ☆**2** a number of things offered together as one [a retirement *package*] ◆☆*v.* to put into a package —**pack′aged, pack′ag·ing**

pain (pān) *n.* **1** a feeling of hurting in some part of the body [a sharp *pain* in a tooth] **2** suffering of the mind; sorrow [The memory of that loss brought us *pain*.] ◆*v.* to give pain to; cause to suffer; hurt [The wound *pains* me. Their insults *pained* us.]

pain·ful (pān′ fəl) *adj.* causing pain; hurting; unpleasant [a *painful* wound; *painful* embarrassment] —**pain′ful·ly** *adv.* —**pain′ful·ness** *n.*

pan·cake (pan′ kāk) *n.* a thin, flat cake made by pouring batter onto a griddle or into a pan and frying it; flapjack

pan·cre·as (pan′ krē əs) *n.* a large gland behind the stomach that sends a juice into the small intestine to help digestion —**pan·cre·at·ic** (pan′ krē at′ik) *adj.*

pan·el (pan′ əl) *n.* **1** a flat section or part of a wall, door, etc., either raised above or sunk below the surfaces around it **2** a board or section containing dials, controls, etc. as for an airplane or a system of electric wiring **3** a picture or painting that is long and narrow **4** a strip of different material sewn lengthwise into a skirt or dress —**pan′eled** or **pan′elled, pan′el·ing** or **pan′el·ling** *v.*

pa·pa·ya (pə pī′ə) *n.* **1** a tree of tropical America, a little like the palm, with a yellowish-orange fruit like a small melon **2** this fruit, used as food

pa·per·back (pā′ pər bak) *n.* a book bound in paper, instead of cloth, leather, etc.

par·a·graph (per′ ə graf) *n.* **1** a separate section of a piece of writing, that deals with a particular point and is made up of one or more sentences: each paragraph begins on a new line that is usually moved in from the margin **2** a short note or item in a newspaper or magazine

par·al·lel (per′ə lel) *adj.* **1** moving out in the same direction and always the same distance apart so as to never meet, as the tracks of a sled in the snow **2** similar or alike [Their lives followed *parallel* courses.] ◆*n.* **1** a parallel line, plane, etc. **2** something similar to or like something else [Your experience is a *parallel* to mine.] —**par′al·leled** or **par′al·lelled, par′al·lel·ing** or **par′al·lel·ling** *v.*

par·ent (per′ənt) *n.* **1** a father or mother **2** any animal or plant as it is related to its offspring **3** anything from which other things come; source; origin [Latin is the *parent* of various languages.] —**par′ent·hood**

par·tic·i·pant (pär tis′ə pənt) *n.* a person who takes part in something

part·ner (pärt′nər) *n.* **1** a person who takes part in something with another or others; especially, one of the owners of a business who shares in its profits and risks **2** either of two players on the same side or team [my tennis *partner*] **3** either of two persons dancing together **4** a husband or wife

part·ner·ship (pärt′nər ship) *n.* **1** the condition or relationship of being a partner **2** a business firm made up of two or more partners

pas·sage (pas′ij) *n.* the act of passing [the *passage* of a bill into law]

pat·tern (pat′ərn) *n.* **1** a plan or model used as a guide for making things [a dress *pattern*] **2** a person or thing taken as a model or example [Sir Galahad was the *pattern* of the pure knight.] **3** the arrangement of parts; design [wallpaper *patterns*] **4** a habit or way of acting that does not change [the migration *pattern* of the swallow]

pause (pôz *or* päz) *n.* **1** a short stop, as in speaking or working **2** a musical sign (⌒) placed above a note or rest that is to be held longer ◆*v.* to make a pause; stop for a short time [He *paused* to catch his breath.] —**paused, paus′ing**

pay·ee (pā ē′) *n.* the person to whom a check, money, etc. is to be paid

pay·ment (pā′mənt) *n.* **1** a paying or being paid [the *payment* of taxes] **2** something paid [a monthly rent *payment* of $168]

peace·ful (pēs′fəl) *adj.* **1** free from noise or disorder; quiet; calm [the *peaceful* countryside] **2** fond of peace; not fighting [a *peaceful* people] **3** of or fit for a time of peace [*peaceful* trade between nations] —**peace′ful·ly** *adv.* —**peace′ful·ness** *n.*

peas·ant (pez′ənt) *n.* mainly in Europe and Asia, a member of the class of farm workers and farmers with small farms

peck (pēk) *n.* **1** a measure of volume for grain, fruit, vegetables, etc.: it is equal to 1/4 bushel or eight quarts **2** a basket, etc. that holds a peck

pent·a·gon (pen′tə gän) *n.* **1** a flat figure having five sides and five angles ☆**2 Pentagon**, the five-sided office building of the Defense Department, near Washington, D.C. —**pen·tag·o·nal** (pen tag′ə n'l) *adj.*

per·form (pər fôrm′) *v.* **1** to do or carry out [to *perform* a task; to *perform* a promise] **2** to do something to entertain an audience; act, play, music, sing, etc. —**per·form′er** *n.*

pe·ri·od·i·cal (pir′ē ad′i kəl) *n.* a magazine published every week, month, etc. ◆*adj.* **1** published every week, month, etc. **2** of periodicals [a *periodical* index] —**pe′ri·od′i·cal·ly** *adv.*

per·sist·ent (pər sis′tənt) *adj.* refusing to give up; steady and determined [a *persistent* job seeker] —**per·sist′ent·ly** *adv.*

per·son·al·ly (pur′sə nəl ē) *adv.* **1** by oneself, without the help of others [I'll ask them *personally*.] **2** as a person [I dislike the artist *personally*, but I admire her paintings.] **3** speaking for oneself [*Personally*, I think you're right.] **4** as though aimed at oneself [You should not take my remarks *personally*.]

per·suade (pər swād′) *v.* to get someone to do or believe something, as by making it seem like a good idea; convince —**per·suad′ed, per·suad′ing**

pes·ti·cide (pes′tə sīd) *n.* any poison used to kill insects, weeds, etc.

pet·al (pet′l) *n.* any of the brightly colored leaves that make up the flower of a plant

pho·no·graph (fō′nə graf) *n.* an instrument for playing records with a spiral groove on them in which sounds of music or speech have been recorded

pho·tog·ra·phy (fə täg′rə fē) *n.* the art or method of making pictures by means of a camera

phys·i·cal (fiz′i kəl) *adj.* **1** of nature or matter; material; natural [the *physical* universe] **2** of the body rather than the mind [Swimming is good *physical* exercise.] **3** of or having to do with the natural sciences or the laws of nature [the *physical* force that makes an object move] ➙*n.* ☆a medical examination of the whole body

pic·co·lo (pik′ə lō) *n.* a small flute that sounds notes an octave higher than an ordinary flute does —*pl.* **pic′co·los**

pick·le (pik′el) *n.* **1** a cucumber or other vegetable preserved in salt water, vinegar, or spicy liquid **2** a liquid of this kind used to preserve food ➙*v.* to preserve in a pickle liquid [*pickled* beets] —**pick′led, pick′ling**

piece (pēs) *n.* **1** a part broken or separated from a whole thing [The glass shattered and I swept up the *pieces*.] **2** a part or section of a whole, thought of as complete by itself [a *piece* of meat; a *piece* of land] **3** any one of a set or group of things [a dinner set of 52 *pieces*; a chess *piece*] **4** a work of music, writing, or art [a *piece* for the piano] —**pieced, piec′ing** *v.*

pis·til (pis′təl) *n.* the part of a flower in which the seeds grow: a single pistil is made up of a stigma, style, and ovary

plan (plan) *n.* **1** a method or way of doing something, that has been thought out ahead of time [vacation *plans*] **2** a drawing that shows how the parts of a building or piece of ground are arranged [floor *plans* of a house; a *plan* of the battlefield] ➙*v.* **1** to think out a way of making or doing something [They *planned* their escape carefully.] **2** to make a drawing or diagram of beforehand [An architect is *planning* our new school.] —**planned, plan′ning**

plas·tic (plas′tik) *adj.* **1** that can be shaped or molded [Clay is a *plastic* material.] **2** that gives form or shape to matter [Sculpture is a *plastic* art.] **3** made of plastic [a *plastic* comb] ➙*n.* a substance, made from various chemicals, that can be molded and hardened into many useful products —**plas·tic·i·ty** (plas tis′ə tē) *n.*

Platte (plat) a river in central Nebraska

pleas·ant (plez′ənt) *adj.* **1** giving pleasure; bringing happiness; enjoyable [a *pleasant* day in the park] **2** having a look or manner that gives pleasure; likable [a *pleasant* person]

pleas·ing (plēz′iŋ) *adj.* giving pleasure; enjoyable [a *pleasing* smile]

pleas·ure (plezh′ər) *n.* **1** a feeling of delight or satisfaction; enjoyment [I get *pleasure* from taking long walks.] **2** a thing that gives pleasure [Her voice is a *pleasure* to hear.] **3** one's wish or choice [For dessert, what is your *pleasure*?]

pledge (plej) *n.* **1** a promise or agreement [the *pledge* of allegiance to the flag] **2** something promised, especially money to be given as to a charity **3** a thing given as a guarantee or token of something [They gave each other rings as a *pledge* of their love.] ➙*v.* to promise to give [to *pledge* $100 to a building fund] —**pledged, pledg′ing**

plen·ti·ful (plen′ti fəl) *adj.* great in amount or number; more than enough [a *plentiful* food supply] —**plen′ti·ful·ly** *adv.*

pli·ers (plī′ərz) *pl.n.* a tool like small pincers, used for gripping small objects or bending wire

plu·ral (ploor′əl) *adj.* showing that more than one is meant [The *plural* form of "box" is "boxes."] ➙*n.* the form of a word which shows that more than one is meant

poach (pōch) *v.* to cook an egg without its shell, in boiling water or in a small cup put over boiling water

poise (poiz) *n.* **1** balance, as in the way one carries oneself [the perfect *poise* of a tiger that is ready to spring] **2** calmness and easiness of manner; self-control [I lost my *poise* when they laughed at me.] ➙*v.* to balance or be held balanced [The stork *poised* itself on one leg. The earth is *poised* in space.] —**poised, pois′ing**

poi·son·ous (poi′zə nəs) *adj.* that is a poison; harming or killing by poison [a *poisonous* berry]

po·lar (pō′lər) *adj.* **1** of or near the North or South Pole **2** of a pole or poles

Pol·ish (pōl′ish) *adj.* of Poland, its people, language, etc. ➙*n.* the language of Poland

po·lite (pə līt′) *adj.* **1** having or showing good manners; thoughtful of others; courteous [a *polite* note of thanks] **2** behaving in a way that is considered refined or elegant [Such things aren't done in *polite* society.] —**po·lite′ly** *adv.* —**po·lite′ness** *n.*

a	ask, fat
ā	ape, date
ä	car, lot
e	elf, ten
ē	even, meet
i	is, hit
ī	ice, fire
ō	open, go
ô	law, horn
oi	oil, point
oo	look, pull
o͞o	ooze, tool
ou	out, crowd
u	up, cut
ʉ	fur, fern
ə	a in ago
	e in agent
	e in father
	i in unity
	o in collect
	u in focus
ch	chin, arch
ŋ	ring, singer
sh	she, dash
th	thin, truth
th	then, father
zh	s in pleasure

pol·li·nate (päl′ə nāt) *v.* to place pollen on the pistil of a flower; fertilize
—**pol′li·nat·ed, pol′li·nat·ing**
—**pol′li·na′tion** *n.*

pol·y·es·ter (päl′ē es′tər) *n.* an artificial resin used in making plastics, fibers for fabrics, etc.

pop·u·lar (päp′yoo lər) *adj.* **1** having many friends; very well liked **2** liked by many people **3** of, for, or by all the people or most people —**pop·u·lar·i·ty** (päp′yə lar′ə tē) *n.* —**pop′u·lar·ly** *adv.*

pop·u·la·tion (päp′yoo lā′shən) *n.* **1** the people living in a country, city, etc.; especially, the total number of these **2** the act of populating or the fact of being populated

pos·si·ble (päs′ə bəl) *adj.* **1** that can be [The highest *possible* score in bowling is 300.] **2** that may or may not happen [colder tomorrow, with *possible* showers] **3** that can be done, known, got, used, etc. [two *possible* routes to Denver]

post·game (pōst′gām′) *adj.* having to do with activities after a game

post·pone (pōst pōn′) *v.* to put off until later; delay [I *postponed* my trip because of illness.] —**post·poned′, post·pon′ing** —**post·pone′ment** *n.*

pos·ture (päs′chər) *n.* **1** the way one holds the body in sitting or standing; carriage [good *posture* with the back held straight] **2** a special way of holding the body or of acting, as in posing [Doubling up a fist is a *posture* of defiance.] ◆*v.* to take on a posture; pose —**pos′tured, pos′tur·ing**

post·war (pōst′wôr′) *adj.* after the war

po·ta·to (pə tāt′ō) *n.* **1** a plant whose tuber, or thick, starchy underground stem, is used as a vegetable **2** this tuber —*pl.* **po·ta′toes**

pow·der (pou′dər) *n.* a dry substance in the form of fine particles like dust, made by crushing or grinding [talcum *powder*; baking *powder*; gun*powder*] ◆*v.* to sprinkle, dust, or cover as with powder [Snow *powdered* the rooftops.]

pow·er·ful (pou′ər fəl) *adj.* having much power; strong or influential [a *powerful* leader] —**pow′er·ful·ly** *adv.*

☆**prai·rie** (prer′ē) *n.* a large area of level or rolling grassy land without many trees

preach·er (prēch′ər) *n.* a person who preaches; especially, a clergyman

pre·pare (prē per′) *v.* **1** to make or get ready [to *prepare* for a test; to *prepare* ground for planting] **2** to furnish with what is needed; equip [to *prepare* an expedition] **3** to make or put together out of parts or materials [to *prepare* a medicine] —**pre·pared′, pre·par′ing**

pre·serv·a·tive (prē zurv′ə tiv) *n.* anything that preserves; especially, a substance added to food to keep it from spoiling

pre·serve (prē zurv′) *v.* **1** to protect from harm or damage; save [to *preserve* our national forests] **2** to keep from spoiling or rotting **3** to prepare food for later use by canning, pickling, or salting it —**pre·served′, pre·serv′ing** ◆*n. usually* **preserves**, *pl.* fruit preserved by cooking it with sugar and canning it

pres·i·dent (prez′i dənt) *n.* ☆**1** the highest officer of a company, club, college, etc. **2** *often* **President**, the head of government in a republic

pres·sure (presh′ər) *n.* **1** a pressing or being pressed; force of pushing or of weight [the *pressure* of the foot on the brake] **2** a condition of trouble, strain, etc. that is hard to bear [She never gave in to the *pressure* of her grief.] **3** influence or force to make someone do something [His friends put *pressure* on him to resign as president.] **4** urgent demands; urgency [She neglected her homework and now has to work under *pressure* of time.] —**pres′sured, pres′sur·ing** *v.*

pre·tend (prē tend′) *v.* **1** to make believe, as in play [Let's *pretend* we're cowboys.] **2** to claim or act in a false way [She *pretended* to be angry, but she wasn't.] —**pre·tend′ed** *adj.*

pre·vail (prē vāl′) *v.* **1** to be successful or win out [to *prevail* over an enemy] **2** to be or become more common or widespread, as a custom or practice

pre·vent (prē vent′) *v.* **1** to stop or hinder [A storm *prevented* us from going.] **2** to keep from happening [Careful driving *prevents* accidents.] —**pre·vent′ed, pre·vent′ing**

pris·on·er (priz′ən ər *or* priz′nər) *n.* a person who is kept shut up, as in a prison, or held as a captive, as in war

prob·lem (präb′ləm) *n.* **1** a condition, person, etc. that is difficult to deal with or hard to understand [Getting the table through that narrow door will be a *problem*.] **2** a question to be solved or worked out [an arithmetic *problem*; the problem of reckless drivers]

pro·ceed (prō sēd′) *v.* to go on, especially after stopping for a while [After eating, we *proceeded* to the next town.] —**pro·ceed′ed, pro·ceed′ing**

pro·ces·sion (prə sesh′ən) *n.* **1** a number of persons or things moving forward in an orderly way **2** the act of moving in this way

pro·duce (prə doos′ *or* prə dyoos′) *v.* **1** to bring forth; bear; yield [trees *producing* apples; a well that *produces* oil] **2** to make or manufacture [a company that *produces* bicycles] **3** to bring out into view; show [*Produce* your fishing license.] **4** to get ready and bring to the public, as a play, movie, etc. —**pro·duced′, pro·duc′ing** ◆*n.* (prō′ doos) —**pro·duc′er**

pro·fes·sion·al (prə fesh'ən əl) *adj.* **1** of or in a profession [the *professional* ethics of a lawyer] **2** earning one's living from a sport or other activity not usually thought of as an occupation [a *professional* golfer] **3** engaged in by professional players [*professional* football] —**pro·fes′ sion·al·ism** *n.* —**pro·fes′ sion·al·ly** *adv.*

prof·it·a·ble (präf'it ə bəl) *adj.* that brings profit or benefit [a *profitable* sale; a *profitable* idea] —**prof′ it·a·bly** *adv.*

pro·mote (prə mōt') *v.* **1** to raise to a higher rank, grade, or position [She was *promoted* to manager.] **2** to help to grow, succeed, etc. [New laws were passed to *promote* the general welfare.] ☆**3** to make more popular, increase the sales of, etc. by advertising or giving publicity [to *promote* a product] ☆**4** to move a student forward a grade in school —**pro·mot′ ed, pro·mot′ ing** —**pro·mot′ er, pro·mo′ tion** *n.*

pro·pose (prə pōz') *v.* **1** to suggest for others to think about, approve, etc. [We *propose* that the city build a zoo. I *propose* Robin for treasurer.] **2** to plan or intend [Do you *propose* to leave us?] **3** to make an offer of marriage —**pro·posed′, pro·pos′ ing**

pro·tec·tion (prō tek'shən) *n.* **1** a protecting or being protected [The guard carried a club for *protection*.] **2** a person or thing that protects [Being careful is your best *protection* against accidents.]

pro·test (prō test' *or* prō' test) *v.* **1** to speak out against; object [They joined the march to *protest* against injustice.] **2** to say in a positive way; insist [Bill *protested* that he would be glad to help.] ◆*n.* (prō' test) the act of protesting; objection [They ignored my *protest* and continued hammering.] —**pro·test′ er** *or* **pro·tes′ tor**

pro·trac·tor (prō trak' tər *or* prō' trak tər) *n.* an instrument used for drawing and measuring angles: it is in the form of a half circle marked with degrees

pro·vide (prō vīd') *v.* **1** to give what is needed; supply; furnish [The school *provides* free books.] **2** to furnish the means of support [How large a family do you *provide* for?] **3** to get ready ahead of time; prepare [You'd better *provide* for rain by taking umbrellas.] **4** to set forth as a condition, as in a contract [Our lease *provides* that rent will be paid monthly.] —**pro·vid′ ed, pro·vid′ ing**

prune (prōōn) *v.* **1** to cut off or trim branches, twigs, etc. from [to *prune* hedges] **2** to make shorter by cutting out parts [to *prune* a novel] —**pruned, prun′ ing**

psy·chol·o·gy (sī käl' ə jē) *n.* **1** the science that studies the mind and the reasons for the ways that people think and act **2** the ways of thinking and acting of a person or group [the *psychology* of the child; mob *psychology*] —*pl.* **psy·chol′ o·gies** —**psy·chol′ o·gist** *n.*

pub·lic (pub' lik) *adj.* **1** of or having to do with the people as a whole [*public* affairs; *public* opinion] **2** for the use or the good of everyone [a *public* park] **3** acting for the people as a whole [a *public* official] **4** known by all or most people; open [a *public* figure; a *public* scandal]

pump·kin (pum' kin *or* pump' kin) *n.* a large, round, orange fruit that grows on a vine and has many seeds: the pulp is much used as a filling for pies

punc·tu·a·tion (puŋk' chōō ā' shən) *n.* **1** the use of commas, periods, etc. in writing [rules of *punctuation*] **2** punctuation marks [What *punctuation* is used to end sentences?]

pup·pet·eer (pup ə tir') *n.* a person who works the strings that make puppets move or one who puts on puppet shows

pyr·a·mid (pir' ə mid) *n.* **1** a solid figure whose sloping sides are triangles that come together in a point at the top **2** anything having this shape; especially, any of the huge structures with a square base and four sides in which ancient Egyptian rulers were buried ◆*v.* to build up or heap up in the form of a pyramid

qual·i·fi·ca·tion (kwôl' ə fi kā' shən *or* kwä' lə fi kā' shən) *n.* **1** a qualifying or being qualified **2** a thing that changes, limits, or holds back [I can recommend the book without any *qualification*.] **3** any skill, experience, special training, etc. that fits a person for some work, office, etc.

qual·i·fy (kwôl' ə fī *or* kwä' lə fī) *v.* to make or be fit or suitable for a particular role, job, or activity [Your training and education *qualify* you for the job.] —**qual′ i·fied, qual′ i·fy·ing**

quar·rel (kwôr' əl) *n.* **1** an argument or disagreement, especially an angry one; dispute **2** a reason for arguing [I have no *quarrel* with the way things are being done.] ◆*v.* **1** to argue or disagree in an angry way **2** to find fault; complain [She *quarrels* with his methods, not with his results.] —**quar′ reled** *or* **quar′ relled, quar′ rel·ing** *or* **quar′ rel·ling**

quar·ter (kwôrt' ər) *n.* **1** any of the four equal parts of something; fourth [a *quarter* of a mile; the third *quarter* of a football game] **2** one-fourth of a year; three months **3** the point fifteen minutes before or after any given hour [It's a *quarter* after five.] **4** a coin of the U.S. or Canada, worth 25 cents; one-fourth of a dollar

a	ask, fat
ā	ape, date
ä	car, lot
e	elf, ten
ē	even, meet
i	is, hit
ī	ice, fire
ō	open, go
ô	law, horn
oi	oil, point
͞oo	look, pull
o͞o	ooze, tool
ou	out, crowd
u	up, cut
ʉ	fur, fern
ə	a in ago
	e in agent
	e in father
	i in unity
	o in collect
	u in focus
ch	chin, arch
ŋ	ring, singer
sh	she, dash
th	thin, truth
th	then, father
zh	s in pleasure

ques·tion (kwes′chən) *n.* **1** something that is asked in order to learn or know [The athlete refused to answer the reporter's *questions*.] **2** doubt [There is no *question* about his honesty.] **3** a matter to be considered; problem [It's not a *question* of money.] ◆*v.* to ask questions of [The lawyer started to *question* the witness.] —**ques′tion·er** *n.*

quick (kwik) *adj.* **1** done with speed; rapid; swift [We took a *quick* trip.] **2** done or happening at once; prompt [I was grateful for her *quick* reply.] **3** able to learn or understand easily [You have a *quick* mind.] **4** easily stirred up; touchy [Lynn has a *quick* temper.] —**quick′ly** *adv.* —**quick′ness** *n.*

qui·et (kwī′ət) *adj.* **1** not noisy; hushed [a *quiet* motor] **2** not talking; silent [She was *quiet* during dinner.] **3** not moving; still; calm [a *quiet* pond] **4** peaceful and relaxing [We spent a *quiet* evening at home.] —**qui′et·ly** *adv.* —**qui′et·ness** *n.*

ra·dar (rā′där) *n.* a device or system that sends out radio waves and picks them up after they strike some object and bounce back

☆**ra·di·o** (rā′dē ō′) *n.* **1** a way of sending sounds through space by changing them into electric waves which are sent and picked up, without wires, by a receiver that changes them back to sounds **2** the act or business of broadcasting news, music, talks, etc. by radio —*pl.* **ra′di·os′** —**ra′di·oed′, ra′di·o′ing** *v.*

ra·di·us (rā′dē əs) *n.* **1** any straight line that goes from the center to the outside of a circle or sphere **2** a round area as measured by its radius [no houses within a *radius* of five miles] **3** the thicker of the two bones in the forearm —*pl.* **ra·di·i** (rā′dē ī′) or **ra′di·us·es**

rail·way (rāl′wā) *n.* a track made up of parallel steel rails along which trains run

rain·bow (rān′bō) *n.* a curved band across the sky with all the colors of the spectrum in it: it is seen when the sun's rays pass through falling rain or mist

rai·sin (rā′zən) *n.* a sweet grape dried for eating

rasp·ber·ry (raz′ber′ ē) *n.* **1** a small, juicy, red or black fruit with many tiny seeds **2** the shrub it grows on —*pl.* **rasp′ber′ries**

☆**ray·on** (rā′än) *n.* a fiber made from cellulose, or a fabric woven from such fibers

read·i·ly (red′əl ē) *adv.* **1** without hesitation; willingly **2** without difficulty; easily

re·al·ist (rē′ə list) *n.* a person who sees things as they really are; practical person

re·ap·pear (rē ə pir′) *v.* to appear again —**re′ap·pear′ance** *n.*

re·ar·range (rē ə rānj′) *v.* to arrange again or in a different way —**re·ar·ranged′, re·ar·rang′ing** —**re′ar·range′ment** *n.*

re·ceive (rē sēv′) *v.* **1** to take or get what has been given or sent to one [to *receive* a letter] **2** to meet with; be given; undergo [to *receive* punishment; to receive applause] **3** to find out about; learn [He *received* the news calmly.] **4** to greet guests and let them come in [Our hostess *received* us at the door.] —**re·ceived′, re·ceiv′ing**

re·cent (rē′sənt) *adj.* of a time just before now; made or happening a short time ago [*recent* news; a *recent* storm] —**re′cent·ly** *adv.*

rec·og·nize (rek′əg nīz) *v.* **1** to be aware of as something or someone seen, heard, etc. before; know again [to *recognize* a street; to *recognize* a tune] **2** to know by a certain feature; identify [to *recognize* a giraffe by its long neck] **3** to take notice of; show approval of [a ceremony to *recognize* those employees with ten years or more of service] **4** to admit as true; accept [to *recognize* defeat] —**rec′og·nized, rec′og·niz·ing**

rec·om·mend (rek ə mend′) *v.* **1** to speak of as being good for a certain use, job, etc.; praise [to *recommend* a good plumber; to *recommend* a book] **2** to make pleasing or worth having [That summer camp has much to *recommend* it.] **3** to give advice; advise [I *recommend* that you study harder.]

rec·re·a·tion (rek′ rē ā′shən) *n.* **1** the act of refreshing one's body or mind, as after work [He plays chess for *recreation*.] **2** any sport, exercise, hobby, amusement, etc. by which one does this —**rec′re·a′tion·al** *adj.*

rec·tan·gle (rek′ tan′gəl) *n.* any flat figure with four right angles and four sides

re·cy·cle (rē sī′kəl) *v.* to use again and again, as a single supply of water in a fountain or for cooling, metal to be melted down and recast, or paper processed for use again —**re·cy′cled, re·cy′cling**

re·duce (rē do͞os′ *or* rē dyo͞os′) *v.* **1** to make smaller, less, fewer, etc.; decrease [to *reduce* speed; to *reduce* taxes] **2** to lose weight, as by dieting **3** to make lower, as in rank or condition; bring down [to *reduce* a major to the rank of captain; a family *reduced* to poverty] **4** to change into a different form or condition [to *reduce* peanuts to a paste by grinding] —**re·duced′, re·duc′ing** —**re·duc′er** *n.* —**re·duc′i·ble** *adj.*

ref·er·ence (ref′ər əns *or* ref′rəns)
n. **1** the act or fact of referring; mention
[They made no *reference* to the accident.]
2 the fact of having to do with; relation;
connection [I am writing in *reference* to
your letter.] **3** a mention, as in a book, of
some other work where information can be
found; also, the work so mentioned [Most of
the author's *references* are useful.]
4 something that gives information [Look in
the encyclopedia and other *references*.]

re·flect (rē flekt′) *v.* **1** to throw back or be
thrown back, as light, heat, or sound
[A polished metal surface *reflects* both light
and heat.] **2** to give back an image of
[The calm lake *reflected* the trees on the
shore.] **3** to bring as a result [Your success
reflects credit on your teachers.] **4** to bring
blame, doubt, etc.

reg·u·lar (reg′yə lər) *adj.* **1** formed or
arranged in an orderly way; balanced
[a *regular* pattern; a face with *regular*
features] **2** according to some rule or habit;
usual; customary [Sit in your *regular* place.]
3 steady and even; not changing [a *regular*
rhythm] **4** in grammar, changing form in
the usual way in showing tense, number,
etc. ["Walk" is a *regular* verb, but "swim" is
not.] —**reg·u·lar·i·ty** (reg′yə lar′ə tē) *n.*
—**reg′u·lar·ly** *adv.*

rel·a·tive (rel′ə tiv) *n.* a person of the same
family by blood or by marriage

re·lax (rē laks′) *v.* **1** to make or become less
firm, tense, or strict; loosen up [The body
relaxes in sleep. The parents never *relaxed*
their watch over their child.] **2** to rest from
work or effort [He *relaxes* by going fishing.]
—**re·lax·a·tion** *n.*

re·lay (rē′lā) *n.* **1** a fresh group that takes
over some work from another group; shift
[The carpenters worked in *relays* to finish
the project on time.] **2** a race in which each
member of a team runs only a certain part
of the whole distance: the full name is **relay
race** ◆*v.* to get and pass on [to *relay* a
message] —**re′layed, re′lay·ing**

re·li·ant (rē lī′ənt) *adj.* having or showing
trust or confidence; depending [The needy
are *reliant* on our help.]

re·lieve (rē lēv′) *v.* **1** to reduce or ease pain
or worry [Cold water *relieves* a swelling.]
2 to free from pain or worry [We were
relieved of our fear when the danger
passed.] —**re·lieved′, re·liev′ing**

re·li·gion (rē lij′ən) *n.* **1** belief in, or the
worship of, God or a group of gods
2 a particular system of belief or worship
built around God, moral ideas, a philosophy
of life, etc.

re·mem·ber (rē mem′bər) *v.* **1** to think of
again [I suddenly *remembered* I was
supposed to mow the lawn.] **2** to bring back
to mind by trying; recall [I just can't
remember your name.] **3** to be careful not
to forget [*Remember* to look both ways
before crossing.] **4** to mention as sending
greetings [*Remember* me to your family.]

re·mote (rē mōt′) *adj.* **1** far off or far
away in space or time; distant **2** not closely
related **3** slight or faint —**re·mot′er,
re·mot′est** —**re·mote′ly** *adv.*
—**re·mote′ness** *n.*

re·pel·lent (rē pel′ənt) *adj.* that repels in
any of various ways [a *repellent* smell; a
water-*repellent* jacket] ◆*n.* something that
repels, as a spray that keeps insects away

re·print (rē print′) *v.* to print again [The
book was *reprinted*.] —**re·print′ed,
re·print′ing**

re·quire (rē kwīr′) *v.* **1** to be in need of
[Most plants *require* sunlight.] **2** to order,
command, or insist upon [He *required* us to
leave.] —**re·quired′, re·quir′ing**

res·cue (res′kyoo) *v.* to free or save from
danger, evil, etc. [to *rescue* people from a
burning building] ◆*n.* the act of rescuing
—**res′cued, res′cu·ing** —**res′cu·er** *n.*

res·i·dent (rez′i dənt) *n.* a person who
lives in a place, not just a visitor ◆*adj.*
living or staying in a place, as while
working

re·sign (rē zin′) *v.* to give up one's office,
position, membership, etc. [We *resigned*
from the club.]

re·source·ful (rē sôrs′fəl) *adj.* skillful
at solving problems or getting out of
trouble —**re·source′ful·ly** *adv.*
—**re·source′ful·ness** *n.*

re·spon·si·ble (rē spän′sə bəl) *adj.*
1 supposed or expected to take care of
something or do something [Harry is
responsible for mowing the lawn.] **2** that
must get the credit or blame [All of us are
responsible for our own actions.] **3** having
to do with important duties [a *responsible*
job] **4** that can be trusted or depended
upon; reliable [a *responsible* person]

re·turn (rē turn′) *v.* **1** to go or come back
[When did you *return* from your trip?]
2 to bring, send, carry, or put back [Our
neighbor *returned* the ladder.] **3** to pay
back by doing the same [to *return* a visit; to
return a favor] **4** to throw, hit, or run back a
ball —**re·turned′, re·turn′ing, re·turns′**

re·view (rē vyoo′) *v.* **1** to go over or study
again [to *review* a subject for a test]
2 to think back on [She *reviewed* the events
that led to their quarrel.] **3** to inspect or
examine in an official way [to *review*
troops] **4** to tell what a book, play, etc. is
about and give one's opinion of it

rev·o·lu·tion (rev′ə loo′shən) *n.*
1 overthrow of a government or a social
system, with another taking its place
[the American *Revolution*; the Industrial
Revolution] **2** a complete change of any
kind [The telephone caused a *revolution* in
communication.] **3** the act of revolving;
movement in an orbit [the *revolution* of
the moon around the earth] **4** a turning
motion of a wheel, etc. around a center
or axis; rotation

a	ask, fat
ā	ape, date
ä	car, lot
e	elf, ten
ē	even, meet
i	is, hit
ī	ice, fire
ō	open, go
ô	law, horn
oi	oil, point
oo	look, pull
o͞o	ooze, tool
ou	out, crowd
u	up, cut
ʉ	fur, fern
ə	a in ago
	e in agent
	e in father
	i in unity
	o in collect
	u in focus
ch	chin, arch
ŋ	ring, singer
sh	she, dash
th	thin, truth
th	then, father
zh	s in pleasure

re·ward (rē wôrd′) *n.* **1** something given in return, especially for good work or a good deed [a *reward* for bravery] **2** money offered, as for returning something lost

ridge (rij) *n.* **1** a top or high part that is long and narrow; crest [the *ridge* of a roof] **2** a range of hills or mountains **3** any narrow, raised strip [Waves made tiny *ridges* in the sand.]

roast (rōst) *v.* **1** to cook with little or no liquid, as in an oven or over an open fire [to *roast* a chicken or a whole ox] **2** to dry or brown with great heat [to *roast* coffee] **3** to make or become very hot —**roast′ed, roast′ing**

rot (rät) *v.* to fall apart or spoil by the action of bacteria or dampness; to decay [A dead tree will *rot*.] —**rot′ted, rot′ting**

rub·ble (rub′əl) *n.* **1** rough, broken pieces of stone, brick, etc. **2** masonry made up of such pieces **3** broken pieces from buildings, etc. damaged or destroyed by an earthquake, bombing, etc.

Rus·sian (rush′ən) *n.* **1** a person born or living in Russia **2** the chief language of Russia ←*adj.* of Russia, its people, their language, etc.

sa·li·va (sə lī′və) *n.* the watery liquid produced in the mouth by certain glands; spit: it helps to digest food

salm·on (sam′ən) *n.* a large food fish with silver scales and flesh that is orange-pink when cooked: salmon live in the ocean but swim up rivers to lay their eggs —*pl.* **salm′on** or **salm′ons**

sat·in (sat′n) *n.* a cloth of silk, nylon or rayon having a smooth finish, glossy on the front side and dull on the back

sat·u·rate (sach′ər āt) *v.* **1** to soak through and through [The baby's bib was *saturated* with milk.] **2** to fill so completely or dissolve so much of something that no more can be taken up [to *saturate* water with salt] —**sat′u·rat·ed, sat′u·rat·ing** —**sat′u·ra′tion** *n.*

sau·cer (sô′sər *or* sä′sər) *n.* **1** a small, shallow dish, especially one for a cup to rest on **2** anything round and shallow like this dish

sau·sage (sô′sij *or* sä′sij) *n.* pork or other meat, chopped up and seasoned and, usually, stuffed into a tube made of thin skin

scan (skan) *v.* **1** to look at very carefully; examine [Columbus *scanned* the horizon for land.] ☆**2** to glance at or look over quickly [I *scanned* the list of names to find yours.] **3** to show the pattern of rhythm in the lines of a poem [We can *scan* a line this way: Má rÿ Má rÿ quíte cŏn trár ў.] —**scanned, scan′ning** —**scan′ner** *n.*

scare·crow (sker′krō) *n.* a figure of a man made with sticks, old clothes, etc. and set up in a field to scare birds away from crops

scarf (skärf) *n.* **1** a long or broad piece of cloth worn about the head, neck, or shoulders for warmth or decoration **2** a long, narrow piece of cloth used as a covering on top of a table, bureau, etc. —*pl.* **scarves** or **scarfs** (skärvz)

scar·y (sker′ē) *adj.* causing fear; frightening —**scar′i·er, scar′i·est** —**scar′i·ness** *n.*

schol·ar·ship (skä′lər ship) *n.* **1** the knowledge of a learned person; great learning **2** the kind of knowledge that a student shows [Her paper shows good *scholarship*.]

sci·ence (sī′əns) *n.* knowledge made up of an orderly system of facts that have been learned from study, observation, and experiments [*Science* helps us to understand how things happen.]

sci·en·tist (sī′ən tist) *n.* an expert in science, such as a chemist, biologist, etc.

scram·ble (skram′bəl) *v.* **1** to climb or crawl in a quick, rough way [The children *scrambled* up the steep hill.] **2** to struggle or scuffle for something [The puppies *scrambled* for the meat.] ☆**3** to cook eggs while stirring the mixed whites and yolks **4** to mix up electronic signals, as those containing a secret message, so that the message cannot be understood without special equipment —**scram′bled, scram′bling**

scrape (skrāp) *v.* **1** to make smooth or clean by rubbing with a tool or with something rough [to *scrape* the bottom of a ship] **2** to remove in this way [*Scrape* off the old paint.] **3** to scratch or rub the skin from [He fell and *scraped* his knee.] **4** to rub with a harsh or grating sound [The shovel *scraped* across the sidewalk.] —**scraped, scrap′ing**

☆**screen·play** (skrēn′plā) *n.* the written script from which a movie is made

sec·re·tar·y (sek′rə ter′ē) *n.* **1** a person whose work is keeping records, writing letters, etc. for a person, organization, etc. **2** the head of a department of government [the *Secretary* of State] **3** a writing desk, especially one with a bookcase built at the top —*pl.* **sec·re·tar′ies** —**sec·re·tar·i·al** (sek′rə ter′ē əl) *adj.*

seek (sēk) *v.* to try to find; search for [to *seek* gold] —**sought, seek′ing**

seize (sēz) *v.* to take hold of in a sudden, strong, or eager way; grasp [to *seize* a weapon and fight] —**seized, seiz´ing**

se·lec·tive (sə lek´tiv) *adj.* 1 of or set apart by selection 2 tending to select 3 having the power to select [A *selective* radio set brings in each station clearly.] —**se·lec´tive·ly** *adv.* —**se·lec·tiv·i·ty** (se lek´ tiv´ə tē) *n.*

self-con·trol (self´kən trōl´) *n.* control of oneself or of one's feelings and actions

self-pres·er·va·tion (self´prez ər vā´shən) *n.* the act or instinct of keeping oneself safe and alive

sen·ate (sen´ət) *n.* 1 an assembly or council 2 **Senate**, the upper and smaller branch of Congress or of a state legislature

sen·a·tor (sen´ə tər) *n.* a member of a senate —**sen·a·to·ri·al** (sen´ə tôr´ē əl) *adj.*

sen·si·ble (sen´sə bəl) *adj.* 1 having or showing good sense; reasonable; wise [*sensible* advice] 2 having understanding; aware [She was *sensible* of his unhappiness.] 3 that can be felt or noticed by the senses [a *sensible* change in temperature] 4 that can receive sensation [The eye is *sensible* to light rays.] —**sen·si·ble·ness** *n.* —**sen·si·bly** *adv.*

se·pal (sē´pəl) *n.* any of the leaves that form the calyx at the base of a flower

sep·a·rate (sep´ər āt) *v.* 1 to set apart; divide into parts or groups [*Separate* the good apples from the bad ones.] 2 to keep apart or divide by being or putting between [A hedge *separates* his yard from ours.] 3 to go apart; stop being together or joined [The friends *separated* at the crossroads.] —**sep´a·rat·ed, sep´a·rat·ing** *adj.* (sep´ər ət *or* sep´ rət) single or individual [the body's *separate* parts] —**sep´a·rate·ly** *adv.* —**sep´a·ra´tion** *n.*

se·quence (sē´kwens) *n.* 1 the following of one thing after another; succession [The *sequence* of events in their lives led to marriage.] 2 the order in which things follow one another [Line them up in *sequence* from shortest to tallest.] 3 a series of things that are related [a *sequence* of misfortunes]

se·ri·ous (sir´ē əs) *adj.* 1 having or showing deep thought; not frivolous; solemn; earnest [a *serious* student] 2 not joking or fooling; sincere [Is she *serious* about wanting to help?] 3 needing careful thought; important [a *serious* problem] 4 that can cause worry; dangerous [a *serious* illness] —**se´ri·ous·ly** *adv.* —**se´ri·ous·ness** *n.*

set·tle·ment (set´l mənt) *n.* a place where people have gone to settle; colony [early English *settlements* in Virginia]

shake (shāk) *v.* 1 to move quickly up and down, back and forth, or from side to side [to *shake* one's head in approval] 2 to clasp another's hand, as in greeting 3 to bring, force, throw, stir up, etc. by short, quick movements [I'll *shake* salt on the popcorn. *Shake* the medicine well before taking it.] 4 to tremble or make tremble [His voice *shook* with fear. Chills *shook* his body.] —**shook, shak·en** (shak´'n), **shak´ing**

shal·low (shal´ō) *adj.* 1 not deep [a *shallow* lake] 2 not serious in thinking or strong in feeling [a *shallow* mind] ◆*n.* a shallow place, as in a river

shame·ful (shām´fəl) *adj.* 1 bringing shame or disgrace 2 not moral or decent —**shame´ful·ly** *adv.*

sharp·en (shärp´ən) *v.* to make or become sharp or sharper —**sharp´en·er** *n.*

she'll (shēl) *contraction* 1 she will 2 she shall

sher·bet (shur´bət) *n.* a frozen dessert of fruit juice, sugar, and water or milk

☆**sher·iff** (sher´if) *n.* the chief officer of the law in a county

shield (shēld) *n.* 1 a piece of armor carried on the arm to ward off blows in battle 2 something that guards or protects, as a safety guard over machinery 3 anything shaped like a shield, as a coat of arms ◆*v.* to guard or protect [Trees *shield* our house from the sun.]

ship (ship) *n.* 1 any vessel, larger than a boat, for traveling on deep water 2 the crew of a ship 3 an aircraft or spaceship ◆*v.* to put, take, go, or send in a ship or boat [The cargo was *shipped* from New York.] —**shipped, ship´ping**

ship·wreck (ship´rek) *n.* 1 the remains of a wrecked ship 2 the loss or ruin of a ship, as in a storm or crash ◆*v.* to wreck or destroy a ship

shoe·lace (shoo´lās) *n.* a lace of cord, leather, etc. used for fastening a shoe

shore·ward (shôr´wərd) *adj., adv.* toward the shore [Two boats were headed *shoreward*.]

☆**short·age** (shôrt´ij) *n.* a lack in the amount that is needed or expected [a *shortage* of help]

shred (shred) *n.* 1 a long, narrow strip or piece cut or torn off [My shirt was torn to *shreds*.] 2 a tiny piece or amount; fragment [a story without a *shred* of truth] ◆*v.* to cut or tear into shreds [*shredded* coconut] —**shred´ded** or **shred, shred´ding**

shy (shī) *adj.* 1 easily frightened; timid [a *shy* animal] 2 not at ease with other people; bashful [a *shy* child] —**shi´er** or **shy´er, shi´est** or **shy´est** —**shied, shy´ing** *v.* —**shy´ly** *adv.* —**shy´ness** *n.*

a	ask, fat
ā	ape, date
ä	car, lot
e	elf, ten
ē	even, meet
i	is, hit
ī	ice, fire
ō	open, go
ô	law, horn
σi	oil, point
σ͞σ	look, pull
o͞o	ooze, tool
ou	out, crowd
u	up, cut
u	fur, fern
ə	a in ago
	e in agent
	e in father
	i in unity
	o in collect
	u in focus
ch	chin, arch
ŋ	ring, singer
sh	she, dash
th	thin, truth
th	then, father
zh	s in pleasure

signal/splendid

sig·nal (sig′nəl) *n.* **1** something that tells when some action is to start or end, or is used as a warning or direction [A loud bell is the *signal* for a fire drill. The traffic *signal* is green, telling us to go.] **2** the electrical waves sent out or received as sounds or pictures in radio and television —**sig′naled** or **sig′nalled, sig′nal·ing** or **sig′nal·ling** *v.*

si·lence (sī′ləns) *n.* **1** a keeping still and not speaking, making noise, etc. [His *silence* meant he agreed.] **2** absence of any sound or noise; stillness [There was complete *silence* in the deep forest.] —**si′lenc·er** —**si′lenced, si′lenc·ing** *v.*

sin·cere (sin sir′) *adj.* not pretending or fooling; honest; truthful [Are you *sincere* in wanting to help?] —**sin·cer′er, sin·cer′est**

sin·cer·i·ty (sin ser′ə tē) *n.* the condition of being sincere; honesty; good faith

six (siks) *n., adj.* one more than five; the number 6

six·ty-four (siks′tē fôr) *n., adj.* the cardinal number that is equal to six times ten plus four; 64

skid (skid) *n.* ☆**1** a plank, log, etc. used as a support or as a track on which to slide something heavy **2** a sliding wedge used as a brake on a wheel ►*v.* to slide without turning, as a wheel does on ice when it is held by a brake —**skid′ded, skid′ding**

slaugh·ter (slôt′ər *or* slät′ər) *n.* the act of killing people or animals in a cruel way or in large numbers ►*v.* to kill for food; butcher [to *slaughter* a hog] —**slaugh′tered, slaugh′ter·ing**

sleep·y (slē′pē) *adj.* **1** ready or likely to fall asleep; drowsy **2** not very active; dull; quiet [a *sleepy* little town] —**sleep′i·er, sleep′i·est** —**sleep′i·ly** *adv.* —**sleep′i·ness** *n.*

slight (slīt) *adj.* **1** small in amount or degree; not great, strong, important, etc. [a *slight* change in temperature; a *slight* advantage; a *slight* bruise.] **2** light in build; slender [Most jockeys are short and *slight*.] ►*v.* to pay little or no attention to; neglect, snub, etc. [to *slight* one's homework; to *slight* a neighbor] —**slight′ly** *adv.* —**slight′er, slight′est** *adj.*

snout (snout) *n.* the part, including the nose and jaws, that sticks out from the face of pigs, dogs, and certain other animals

snow·drift (snō′drift) *n.* a bank or pile of snow heaped up by the wind

soil (soil) *n.* the act of soiling or a soiled spot; stain ►*v.* **1** to make or become dirty; stain; spot **2** to disgrace [to *soil* one's honor] —**soiled**

sor·row (sär′ō) *n.* a sad or troubled feeling; sadness; grief

spa·ghet·ti (spə get′ē) *n.* long, thin strings of dried flour paste, cooked by boiling or steaming and served with a sauce

Span·ish (span′ish) *adj.* of Spain, its people, etc. ►*n.* the language of Spain and Spanish America —**the Spanish**, the people of Spain

spark·le (spär′kəl) *v.* **1** to give off sparks or flashes of light; glitter; glisten [A lake *sparkles* in sunlight.] **2** to be lively and witty [There was much *sparkling* talk at the party.] **3** to bubble as ginger ale does —**spar′kled, spar′kling**

spar·row (sper′ō) *n.* a small, often brown or gray songbird with a short beak

speak·er (spē′kər) *n.* **1** a person who speaks or makes speeches **2** the person who serves as chairman of a group of lawmakers, especially ☆**Speaker**, the chairman of the U.S. House of Representatives: *the full name is* **Speaker of the House 3** a device that changes electric current into sound waves, used as part of a hi-fi system, radio, etc.

spe·cies (spē′shēz *or* spē′sēz) *n.* **1** a group of plants or animals that are alike in certain ways [The lion and tiger are two different *species* of cat.] **2** a kind or sort [a *species* of bravery] —*pl.* **spe′cies** —**the species**, the human race

speech (spēch) *n.* **1** the act or way of speaking [We knew from their *speech* that they were from the South.] **2** the power to speak [She lost her *speech* from a stroke.] **3** something spoken; remark, utterance, etc. **4** a talk given in public [political *speeches* on TV]

spell·bound (spel′bound) *adj.* held fast as if by a spell; fascinated; enchanted

spin (spin) *v.* **1** to draw out the fibers of and twist into thread [to *spin* cotton, wool, flax, etc.] **2** to make from a thread given out by the body [Spiders *spin* webs.] **3** to tell slowly, with many details [to *spin* out a story] **4** to whirl around swiftly [The earth *spins* in space. *Spin* the wheel.] —**spun, spin′ning** —**spin′ner** *n.*

spi·ral (spī′rəl) *adj.* circling around a center in a flat or rising curve that keeps growing larger or smaller, as the thread of a screw, or that stays the same, as the thread of a bolt ►*n.* a spiral curve or coil [The mainspring of a watch is a *spiral*.] ►*v.* to move in or form into a spiral —**spi′raled** or **spi′ralled, spi′ral·ing** or **spi′ral·ling** —**spi′ral·ly** *adv.*

splen·did (splen′did) *adj.* **1** very bright, brilliant, showy, magnificent, etc. [a *splended* display; a *splendid* gown] **2** deserving high praise; glorious; grand [your *splendid* courage] **3** very good; excellent; fine; *used only in everyday talk* [a *splended* trip] —**splen′did·ly** *adv.*

spoil (spoil) *v.* to make or become useless, worthless or rotten; to damage; to ruin [Meat *spoils* fast in warm weather.] —**spoiled** or **spoilt, spoil´ing**

spo·ken (spō´kən) *v. past participle of* **speak** ➛*adj.* said aloud; oral [a *spoken* order]

sprawl (sprôl) *v.* to sit or lie with the arms and legs spread out in a relaxed or awkward way [He *sprawled* on the grass.] —**sprawled, sprawl´ing**

squawk (skwôk *or* skwäk) *n.* a loud, harsh cry such as a chicken or parrot makes ➛*v.* ☆to complain loudly: *used only in everyday talk* —**squawk´er** *n.*

sta·di·um (stā´dē əm) *n.* a place for outdoor games, meetings, etc., with rising rows of seats around the open field

stain (stān) *v.* to spoil with dirt or a patch of color; to soil or spot [The rug was *stained* with ink.] —**stained, stain´ing** ➛*n.* a dirty or colored spot [grass *stain*]

sta·men (stā´mən) *n.* the part of a flower in which the pollen grows, including the anther and its stem

state·ment (stāt´mənt) *n.* **1** the act of stating **2** something stated or said [May we quote your *statement*?] **3** a report or record, as of money owed [The customers receive monthly *statements*.]

sta·tion·ar·y (stā´shə ner´ē) *adj.* **1** not to be moved; fixed [*stationary* seats] **2** not changing in condition, value, etc. [*stationary* prices]

stat·ue (stach´o͞o) *n.* the form or likeness of a person or animal carved in wood, stone, etc., modeled in clay, or cast in plaster or a metal

stead·y (sted´ē) *adj.* **1** firm; not shaky [a *steady* chair] **2** not changing or letting up; regular [a *steady* gaze; a *steady* worker] **3** not easily excited; calm [*steady* nerves] **4** serious and sensible; reliable [a *steady* young person] —**stead´i·er, stead´i·est** —**stead´ied, stead´y·ing** *v.* —**stead´i·ly** *adv.* —**stead´i·ness** *n.*

stick·y (stik´ē) *adj.* **1** that sticks; gluey; clinging [His fingers were *sticky* with candy.] **2** hot and damp; humid; *used only in everyday talk* [a *sticky* August day] —**stick´i·er, stick´i·est** —**stick´i·ness** *n.*

stiff·ness (stif´nəs) *n.* the condition of being hard to bend or stretch

stom·ach (stum´ək) *n.* **1** the large, hollow organ into which food goes after it is swallowed: food is partly digested in the stomach **2** the belly, or abdomen [The fighter was hit in the *stomach*.]

strange (strānj) *adj.* **1** not known, seen, or heard before; not familiar [I saw a *strange* person at the door.] **2** different from what is usual; peculiar; odd [wearing a *strange* costume] **3** not familiar; without experience [She is *strange* to this job.] —**strang´er, strang´est** —**strange´ly** *adv.*

straw·ber·ry (strô´ber´ē *or* strä´ber´ē) *n.* **1** the small, red, juicy fruit of a low plant of the rose family **2** this plant —*pl.* **straw´ber´ries**

strut (strut) *v.* to walk in a self-confident way, usually as if to attract attention [The famous singer *strutted* across the stage.] —**strut´ted, strut´ting**

stur·dy (stur´dē) *adj.* **1** strong and hardy [a *sturdy* oak] **2** not giving in; firm [*sturdy* defiance] —**stur´di·er, stur´di·est** —**stur´di·ly** *adv.* —**stur´di·ness** *n.*

sub·due (səb do͞o´ *or* səb dyo͞o´) *v.* **1** to conquer or overcome; get control over [to *subdue* an invading army; to *subdue* a bad habit] **2** to make less strong or harsh; soften [*subdued* anger; *subdued* light; *subdued* colors] —**sub·dued´, sub·du´ing**

sub·ject (sub´jekt) *adj.* **1** under the power or control of another [The *subject* peoples in colonies often revolt.] **2** likely to have; liable [He is *subject* to fits of anger.] ➛*n.* **1** a person under the power or control of a ruler, government, etc. **2** a course of study, as in a school [What is your favorite *subject*?] —**sub·jec´tion** *n.*

sub·ma·rine (sub´mə rēn) *n.* a kind of ship that can travel underwater

sub·merge (sub murj´) *v.* to put, go, or stay underwater [Whales can *submerge* for as long as half an hour.] —**sub·merged´, sub·merg´ing**

sub·mit (sub mit´) *v.* **1** to give or offer to others for them to look over, decide about, etc.; refer [A new tax law was *submitted* to the voters.] **2** to give in to the power or control of another; surrender [We will never *submit* to the enemy.] —**sub·mit´ted, sub·mit´ting**

sub·scribe (səb skrīb´) *v.* **1** to agree to take and pay for [We *subscribed* to the magazine for a year.] **2** to promise to give [She *subscribed* $100 to the campaign for a new museum.] **3** to agree with or approve of [I *subscribe* to the principles in the Constitution.] —**sub·scribed´, sub·scrib´ing** —**sub·scrib´er** *n.*

sub·side (səb sīd´) *v.* **1** to sink to a lower level; go down [In June the river began to *subside*.] **2** to become quiet or less active [The angry waves *subsided*. The teacher's temper *subsided*.] —**sub·sid´ed, sub·sid´ing**

sub·sti·tute (sub´stə to͞ot *or* sub´stə tyo͞ot) *n.* a person or thing that takes the place of another [He is a *substitute* for the regular teacher.] ➛*v.* to use as or be a substitute [to *substitute* vinegar for lemon juice; to *substitute* for an injured player] —**sub´sti·tut·ed, sub´sti·tut·ing** —**sub´sti·tu´tion** *n.*

sub·tract (səb trakt´) *v.* to take away, as a part from a whole or one number from another [If 3 is *subtracted* from 5, the remainder is 2.]

a	ask, fat
ā	ape, date
ä	car, lot
e	elf, ten
ē	even, meet
i	is, hit
ī	ice, fire
ō	open, go
ô	law, horn
oi	oil, point
o͝o	look, pull
o͞o	ooze, tool
ou	out, crowd
u	up, cut
ʉ	fur, fern
ə	a in ago
	e in agent
	e in father
	i in unity
	o in collect
	u in focus
ch	chin, arch
ŋ	ring, singer
sh	she, dash
th	thin, truth
th	then, father
zh	s in pleasure

suc·ceed (sək sēd′) **v. 1** to manage to do or be what was planned; do or go well [I *succeeded* in convincing them to come with us.] **2** to come next after; follow [Carter *succeeded* Ford as president.]

suc·cess (sək ses′) **n. 1** the result that was hoped for; satisfactory outcome [Did you have *success* in training your dog?] **2** the fact of becoming rich, famous, etc. [Her *success* did not change her.] **3** a successful person or thing [Our play was a *success*.]

suf·fer (suf′ər) **v. 1** to feel or have pain, discomfort, etc. [to *suffer* from a headache] **2** to experience or undergo [The team *suffered* a loss when Sal was hurt.] **3** to become worse or go from good to bad [Her grades *suffered* when she didn't study.] **4** to put up with; bear [He won't *suffer* criticism.]

sug·gest (səg jest′) **v. 1** to mention as something to think over, act on, etc. [I *suggest* we meet again.] **2** to bring to mind as something similar or in some way connected [The white dunes *suggested* snow-covered hills. Clouds *suggest* rain.]

sun·ny (sun′ē) **adj. 1** bright with sunlight [Today is a *sunny* day.] **2** like or from the sun [A *sunny* beam shone through.] **3** cheerful; bright [Lynn has a *sunny* smile.] —**sun′ni·er, sun′ni·est**

sun·shine (sun′shīn) **n. 1** the shining of sun **2** the light and heat from the sun **3** cheerfulness, happiness, etc. —**sun′shin·y adj.**

sup·ply (sə plī′) **v. 1** to give what is needed; furnish [The camp *supplies* sheets and towels. The book *supplied* us with the facts.] **2** to take care of the needs of [to *supply* workers with tools] **3** to make up for; fill [These pills *supply* a deficiency of iron.] —**sup·plied′, sup·ply′ing**

sup·port (sə pôrt′) **v. 1** to carry the weight or burden of; hold up [Will that old ladder *support* you?] **2** to take the side of; uphold or help **3** to earn a living for; provide for [He *supports* a large family.] **4** to help prove [Use examples to *support* your argument.] —**sup·port′er n.**

sur·prise (sər prīz′) **v. 1** to cause to feel wonder by being unexpected [Her sudden anger *surprised* us.] **2** to come upon suddenly or unexpectedly [I *surprised* him in the act of stealing the watch.] **3** to attack or capture suddenly —**sur·prised′, sur·pris′ing**

sur·round (sər round′) **v.** to form or arrange around on all or nearly all sides; enclose [The police *surrounded* the criminals. The house is *surrounded* with trees.]

sur·vey (sər vā′ *for v.*; sur′vā *for n.*) **v.** to look over in a careful way; examine; inspect [The lookout *surveyed* the horizon.] —**sur·veyed′, sur·vey′ing n.** a detailed study or inspection made from gathering and analyzing evidence [We made a *survey* of the class's favorite hobbies.]

sur·vive (sər vīv′) **v. 1** to continue to live or exist [Thanksgiving is a Pilgrim custom that *survives* today.] **2** to live or last longer than; outlive [Most people *survive* their parents.] **3** to continue to live or exist in spite of [We *survived* the fire.] —**sur·vived′, sur·viv′ing**

swal·low (swä′lō) **v. 1** to let food, drink, etc. go through the throat into the stomach **2** to move the muscles of the throat as in swallowing something [I *swallowed* hard to keep from crying.] **3** to take in; engulf [The waters of the lake *swallowed* him up.] **4** to put up with; bear with patience [We refused to *swallow* their insults.]

sweat·er (swet′ər) **n.** a knitted outer garment for the upper part of the body

Swed·ish (swēd′ish) **adj.** of Sweden or the Swedes ▸**n.** the language of the Swedes

sweep (swēp) **v. 1** to clean as by brushing with a broom [to *sweep* a floor] **2** to clear away as with a broom [*Sweep* the dirt from the porch.] **3** to carry away or destroy with a quick, strong motion [The tornado *swept* the shed away.] —**swept, sweep′ing** ▸**n.** the act of sweeping, as with a broom

sweep·er (swēp′ər) **n. 1** a person or thing that sweeps **2** a device for cleaning floors

sweet (swēt) **adj. 1** having the taste of sugar; having sugar in it [a *sweet* apple] **2** pleasant in taste, smell, sound, manner, etc. [*sweet* perfume; *sweet* music; a *sweet* child] ▸**adv.** in a sweet manner —**sweet′er, sweet′est** —**sweet′ish adj.** —**sweet′ly adv.** —**sweet′ness n.**

sym·bol (sim′bəl) **n.** an object, mark, sign, etc. that stands for another object, or for an idea, quality, etc. [The dove is a *symbol* of peace. The mark $ is the *symbol* for dollar or dollars.]

sym·pho·ny (sim′fə nē) **n. 1** a long piece of music for a full orchestra, usually divided into four movements with different rhythms and themes **2** a large orchestra for playing such works: *its full name is* **symphony orchestra 3** harmony, as of sounds, color, etc. [The dance was a *symphony* in motion.] —*pl.* **sym′pho·nies** —**sym·phon·ic** (sim fän′ik) **adj.** —**sym·phon′i·cal·ly adv.**

tar·dy (tär′dē) **adj.** not on time; late; delayed [to be *tardy* for class] —**tar′di·er, tar′di·est**

tel·e·graph (tel′ə graf) **n.** a device or system for sending messages by a code of electrical signals that are sent over a wire, by radio or by microwave

☆**tel·e·phone** (tel′ə fōn) *n.* **1** a way of sending sounds over distances by changing them into electric signals which are sent through a wire and then changed back into sounds **2** a device for sending and receiving sounds in this way —**tel′e·phoned, tel′e·phon·ing** *v.* —**tel·e·phon·ic** (tel′ə fän′ ik) *adj.*

tem·per·a·ture (tem′prə chər *or* tem′pər ə chər) *n.* **1** the degree of hotness or coldness, as of air, liquids, the body, etc., usually as measured by a thermometer **2** a body heat above the normal, which is about 37°C or 98.6°F; fever

ter·ri·ble (ter′ə bəl) *adj.* **1** causing great fear or terror; dreadful [a *terrible* flood] **2** very great; severe [*terrible* suffering] **3** very bad or unpleasant: *used only in everyday talk* [Our guest had *terrible* manners.] —**ter′ri·bly** *adv.*

Tex·as (teks′əs) a state in the south central part of the U.S.: abbreviated **Tex., TX** —**Tex′an** *adj., n.*

thaw (thô *or* thä) *v.* to melt [The snow *thawed*.] —**thawed, thaw′ ing**

the·o·ry (thē′ē rē *or* thir′ē) *n.* an explanation of how or why something happens, especially one based on scientific study and reasoning [Einstein's *theory* of relativity] —*pl.* **the′o·ries**

they've (thāv) *contraction* they have

thick·en (thik′ən) *v.* to make or become thick or thicker [Adding flour will *thicken* the gravy.] —**thick′ened, thick′en·ing**

thief (thēf) *n.* a person who steals, especially one who steals secretly —*pl.* **thieves** (thēvz)

throb (thräb) *v.* to beat or vibrate hard or fast, as the heart does when one is excited —**throbbed, throb′bing** ➛*n.* the act of throbbing; a strong beat

throw (thrō) *v.* **1** to send through the air by a fast motion of the arm; hurl, toss, etc. [to *throw* a ball] **2** to make fall down; upset [to *throw* someone in wrestling] **3** to send or cast in a certain direction, as a glance, light, shadow, etc. **4** to put suddenly into some condition or place [to *throw* into confusion; to throw into prison] —**threw, thrown, throw′ ing**

tick·le (tik′əl) *v.* **1** to touch or stroke lightly, as with a finger or feather, so as to cause twitching, laughter, etc. **2** to have such a scratching or twitching feeling [The dust makes my nose *tickle*.] **3** to give pleasure to; amuse; delight [The joke really *tickled* her.] —**tick′led, tick′ling** —**tick′ler** *n.*

tight (tīt) *adj.* **1** made so that water, air, etc. cannot pass through [a *tight* boat] **2** put together firmly or closely [a *tight* knot] **3** fitting too closely [a *tight* shirt] **4** stretched and strained; taut [a *tight* wire; *tight* nerves] —**tight′ ly** *adv.* —**tight′ness** *n.*

tight·en (tīt′n) *v.* to make or become tight or tighter

toad·stool (tōd′stool) *n.* a mushroom, especially one that is poisonous

toast (tōst) *v.* **1** to brown the surface of by heating, as bread **2** to warm [*Toast* yourself by the fire.] ➛*n.* toasted bread —**toast′ er**

toil (toil) *v.* **1** to work hard; labor **2** to go slowly with pain or effort [to *toil* up a hill] ➛*n.* hard work —**toil′ er**

to·ma·to (tə māt′ō *or* tə mät′ō) *n.* **1** a red or yellow, round fruit, with a juicy pulp, used as a vegetable **2** the plant it grows on —*pl.* **to·ma′toes**

to·mor·row (tə′ mär′ō) *adv.* on the day after today ➛*n.* **1** the day after today **2** some future time

tor·na·do (tôr nā′ dō) *n.* a high, narrow column of air that is whirling very fast: it is often seen as a slender cloud shaped like a funnel, that usually destroys everything in its narrow path —*pl.* **tor·na′ does** or **tor·na′dos**

tor·pe·do (tôr pē′ dō) *n.* a large, exploding missile shaped like a cigar: it moves under water under its own power to blow up enemy ships —*pl.* **tor·pe′does**

tor·rent (tôr′ənt) *n.* **1** a swift, rushing stream of water **2** any wild, rushing flow [a *torrent* of insults] **3** a heavy fall of rain

tough (tuf) *adj.* **1** that will bend or twist without tearing or breaking [*tough* rubber] **2** that cannot be cut or chewed easily [*tough* meat] **3** strong and healthy; robust [a *tough* pioneer] **4** very difficult or hard [a *tough* job] —**tough′ness** *n.*

tour·ist (toor′ist) *n.* a person who tours or travels for pleasure ➛*adj.* of or for tourists

tow·el (tou′əl *or* toul) *n.* a piece of soft paper or cloth for drying things by wiping

trans·fer (trans fur′ *or* trans′fər) *v.* **1** to move, carry, send, or change from one person or place to another [He *transferred* his notes to another notebook. Jill has *transferred* to a new school.] **2** to move a picture, design, etc. from one surface to another, as by making wet and pressing ☆**3** to change from one bus, train, etc. to another —**trans·ferred′, trans·fer′ring**

trans·late (trans lāt′ *or* tranz lāt′) *v.* **1** to put into words of a different language [to *translate* a Latin poem into English] **2** to change into another form [to *translate* ideas into action] **3** to change from one place or condition to another; especially, to carry up to heaven —**trans·lat′ed, trans·lat′ing**

trans·mit (trans mit′ *or* tranz mit′) *v.* to send from one person, place, or thing to another; pass on; transfer [to *transmit* a disease] —**trans·mit′ted, trans·mit′ting**

trans·par·ent (trans per′ənt) *adj.* so clear or so fine that objects on the other side can be easily seen [*transparent* glass]

a	ask, fat
ā	ape, date
ä	car, lot
e	elf, ten
ē	even, meet
i	is, hit
ī	ice, fire
ō	open, go
ô	law, horn
oi	oil, point
oo	look, pull
oo	ooze, tool
ou	out, crowd
u	up, cut
ʉ	fur, fern
ə	a in ago
	e in agent
	e in father
	i in unity
	o in collect
	u in focus
ch	chin, arch
ŋ	ring, singer
sh	she, dash
th	thin, truth
th	then, father
zh	s in pleasure

trans·plant (trans plant′) **v. 1** to dig up from one place and plant in another **2** to move tissue or an organ by surgery from one person or part of the body to another; graft ➛**n.** (trans′plant) something transplanted, as a body organ or seedling

trans·port (trans pôrt′) **v. 1** to carry from one place to another [to *transport* goods by train or truck] **2** to cause strong feelings in [*transported* with delight] **3** to send to a place far away as a punishment

treas·ure (trezh′ər) **n. 1** money, jewels, etc. collected and stored up **2** a person or thing that is loved or held dear ➛**v. 1** to love or hold dear; cherish [I *treasure* their friendship.] **2** to store away or save up, as money; hoard —**treas′ured, treas′ur·ing**

tri·an·gle (trī′aŋ′ gəl) **n. 1** a flat figure with three sides and three angles **2** anything shaped like this **3** a musical instrument that is a steel rod bent in a triangle: it makes a high, tinkling sound when struck with a metal rod

tri·o (trē′ō) **n. 1** a piece of music for three voices or three instruments **2** the three people who sing or play it **3** any group of three —*pl.* **tri′os**

tri·ple (trip′əl) **adj. 1** made up of three [A *triple* cone has three dips of ice cream.] **2** three times as much or as many ➛**n. 1** an amount three times as much or as many ☆**2** a hit in baseball on which the batter gets to third base —**tri′pled, tri′pling v.**

tri·plet (trip′lət) **n. 1** any one of three children born at the same time to the same mother **2** any group of three

tri·pod (trī′päd) **n.** a stand, frame, etc. with three legs: cameras and small telescopes are often held up by tripods

tri·umph (trī′əmf) **n. 1** a victory, as in a battle; success [His *triumph* over illness inspired us.] **2** great joy over a victory or success [She grinned in *triumph* when she won the race.] ➛**v.** to be the winner; win victory or success [to *triumph* over an enemy] —**tri·um·phal** (trī um′f′l) **adj.**

trout (trout) **n.** a small food fish of the salmon family, found mainly in fresh water

trudge (truj) **v.** to walk, especially in a tired way or with effort —**trudged, trudg′ing** ➛**n.** a long or tiring walk

☆**type·writ·er** (tīp′rīt′ ər) **n.** a machine with a keyboard for making printed letters or figures on paper

ty·phoid (tī′ foid) **n.** a serious disease that is spread as by infected food or drinking water, and causing fever, sores in the intestines, etc.: *the full name is* **typhoid fever**

ty·phoon (tī foon′) **n.** any violent tropical cyclone that starts in the western Pacific

un- **1** *a prefix meaning* not *or* the opposite of [An *unhappy* person is one who is not happy, but sad.] **2** *a prefix meaning* to reverse or undo the action of [To *untie* a shoelace is to reverse the action of tying it.]

un·a·vail·a·ble (un′ə vāl′ə bəl) **adj.** not able to be gotten, used, or reached [This book is now *unavailable*.]

un·cooked (un kookt′) **adj.** not cooked; raw

un·cov·er (un kuv′ər) **v. 1** to remove the cover or covering from **2** to make known; disclose, as a hidden fact **3** to take off one's hat, as in showing respect

un·der·neath (un′der neth′) **adv., prep.** under; below; beneath

un·der·sea (un′dər sē′) **adj., adv.** beneath the surface of the sea

un·der·wa·ter (un′dər wôt′ər *or* un′dər wät′ər) **adj., adv.** under the surface of the water

un·for·giv·a·ble (un′fər giv′ə bəl) **adj.** not deserving to be pardoned; inexcusable

u·nit (yoon′it) **n. 1** a single person or group, especially as a part of a whole [an army *unit*] **2** a single part with some special use [the lens *unit* of a camera] **3** a fixed amount or measure used as a standard [The ounce is a *unit* of weight.] **4** the smallest whole number; one

un·just (un just′) **adj.** not just or right; unfair [an *unjust* rule] —**un·just′ly adv.**

un·law·ful (un lô′fəl *or* un lä′fəl) **adj.** against the law; illegal —**un·law′ful·ly adv.** —**un·law′ful·ness n.**

un·like·ly (un līk′lē) **adj. 1** not likely to happen or be true [an *unlikely* story] **2** not likely to be right or successful [an *unlikely* place to dig for gold]

un·sel·fish (un sel′fish) **adj.** not selfish; putting the good of others above one's own interests —**un·self′ish·ly adv.** —**un·self′ish·ness n.**

un·u·su·al (un yoo′zhoo əl) **adj.** not usual or common; rare; remarkable —**un·u′su·al·ly adv.**

us·a·ble or **use·a·ble** (yoo′zə bəl) **adj.** that can be used; fit or ready for use

va·ca·tion (vā kā′shən) **n.** a period of time when one stops working, going to school, etc. in order to rest and have recreation ➛**v.** to take one's vacation

val·u·a·ble (val′yσͬ ə bəl *or* val′yə bəl) *adj.* **1** having value or worth; especially, worth much money **2** thought of as precious, useful, worthy, etc. ➜*n.* something of value, as a piece of jewelry

valve (valv) *n.* **1** a device, as in a pipe, that controls the flow of a gas or liquid by means of a flap, lid, or plug that closes off the pipe **2** a membrane in the body that acts in this way [The *valves* of the heart let the blood flow in one direction only.] **3** a device, as in a trumpet, that opens a branch to the main tube so as to change the pitch **4** one of the parts making up the shell of a clam, oyster, etc.

va·por (va′pər) *n.* **1** a thick mist or mass of tiny drops of water floating in the air, as steam or fog **2** the gas formed when a substance that is usually liquid or solid is heated [Mercury *vapor* is used in some lamps.]

vault (vôlt) *n.* **1** an arched ceiling or roof **2** a room with such a ceiling, or a space that seems to have an arch [the *vault* of the sky] ☆**3** a room for keeping money, valuable papers, etc. safe, as in a bank

ve·hi·cle (vē′i kəl *or* vē′hi kəl) *n.* **1** a means of carrying persons or things, especially over land or in space, as an automobile, bicycle, spacecraft, etc. **2** a means by which something is expressed, passed along, etc. [TV is a *vehicle* for advertising.] **3** a liquid, as oil or water, with which pigments are mixed to make paint

vein (vān) *n.* **1** any blood vessel that carries blood back to the heart from some part of the body **2** any of the fine lines, or ribs, in a leaf or in an insect's wing **3** a layer of mineral, rock, etc. formed in a crack in different rock [a *vein* of silver or of coal]

ver·dict (vʉr′dikt) *n.* **1** the decision reached by a jury in a law case [a *verdict* of "not guilty"] **2** any decision or opinion

vet·er·an (vet′ər ən *or* ve′trən) *n.* **1** a person who has served in the armed forces **2** a person with much experience in some kind of work ➜*adj.* having had long experience in some work or service [*veteran* troops; a *veteran* diplomat]

vic·tim (vik′tim) *n.* **1** someone or something killed, hurt, sacrificed, etc. [a *victim* of the storm; the *victims* of prejudice] **2** a person who is cheated or tricked [a *victim* of swindlers]

vic·to·ry (vik′tər ē) *n.* the winning of a battle, struggle, or contest; success in defeating an enemy or rival —*pl.* **vic′to·ries**

vil·lage (vil′ij) *n.* **1** a group of houses in the country, smaller than a town **2** the people of a village —**vil′lag·er**

vi·o·lence (vī′ə ləns) *n.* great strength or force [the *violence* of a tornado]

vi·o·lent (vī′ə lənt) *adj.* showing or acting with great force that causes damage or injury [*violent* winds] —**vi′o·lent·ly** *adv.*

vis·i·ble (viz′ə bəl) *adj.* that can be seen or noticed; evident [a barely *visible* scar; a *visible* increase in crime] —**vis′i·bly** *adv.*

vo·cal·ist (vō′kəl ist) *n.* a person who sings; singer

vol·ca·no (vôl kā nō *or* väl kā′nō) *n.* **1** an opening in the earth's surface through which molten rock from inside the earth is thrown up **2** a hill or mountain of ash and molten rock built up around such an opening —*pl.* **vol·ca′noes** *or* **vol·ca′nos**

vol·ume (väl′yσͬm) *n.* **1** a book [You may borrow four *volumes* at a time.] **2** one of the books of a set [*Volume* III of the encyclopedia] **3** the amount of space inside something, measured in cubic inches, feet, etc. [The *volume* of this box is 27 cubic feet, or .756 cubic meter.]

vol·un·teer (väl ən tir′) *n.* a person who offers to do something of his or her own free will, as one who enlists in the armed forces by choice ➜*adj.* of or done by volunteers [a *volunteer* regiment; *volunteer* help]

vot·er (vōt′ər) *n.* a person who votes or has the right to vote

voy·age (voi′ij) *n.* **1** a journey by water [an ocean *voyage*] **2** a journey through the air or through outer space [a *voyage* by rocket] ➜*v.* to make a voyage —**voy′aged, voy′ag·ing** —**voy′ag·er** *n.*

waf·fle (wäf′əl) *n.* a crisp cake with small, square hollows, cooked in a waffle iron

walk·way (wôk′wā) *n.* a passage for walking

war·ri·or (wôr′ē ər) *n.* a soldier: not often used today

wash·a·ble (wôsh′ə b′əl *or* wäsh′ə bəl) *adj.* able to be washed without being damaged

wa·ter·mel·on (wôt′ər mel ən *or* wät′ər mel ən) *n.* a large melon with a green rind and juicy, red pulp with many seeds

wealth (welth) *n.* **1** much money or property; riches **2** a large amount [a *wealth* of ideas] **3** any valuable thing or things [the *wealth* of the oceans]

weath·er (we*th*′er) *n.* the conditions outside at any particular time with regard to temperature, sunshine, rainfall, etc. [We have good *weather* today for a picnic.] ➜*v.* to pass through safely [to *weather* a storm]

weird (wird) *adj.* **1** strange or mysterious in a ghostly way [*Weird* sounds came from the cave.] **2** very odd, strange, etc. [What a *weird* hat! What *weird* behavior!] —**weird′ly** *adv.* —**weird′ness** *n.*

wheel·bar·row (hwēl′bar′ō *or* wēl′ber′ō) *n.* a small kind of cart pushed or pulled by hand and having a single wheel

a	ask, fat
ā	ape, date
ä	car, lot
e	elf, ten
ē	even, meet
i	is, hit
ī	ice, fire
ō	open, go
ô	law, horn
oi	oil, point
σͬ	look, pull
σͬσͬ	ooze, tool
ou	out, crowd
u	up, cut
ʉ	fur, fern
ə	a in ago
	e in agent
	e in father
	i in unity
	o in collect
	u in focus
ch	chin, arch
ŋ	ring, singer
sh	she, dash
th	thin, truth
th	then, father
zh	s in pleasure

whis·tle (hwis′əl *or* wis′əl) **v.** **1** to make a high, shrill sound as by forcing breath through puckered lips or by sending steam through a small opening **2** to move with a high, shrill sound [The arrow *whistled* past her ear.] **3** to blow a whistle **4** to produce by whistling [to *whistle* a tune] —**whis′tled, whis′tling** ►**n.** a device for making whistling sounds —**whis′tler**

whole·sale (hōl′sāl) **n.** the sale of goods in large amounts, especially to retail stores that resell them to actual users ►**adj.** **1** of or having to do with such sale of goods [a *wholesale* dealer; a *wholesale* price] **2** widespread or general [*wholesale* destruction by the volcano] ►**adv.** **1** in wholesale amounts or at wholesale prices [We are buying the clothes *wholesale*.] **2** in a widespread or general way [The members refused to obey the new rules *wholesale*.] ►**v.** to sell or be sold in large amounts, usually at lower prices —**whole′saled, whole′sal·ing** —**whole′sal·er n.**

who'll (hōōl) *contraction* **1** who shall **2** who will

wil·der·ness (wil′dər nəs) **n.** a wild region; wasteland or overgrown land with no settlers

wis·dom (wiz′dəm) **n.** **1** the quality of being wise; good judgment, that comes from knowledge and experience in life [She had the *wisdom* to save money for her old age.] **2** learning; knowledge [a book filled with the *wisdom* of India]

with·draw (with drô′ *or* with drô′) **v.** **1** to take or pull out; remove [to *withdraw* one's hand from a pocket] **2** to move back; go away; retreat [She *withdrew* behind the curtain.] **3** to leave; retire or resign [to *withdraw* from school] **4** to take back; recall [I *withdraw* my statement.] —**with·drew′, with·drawn′, with·draw′ing**

wolf (wŏŏlf) **n.** **1** a wild animal that looks like a dog: it kills other animals for food **2** a person who is fierce, cruel, greedy, etc. —*pl.* **wolves**

wolves (wŏŏlvz) **n.** *plural of* **wolf**

wom·an (wŏŏm′ən) **n.** **1** an adult, female human being **2** women as a group **3** a female servant —*pl.* **wom′en**

wom·en (wim′ən) **n.** *plural of* **woman**

won·der·ful (wun′dər fəl) **adj.** **1** that causes wonder; marvelous; amazing **2** very good; excellent: *used only in everyday talk* —**won′der·ful·ly adv.**

wor·ry (wʉr′ē) **v.** **1** to be or make troubled in mind; feel or make uneasy or anxious [Don't *worry*. Her absence *worried* us.] **2** to annoy, bother, etc. [Stop *worrying* me with such unimportant matters.] **3** to bite at and shake about with the teeth [The dog *worried* an old shoe.] —**wor′ried, wor′ry·ing** ►**n.** a troubled feeling; anxiety; care —*pl.* **wor′ries**

wrap·per (rap′ər) **n.** **1** a person or thing that wraps **2** a covering or cover [a newspaper mailed in a paper *wrapper*] **3** a woman's dressing gown

wrath (ra*th*) **n.** great anger; rage; fury

wreath (rēth) **n.** **1** a ring of leaves, flowers, etc. twisted together **2** something like this [*wreaths* of smoke] —*pl.* **wreaths** (rē*th*z)

wres·tle (res′əl) **v.** **1** to struggle with, trying to throw or force to the ground without striking blows with the fists **2** to struggle hard, as with a problem; contend —**wres′tled, wres′tling** ►**n.** **1** the action or a bout of wrestling **2** a struggle or contest —**wres′tler**

wrin·kle (riŋ′kəl) **n.** a small or uneven crease or fold [*wrinkles* in a coat; *wrinkles* in skin] ►**v.** **1** to make wrinkles in [a brow *wrinkled* with care] **2** to form wrinkles [This cloth *wrinkles* easily.] —**wrin′kled, wrin′kling**

write (rīt) **v.** **1** to form words, letters, etc., as with a pen or pencil **2** to form the words, letters, etc. of [*Write* your address here.] **3** to be the author or composer of [Dickens *wrote* novels. Mozart *wrote* symphonies.] —**wrote, writ′ten, writ′ing**

writ·ten (rit′n) *past participle of* **write**

yes·ter·day (yes′tər dā) **adv.** on the day before today ►**n.** **1** the day before today **2** some time in the past

yield (yēld) **v.** **1** to give up; surrender [to *yield* to a demand; to *yield* a city] **2** to give or grant [to *yield* the right of way; to *yield* a point] **3** to give way [The gate would not *yield* to our pushing.] **4** to bring forth or bring about; produce; give [The orchard *yielded* a good crop. The business *yielded* high profits.]

yolk (yōk) **n.** the yellow part of an egg

you'd (yōōd) *contraction* **1** you had **2** you would

you've (yōōv) *contraction* you have

zo·ol·o·gy (zō äl′ə jē) **n.** the science that studies animals and animal life —**zo·ol′o·gist**

Level E Student Record Chart

Name _____

		Pretest	Final Test
Lesson 1	Words with the Sound of **k**, **kw**, and **n**		
Lesson 2	Hard and Soft **c** and **g**		
Lesson 3	Words with the Sound of **f**		
Lesson 4	Words with **kn**, **gn**, **wr**, and **rr**		
Lesson 5	Words with the Sound of **el** and **l**		
Lesson 6	Lessons 1–5 • Review	■■■■■	
Lesson 7	Vowel Pairs **ai**, **ay**, **oa**, and **ow**		
Lesson 8	Vowel Pairs **ee** and **ea** and Vowel Digraph **ea**		
Lesson 9	Vowel Digraphs **au** and **aw**		
Lesson 10	Vowel Digraphs **ie** and **ei** and Vowel Pair **ei**		
Lesson 11	Diphthongs **ou**, **ow**, **oi**, and **oy**		
Lesson 12	Lessons 7–11 • Review	■■■■■	
Lesson 13	Prefixes **un**, **in**, **dis**, and **trans**		
Lesson 14	Prefixes **en**, **im**, and **mis**		
Lesson 15	Prefixes **pre**, **pro**, **re**, and **ex**		
Lesson 16	Prefixes **fore**, **post**, **over**, **co**, **com**, and **con**		
Lesson 17	Prefixes **sub**, **mid**, **bi**, and **tri**		
Lesson 18	Lessons 13–17 • Review	■■■■■	
Lesson 19	Compound Words		
Lesson 20	Possessives and Contractions		
Lesson 21	Syllables		
Lesson 22	Syllables		
Lesson 23	Syllables		
Lesson 24	Lessons 19–23 • Review	■■■■■	
Lesson 25	Suffixes **er**, **est**, **or**, and **ist**		
Lesson 26	Suffixes **ee**, **eer**, **ent**, and **ant**		
Lesson 27	Suffixes **ward**, **en**, **ize**, **ful**, and **ness**		
Lesson 28	Suffixes **hood**, **ship**, **ment**, **able**, and **ible**		
Lesson 29	Suffixes **ion**, **tion**, **ance**, **ence**, **ity**, and **ive**		
Lesson 30	Lessons 25–29 • Review	■■■■■	
Lesson 31	Doubling Final Consonants; Adding Suffixes and Endings to Words Ending in **e**		
Lesson 32	Adding Suffixes and Endings to Words Ending in **y**		
Lesson 33	Plurals of Words Ending in **y**		
Lesson 34	Irregular Plurals		
Lesson 35	Challenging Words		
Lesson 36	Lessons 31–35 • Review	■■■■■	

Lesson	6	12	18	24	30	36
Standardized Review Test						

Review Test
Answer Key

Lesson 6

1. a	11. d	21. c
2. c	12. c	22. d
3. c	13. d	23. a
4. b	14. a	24. c
5. b	15. d	25. b
6. a	16. d	
7. c	17. a	
8. b	18. c	
9. d	19. b	
10. a	20. b	

Lesson 12

1. d	11. a	21. c
2. a	12. b	22. c
3. c	13. c	23. b
4. b	14. a	24. b
5. c	15. d	25. d
6. b	16. b	
7. a	17. b	
8. d	18. c	
9. a	19. a	
10. d	20. d	

Lesson 18

1. b	11. b
2. a	12. a
3. d	13. b
4. c	14. d
5. b	15. b
6. c	
7. d	
8. b	
9. c	
10. c	

Lesson 24

1. b	11. a	21. b
2. c	12. c	22. a
3. a	13. b	23. c
4. d	14. c	24. d
5. a	15. a	25. c
6. c	16. d	
7. b	17. a	
8. d	18. b	
9. a	19. c	
10. c	20. a	

Lesson 30

1. a	11. c	21. d
2. b	12. d	22. d
3. c	13. d	23. b
4. b	14. a	24. c
5. d	15. b	25. a
6. c	16. d	
7. a	17. a	
8. d	18. c	
9. b	19. c	
10. a	20. a	

Lesson 36

1. a	11. d
2. b	12. c
3. a	13. d
4. d	14. c
5. b	15. a
6. c	
7. a	
8. d	
9. c	
10. d	

List Words

Word	Lesson
absentee	26
abundant	26
accountant	26
aches	1
achieve	10
activities	33
afterward	27
agreeable	28
agreement	8
aisle	5
allowance	29
alphabetize	27
amazing	31
America's	20
angrily	32
animal	23
answers	22
apologies	33
applicant	26
arrow	4
artistic	23
assign	4
assistant	26
athletic	23
atmosphere	3
attendance	29
author	9
authorities	33
autographs	3
avoid	11
awfully	9
awkward	9
backward	27
bakeries	33
ballet	35
beautiful	23
beliefs	34
believe	10
biceps	17
bicycles	17
bisect	17
blue-green	19
boast	7
borrow	7
boundary	11
braid	7
breathe	8
brief	10
broccoli	34
broiled	11

Word	Lesson
busiest	25
calves	34
campaign	4
Canada's	20
cancel	5
captive	29
cartoonist	25
cassette	21
caution	9
cavities	33
celebrate	2
centuries	33
certain	2
challenge	21
champion's	20
championship	28
channel	5
character	1
cheerful	27
cheerily	32
chiefs	34
chocolate	23
choir	11
chosen	35
circus	2
citizen	23
class's	20
classified	32
closet	22
coast	7
cocoa	7
collect	21
college's	20
cologne	4
column	35
comfortable	28
command	21
commend	16
committee	16
company	16
compete	16
competent	26
complain	7
conceive	10
concert	2
conditions	16
confidence	29
conquer	16
conserve	16
consoled	16

Word	Lesson
contribute	16
cooperate	16
cornbread	19
correct	4
counselor	25
countdown	19
counted	11
countries	33
couple	2
coupon	2
courageous	11
cover	22
cranberries	33
creature	8
credit	2
crowded	11
cuffs	34
dangerous	2
darken	27
daughter	9
decay	7
deceit	10
deceived	10
decided	31
decoys	33
delays	33
delightful	27
dependable	28
designed	4
direction	29
director	25
disapproved	31
discontinue	13
discovered	13
disgrace	13
distance	13
disturb	13
divide	22
dolphins	3
dominant	26
double	5
dozen	22
drains	7
drawer	9
drearier	25
durable	28
earthquake	1
effort	3
eighty	10
either	10

Word	Lesson
election	29
electric	23
emperor	25
employee	26
enable	14
encourage	14
endangered	14
endure	14
enforce	14
engage	14
engineer	26
enjoyable	11
enough	3
envied	32
equality	29
equals	5
equipment	28
exactly	15
excellent	26
exchange	15
excitement	28
exclaim	15
exhaust	9
exist	15
expert	21
explain	15
export	15
fainted	7
falsehood	28
familiar	35
families	33
famous	35
farmers'	20
fashion	35
faucet	9
feather	8
February	35
final	5
fingernail	19
fingerprints	22
flawless	3
foamy	7
forbid	21
forearm	16
forecast	16
foreign	4
foresee	16
forewarn	16
forfeit	35
forty-six	19

List Words

Word	Lesson
forward	27
fossil	21
freight	10
friendlier	32
friendliness	27
frightened	3
fuel	5
gadget	2
gained	7
garage	2
generous	2
geography	3
Georgia's	20
gesture	2
gnawing	9
governor's	20
graduate	2
grandparents	22
grapefruit	19
grateful	2
greater	25
greedily	32
grief	10
groceries	33
haircut	19
hallway	19
halves	34
hastily	32
hauled	9
hawk	9
healthy	8
heavier	32
helmet	22
history	23
hoax	7
hoping	31
horrible	23
humanity	29
humidity	29
hungrier	25
hyphen	3
icicles	2
igloos	34
imagination	31
imitation	29
immerse	14
immobile	14
impolite	14
importance	29
impossible	14

Word	Lesson
impression	23
improper	14
improve	14
include	13
incomplete	13
increase	13
independence	29
inexpensive	13
infield	10
inhale	13
injuries	33
inquire	1
insecure	13
inspector	25
inspire	13
interpreter	25
introducing	31
islands	35
jacket	1
Japan's	20
jellyfish	19
jingle	5
joined	11
joint	11
journeys	33
jungle	5
Kansas'	20
keeping	8
kidneys	33
knead	4
kneecap	19
kneeling	1
knocked	1
knothole	1
knotted	4
knowing	1
known	4
knuckles	4
laughter	3
lawyer	9
leadership	28
leather	8
libraries	33
license	2
likelihood	28
louder	25
loudness	27
loyalty	11
magazine	23
magnifying	32

Word	Lesson
major	22
mammal	5
manners	21
massive	29
mayor's	20
meadows	8
mechanic	1
membership	28
memorize	27
mental	21
merrily	32
Mexico's	20
midair	17
midday	17
middle	17
midnight	17
midstream	17
midwinter	17
mirror	4
misbehave	14
misjudge	14
misplaced	14
mispronounce	14
mission	22
misspelled	35
mistake	14
mistook	14
mistrust	14
misunderstand	14
modern	22
moisture	11
Montreal's	20
moose	34
motherhood	28
mountaineer	26
mountainous	11
mysteries	33
naughty	9
needles	8
neighborhood	28
neither	10
niece	10
noisily	32
normal	21
northeast	8
novelist	25
obeying	32
objection	29
occupying	32
opinion	29

Word	Lesson
opposite	23
orchestra	1
originality	29
oval	5
overboard	16
overcome	16
overlooked	16
overreact	16
ownership	28
oyster	11
painful	7
pancakes	19
panel	5
paperback	19
paragraph	3
parent's	20
participant	26
partner	21
pause	9
payee	26
peaceful	27
perform	21
persuaded	31
photography	3
physical	3
pickle	5
pieces	10
planned	31
plastic	22
pleasant	26
pleasing	31
pleasure	8
pledged	31
plentiful	27
plural	5
poach	7
poise	11
poisonous	11
politeness	27
popular	23
population	29
possible	28
postpone	16
posture	22
postwar	16
potatoes	34
powder	11
prairie	35
preacher	8
prepare	15

List Words

Word	Lesson	Word	Lesson	Word	Lesson	Word	Lesson
preserve	15	scarves	34	subject	17	typhoid	3
pretend	15	scientist	25	submit	17	typhoon	3
prisoner	25	scramble	5	subscribe	17	uncooked	13
problem	21	scraping	31	subside	17	uncovered	13
produce	15	secretaries	33	substitute	17	underneath	8
professional	15	selective	29	subtract	17	underwater	19
profitable	28	self-control	19	succeed	8	unforgivable	31
promote	15	senator's	20	success	22	unit	22
propose	15	sensible	28	suffer	3	unjust	13
protection	29	separate	35	suggest	21	unlawful	9
protest	15	sequence	1	sunniest	32	unlikely	23
provide	15	serious	23	sunshine	19	unselfish	13
punctuation	35	shake	1	supplying	32	unusual	13
puppeteer	26	shallow	21	support	21	usable	31
quarrel	1	shameful	27	surprises	35	vacation	29
quarter	1	sharpen	27	surround	4	valuable	31
questions	1	sheriffs	34	swallows	7	vault	9
quickly	1	shield	10	sweater	8	vehicle	23
quiet	1	shipping	31	sweeper	25	vein	10
radios	34	shipwreck	19	sweeter	8	victories	33
rainbows	19	shoelaces	19	symbol	21	village	2
readily	32	shortage	2	symphony	3	violent	26
reappear	15	shredded	31	telephone	3	visible	28
rearrange	15	shyness	27	terrible	28	vocalist	25
received	10	signal	21	Texas'	20	volcanoes	34
recognize	27	silence	22	they've	20	volunteer	26
recommend	35	skidded	31	thief	10	voyage	11
reduce	22	sleepiest	32	throbbing	31	warrior	25
reflect	15	slightest	25	throwing	7	watermelon	22
regular	2	snowdrift	19	tickle	5	wealth	8
relays	33	soiled	11	tighten	27	weather	35
reliant	26	spaghetti	34	toasted	7	weird	35
religion	23	sparkled	5	toiled	11	whistle	5
remember	23	speaker	1	tomatoes	34	who'll	20
repellent	26	species	34	tomorrow	7	wilderness	27
require	1	speech	8	tornadoes	34	wisdom	35
rescue	21	spellbound	19	tough	3	withdraw	9
resident	26	spinning	31	tourist	25	wolves	34
resign	4	spiral	5	towels	5	women's	20
returning	15	splendid	22	transfer	13	wonderful	27
review	10	squawk	9	transplant	13	worrying	32
reward	15	stadium	23	transport	13	wrapper	4
roasting	7	statement	28	treasure	8	wreath	4
rubble	22	steady	8	triangle	17	wrestler	4
salmon	34	stickiest	32	trio	17	wrinkled	4
saucers	9	stomach	35	triple	17	written	4
sausage	2	strangest	31	tripod	17	yesterday	23
scanner	21	strawberries	9	triumph	3	yield	10
scarecrow	7	sturdier	32	trout	34	yolk	35
scariest	25	subdue	17	typewriters	4	you'd	20

Bonus Words

Word	Lesson
absorbent	26
acceptance	29
adhere	21
adoption	29
advance	21
advanced	31
align	4
alloys	33
appointee	26
attorneys	33
auctioneer	26
audience	9
aviator	25
awe	9
basically	35
betray	7
bifocals	17
bookkeeper	22
broadcast	19
brotherhood	28
casual	2
commence	16
concern	2
connect	16
conscience	35
cough	3
degree	8
destroyed	11
disbelief	10
dismal	5
display	13
displayed	32
easel	5
eerie	35
eighteen	10
electronic	23
enrich	14
errand	4
exceed	15
extend	15
fanciest	25
ferry	4
festival	3
foresight	16
forgivable	31
geese's	20

Word	Lesson
general	5
gorge	2
granite	22
grieve	10
guilty	21
hamburger	23
hammock	1
harsher	25
heal	8
impose	14
impure	14
invisible	13
kindness	1
knob	1
knowledge	4
ladies'	20
legible	28
leisure	10
leprechaun	1
levying	32
loaves	34
mammoth	21
manager	23
mantle	23
measure	8
medical	23
midway	17
minimize	27
misfortune	14
mislead	14
missionaries	33
modified	32
muscle	5
noble	5
observation	31
occupant	26
orchid	35
Oregon's	20
outrageous	11
overdue	16
passage	2
peasant	8
persistent	26
phonograph	3
piccolos	34
pliers	34

Word	Lesson
postgame	16
powerful	11
prevent	15
proceed	15
qualify	1
radar	22
railway	19
realist	25
relative	29
relieved	10
reprint	15
resourceful	27
rotting	31
satin	22
scholarship	28
seek	8
seize	35
self-preservation	19
settlement	28
she'll	20
sherbet	21
shoreward	27
sincere	2
sincerity	29
sixty-four	19
slaughter	9
snout	11
sorrow	7
sparrow	7
spoiled	11
spoken	22
sprawl	9
stain	7
stiffness	27
strutted	31
submarine	17
submerge	17
surveying	32
tardiest	32
telegraph	3
thawed	9
theories	33
thicken	27
thieves	34
toadstool	7
torpedoes	34

Word	Lesson
transmit	13
transparent	13
triplets	17
unavailable	13
undersea	19
violence	29
voter	25
waffle	3
walkways	33
washable	28
wrath	4
you've	20

Spelling Enrichment

Bulletin Board Suggestion

Shoot for the Stars in Spelling Prepare a large rocket ship out of tagboard. Display it on the lower corner of a bulletin board so that it looks as if it is blasting off into space. Then cut large stars out of brightly colored construction paper. Encourage students to write spelling hints on the stars and add them to the bulletin board. The hint might be a spelling rule such as "*i* before *e* except after *c* . . . " or it might suggest a funny pronunciation for one of the list words that will help students with an unusual spelling.

Group Practice

Fill-In Write spelling words on the board. Omit some of the letters and replace them with dashes. Have the first student in Row One come to the board to fill in one of the missing letters in any of the words. Then, have the first student in Row Two continue the procedure. Continue having students in each row take turns coming up to the board to fill in letters until all the words are completed. Any student who is able to correctly fill in a word earns a point for his or her row. The row with the most points at the end of the game wins.

Erase Write list words on the board. Then, ask the class to put their heads down while you call on a student to come to the board and erase one of the words. This student then calls on a class member to identify the erased word. The identified word is then restored and the student who correctly identified the erasure can be the person who erases next.

Crossword Relay First draw a large grid on the board. Then, divide the class into several teams. Teams compete against each other to form separate crossword puzzles on the board. Individuals on each team take turns racing against members of the other teams to join list words until all possibilities have been exhausted. A list word may appear on each crossword puzzle only once. The winning team is the team whose crossword puzzle contains the greatest number of correctly spelled list words or the team who finishes first.

Scramble Prepare letter cards sufficient to spell all the list words. Distribute letter cards to all students. Some students may be given more than one letter card. The teacher then calls out a list word. Students holding the letters contained in the word race to the front of the class to form the word by standing in the appropriate sequence with their letter cards.

Proofreading Relay Write two columns of misspelled list words on the board. Although the errors can differ, be sure that each list has the same number of errors. Divide the class into two teams and assign each team to a different column. Teams then compete against each other to correct their assigned lists by team members taking turns erasing and replacing an appropriate letter. Each member may correct only one letter per turn. The team that corrects its entire word list first wins.

Detective Call on a student to be a detective. The detective must choose a spelling word from the list and think of a structural clue, definition, or synonym that will help classmates identify it. The detective then states the clue using the format, "I spy a word that. . . ." Students are called on to guess and spell the mystery word. Whoever answers correctly gets to take a turn being the detective.

Spelling Tic-Tac-Toe Draw a tic-tac-toe square on the board. Divide the class into X and O teams. Take turns dictating spelling words to members of each team. If the word is spelled correctly, allow the team member to place an X or O on the square. The first team to place three X's or O's in a row wins.

Words of Fortune Have students put their heads down while you write a spelling word on the board in large letters. Then, cover each letter with a sheet of sturdy paper. The paper can be fastened to the board with magnets. Call on a student to guess any letter of the alphabet the student thinks may be hidden. If that particular letter is hidden, then reveal the letter in every place where it appears in the word by removing the paper.

The student continues to guess letters until an incorrect guess is made or the word is revealed. In the event that an incorrect guess is made, a different student continues the game. Continue the game until every list word has been hidden and then revealed.

Dictionary Activities

Around the World Designate the first person in the first row to be the traveler. The traveler must stand next to the student seated behind him or her. Then, dictate any letter of the alphabet at random. Instruct the two students to quickly name the letter of the alphabet that precedes the given letter. The student who is first to respond with the correct answer becomes the traveler while the other student sits at that desk. The traveler

Spelling Enrichment

then moves to compete with the next person in the row. The game continues with the traveler moving up and down the rows as the teacher dictates various alphabet letters. See who can be the traveler who has moved the farthest around the classroom. For variety, you may want to require students to state the letter that follows the given letter. You may also want to dictate pairs of list words and have students name which word comes first.

Stand-Up While the teacher pronounces a word from the spelling dictionary, students look up the entry word and point to it. Tell students to stand up when they have located the entry. See who is the first student to stand up.

This game can be played using the following variations:

1. Have students stand when they have located the guide words for a given word.

2. Have students stand when they are able to tell on what page a given list word appears in the dictionary.

Guide Word Scramble Prepare tagboard cards with spelling words written on them in large letters. Distribute the cards to students. Call on two students to come to the front of the room to serve as guide words. Then, call one student at a time to hold their word card either in front of, in between, or behind the guide words so that the three words are in alphabetical order. You may want to vary the guide words occasionally.

Cut-Off Distribute a strip of paper to each student. Instruct students to write any four spelling words on the strip. All but one of the words should be in alphabetical order. Then, have students exchange their strip with a partner. Students use scissors to cut off the word that is not in alphabetical sequence and tape the remaining word strips together. If students find this activity too difficult, you might have them cut all four words off the strip and arrange them alphabetically on their desks.

Applied Spelling

Journal Allow time each day for students to write in a journal. A spiral bound notebook can be used for this purpose. Encourage students to express their feelings about events that are happening in their lives at home or at school, or they could write about what their plans are for the day. To get them started, you may have to provide starter phrases. Allow them to use "invented" spelling for words they can't spell.

Collect the journals periodically to write comments that echo what the student has written. For example, a student's entry might read, "I'm hape I gt to plae bazball todae." The teacher's response could be "Baseball is my favorite game, too. I'd be happy to watch you play baseball today at recess." This method allows students to learn correct spelling and sentence structure without emphasizing their errors in a negative way.

Letter to the Teacher On a regular basis, invite students to write a note to you. At first you may have to suggest topics or provide a starter sentence. It may be possible to suggest a topic that includes words from the spelling list. Write a response at the bottom of each letter that provides the student with a model of any spelling or sentence structure that apparently needs improvement.

Daily Edit Each day, provide a brief writing sample on the board that contains errors in spelling, capitalization, or punctuation. Have students rewrite the sample correctly. Provide time later in the day to have the class correct the errors on the board. Discuss why the spelling is as it is while students self-correct their work.

Acrostic Poems Have students write a word from the spelling list vertically. Then, instruct them to join a word horizontally to each letter of the list word. The horizontal words must begin with the letters in the list word. They also should be words that describe or relate feelings about the list word. Encourage students to refer to a dictionary for help in finding appropriate words. Here is a sample acrostic poem:

Zebras
Otters
Ostriches

Words-in-a-Row Distribute strips of writing paper to each student. Ask students to write three spelling words in a row. Tell them to misspell two of the words. Then, have students take turns writing their row of words on the board. They can call on a classmate to identify and underline the correctly spelled word in the row. Continue until all students have had a chance to write their row of words.

Spelling Enrichment

Partner Spelling Assign spelling buddies. Allow partners to alternate dictating or writing sentences that contain words from the spelling list. The sentences can be provided by the teacher or generated by students. Have students check their own work as their partner provides the correct spelling for each sentence.

Scrap Words Provide each student with several sheets of tagboard, scraps of fabric or wallpaper, and some glue. Ask students to cut letters out of the scrap materials and glue them to the tagboard to form words from the spelling list. Display the colorful scrap words around the classroom.

Punch Words Set up a work center in the classroom with a supply of construction paper strips, a hole puncher, sheets of thin paper, and crayons. Demonstrate to students how the hole puncher can be used to create spelling words out of the construction paper. Permit students to take turns working at the center in their free time. Students may also enjoy placing a thin sheet of paper over the punch words and rubbing them with a crayon to make colorful word designs. You can then display their punch word and crayon creations.

Word Cut-Outs Distribute scissors, glue, a sheet of dark-colored construction paper, and a supply of old newspapers and magazines to the class. Have students look through the papers and magazines for list words. Tell them to cut out any list words they find and glue them on the sheet of construction paper. See who can find the most list words. This technique may also be used to have students construct sentences or cut out individual letters to form words.

Word Sorts Invite students to write each list word on a separate card. Then, ask them how many different ways the words can be organized (such as animate vs. inanimate, past-tense or vowel patterns, similarity or contrast in meaning). As students sort the words into each category, have them put words that don't belong in a category into an exception pile.

Spelling Notebook

Spelling Notebook

Definitions and Rules

The alphabet has two kinds of letters—**vowels** and **consonants**. The **vowels** are **a**, **e**, **i**, **o**, and **u** (and sometimes **y**). All the rest of the letters are **consonants**.

Each **syllable** in a word must have a vowel sound. If a word or syllable has only one vowel and it comes at the beginning or between two consonants, the vowel usually stands for a **short-vowel** sound.

cat   sit   cup

A **long-vowel** sound usually has the same sound as its letter name.

When **y** comes at the end of a word with one syllable, the **y** at the end usually has the sound of long **i**, as in *dry* and *try*. When **y** comes at the end of a word with more than one syllable, it usually has the sound of long **e**, as in *city* and *funny*.

When two or more **consonants** come together in a word, their sounds may blend together. In a **consonant blend**, you can hear the sound of each letter.

smile   **sl**ide   frie**nd**

A **consonant digraph** consists of two consonants that go together to make one sound.

sharp   four**th**   **ea**ch

A **consonant cluster** consists of three consonants together in one syllable.

thrills   pa**tch**   **spl**ash

A **vowel pair** consists of two vowels together where the first vowel stands for the long sound and the second vowel is silent.

t**ea**cher   f**ai**l   s**oa**k

A **vowel digraph** consists of two vowels that together make a long-vowel sound, a short-vowel sound or a special sound of their own.

br**ea**d   s**oo**ner   a**u**to

A **diphthong** consists of two vowels that blend together to make one sound.

b**oy**   **oi**l   cl**ou**d

A **base word** is a word to which a prefix or suffix may be added to change its meaning.

un**lawful**   re**place**   **shyness**

A **root** is a word part to which a prefix or suffix may be added to change its meaning.

in**duct**ion   re**pel**   con**duct**

An **ending** is a letter or group of letters added to the end of a base word to make the word singular or plural or to tell when an action happened.

hat**s**   fox**es**   run**s**   rain**ed**   help**ing**

A **prefix** is a word part that is added to the beginning of a base word or a root. A prefix changes the meaning of the base word.

unhappy   **dis**trust   **re**pel   **con**duct

A **suffix** is a word part that is added to the end of a base word or root to make a new word.

cheer**ful**   agree**able**   dic**tion**   port**able**

When you write words in **alphabetical order**, use these rules:

1. If the *first letter* of two words is the same, use the second letter.
2. If the *first two letters* are the same, use the third letter.

There are two **guide words** at the top of each page in the dictionary. The word on the left tells you the first word on the page. The word on the right tells you the last word on the page. All the words in between are in alphabetical order.

The dictionary puts an **accent mark** (′) *after* the syllable with the strong sound.

pᴇr′sən

There is a vowel sound that can be spelled by any of the vowels. It is often found in a syllable that is not accented, or stressed, in a word. This vowel sound has the sound-symbol /ə/. It is called the **schwa**.

The word *I* is always a **capital** letter.

A **contraction** is a short way of writing two words. It is formed by writing two words together and leaving out one or more letters. Use an **apostrophe** (′) to show where something is left out.

it is = it's   we will = we'll

A **compound word** is a word made by joining two or more words.

cannot   anyway   maybe   firehouse

Teacher Notes